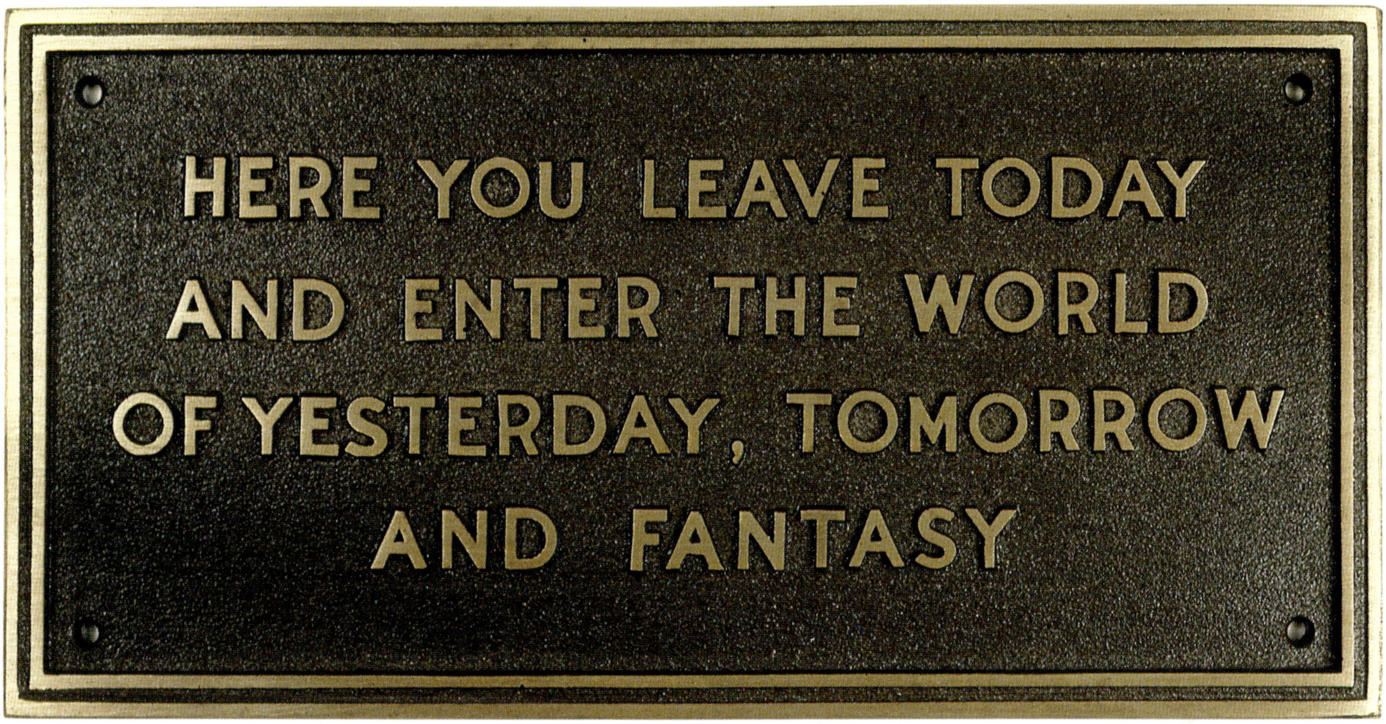
HERE YOU LEAVE TODAY
AND ENTER THE WORLD
OF YESTERDAY, TOMORROW
AND FANTASY

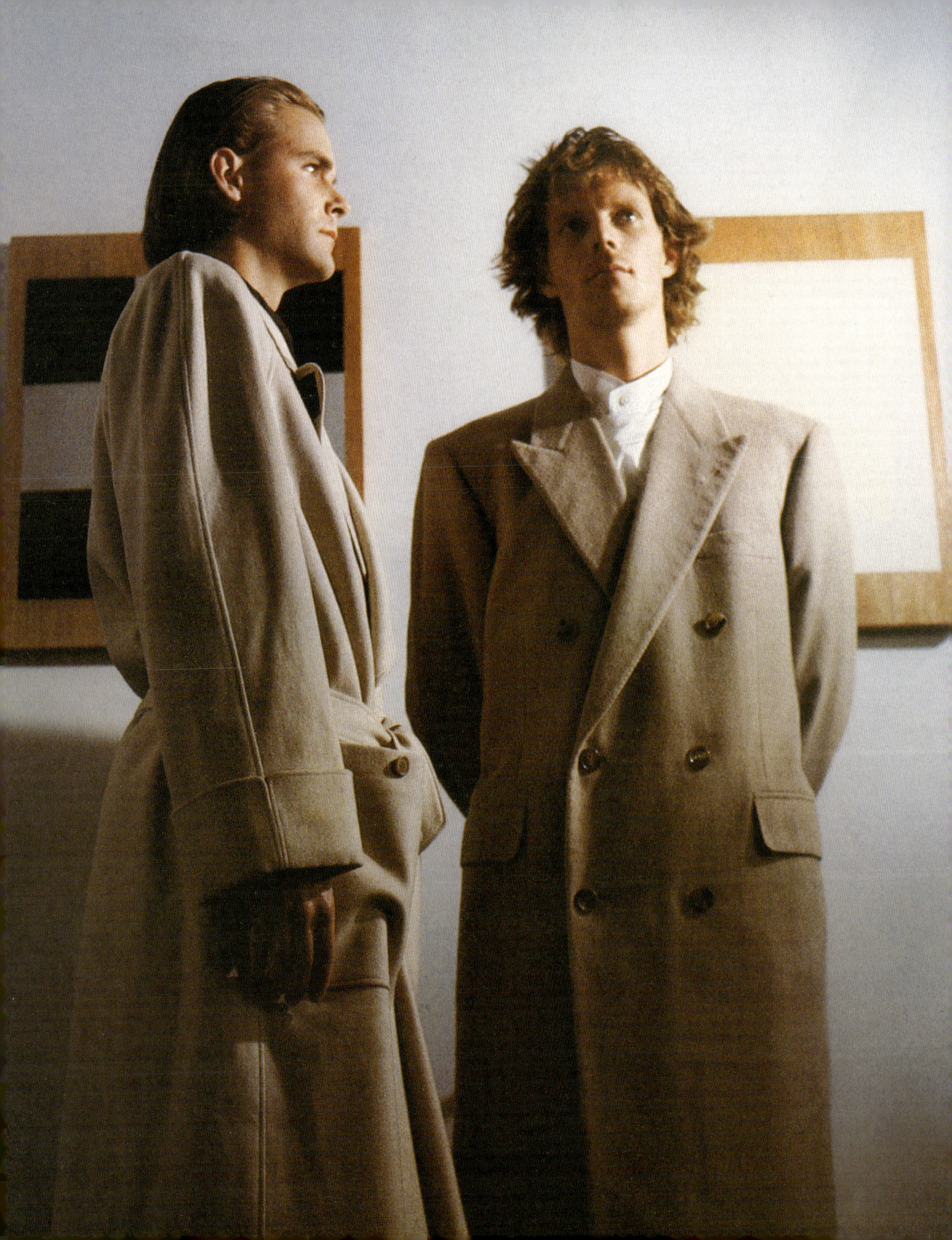

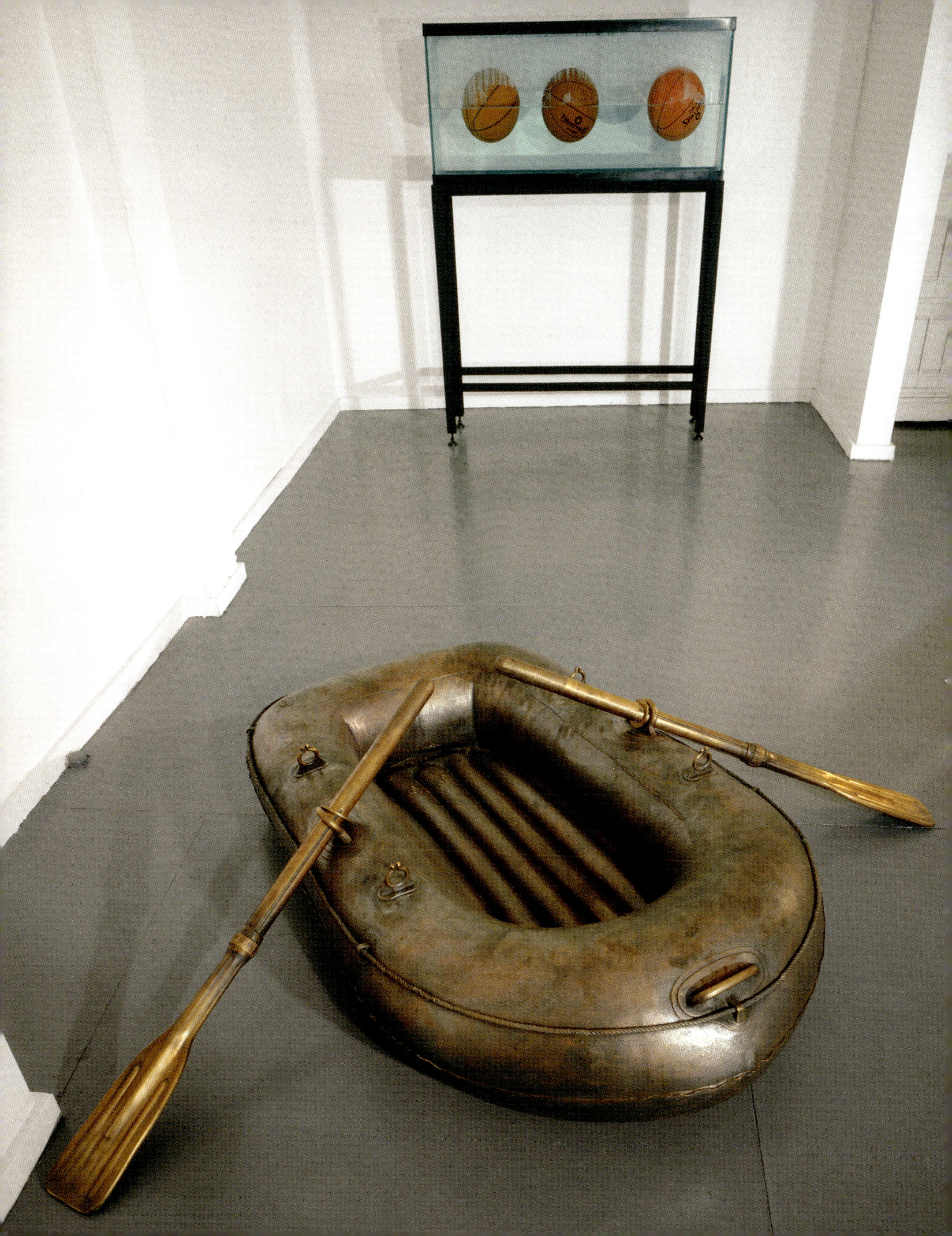

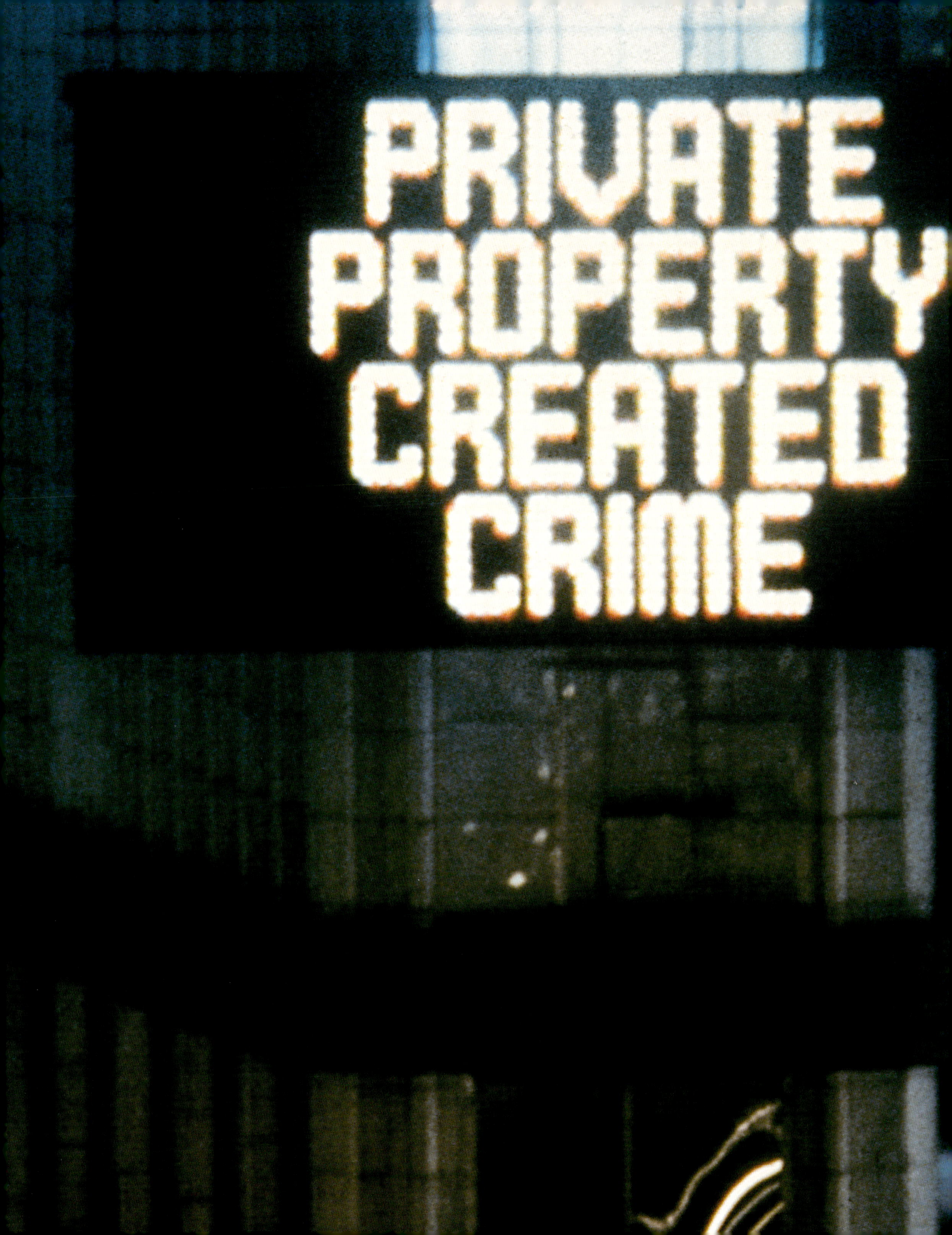
PRIVATE
PROPERTY
CREATED
CRIME

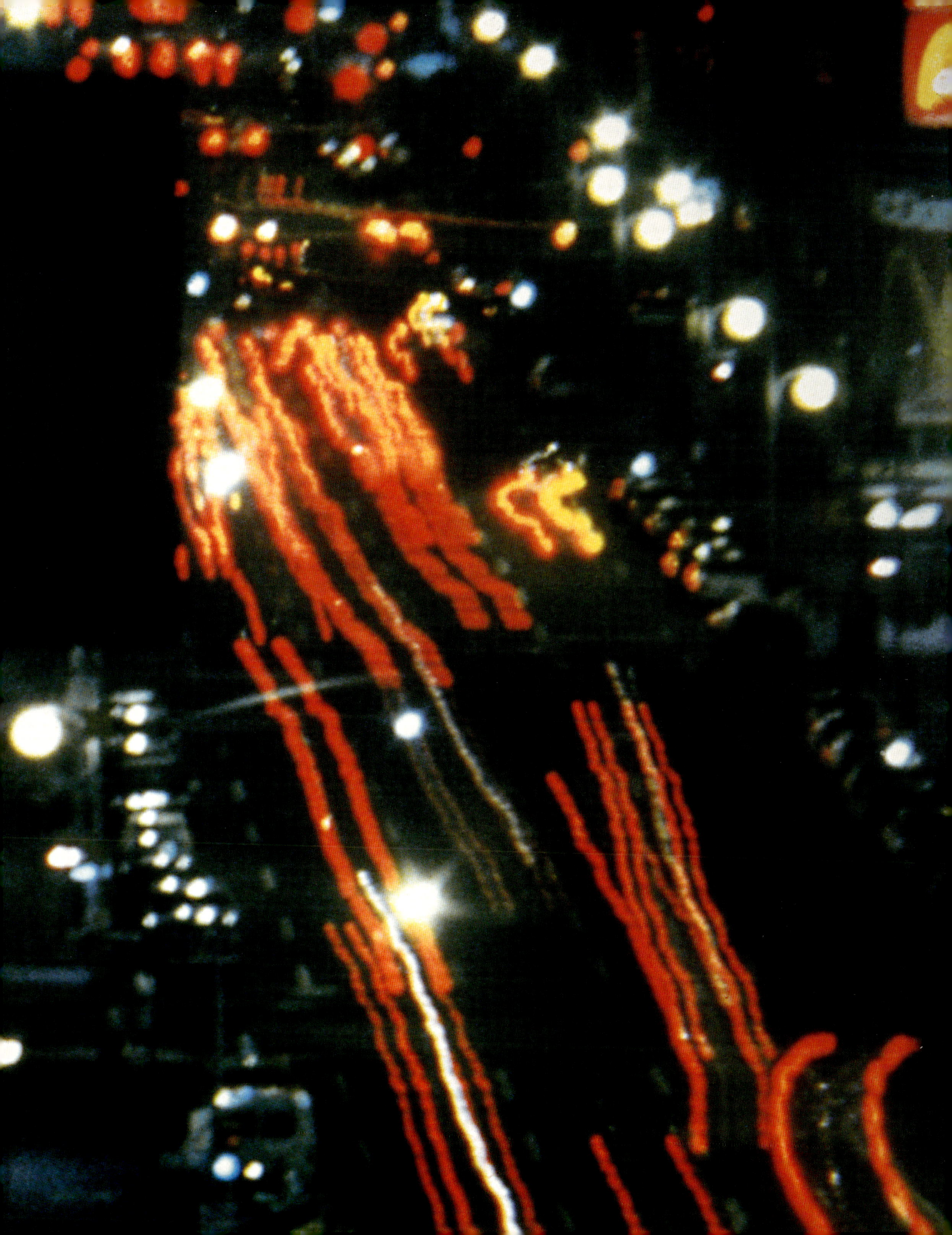

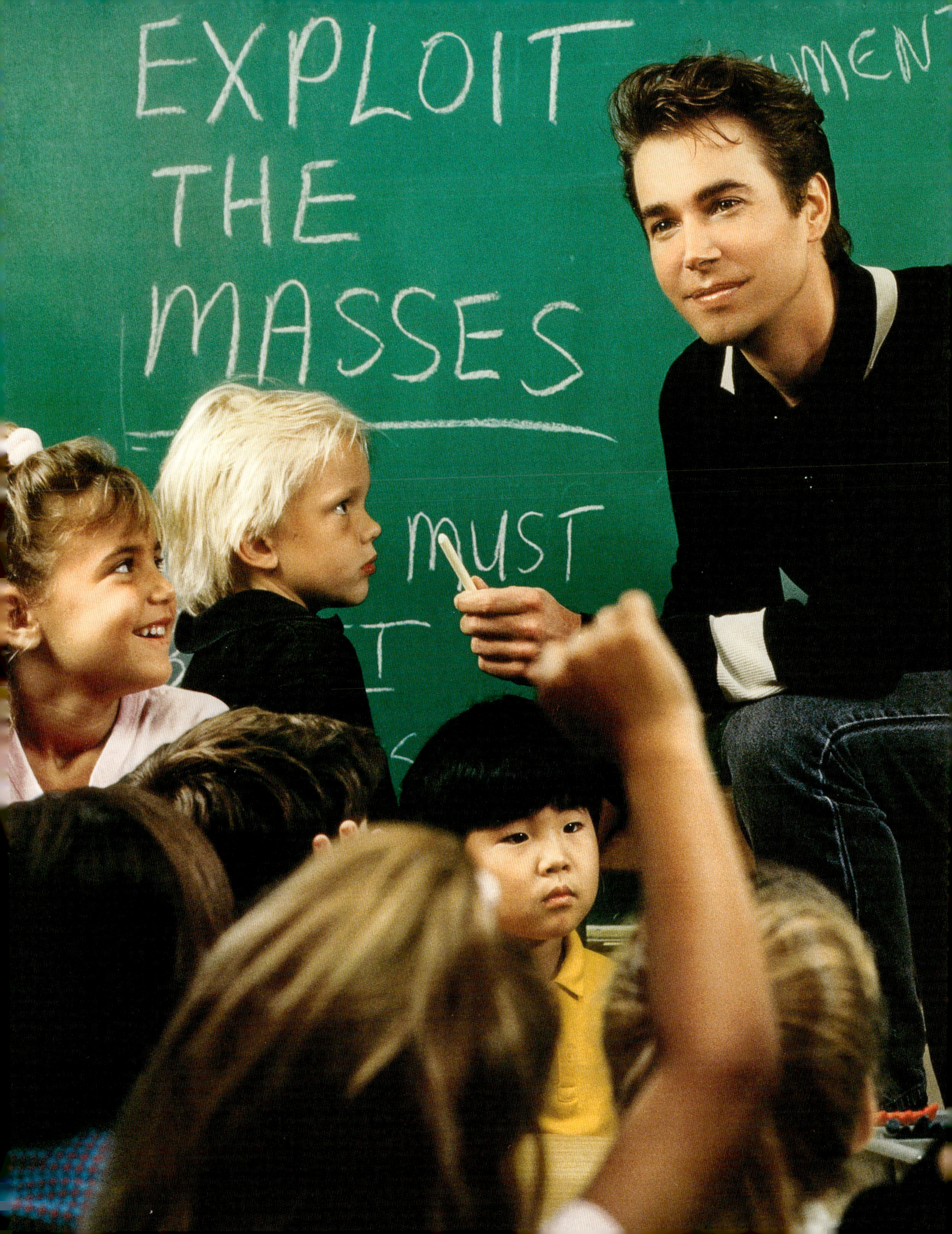
EXPLOIT THE MASSES
MUST

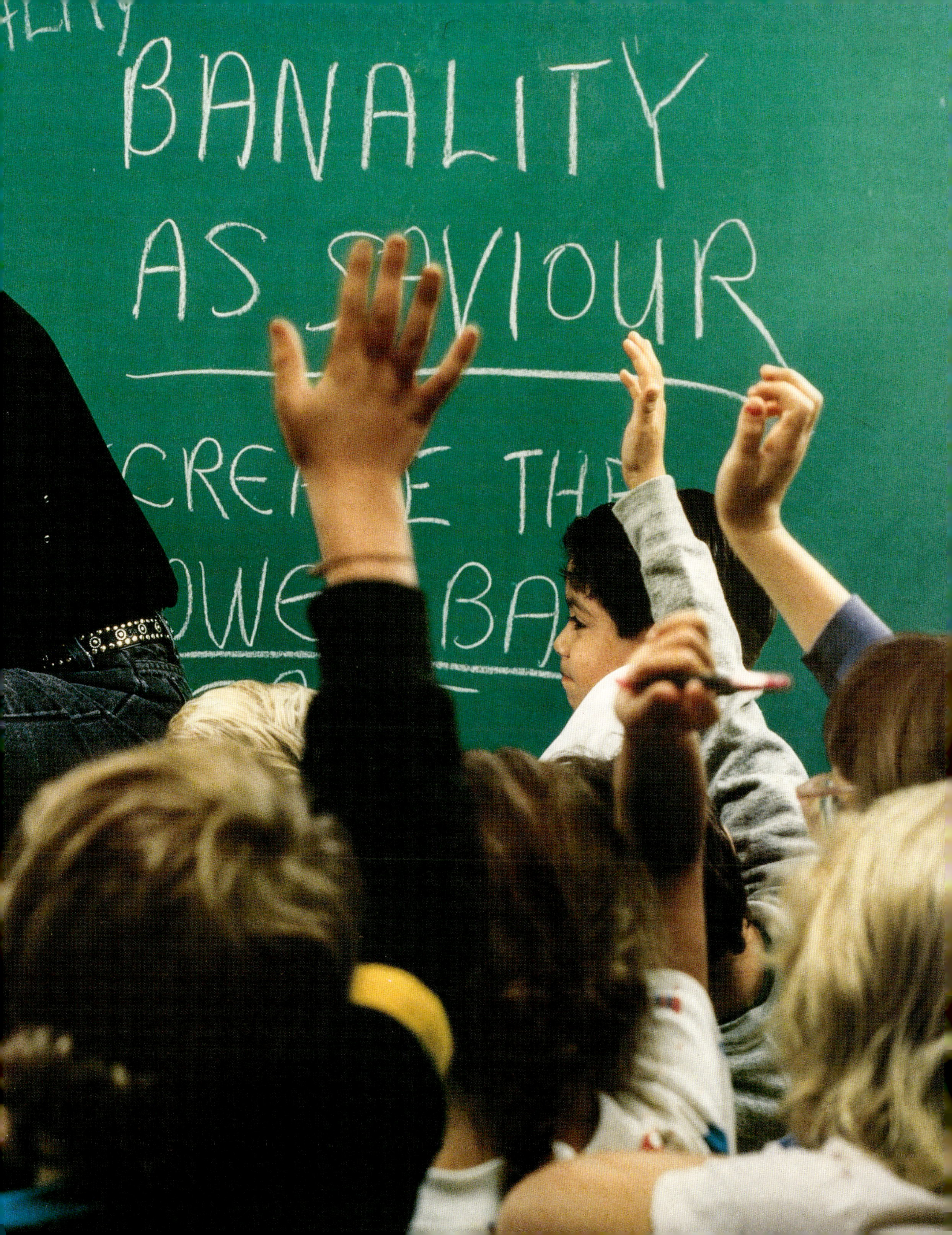
BANALITY

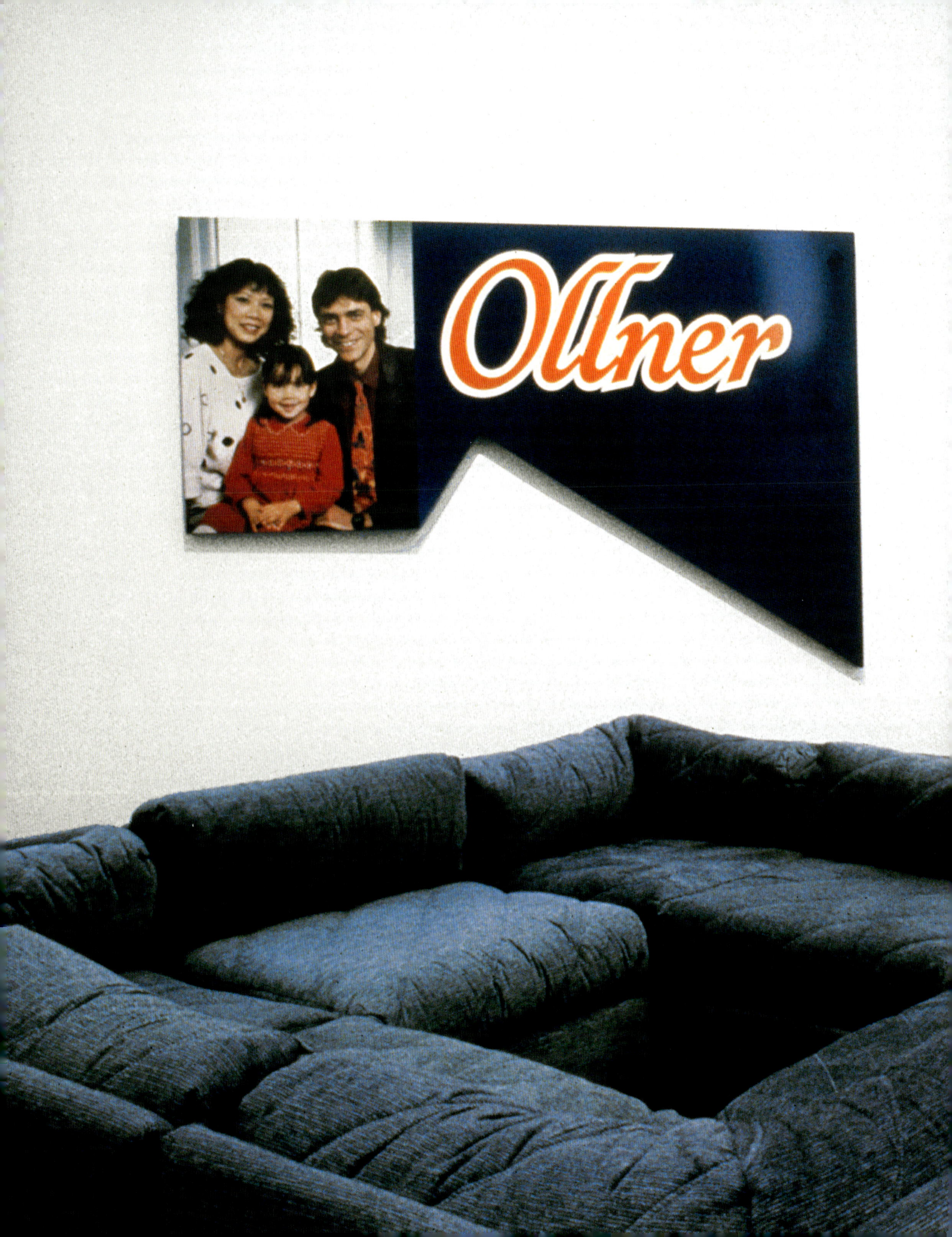
Ollner

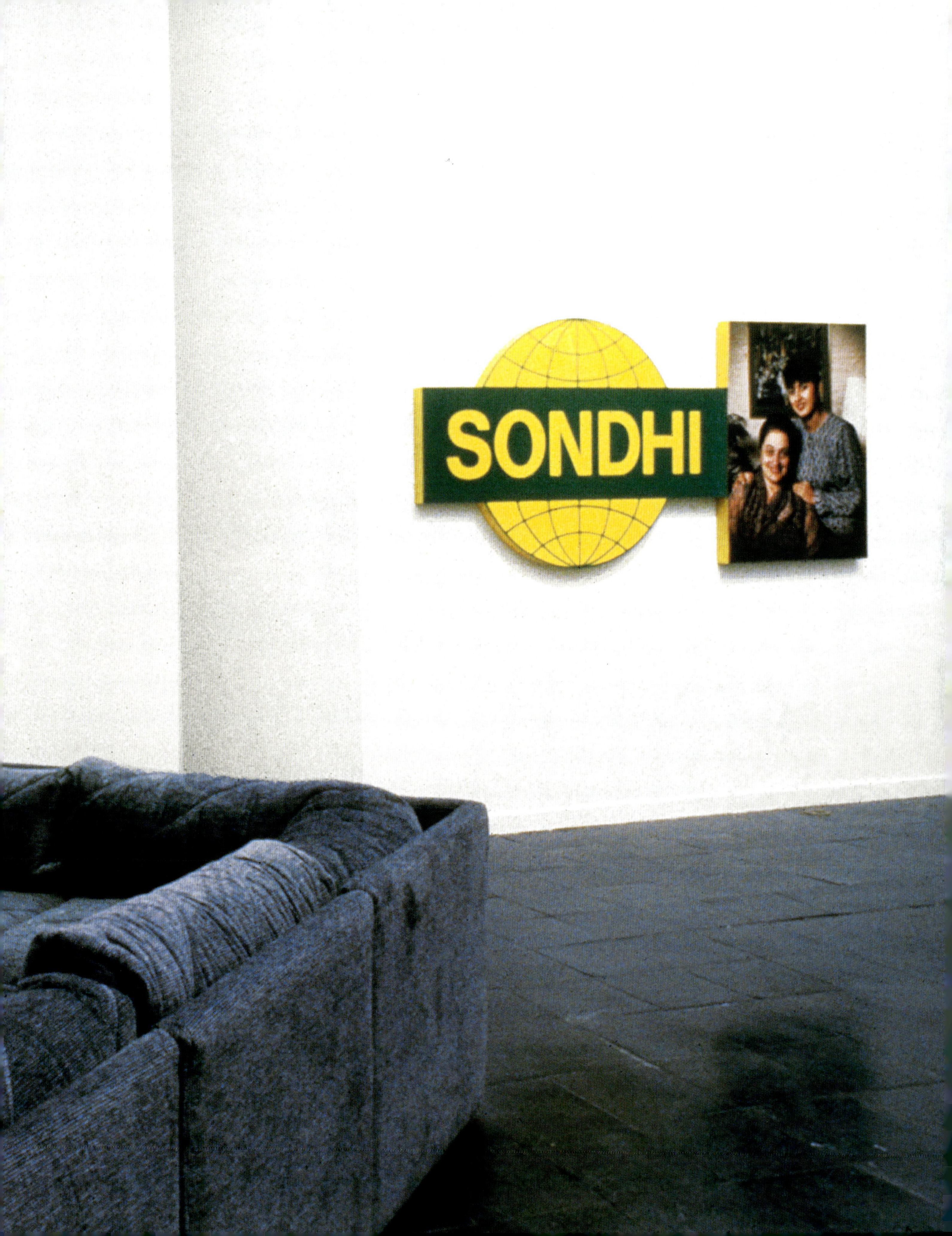
SONDHI

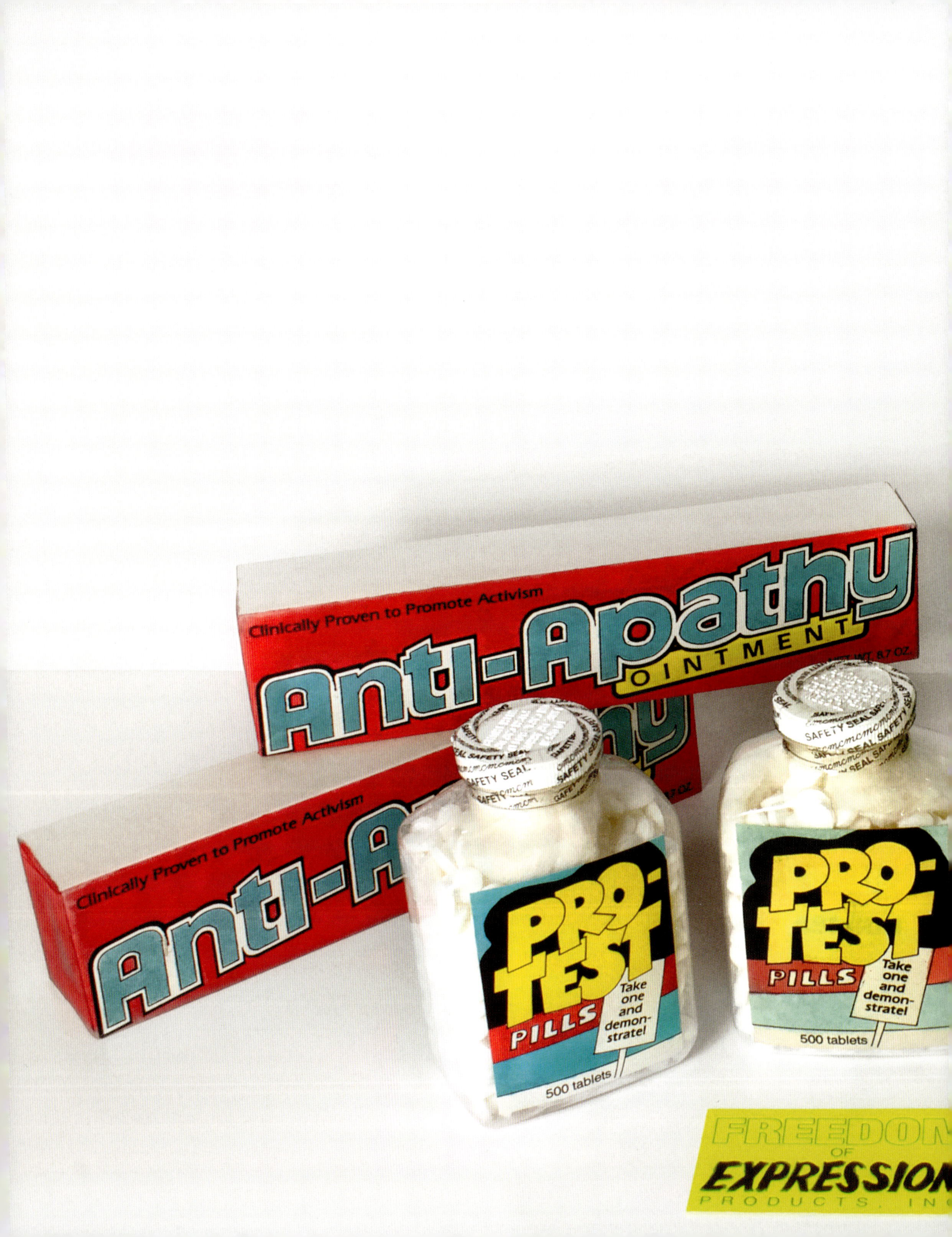
Clinically Proven to Promote Activism
Anti-Apathy
OINTMENT
NET WT. 8.7 OZ.
Clinically Proven to Promote Activism
SAFETY SEAL
PRO-TEST
PILLS
Take one and demon-strate!
500 tablets
FREEDOM
OF
EXPRESSION
PRODUCTS, INC

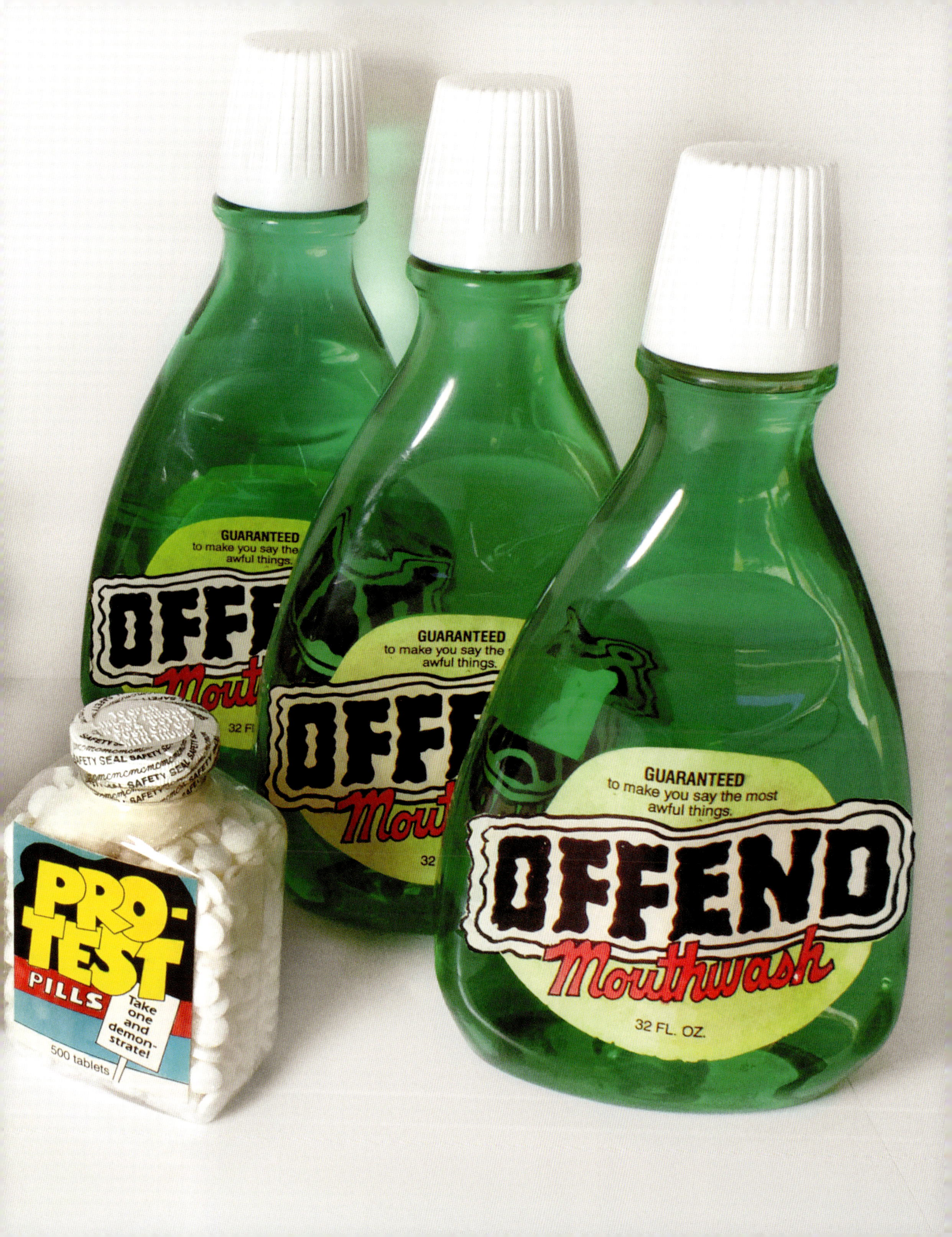
GUARANTEED
to make you say the most
awful things.
OFFEND
Mouthwash
32 FL. OZ.
PRO-TEST
PILLS
Take one and demon-strate!
500 tablets
SAFETY SEAL

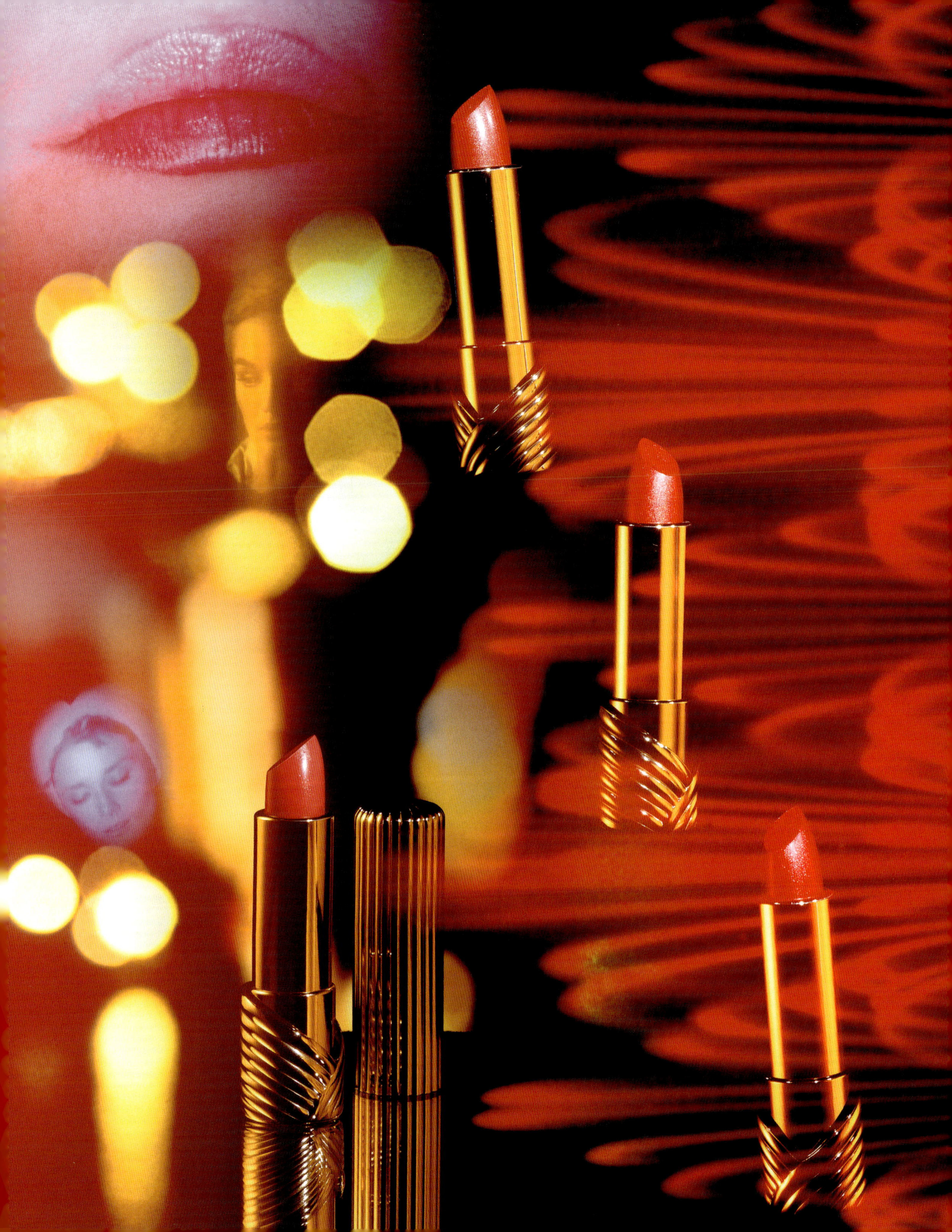

Brand New

Art & Commodity in the 1980s

Edited by
Gianni Jetzer

With essays by
Gianni Jetzer
Bob Nickas
Leah Pires

Chronology by
Patrick Jaojoco

Rizzoli Electa

Hirshhorn Museum
and Sculpture Garden
Washington, DC

This book is published in conjunction with the exhibition *Brand New: Art and Commodity in the 1980s*, organized by the Hirshhorn Museum and Sculpture Garden, Smithsonian Institution, Washington, DC, February 14–May 13, 2018.

Brand New: Art and Commodity in the 1980s has been made possible with support from the Hirshhorn International Council and the Hirshhorn Collectors' Council.

Library of Congress Control Number: 2017953574
ISBN: 978-0-8478-6241-2

First published in the United States of America in 2018 by
Rizzoli Electa
A Divison of Rizzoli International Publications, Inc.
300 Park Avenue South
New York, NY 10010
www.rizzoliusa.com

in association with
Hirshhorn Museum and Sculpture Garden

HIRSHHORN
Smithsonian

For the Hirshhorn Museum and Sculpture Garden:
Rhys Conlon, Editor and Publications Manager
Amy Pastan, Editor
Tyler Laminack, Associate Editor
Sandy Guttman, Curatorial Assistant

For Rizzoli Electa:
Charles Miers, Publisher
Margaret Rennolds Chace, Associate Publisher
Jennifer Bernstein, Tenacious Editorial, Editor

Design: Project Projects
(Adam Michaels, Siiri Tännler)

2018 2019 2020 2021 / 10 9 8 7 6 5 4 3 2 1

Printed in China

On the jacket front: **Barbara Kruger, *I Shop therefore I am***, 1987 (see p. 177)

On pages 1–16: **David Robbins. *Prop***, 1987. Bronze, 6 × 12 × 3⁄8 in. (15.4 × 30.5 × 1 cm). MAMCO (Musée d'art moderne et contemporain), Geneva, Gift of Galerie 1900–2000, Paris. **Stefan Lupino.** Photograph of Peter Nagy and Alan Belcher at Sherrie Levine's exhibition *1917*, Gallery Nature Morte, New York, published in *L'Uomo Vogue*, December 1984. Courtesy of Alan Belcher. **Jeff Koons. *Lifeboat***, 1985. Bronze, 12 × 80 × 60 in. (30.5 × 203.2 × 152.4 cm). Ed. of 3. In background: *Three Ball 50/50 Tank*, 1985. Installation view, *Equilibrium*, International With Monument, New York, May 4–June 2, 1985. © Jeff Koons. **Jenny Holzer. *Untitled***, 1982. Spectacolor light board with computer animation. Installation view, *Messages to the Public*, March 1–31, 1982. Photo: John Marchael. Artwork courtesy of Jane Dickson, Project Initiator and Animator. Courtesy of Public Art Fund, NY. **Jeff Koons. *Art Magazine Ad (Artforum)*** (detail), 1988–89. Lithographic print, 45 × 37¼ in. (114.3 × 94.6 cm). Rubell Family Collection, Miami. © Jeff Koons. **Ken Lum. *Square***, 1986. Furniture installation, dimensions variable. On back wall: *Ollner Family*, 1986; *Amrita and Mrs. Sondhi*, 1986. Installation view, *Damaged Goods: Desire and the Economy of the Object*, New Museum of Contemporary Art, New York, 1986. Courtesy of the artist and New Museum, New York. **Erika Rothenberg. *Freedom of Expression Drugs***, 1989. Three pill bottles, three mouthwash bottles, two ointment boxes, hand-colored printed sign (9 parts), overall 14 × 18 × 24 in. (35.6 × 45.7 × 61 cm). Collection of the artist. **Frank Majore. *Crimson Splendor***, 1987. Silver-dye bleach print, 60 × 48 in. (152.4 × 121.9 cm). Collection of the artist. **James Welling. *Tile Photograph 3***, 1985. Vintage gelatin silver print, 20 × 16 in. (50.8 × 40.6 cm). Ed. of 3 with 2 artist's proofs. Courtesy of the artist and David Zwirner, New York/London

Photograph and Reproduction Credits

Credits for images on pages 36–39, 74–77, and 150–53 appear on page 188.

Page 21: Courtesy of the artist, 47 Canal, New York, and Friends of the High Line. **22:** Courtesy of the artist and New Museum, New York. **23:** © 1996 Jasper Johns/Licensed by VAGA, New York, NY. **24, 33, 88, 94:** © 2017 The Andy Warhol Foundation for the Visual Arts, Inc. / Artists Rights Society (ARS), New York. **25:** Photo: Paula Court. **26–27:** © ARS, NY and DACS, London 2017. **28, 67, 70, 71, 73:** Courtesy of the artist [Louise Lawler] and Metro Pictures, New York. **30:** Image courtesy of White Columns, New York. **31:** Image courtesy of the Modern Archive. **34:** Photo: NGC. **35, 169, 172, 173:** © Krzysztof Wodiczko. Courtesy of Galerie Lelong, New York. **41, 61, 95–97, 112–13, 119:** © Jeff Koons. **44:** © Barbara Kruger. Courtesy of Mary Boone Gallery, New York. Image courtesy of Board of Trustees of the University of Illinois on behalf of its Krannert Art Museum. **49:** Courtesy of the artist. **56–57:** Photo: Matthew Herrmann. **59:** *Inflammatory Essays*, 1979–82 © 2017 Jenny Holzer, member Artists Rights Society (ARS), NY. **63 top, 66:** Courtesy of Coleen Fitzgibbon. **63 bottom, 109:** Digital image © The Museum of Modern Art / Licensed by SCALA / Art Resource, NY. **64:** Courtesy of Peter Nadin. **68, 69:** Courtesy of the artists [Louise Lawler and Sherrie Levine] and Metro Pictures, New York. **72:** Photo: Louise Lawler. Courtesy of *REALLIFE Magazine*. **91, 92, 158:** Photo: Etienne Frossard. **93:** © Guerrilla Girls. **105:** © Philip Taaffe. Courtesy of the artist and Luhring Augustine, New York. **107, 108, 168, 170–71, 179:** Photo: Malcolm Varon, NYC. **114–15:** Photo: Witte de With Center for Contemporary Art, Rotterdam. **120:** Photo: Rémi Villaggi © MUDAM Luxembourg. **125:** © APRA Foundation. **126:** © Clegg & Guttmann 1986/2012. Image © The Metropolitan Museum of Art. Image source: Art Resource, NY. **135:** Photo: Charles Benton. **137, 180:** Courtesy of the artist and David Zwirner, New York/London. **138:** Courtesy of the artist and David Zwirner, New York/London. Image courtesy of the Art Institute of Chicago / Art Resource, NY. **140:** © Jeff Koons. Photo: Laurent Lecat. **143:** Courtesy of Alan Belcher. **144:** © Barbara Kruger. Courtesy of Mary Boone Gallery, New York. **146–49:** Courtesy of Alan Belcher and *REALLIFE Magazine*. **156–57:** © The Felix Gonzalez-Torres Foundation. Courtesy of Andrea Rosen Gallery, New York. **162–63:** Courtesy of the artist and Tanya Bonakdar Gallery, New York. **174–75:** © Donald Moffett. Courtesy of the artist and Marianne Boesky Gallery, New York and Aspen. **177:** © Barbara Kruger. Image courtesy of Glenstone, Potomac, Maryland. Photo: Tim Nighswander / Imaging4Art.com. **178:** Photo: Eeva Inkeri. **183:** Courtesy of the artist and Lehmann Maupin, New York and Hong Kong

Contents

Foreword 17

Acknowledgments 18

Brand New
Art and Commodity in the 1980s
Gianni Jetzer 20

1979–82
DIY 36

Pleasure/Function
Aesthetic Services circa 1980
Leah Pires 62

1983–86
The New Capital 74

Trading in Futures
Bob Nickas 136

1987–89
Dissemination & Contamination 150

Chronology Endnotes 188

Works in the Exhibition 189

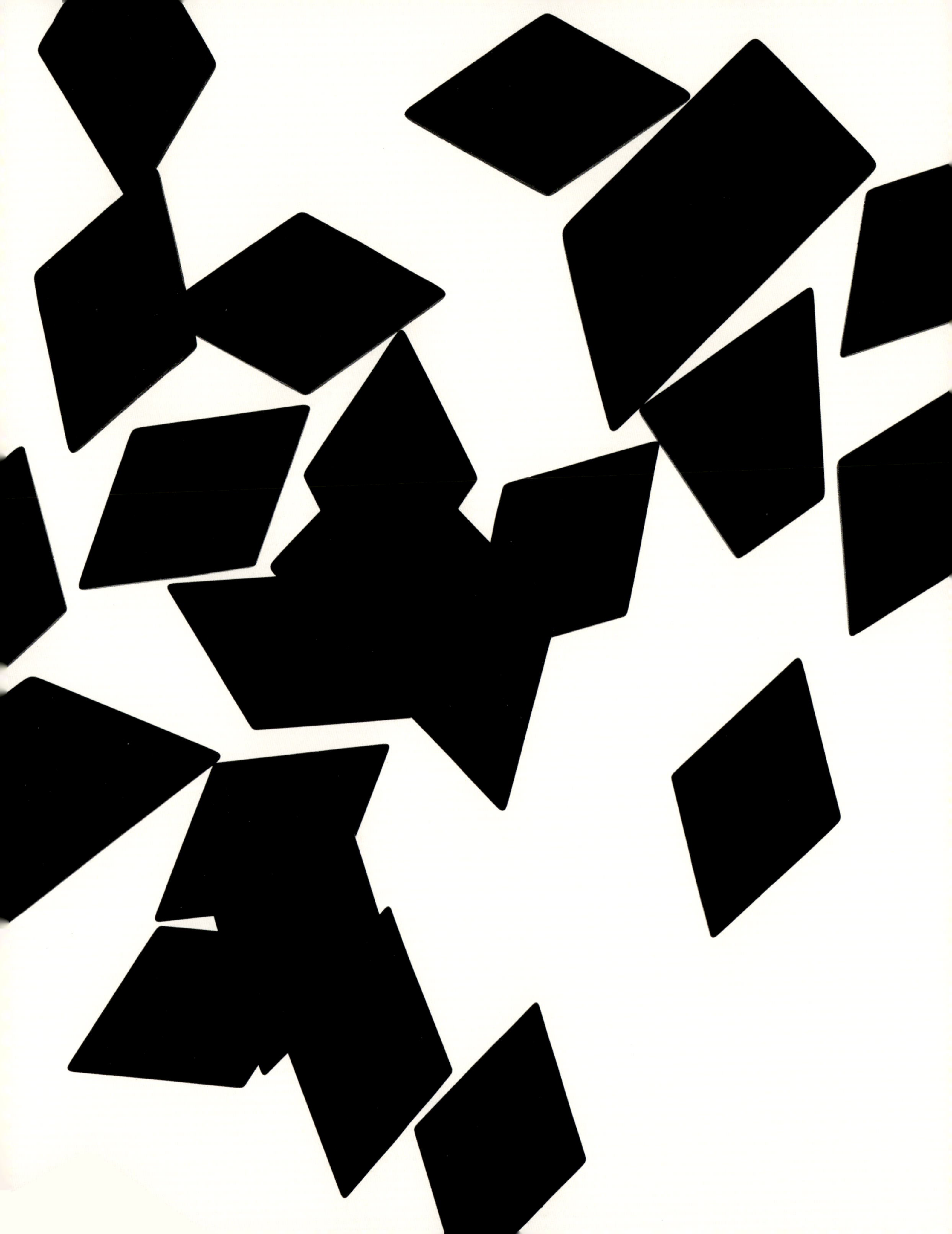

Foreword

Brand New: Art and Commodity in the 1980s accompanies an exhibition at the Hirshhorn Museum and Sculpture Garden that offers a fresh perspective on the artistic appropriation of commercial products in the late twentieth century—a decisive moment when artwork became a commodity and the artist became a brand. During the pivotal decade of the 1980s, New York City's East Village emerged as a creative center for the individuals and collectives who first embraced this radical approach. *Brand New* reexamines the work of celebrated artists such as Jeff Koons, Barbara Kruger, Richard Prince, and Cindy Sherman in this illuminating context and reflects new research on a number of their contemporaries, including Alan Belcher, Julia Wachtel, and Erika Rothenberg. The Hirshhorn, as the national museum of contemporary art, is proud to present this reappraisal of a critical period that shaped our understanding of art's role within the new globalized economy.

The title *Brand New* can be read ironically, as a reference to an insatiable consumer culture that can't get enough of the latest products. Yet it also intends to convey the genuine, fresh excitement of an era driven by desire and gratification. In the 1980s, the nation's newfound economic prosperity set the stage for a reevaluation of the art object. Within this environment, material goods were seen as a demonstration of power and financial wealth, while artists were associated with cultural capital. Everyday objects, such as vacuum cleaners, clocks, and tires, served as vehicles for storytelling, political expression, and satire; at the same time, artists themselves took on public personas that were inseparable from their artistic output. In addition to revealing this abrupt shift in the fabric of art, *Brand New* documents the unique collaborations taking place at a time when disparate, multigenerational circles of artists worked and exhibited together. Artist-run galleries played a critical role in the emergence of new voices and helped to form influential communities.

A show of this scale requires the dedication and cooperation of many people. I am indebted to Gianni Jetzer, the Hirshhorn's curator-at-large, who conceived and organized this challenging project. Bringing together the work of more than fifty artists is no small task, and coordinating the installation of such diverse material while writing a critical and enlightening book is a feat.

Brand New: Art and Commodity in the 1980s is organized by the Hirshhorn Museum and Sculpture Garden and has been made possible with support from the Hirshhorn International Council and the Hirshhorn Collectors' Council. I speak for the Museum staff and Trustees when I say that we could not have realized a venture of this magnitude without the cooperation and support of the many lenders to the exhibition. Thank you for your generosity and for enabling us to introduce our visitors to a significant and spirited period in the history of art and American culture.

Melissa Chiu
Director
Hirshhorn Museum and Sculpture Garden

Acknowledgments

This book and the associated exhibition, *Brand New: Art and Commodity in the 1980s*, would not have been possible without the generosity, advice, and collaboration graciously offered by myriad institutions and individuals who broke new ground in the 1980s. My deepest admiration goes to all the artists, gallerists, writers, and curators who have continued to work since the end of that decade to profoundly shape how we look at art today. I am particularly grateful to Bob Nickas, who provided mentorship and support on this project and who generously contributed a new text to this publication. I am also indebted to Jeffrey Deitch and Lisa Phillips for their eyewitness accounts of what was so unusual, and so appealing, in the downtown New York art scene of the 1980s.

I would like to thank personally those artists who not only agreed to display their work in this context but also directly aided in the conceptualization of the exhibition through our discussions and correspondence. To Alan Belcher, Ashley Bickerton, Mike Bidlo, Barbara Bloom, Jennifer Bolande, AA Bronson, Jessica Diamond, the Guerrilla Girls, Peter Halley, Tishan Hsu, Barbara Kruger, Louise Lawler, Ken Lum, Frank Majore, Carole Ann Klonarides, Peter Nagy, Joel Otterson, David Robbins, Walter Robinson, Julia Wachtel, James Welling, and Krzysztof Wodiczko: you have my unending gratitude and utmost respect. As regards the artists who are no longer with us, I am humbled and astounded by the integrity of Matthew C. Lange at the Sarah Charlesworth Estate; Cay-Sophie Rabinowitz and Kenta Murakami at the Gretchen Bender Estate; and Emilie Keldie and Caitlin Burkhart at the Felix Gonzalez-Torres Foundation. I truly appreciate the hard work performed by the artists' assistants: everyone at the Mike Bidlo Studio; Scott Dixon and Leigh Mozes at the Peter Halley Studio; Jenny Mushkin, Lauran Rothstein, and Sophia Alexandrov at the Jeff Koons Studio; and Raymond Foye at the Philip Taaffe Studio. Finally, I could not be more thankful for the coordination and assistance extended by many galleries, including David Lewis, David Zwirner, Elizabeth Dee, Galerie Lelong, Hauser & Wirth, Lehmann Maupin, Maccarone, Magenta Plains, Mai 36 Galerie, Marianne Boesky Gallery, Metro Pictures, P•P•O•W, Peter Freeman, Inc., Tanya Bonakdar Gallery, and Venus Over Manhattan.

I am immensely grateful to the private collectors, museums, and artists who were willing to lend singularly important works of art to the exhibition: 98 Bowery and Marc Miller; David Amico; Art Gallery of Ontario, Toronto; Michael Asher Foundation; Lisa Beck and Kevin Jones; Alan Belcher; Barbara Bloom; Jennifer Bolande; CAPC musée d'art contemporain de Bordeaux; Des Moines Art Center; Bil Ehrlich; Electronic Arts Intermix (EAI), New York; Coleen Fitzgibbon; Glenstone, Potomac, Maryland; Peter Halley; Hessel Museum of Art, Bard College, Annandale-on-Hudson, New York; Tishan Hsu; Pierre Huber; Institute of Contemporary Art, Boston; Jeff Koons; Krannert Art Museum, University of Illinois at Urbana-Champaign; Louise Lawler; Thomas Lawson and Susan Morgan; Frank Majore; MAMCO (Musée d'art moderne et contemporain), Geneva; Gracie Mansion; José Martos; The Metropolitan Museum of Art, New York; MUDAM Luxembourg, Musée d'Art Moderne Grand-Duc Jean; The Museum of Modern Art, New York; Peter Nadin; Peter Nagy; New Museum, New York; Rubell Family Collection, Miami; Richard and Ellen Sandor; B. Z. and Michael Schwartz; Philip Taaffe; Julia Wachtel; Walker Art Center, Minneapolis; Tom Warren; Robin Weglinski; James Welling; Whitney Museum of American Art, New York; Jessica R. Wolff and Stephen A. Wanta; and those lenders who wish to remain anonymous.

A prodigious amount of research went into this project, which would not have been nearly as comprehensive or extensive without the help of research/curatorial assistants Patrick Jaojoco and Sandy Guttman. This research was further inspired by a panel discussion held in February 2017 at the School of Visual Arts in association with the Master of Arts program in curatorial practice, hosted by Steven Henry Madoff and featuring myself, Julia Wachtel, and Leah Pires. An informal roundtable discussion among Mera and Don Rubell, Walter Robinson, Jay Gorney,

Julia Wachtel, Alexandre Stipanovich, and myself at the Café Odeon in Manhattan was another incredible source of information. Thank you all for your help in formulating the historical context and trajectory of the exhibition and publication. As for the meat of this volume, it is largely ascribable to the efforts of my fellow authors, Patrick Jaojoco, Bob Nickas, and Leah Pires, who connected thousands of dots within this challenging and formidably political decade and contributed their expertise and scholarship to these pages. Generously, Leah Pires shared her knowledge by curating one of the exhibition's vitrines, bringing some important printed matter into the game.

The team at the Hirshhorn Museum and Sculpture Garden was essential to the organization of both the exhibition and the book: thank you for your advice, encouragement, analysis, help, and logistical brilliance. This ambitious show would not have seen the light of day without the practical leadership of the Hirshhorn's director, Melissa Chiu, and would not have shone so brightly without the guidance of Chief Curator Stéphane Aquin. Lawrence Hyman, manager of exhibition and curatorial planning, remained a steadfast organizer and was key to assembling the exhibition's many moving parts. Stefan Gibson, project manager and designer, was responsible for ensuring the production of the exhibition, and his ideas were invaluable in making the show as beautiful as possible. Registrars Melissa Sapsford and Rajshree Solanki laid the groundwork for this complex show. Again, I offer special thanks to Sandy Guttman, curatorial assistant, who deftly coordinated ideas, data, and logistics.

Of course, this publication was a project in and of itself. It would not have been possible without the exertions of the patient and capable Rhys Conlon, former editor and publications manager at the Hirshhorn, or those of Tyler Laminack, associate editor at the museum. I also thank freelance editors Jennifer Bernstein, Susan Delson, Rachel Julia Engler, and Amy Pastan for their valuable input and for enlightening *Brand New* with their expertise and imagination. I am grateful to Malcolm Varon, who graciously photographed several works for the book on a very hectic schedule. Special thanks go to Adam Michaels, Siiri Tännler, and the Project Projects team, who are responsible for the breathtaking design of this book. Last but not least, I extend my sincerest gratitude to Margaret Rennolds Chace and the entire Rizzoli team for publishing what we hoped would be—and are now proud to call—a stunning and important art publication.

Gianni Jetzer
Curator-at-Large
Hirshhorn Museum and Sculpture Garden

Brand New
Art and Commodity in the 1980s

Gianni Jetzer

In the summer of 2014, a glass-fronted commercial refrigerator on Manhattan's High Line displayed ranks of colorful bottles hypothetically waiting for thirsty passersby to purchase them (see fig. 1). Created by the American artist Josh Kline, this work, *Skittles*, contained "smoothies" of fifteen varieties, each representing, through its name and ingredients, a particular mindset or aspect of urban living. The label of the "anarchy" smoothie, for example, proclaimed that it was made of infused vodka, Axe body wash, protein powder, Red Bull energy drink, self-tanner, bananas, and DHEA hormone. The rows of beverages reflected a collection of stereotypes, mirroring the ways in which marketing shapes the mind and body and the parallel process by which we employ products to continually reinvent ourselves.

Kline belongs to a new generation of artists who explore branding and identity in their work. Contemporaries of Kline's whose work shares this emphasis are the European artists Yngve Holen, Pamela Rosenkranz, and Antoine Catala and the American collective DIS, all of whom deftly navigate the network of the global art world and its maze of museums, galleries, biennials, private foundations, and art fairs. This interrelated system, which seamlessly integrates nonprofit organizations and commercial realities, developed most rapidly in the 1980s, when contemporary art, once a hermeneutic circle, became big business, and artists came not just to accept but to revel in the commerce of art. By branding themselves personally, appropriating forms and images from art history, and evoking and embracing consumer goods, a group of New York artists strategically positioned themselves within a market that had recently opened up to emerging art. While the previous generation of artists had relied on day jobs, grants from the National Endowment for the Arts, and income from small, DIY editions and merchandise, this group benefited from the emergence of a multitude of ambitious new galleries, centered in New York's East Village. As the art historian Jaimey Hamilton Faris recounts, "[The] heightened commodification of contemporary art was the result of a specific historical moment in which the seventies economic malaise made it appealing to find new 'local' talent rather than purchasing modern or Old Master art. With the advent of the Reagan-Thatcher era and stock market speculation, the global contemporary art market was born."[1]

The title of this publication and the associated exhibition, *Brand New*, is ambivalent in nature, yoking two words that were immanent in both art and commerce in the 1980s. Jean-Marie Dru, a leader in the global advertising industry, has posited the "brand" as the new standard that came into being at that time, overruling commodities themselves: "The notion of ideas in advertising really took off with the advent of TV advertising.... There was a premium on brevity.... It had to be based on a strong idea, an idea that struck the imagination.... The idea is not just about creatively expressing a message about the product, it's now about finding a convincing way of communicating the present or future essence of a brand."[2] As both advertising and art came to rely more on concepts and ideas than on tangible characteristics, the two fields converged to an unprecedented degree.

In the 1980s, "new," and even "brand new," no longer stood for genuine innovation but served instead as cultural shorthand for the excitement and amazement that perpetuated a cycle of desire, consumption, and instant gratification. In one of the classic art-world takes on this shift, Jeff Koons created various works incorporating the phrase "The New" into their titles or visible structure. From a studio portrait of himself as a child with a box of crayons (see p. 41) to a lightbox in the window of a museum, these works playfully undermined the notion of "newness" while accentuating the artificiality of marketing promises. As Faris puts it, "What would be 'the new' common thing that could feed the voracious engine of market expansion?"[3]

The process of commodification reached beyond actual consumer goods. As the critic and theorist Fredric Jameson recognized in 1984, the production of aesthetic and commodity signs was

1 Jaimey Hamilton Faris, *Uncommon Goods: Global Dimensions of the Readymade* (Chicago: University of Chicago Press, 2013), p. 38.

2 Jean-Marie Dru, *Jet Lag: An Adman's View of the World* (Brooklyn, NY: powerHouse Books, 2012), pp. 121-22.

3 Hamilton Faris, *Uncommon Goods*, p. 39.

4 Fredric Jameson, "Postmodernism, or, The Cultural Logic of Late Capitalism," *New Left Review* I, no. 146 (July-August 1984), p. 58.

5 See Steven A. Taubeneck, "The Subversive Quotation as a Postmodernist Pattern," *Pacific Coast Philology* 22, no. 1/2 (November 1987), pp. 88-97.

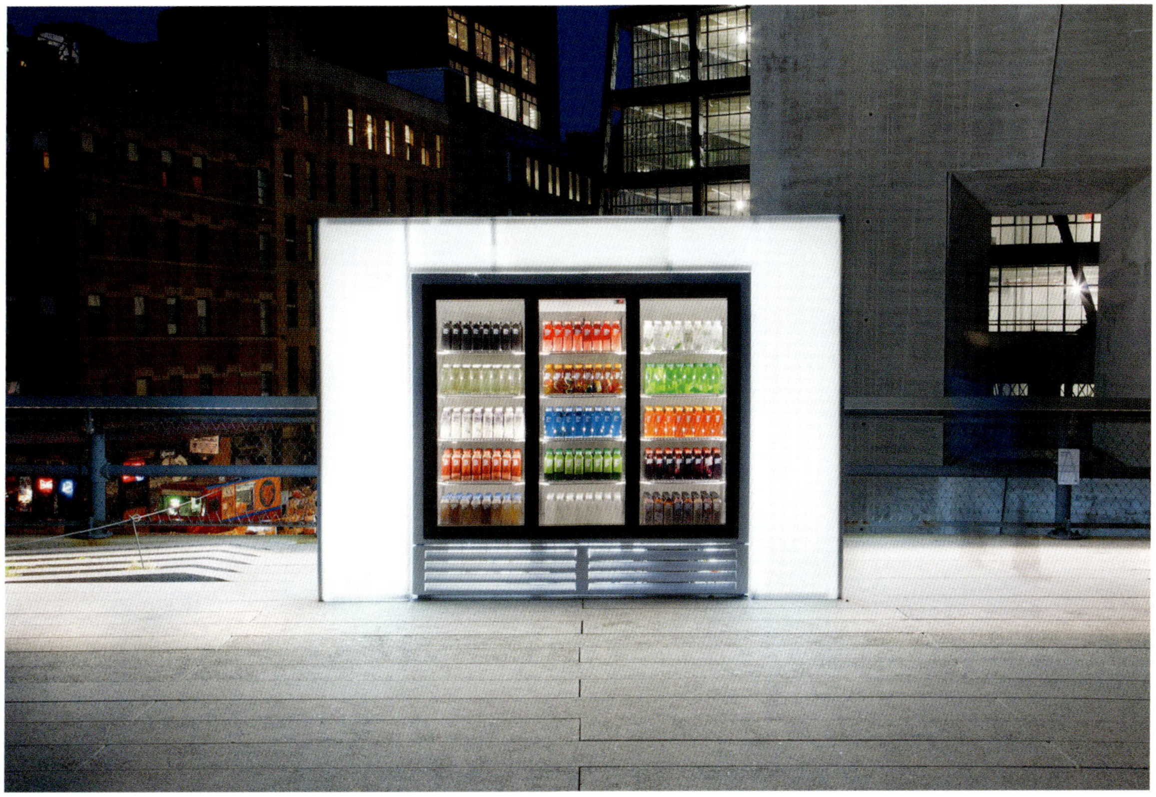

Fig. 1 Josh Kline. *Skittles*, 2014. Commercial refrigerator, lightbox, blended liquids in bottles. Commissioned and produced by Friends of the High Line. Installation view, *Archeo*, The High Line, New York, 2014

becoming increasingly entangled: "The frantic economic urgency of producing fresh waves of ever more novel-seeming goods (from clothing to airplanes), at ever greater rates of turnover, now assigns an increasingly essential structural function and position to aesthetic innovation and experimentation."[4] In light of this rampant commodification, the status of the object underwent a profound shift. As the 1980s proceeded, the public grew fascinated with brands as identities to appropriate, and artists saw an opportunity. Commercial identity was not the only field from which to borrow. A parallel profanation of high culture rendered art history a resource to be ransacked–a pastiche that could be grafted onto contemporary reality, making the use of visual quotations a hallmark of postmodernism.[5] Artists often appropriated familiar images from art history or created paintings that highlighted their quality as objects. Acknowledging the blatant realities of artistic and commercial production turned into a strategy for creating complex chains of signification pointing beyond the object itself.

Even the individual artists, as public figures, felt the impact of the prevailing marketing ethos. From the creation of signature artistic styles and personal logos to performances and other events, the line between artists and their "brands" began to blur. Political issues were also expressed through commodity signs as artists engaged with the social challenges that followed the collapse of Reaganomics and the acute AIDS crisis. At this historical moment, commodities proved to be a surprisingly sturdy vehicle for the expression and interrogation of pressing social and political matters.

In our current century, several group shows–including the New Museum of Contemporary Art's 2004 exhibition *East Village USA* in New York and the Modern Art Museum of Fort Worth's 2014 exhibition *Urban Theater: New York Art in the 1980s*–have taken a geographical approach to the period in question. Others have emphasized specific themes. Tate Modern's 2009 exhibition *Pop Life: Art in a Material World* considered Pop art and its influence, and in the same year, the Metropolitan Museum of Art organized *The Pictures Generation, 1974-1984*, which examined in detail a loose group of New York artists who touched on the subject of commercialism by appropriating media imagery, without placing actual consumer goods in their work. Finally, a 2012 exhibition at the Museum of Contemporary Art, Chicago, *This Will Have Been: Art, Love and Politics in the 1980s*, highlighted larger sociocultural impacts on art.

The true precedents for *Brand New*, however, are a pair of important exhibitions, both held in 1986, that focused solely on the commodity aspect of the art object. At the New Museum, Brian Wallis organized *Damaged Goods: Desire and the Economy of the Object*, which looked behind the facade of consumerism while questioning "the conventionalized assumptions of the systems [consumer objects]

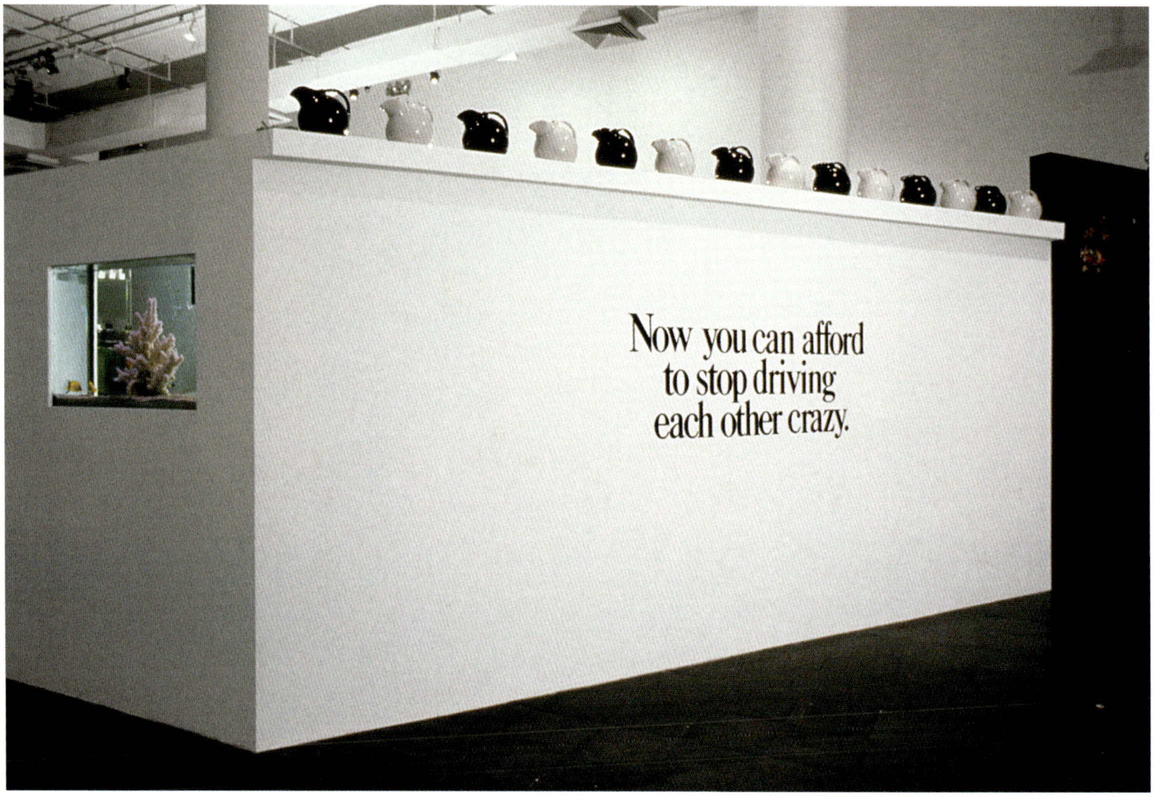

Fig. 2 **Haim Steinbach.** ***announcing something*****, 1986. Installation with variable components. Installation view,** ***Damaged Goods: Desire and the Economy of the Object*****, New Museum of Contemporary Art, New York, 1986**

inhabit"[6] **(see fig. 2)**. In parallel, *Endgame: Reference and Simulation in Recent Painting and Sculpture*, curated by David Joselit, Elisabeth Sussman, and Bob Riley at the Institute of Contemporary Art, Boston, explored the shifting status of the object and what the curators described at the time as the "political economy of the image" in the context of sociocultural and economic changes.

Brand New enlarges on these exhibitions' visions of what commodities represented as a signifying language in the art of the 1980s. In scholarship and criticism to date, postmodern art has been discussed primarily in its expression via photography, particularly as practiced by those artists who relied on commercial sources and were championed by curators and intellectuals alike. *Brand New* acknowledges the crucial contributions of artists beyond this limited scope, including postmodern artists who used marketing strategies to mirror a material world that remains, somehow, the measure of all things.

Today, we no longer see commodities as foreign objects introduced into high art but, rather, as crucial vessels for ideas. By rethinking the connection between the material world and conceptualism, New York artists in the 1980s opened the way for commercial signs to become mediums of self-projection. Eventually, the origin of an object no longer mattered–what was crucial was what it signified, to whom, and for what reasons. To understand this far-reaching shift from the readymade to what the art historian Martha Buskirk has called the "contingent object," one must look back at the gradual confluence of art and commodity over the course of the twentieth century.[7]

From Readymade to Pop

Since Marcel Duchamp's conceptualization of the readymade around 1915, the relationship between art and commodity has played a critical role in American art history. There is a direct line of development from Duchamp, who lived in the United States intermittently from 1915 and became an American citizen in 1955, to Warhol and deeper into the 1980s, in the work of artists such as Jeff Koons and Haim Steinbach. Yet, in a recent public discussion, Steinbach stated that the readymade is now obsolete.[8] His provocative assertion mirrors the somewhat complex stature of Duchamp's feat from the standpoint of the present day. In a world in which high and low culture have totally embraced one another, is Duchamp's once-shocking intervention still discernible?

For Duchamp, the readymade was a way to escape the constraints of painting. In a radical move, he chose to present mass-produced items publicly offered on the market–a urinal, a snow shovel, a vinyl typewriter cover–as his own works of art. His trespass of what had been a bold line between the two separate worlds of art and commerce caused a stir

6 Brian Wallis, "A Product You Could Kill For," in *Damaged Goods: Desire and the Economy of the Object*, exh. cat. (New York: New Museum of Contemporary Art, 1986), p. 34.

7 Martha Buskirk, *The Contingent Object of Contemporary Art* (Cambridge, MA: MIT Press, 2003), p. 211. Interestingly, Buskirk does not discuss in depth Jeff Koons's use of the word "contingency" in the 1980s; see p. 28.

8 See "Staging Common Objects" [transcript of panel discussion with John M Armleder, Bob Nickas, and Haim Steinbach, moderated by Gianni Jetzer], in Gianni Jetzer, *The Swiss Institute Experience* (Zurich: JRP Ringier, 2013), p. 400.

9 Joseph Masheck, "Introduction to the Da Capo Edition: Where Were We?" in Joseph Masheck, ed., *Marcel Duchamp in Perspective* (Englewood Cliffs, NJ: Prentice-Hall, 1975), p. xix.

10 Helen Molesworth, "Robert Rauschenberg Combines: Painting + Sculpture" [press release], Baltimore Museum of Art, 2000, http://tfaoi.com/aa/2aa/2aa398.htm.

11 Quoted in Marco Livingston, ed., *Pop Art: An International Perspective*, exh. cat. (London: Royal Academy of Arts, 1991), p. 47.

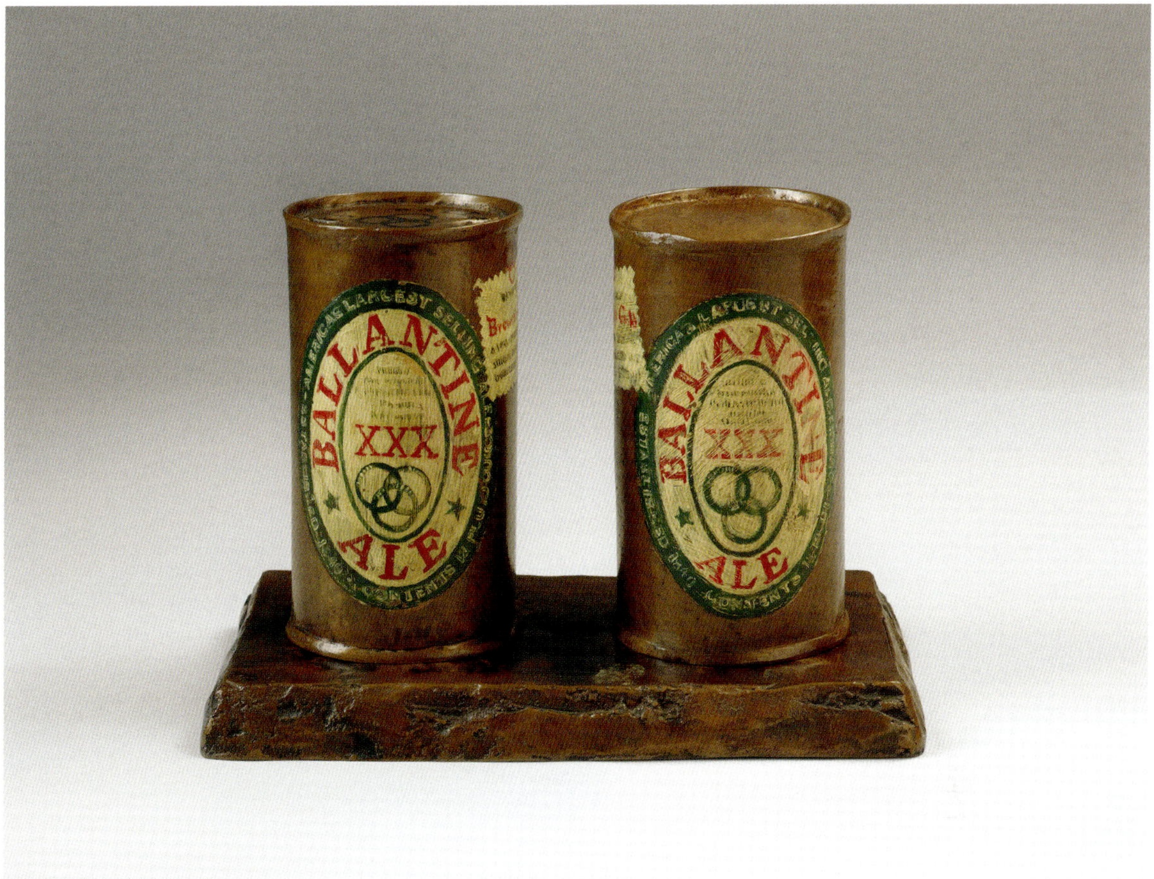

Fig. 3 **Jasper Johns. *Painted Bronze*, 1960. Oil on bronze. Museum Ludwig, Cologne, Ludwig Donation**

at the time and produced a discomfort that remains in the collective unconscious to this day. Still, as the critic and art historian Joseph Masheck pointed out in 1975, Duchamp's readymades are "nothing but art objects, however *naughty*."[9] Duchamp was not making a point of cherishing consumer objects but, rather, was testing the limits of art.

Around 1954, Robert Rauschenberg coined the term "Combine" to describe a series of works that eliminated the distinction between painting and sculpture. He had begun incorporating everyday manufactured objects such as furniture, tires, and clocks, as well as curiosities such as taxidermied animals, into his paintings, creating assemblages that blurred the line between art and commodity. The curator Helen Molesworth has aptly described the Combines as "lush meditations on the complexity of images and objects in everyday life."[10] By augmenting paintings with commonplace items, Rauschenberg ennobled those objects and placed them on an equal footing with more traditional media.

Rauschenberg played an essential role as a forerunner of New York's burgeoning Pop art movement, as did Jasper Johns, another pioneer in the introduction of consumer objects into art. Johns's anecdote about the creation of his 1960 work *Painted Bronze* **(fig. 3)** says much about the increasingly complex state of affairs between art and commodity:

> I was doing at that time sculptures of small objects–flashlights and light bulbs. Then I heard a story about Willem de Kooning. He was annoyed with my dealer, Leo Castelli, for some reason, and said something like, "That son-of-a-bitch; you could give him two beer cans and he could sell them." I heard this and thought, "What a sculpture–two beer cans." It seemed to me to fit in perfectly with what I was doing, so I did them–and Leo sold them.[11]

By painting labels neatly on cast-bronze reproductions of beer cans, Johns created, in a spirit similar to Rauschenberg's Combines, a painting-sculpture hybrid that was still clearly recognizable as a traditional work of art. The inspiration for the work lay in the bullishness of an art market that turned works of art into sheer commodities that could be sold even before their realization. In that sense, *Painted Bronze* was also an early commentary on the power of the market and its implications for artists.

By situating consumer products as a primary topic, Pop art in the 1960s shifted the paradigm even more clearly than Rauschenberg and Johns had already done. Tellingly, Andy Warhol's first jobs were designing window displays for stores and making advertising illustrations. The appearance in his artistic vocabulary around 1962–64 of Campbell's

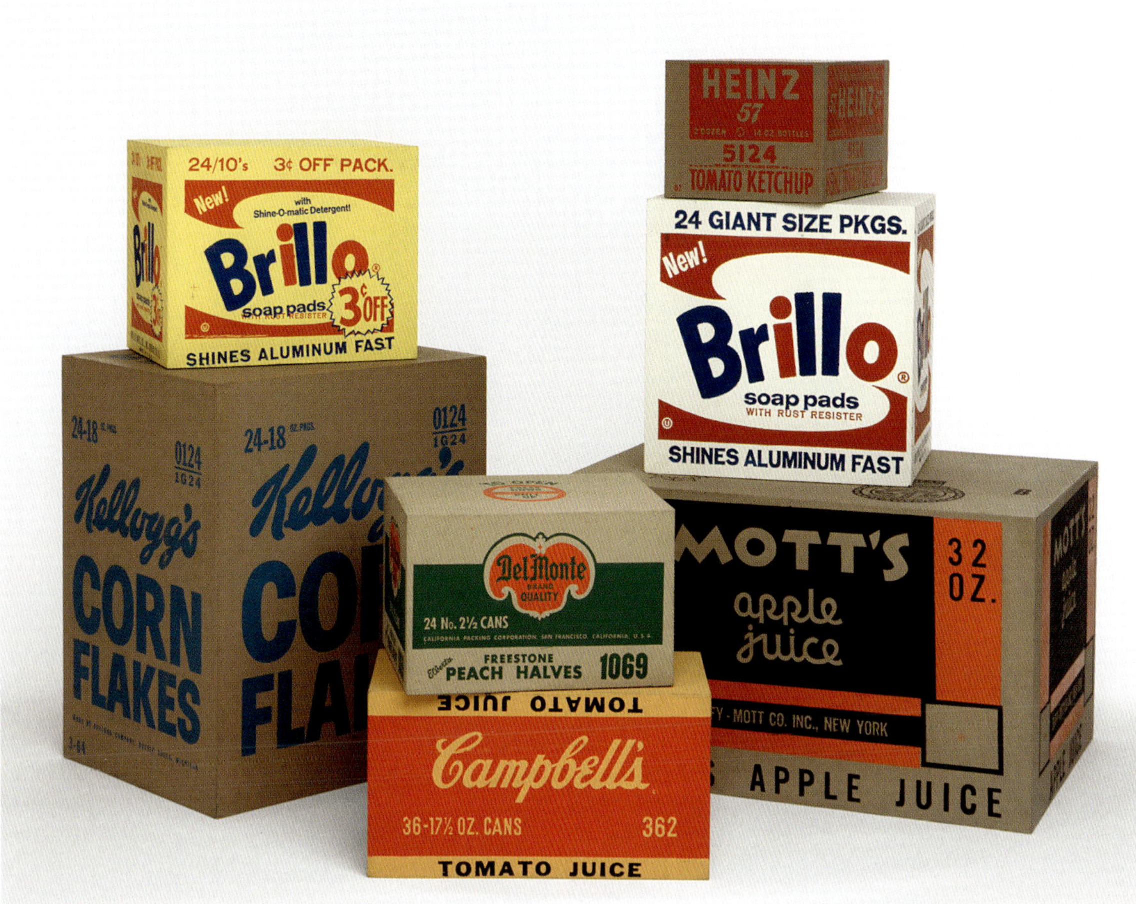

Fig. 4 Andy Warhol. ***Campbell's Tomato Juice Box; Del Monte Peach Halves Box; Heinz Tomato Ketchup Box; Kellogg's Corn Flakes Box; Mott's Apple Juice Box; White Brillo Box; Yellow Brillo Box*, 1964. Synthetic polymer paint, screenprint on wood. Walker Art Center, Minneapolis, Gift of Kate Butler Peterson, 2002**

Soup cans, Coca-Cola bottles, and boxes of Brillo soap pads elevated consumer fetishes to the realm of high art. Unlike those of the artists discussed thus far, Warhol's decision to portray commodities stemmed from his interest in them as icons of consumerism. Yet he never directly integrated actual products into his art, instead projecting them onto the surfaces of canvases or wood blocks (see fig. 4). In the tradition of Johns's beer cans, Warhol's Brillo boxes are not readymades but "re-mades"–hybrid representations, not the products themselves. Although Warhol's life became its own all-embracing brand, his work always fell within the art-historical tradition.

With this lineage in mind, the introduction of actual consumer items into art, as objects to be staged, manipulated, and re-signified, did not occur before the 1980s–not until the activities of the generation of artists foregrounded in this volume. The readymade had burst many boundaries at the beginning of the twentieth century, but in the 1980s, art and commodity became convergent lines.

Pictures and Promises

Warhol, alive and well until 1987, was a crucial figure for the artists who emerged in this period. What made him so was not only his art but also the fact that he had, over the previous twenty years, completely and unapologetically embraced consumerism. He praised the material world's seductive power and shopped constantly as a form of surrogate religion. For artists, a Warholian mindset was de rigueur at a time when the media showed a new interest in them as personalities and creative entrepreneurs. In the mid-1980s, MTV aired the series *Art Break*, in which the likes of Dara Birnbaum, Richard Prince, and Jean-Michel Basquiat presented their artistic brands in short clips. Warhol's "fifteen minutes of fame" were replaced by an endless loop of images that cable television funneled into millions of households. Political, cultural, and technological changes stimulated the social shift from modernity to postmodernity.

By the 1980s, new approaches to the communication, reception, and philosophical justification of knowledge pointed to a thorough restructuring of culture and its diffusion into the worlds of marketing

12 Together with Alan Belcher, Peter Nagy founded Gallery Nature Morte at 204 East Tenth Street in the East Village in 1982. It was one of the new galleries that represented, as Belcher puts it, "a post-modern genre of deconstructionist conceptual photography, sculpture, and painting." See https://www.balanelcher.com/gallery-nature-morte.

13 Guy Debord, *The Society of the Spectacle* (New York: Zone Books, 1994), p. 18.

14 See Jacques Derrida, *Of Grammatology* (Baltimore: Johns Hopkins University Press, 1997), p. 60.

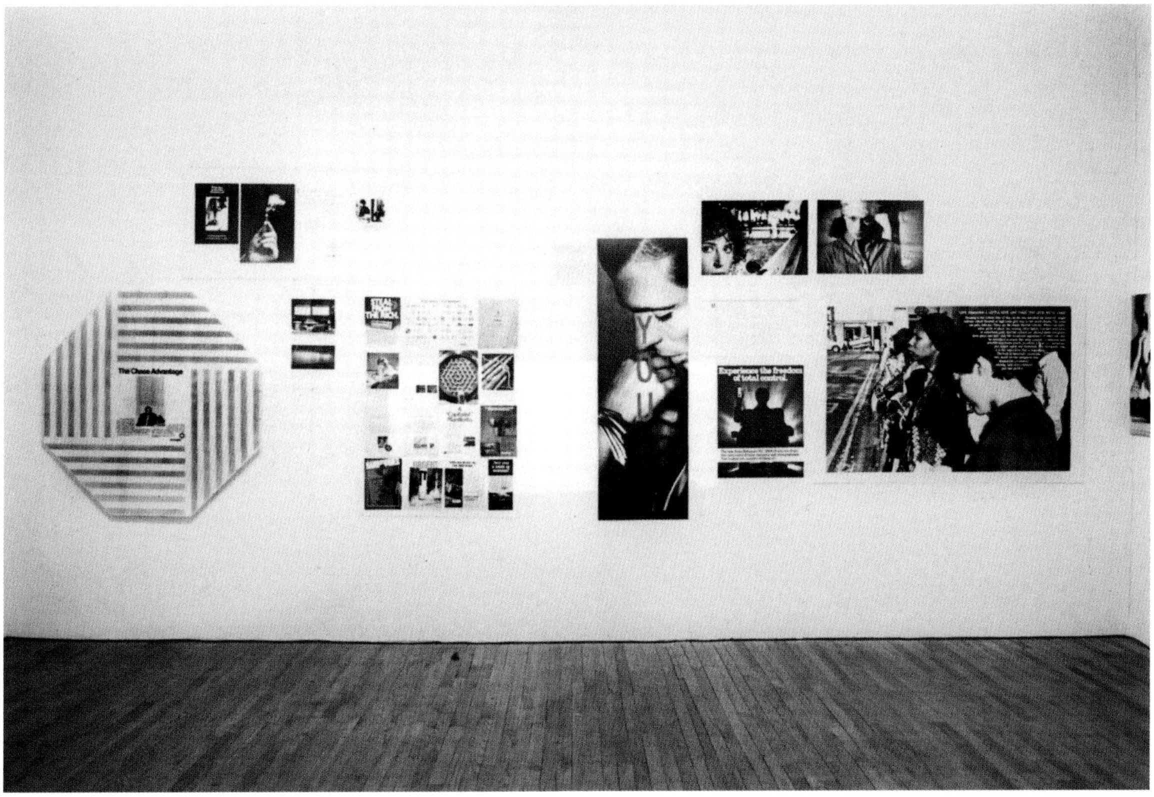

Fig. 5 Installation view, *Pictures and Promises*, The Kitchen, New York, 1981

and entertainment. One example of this development is *Entertainment Erases History*, a so-called Xerox work by the artist Peter Nagy **(see pp. 78–79)**; the works in the series, which he produced from 1982 to 1985, evoke the DIY flyers produced for self-organized art shows, performances, and concerts. Nagy, a cofounder of Gallery Nature Morte, played a crucial role in the era's East Village art scene.[12] In *Entertainment* (1983), he revamped a timeline of modernist art history, replacing the expected thumbnail images of works of art or miniature portraits of artists with graphic representations of electronic products such as computers, cordless phones, and televisions (Bridget Riley's *Current* is the only work of art that survives the alteration).

The value of these objects lay not in their visual appeal but rather in the promise of the tasks they could perform and the ways they altered daily life by providing access to limitless information and entertainment. In *The Society of the Spectacle* (1967)–one of Nagy's, and many other East Village artists', favorite reads of the time–the French philosopher and filmmaker Guy Debord had predicted the mechanisms of the upcoming media society and its impact on reality:

> When the real world changes into simple images, the simple images become real beings and effective motivations of hypnotic behavior. The spectacle, as a tendency *to make one see the world* by means of various specialized mediations (it can no longer be grasped directly), naturally finds vision to be the privileged human sense which the sense of touch was for other epochs.[13]

Following Debord's and Nagy's line of thought, the 1980s may be posited as the moment when consumption and entertainment started to shape reality in a groundbreaking way, eventually becoming the dominant vision of Western society. *Entertainment Erases History* also reflects the theory, as conceived by Jacques Derrida,[14] of "deconstruction," one of the most urgent intellectual concerns of the 1980s. A "deconstructive" analysis questions the already evident understanding of things, particularly insofar as that understanding is expressed in language, or texts, of various kinds. The sophisticated reinterpretation of the material world achieved through deconstruction and other strains of French theory became a new norm, and many once-established categories of knowledge, such as "history," were called into question.

"Representation" was another key word of the 1980s, both for its essential role in the field of semiotics and for its prominence in feminism and gender politics (for example, in such concepts as the "male gaze"); the ways in which commerce and advertising deployed images–especially of women–were interrogated in the work of Barbara Kruger, Martha Rosler, and many of their contemporaries. Parallel and more wide-ranging intellectual investigations were undertaken by writers such as Rosalind E.

Krauss, Annette Michelson, Craig Owens, Hal Foster, Douglas Crimp, and others in the pages of the influential journal *October*.[15] Somewhat controversially, this entire circle was fixated on photographic practice as exemplified in the work of the so-called Pictures Generation (a sobriquet borrowed from *Pictures*,[16] Crimp's seminal 1977 exhibition at Artists Space): as the art historian Johanna Burton has pointed out, "Much of [*October*'s] theorization of 'postmodern' practices hinged on photographic procedures, photography's embeddedness in the repetitions of mechanical reproduction making the medium especially well-equipped for rendering transparent various structures and repetitions, whether art historical, commercial, or social."[17] The *October* writers openly criticized artists who, rather than work through the medium of photography, chose to include actual commodities in their work. Foster, for example, doubted such artists' distance from the commercial world and the possibility of their critical evaluation of it.[18] Hence, the group of New York artists who came after the Pictures Generation turned toward French theorists such as Derrida and Jean Baudrillard, whose works were newly available in English-language translations published in journals such as *Semiotext(e)* and, ironically, *October* itself and who seemed to offer solutions to the vital problem of the commodity in contemporary art.

The impact of such concerns is abundantly clear in a group show curated by Kruger in 1981 at the Kitchen Center for Video and Music (better known simply as the Kitchen), a nonprofit arts space in Soho. *Pictures and Promises: A Display of Advertisings, Slogans and Interventions* (see fig. 5) combined advertisements and art in no particular order or hierarchy: Hans Haacke's critique of capitalism (in the form of an appropriated Chase Bank logo) collided with advertisements for Seagram's liquor, and Matt Mullican's pictograms consorted with Warhol's *Campbell's Soup Can*. Also on view was Dara Birnbaum's film *Rémy/Grand Central: Trains and Boats and Planes* (1980) (see p. 48), which, inspired by Debord's cinematographic collages, depicts a woman flaunting, sipping from, and eventually destroying a bottle of Cognac. Commissioned by the French brand Rémy Martin and previously shown in New York's Grand Central Station, the film was supplemented, at the Kitchen, by a screening of various television commercials. Kruger, as curator-artist, stated in the press release for the exhibition, "The quotational qualities of these words and pictures remove them and their 'originals' from the seemingly 'natural' position within the flow of dominant social directives, into the realm of commentary. This comment, at times, alternates ideas of presentation, seduction, interruption, representation, and the impossibility of opacity."[19]

For commercial signs exhibited in the art space, the decontextualization to which Kruger referred was transformative: in the hands of artists, advertisements became working material for more and less subtle critiques. Art and advertising were now equally entitled to comment on the world. As one reviewer noted, "Kruger has taken the necessary next step in seeing 'art information' and 'commercial information' as (temporarily, perhaps) convergent parallel lines, subsets of an inclusive repository of images."[20]

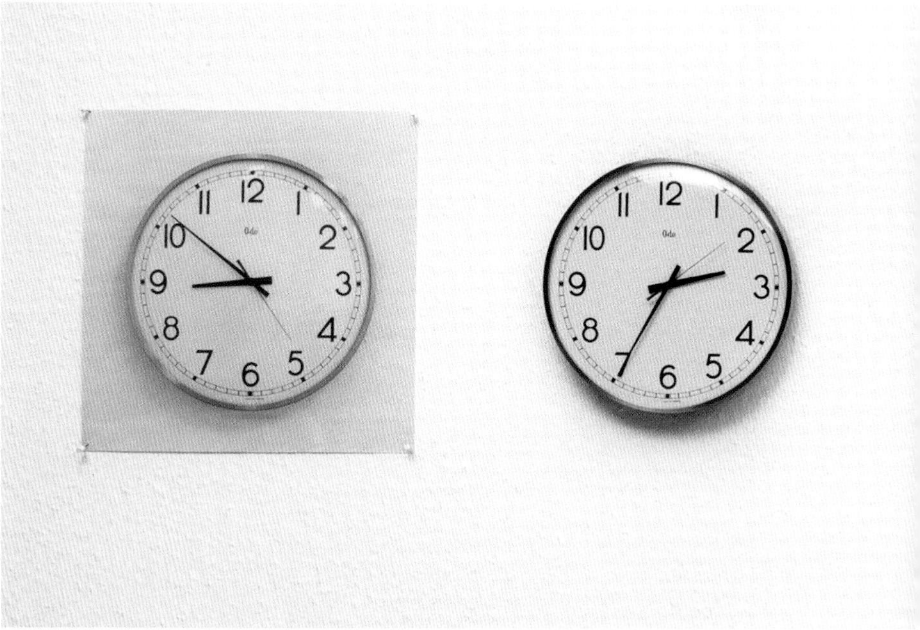

Fig. 6 Joseph Kosuth. *Clock (One and Five), English/Latin Version*, 1965. Wall clock, color photograph, and three printed texts. Tate, London, Purchased 1974

Kruger's approach echoed a new kind of representation that the artists of the Pictures Generation had begun to explore: art could put mass media under critical scrutiny by reproducing its very images. Platforms such as print media and cable television had contributed to the creation of an increasingly pervasive and powerful parallel reality: "Every cigarette, every drink, every love affair echoes down a never-ending passageway of references—to advertisements, to television shows, to movies—to the point where we no longer know if we mimic or get mimicked."[21] By pairing the word "Promises" with the already resonant word "Pictures," Kruger emphasized the aspect of desire so crucial to advertising's all-encompassing impact on the personal lives of consumers. Advertisements were everywhere. They had become a ubiquitous visual form that presumed types of literacy and cultural production that themselves had become a mere matter of codes.

Apart from her curatorial activities, Kruger's own work (see pp. 44, 144, 177) is an exemplary commentary on this new stage in capitalism's development, in which the means of consumption had become the center of attention in the all-embracing spectacle of media. Much as Warhol's early occupations inspired his art, Kruger's was informed by her work as a

15 *October*, founded in 1976 in New York, scrutinized the extra-aesthetic circumstances to which the production of art was exposed and considered many questions of political and economic reality.

16 The participating artists in Crimp's exhibition were Troy Brauntuch, Jack Goldstein, Sherrie Levine, Robert Longo, and Philip Smith.

17 Johanna Burton, "For Presentation and Display: Some Art of the '80s" [press release], Princeton University Art Museum, 2005, http://web.mit.edu/allanmc/www/amcarticles/Burton-80s.pdf.

18 See Hal Foster, "The Future of an Illusion, or the Contemporary Artist as Cargo Cultist," in Yve-Alain Bois et al., *Endgame: Reference and Simulation in Recent Painting and Sculpture*, exh. cat. (Boston: Institute of Contemporary Art; Cambridge, MA: MIT Press, 1986), p. 96.

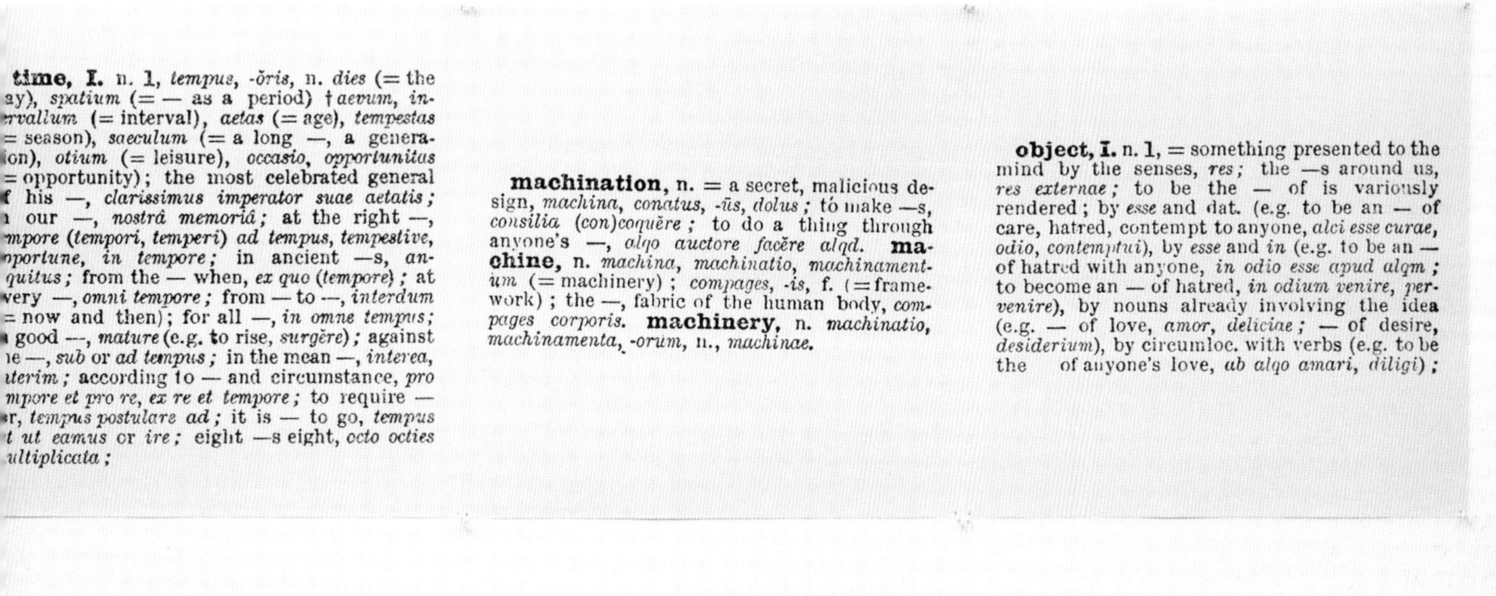

19 Barbara Kruger, "Pictures and Promises" [press release], The Kitchen Center for Video and Music, 1981, http://archive.thekitchen.org/wp-content/uploads/2015/01/PressRelease_Kruger_1981.pdf.

20 Carrie Rickey, "Pictures and Promises," *Artforum* 19, no. 7 (March 1981), p. 84.

21 Thomas Lawson, "A Fatal Attraction," in *A Fatal Attraction: Art and the Media*, exh. cat. (Chicago: Renaissance Society at the University of Chicago, 1982), p. 3.

22 Quoted in Rosetta Brooks, "Spiritual America: No Holds Barred," in Lisa Phillips, ed., *Richard Prince*, exh. cat. (New York: Whitney Museum of American Art, 1992), p. 85.

23 See Ferdinand de Saussure, *Course in General Linguistics*, ed. Charles Bally and Albert Sechehaye in collaboration with Albert Riedlinger, trans. Wade Baskin (New York: McGraw-Hill Book Co., 1966), p. 65.

graphic designer for the magazine publisher Condé Nast: her primary interest became the analysis of how images function in society.

In a somewhat different spin on these issues, the artist Martha Rosler, in 1982, performed *Martha Rosler Reads "Vogue"* live on New York's public-access Paper Tiger Television (see p. 45). Holding a copy of the world's most famous fashion magazine—which happened to be published by Condé Nast—Rosler read aloud and commented on its content, criticizing its unfulfillable promises and underlying commercialism, alluding to the working conditions under which fashion labels were produced in third-world countries, and offering an in-depth analysis of media politics from a feminist perspective.

Another pivotal figure, Richard Prince—whose work was shown in *Pictures and Promises* and repeatedly addressed in *October*—explored the permeability of art and advertising by appropriating commercial photographs in an unprecedented manner. In 1977, the same year in which Crimp's *Pictures* show took place, Prince began rephotographing advertisements, removing the advertising copy, and presenting the cropped images as large photographic prints, which he called "the closest thing to the real thing."[22] Prince's recontextualization of commercial imagery opened up additional layers of meaning, thereby exploring the economy of desire to which the images had originally belonged. In works such as *Untitled (Hand with cigarette and watch)* (1980) (see p. 49), he formally analyzed the iconography of consumerism and power, comparing different male postures. He used the medium of photography as a dissecting table to analyze, expand, and reframe commercial imagery. Appropriation Prince's primary tool at the time—was central to artistic production in the early 1980s. The technique involved seizing what might have been considered intellectual property belonging to someone else—a flat denial of ownership. In contrast to the always hermetic readymade, Prince deconstructed images to break them open and illuminate an inherent discourse of power.

Commodity as Spectacle

Early works by the American conceptual artist Joseph Kosuth such as *Clock (One and Five)* (1965) (fig. 6) illustrate the impact of semiotic theory on contemporary art. In the wall-hung installation, five items are lined up in a row: a black-and-white photograph of a wall clock, an actual wall clock, and three text panels, each bearing the definition of a relevant word. The tautological display owes much to the Swiss linguist Ferdinand de Saussure's notion of the linguistic sign, which is, he argued, a union of the signifier and the signified (whose relationship, however, is almost always arbitrary).[23] Shortly thereafter, Kosuth developed his series *Art as Idea as Idea*, in which dictionary definitions on photostats entirely displaced objects. In these works, a separation could be observed between signifier and signified, which henceforth operated as discrete "entities." The absent object was replaced by its linguistic counterpart, triggering a multitude of images. This development is reminiscent of the radical shift from modernism to postmodernism described by Baudrillard in his book *Symbolic Exchange and Death* (1976): "The end of the signifier/signified dialectic which facilitates the accumulation of knowledge and of meaning. . . . The end of the linear dimension of the commodity. The end of the classical era of the sign. The end of the era of production."[24] The collapse of the sign provoked a reset in the production of meaning, both culturally and economically. From this point forward, any object was entitled to represent any narrative: as such, commodities became open signifiers. Their value was no longer defined by what they might accomplish but rather by what they communicated. Kosuth's metamorphosis of a solid object into an idea could now work in the opposite direction: in the 1980s, artists took the far-reaching step of representing ideas *through* commodities.

By the middle of the decade, Jeff Koons, in turn, had formulated theories around his use of consumer goods. In a series of works (see p. 61), he turned simple vacuum cleaners and floor polishers into vehicles for reflecting on sexuality, eternity, life, and death. "I would like to offer up a term that has had vital currency in the process of my own thinking: contingency," he said in 1986. "I think that through this procession of contingencies, discourses are being pulled together into the object itself, promoting an awareness of the fact that all meanings are contingent upon some other meaning, where meanings are appropriated for their relationship to external forces, the larger social schema in which they're involved."[25]

The concept of contingency was crucial for Koons in liberating the household appliances he showcased in his work from their utilitarian origins. His thinking was related to the "floating signifier," a term used by the French anthropologist Claude Lévi-Strauss in his 1950 text "Introduction à l'oeuvre de Marcel Mauss." For Lévi-Strauss, the floating signifier, because of its contradictory nature, could accommodate different readings in parallel and offer a plethora of interpretations.[26] Koons's "contingency" builds on a similar base: his iterations of the vacuum cleaner hint at the anthropomorphic nature of the machine, which was capable of breath and characterized by a distinct gender attribution. He alluded to contingency as a means of turning commodities into characters that could perform different roles and therefore represent multiple strings of reality. He even considered the vacuum cleaner to be a supreme being: "It's brand new, it's in a position to out-survive you, the viewer. It doesn't have feelings, but it is better prepared to be eternal."[27] Koons's claim for contingency created a multitude of added connotations, creating a structure of diversion and, eventually, spectacle, as Debord described it: "The fetishism of the commodity–the domination of society by 'intangible as well as tangible things'–attains its ultimate fulfillment in the spectacle, where the real world is replaced by a selection of images which are projected above it, yet which at the same time succeed in making themselves regarded as the epitome of reality."[28]

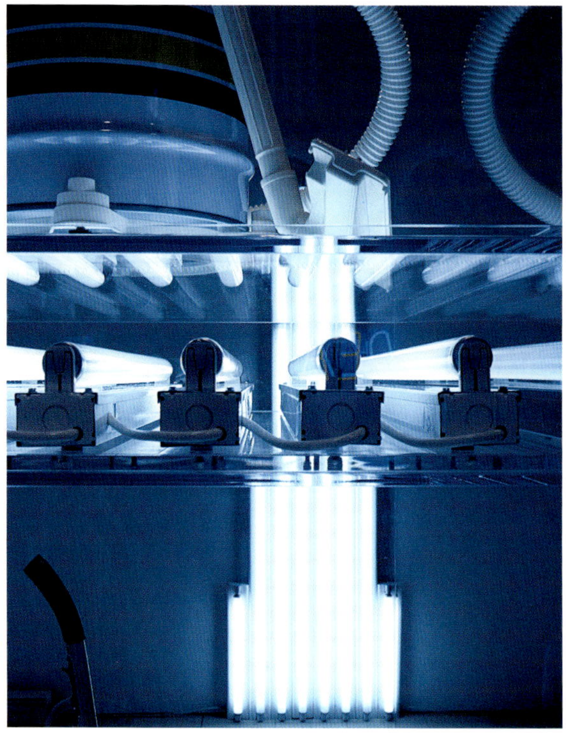

Fig. 7 Louise Lawler. *Closer Than You Thought*, 2004/2005. Cibachrome on aluminum box, laminated

Pre-New and Post-History

In the 1980s, artists' use of art history as source material drew complex lines of signification between original and reproduction, present and past, and even culture and commerce. The American artist Gretchen Bender–who later became known for her multichannel choreographies of recycled television imagery, which she called "electronic theater"–started her career making silkscreen prints. In the series *The Pleasure Is Back* (1982), she paired reproductions of paintings by Neo-Expressionist artists such as Julian Schnabel and Sandro Chia with imagery from iconic advertisements for Dial soap (see p. 43). Organized in a cruciform shape, these source images clash and create a cartography of media reality, in which every image is flattened and streamlined into a larger mass of "infotainment."[29] In the process, the images became paradigmatic samples of representation. While the Pictures Generation deconstructed media reality to see behind its curtain, artists such as Bender appropriated images and reorganized them to reflect the contemporary flux of imagery in which we are all immersed.

In Koons's *Pre-New* series, which preceded the stacked vacuum cleaner works discussed above, he mounted domestic appliances to the front of fluorescent tubes, creating intriguing display mock-ups. In both these and the subsequent series, in which the machines are immortalized in neat acrylic cases with a layer of fluorescent tubing at the bottom, the settings are formally close to the work of artists such

24 Jean Baudrillard, *Symbolic Exchange and Death* (London: Sage Publications, 1993), p. 145.

25 David Robbins, ed., "From Criticism to Complicity" [transcript of panel discussion on May 2, 1986, at Pat Hearn Gallery with Sherrie Levine, Peter Halley, Jeff Koons, Haim Steinbach, Ashley Bickerton, and Philip Taaffe, moderated by Peter Nagy], *Flash Art*, no. 129 (Summer 1986), p. 49.

26 See Jeffrey Mehlman, "The 'Floating Signifier': From Lévi-Strauss to Lacan," *Yale French Studies*, no. 48 (1972), pp. 10–37.

27 Quoted in Michael Archer, *Jeff Koons: One Ball Total Equilibrium Tank* (London: Afterall Books, 2011), p. 80.

28 Debord, *Society of the Spectacle*, p. 36.

29 *Infotainment* was the title of an exhibition organized by the collector Anne Livet in close cooperation with Gallery Nature Morte in New York in 1985. The show, one of the most complete surveys of artists from the East Village scene, toured multiple cities in the United States. The term "infotainment" became popular in the 1980s, when information and entertainment were no longer seen as opposing poles but rather as competing realities. See *Infotainment (18 Artists from New York)*, exh. cat. (New York: J. Berg Press, 1985).

30 James Welling's thesis exhibition at California Institute of the Arts (CalArts) in April 1974 consisted of torn-out ad pages from magazines (of cigarettes and other items), making him a forerunner of the Pictures Generation. By 1985, he was playing with the formal language of Minimalism, putting tiles reminiscent of Carl Andre's work on the surface of photographic paper to create intriguing

photograms (see pp. 16, 132, 133). Rodney Graham placed the twenty-four-volume complete works of Sigmund Freud in a box shaped like a Donald Judd metal shelf, marrying psychoanalysis and specific object. Ashley Bickerton referred to Judd as the point of departure for his wall-hung boxes in conversation with the author on July 12, 2016, in New York.

31 After meeting Richard Prince in the late 1970s, Sherrie Levine began creating work that subtly confronted the subject of gender relations. She produced a groundbreaking series of works that appropriated the renowned noncommercial, government-commissioned work of the photographer Walker Evans and expanded the investigation of image codes to the cultural field. The amount of contrast she used in her prints was lower than that used by Evans; upon inspection, the images are clearly recognizable as Levine's own, even though the subjects and cropping are identical to the originals. Levine understood her work not only as a critique of art as commodity but also as a feminist deconstruction of overwhelmingly male art history.

32 Robbins, "From Criticism to Complicity," p. 48.

33 Walter Benjamin wrote his seminal essay "The Work of Art in the Age of Mechanical Reproduction" in 1935. It influenced several generations of thinkers, from the Frankfurt School to the Situationists. The essay was particularly important within the *October* circle.

as Donald Judd and Dan Flavin, whose Minimalist tropes play into the purity of Koons's displays. In the 1980s, a number of artists shared this fascination with Minimalism and, occupying a posthistorical standpoint, applied formal languages from that earlier movement to make new kinds of art.[30] Louise Lawler exemplified this affiliation in her photograph *Closer Than You Thought* (2004/2005) **(fig. 7)**, which portrays a fluorescent Flavin work through the lit display case of a Koons vacuum cleaner. By pointing her camera at the formal analogies between the two works, Lawler simultaneously revealed their differences. While for Flavin the fluorescent tubes constituted the work of art, in Koons's case, they were a frame of reference.

Jeff Koons's contemporary Peter Halley–both were represented by the up-and-coming East Village gallery International With Monument–developed an interest in geometry that went beyond Minimalist art. In his seminal essay "The Crisis in Geometry," Halley discussed and reproduced works by Donald Judd and Frank Stella as well as post-Minimalist artists such as Robert Smithson and Robert Morris. Halley, like many in his cohort, was heavily influenced by Baudrillard; his primary goal as a painter was to put Baudrillard's theories into practice and to create an art of simulation. Halley's cell-and-conduit series **(see p. 111)** maps out a complex ramification, hinting at the French philosopher's "hyperreality" (an idealized, artificial version of reality). Equally influenced by Michel Foucault and his 1975 opus *Discipline and Punish*, Halley combined social thought with simulation to create a series of works touching on prisons, including *Prison and Cell with Smokestack and Conduit* (1985). The Roll-A-Tex texture and use of Day-Glo colors–Halley's trademark–were references to the facades of suburban homes, to Pop art and psychedelic culture, and to the artificial glow of technology, thus conflating painting, vernacular architecture, nostalgia, and contemporaneity.

Mike Bidlo carried art-historical appropriation to an extreme by restaging Warhol's Factory in his studio at PS1 in Long Island City for one April afternoon in 1984 **(see pp. 86–87)**. In *Mike Bidlo Presents: The Factory at PS1*, Bidlo played Andy, while some of his contemporaries represented other famous figures (David Wojnarowicz, for example, played Lou Reed). The appropriation of an entire artistic scene that had been initiated by a still-living artist was an ambitious act, and it revealed that not just works of art but the visual brands of artists could now be "borrowed." Eventually, it became clear that Warhol and his entourage represented his identity better than any one of his artworks. The appropriation of tangible property was ultimately not enough; in artistic practice, the staging of relational information quickly informed new production.

Painting as Object Lesson

Sherrie Levine's stripe paintings of the mid-1980s represent a slightly different kind of appropriation **(see p. 104)**.[31] They are, as the artist openly stated, a direct take on the works of BMPT, the mid-1960s Parisian group consisting of Daniel Buren, Olivier Mosset, Michel Parmentier, and Niele Toroni, who, in their own estimation, had staked out the "degree zero" of painting. When Mosset borrowed the painted stripes of his colleague Buren to escape the confinement of his own artistic brand–the circle–he provoked a furious reaction from his former ally. Levine spoke of an "object lesson"[32] residing in this historical episode, implying that even paintings had turned into a product that was available for general use. Levine's stripe paintings are miniature vignettes that act as stand-ins for the object lesson they illustrate. In their new identity as commodity, they gain a subversive momentum. They are not, however, "mechanical reproductions" as described by the German critic and philosopher Walter Benjamin in his epochal essay but, rather, casein and wax on wood, carefully painted by hand.[33] This choice of Levine's made her position even more particular, because, by the historical moment in question, the medium of painting was largely considered anachronistic or even simply "over."[34] Thus, these works and their reception in the art world demonstrate that history had reached a critical turning point at which deconstruction had become a new cultural standard. In the words of Peter Halley, "There was an almost complete rejection of this idea of history on the part of both artists and theoreticians, and it, therefore, became necessary to rethink the relationship between artists and the previous art that they had incorporated into their own."[35]

Another artist in this circle, Philip Taaffe, acted on a similar idea, borrowing a subject from the collection of the Museum of Modern Art, New York–Bridget Riley's *Current* (1964)–as the model for his work *Undercurrent* (1984) **(see p. 105)**. Curiously, Taaffe found his source material in the Op art movement, which, by the 1980s, had been marginalized and almost forgotten. He translated the painting of his older colleague into a mixed-media collage, establishing a dialogue between history and representation. Moreover, Op art shared a penchant for black-and-white décor, a dominant design aesthetic of the 1980s **(see fig. 9)**–making Taaffe's appropriations not only a strange replay of history but also an allusion to the many ways that art was now being diffused into everyday life.

The rediscovery and reassessment around this time of the work of the American artist Elaine Sturtevant (who preferred to be identified by her last name alone) can also be related to the developing abolition of history and profanation of earlier works

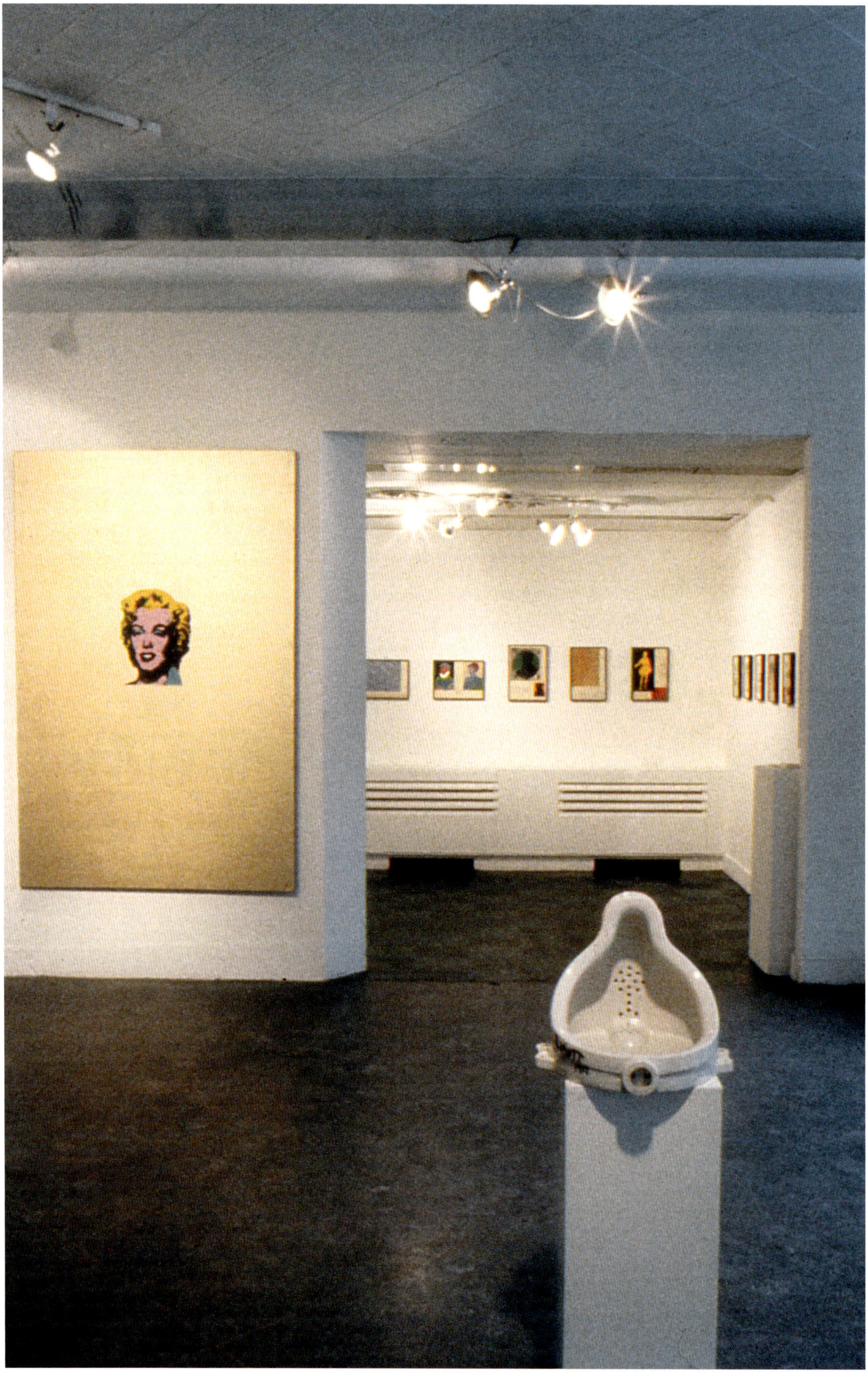

Fig. 8 Installation view, *Sturtevant*, White Columns, New York, 1986

of art into a common language. Sturtevant, whose first one-woman show had taken place in 1965, made appropriation the center of her practice, manually replicating works in various media by, among other male artists, Rauschenberg, Warhol, Roy Lichtenstein, Joseph Beuys, and Claes Oldenburg–often (though not always) with their approval and collaboration. Her spring solo show at White Columns in 1986, which featured her re-creations of Marcel Duchamp's *Fountain* and Warhol's *Gold Marilyn Monroe* **(see fig. 8)**, received considerable attention. Although her borrowing from other artists had been cause for suspicion in the 1960s, Sturtevant–as someone who practiced appropriation *avant la lettre*–was now seen as a luminary.

The Swiss artist John M Armleder, a fixture of the 1980s New York art scene with regular solo shows at John Gibson Gallery in Soho, took the radical step of acting as if he were an interior decorator, carefully delivering paintings that paired, harmoniously or not, with existing furniture (something that most collectors do anyway); in so doing, he further investigated the status of the common object **(see p. 109)**. Chairs, flowerpots, and even surfboards served as points of departure for the paintings he formulated to match them, often borrowing motifs from Russian Constructivism. The resulting nonconformist commodity sculptures, which Armleder called *Furniture Sculptures*, went to the core of his Fluxus-inspired practice–opening up definitions of art by staging unexpected encounters.

Interestingly, in the 1980s, media and art often performed odd dances with one another. After Allan McCollum first showed his *Surrogate Paintings*–a series of handmade wood (later plaster) stand-ins for paintings, essentially solid-black rectangles with glossy white frames **(see pp. 54–55)**–he was watching television one day and noticed framed paintings on film sets that closely resembled his *Surrogates* when viewed in the background of a shot or in the blur of motion. In the series that followed, *Surrogates on Location*, he further analyzed the status of painting in a media-saturated world by photographing the television screen and capturing the stand-ins in "action," thereby ironically reclaiming his *Surrogates*. To McCollum's delight, the *Surrogate* paintings, originally meant to form open signifiers for the gallery visitor to digest, did not exist only there but were strewn throughout the media environment, in countless shows and films, and with a similar aim: to create "tokens of exchange" for the viewer.[36]

Artists such as Levine, Taaffe, and Bidlo, successors to the pioneers Sturtevant and Mosset, attacked the supremacy of painting by disrespecting its presumed inimitability. In similar ways, Armleder and McCollum staged paintings as placeholders and surrogates, undermining their status as originals.

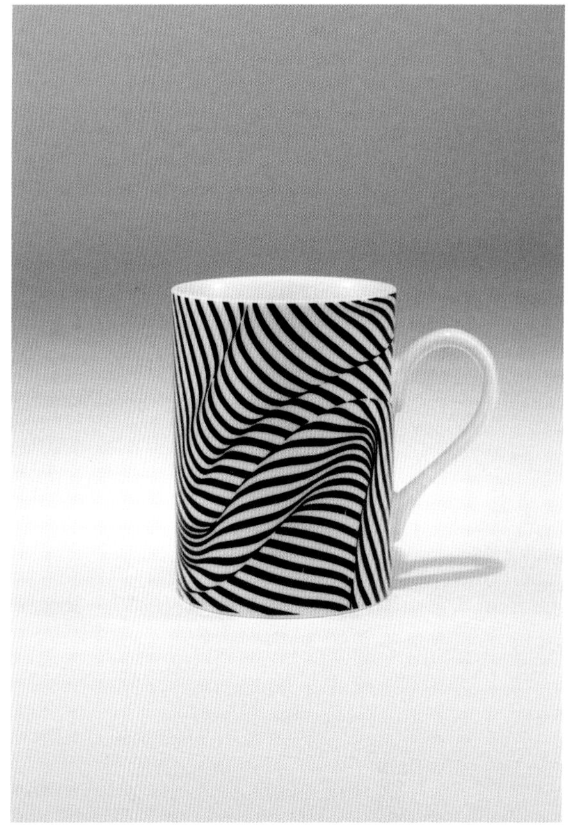

Fig. 9 Robert and Trix Haussmann for Swid Powell. "Black Stripes" mug, 1984

Beyond the Product Itself

In 1981, the artist Haim Steinbach created *Shelf with Ajax* **(see p. 60)**. A plastic *faux bois* ledge supported by several natural branches and lined with floral-print fabric serves as the display for a can of Ajax cleanser. The sharp contrast between the false lushness of the shelf and the simple, bold design of the supermarket product defies easy interpretation. Introduced in 1947, the Ajax brand, owned by Colgate-Palmolive, had become a household name for cleanliness. Here, the can's commodity status is undermined through an almost surreal mise-en-scène that generates an enigmatic presence; yet, the cleanser is still legible as an everyday commodity. Its status as a brand-name object, even removed from its use value, is never eradicated. Unlike Warhol's soup cans, *Shelf with Ajax* is not a representational depiction. The work is not a Rauschenbergian Combine, either, and not even appropriation comes into play. Instead, the thing itself takes the main stage. Steinbach went directly to the actual Ajax, a mass-produced, strongly branded product that anyone with a small amount of money could buy. Furthermore, the staged commodity points beyond its initial context of domestic cleanliness. It indicates the general interest in antiseptic products characteristic of the period and brings to light striking parallels between assertions of cleanness and demonstrations of power. In

34 In "The End of Painting" (*October*, no. 16 [Spring 1981], pp. 69–86), Douglas Crimp stated that it was no longer possible to make relevant contributions to the field. He rejected the work of Frank Stella, considering it pure idiocy, and praised the in-situ works of Daniel Buren because, for Crimp, the confinement of painting did not apply to such simple marks. Thomas Lawson saw painting, in 1985, as the "last exit" in the endgame of postmodernism, arguing that it offered "perfect camouflage" and was a "subversive method from the center of the marketplace." He explicitly excluded those he called "ironic painters," namely Julian Schnabel. See Thomas Lawson, "Last Exit: Painting," in Richard Hertz, ed., *Theories of Contemporary Art* (Upper Saddle River, NJ: Prentice Hall, 1985), pp. 143–55.

35 Peter Halley, *Selected Essays: 1981–2001* (New York: Edgewise Press, 2013), p. 241.

36 D. A. Robbins, "An Interview with Allan McCollum," *Arts Magazine*, October 1985, p. 40.

advertising, sprays that promised to "kill 100% of germs" were so aggressively marketed that the art historian David Joselit compared the ads' language to President Ronald Reagan's war rhetoric. Joselit observed, for example, that "the home can be a place riddled with invisible enemies and troublesome battlefields: a place in which to kill."[37]

Steinbach's *Ajax* emerged alongside the work of other artists, such as Jeff Koons, who used and sometimes glorified cleaning products such as detergents, vacuums, and sponges in their work. Others highlighted hygienic methods in the context of AIDS and the fear of contamination. The sculptor Robert Gober, for instance, started his sink series (see p. 130) in 1984, arguably the darkest year of the AIDS epidemic. The critic Peter Schjeldahl noticed the sinks' "cold air of clinical hygiene,"[38] contextualizing them as a form of poetic activism allied to the art of Felix Gonzalez-Torres. Other American artists expanded the concept of hygiene to the social order. Tishan Hsu covered his sculptures in mass-produced tiles; his *Biocube* (1988) (see p. 159) is a hybrid object that mimics laboratory furniture or surgical fixtures. Its surface, however, is strangely marked by pustules that seem to indicate the outbreak of disease within the sanitized cube. Alan Belcher's *$51.49* (1983) (see p. 134) consists of a dye transfer label that the artist applied to a bottle of Solo fabric softener. The balanced, symmetrical composition, with its integrated text, references the work of Pop artists such as Robert Indiana, but the catchwords themselves—LOGO, COLA, AIDS—underscore the complexity of real life through their controversial juxtaposition.

By the mid-1980s, Haim Steinbach had become famous for his increasingly sophisticated arrangements of mass-produced items on spotlessly clean, Minimalist-inspired wedge shelves. The shelves' Formica-laminated surfaces recalled Donald Judd's reliefs and Richard Artschwager's furniture sculptures, while the displayed consumer items were always neatly organized, like play figurines in a board game. The impact of commercial reality set the tone of the works. Steinbach had made shopping a part of his artistic practice and quoted the aesthetics of mercantile staging, from in-store presentations to window displays. In her review of Steinbach's 1986 show at Cable Gallery in the East Village, Roberta Smith pointed out the historical aspects of *supremely black* (1985) (see p. 117):

> The "Bold" experiment of Constructivist design is recalled, even as its absorption into contemporary design and commercial art is acknowledged. . . . The decoding and recoding of color—the liveliest, most sensuous aspect of Steinbach's work—is terrific, as is the way he uses color as a clue to ideas. When color and subject matter rub together . . . things begin to click, and the area of investigation that Steinbach has demarcated for himself—the overlap of modernism and commerce—becomes visible.[39]

The combination of history, consumerism, and color coding resulted in a synchronization of multiple layers of reality. Steinbach acknowledged that objects are transient and interactive; his works are thus tests of the physical presence of objects.

In parallel, advertising firms were developing branding ideas that went far beyond the products' actual use value. In 1984, Apple Inc. aired one of the most ambitious commercials in the history of advertising. Directed by the Hollywood auteur Ridley Scott, it is today considered a masterpiece. The cofounder of Apple, Steve Jobs, was strongly involved in the creation of the plot, which featured an unnamed heroine who saves humanity from oppression. In an allusion to George Orwell's 1949 novel *Nineteen Eighty-Four*, rows and rows of meek, gray-garbed slaves watch a screen on which "Big Brother" speaks, until the athletic actress runs up the aisle and flings a sledgehammer at the screen, destroying it in a fireball. On her white tank top, we see the silhouette of the new Apple Macintosh computer. An off-screen voice then reads the closing titles on screen: "On January 24th, Apple Computer will introduce Macintosh. And you'll see why 1984 won't be like '1984.'" Never had the public seen such an explicitly ambivalent television advertisement. It contained references not only to literature but also to the Olympic Games that would take place in Los Angeles that summer, and it acknowledged feminism as well as the anxieties surrounding a computer-dominated future. Brands such as Apple came to be fetishized even more than the commodities themselves. Apple situated itself as more than a producer of consumer goods; it was, and is, a lifestyle and a psychological entity. It took another ten years for the company to crystallize its brand into a simple slogan: *Think different*.

By that point, commodities had become thoroughly incorporated into the complex chain of signification and ideation that marked much of 1980s art. Through the creation of brands, the subordinated commodities acquired additional connotations that allowed them to stand in for, or emblematize, *ideas*. The layers of sometimes contradictory reality that were grafted onto material objects to create an all-encompassing vision seemed altogether without boundaries.

The Artist as Entertainer

As the narrative of the brand came to define the act of consumption, many artists saw fit to develop themselves into brands, simultaneously subverting

37 David Joselit, "Modern Leisure," in Bois et al., *Endgame*, p. 82.

38 Peter Schjeldahl, "Found Meanings: A Robert Gober Retrospective," *New York*, October 13, 2014.

39 Roberta Smith, "Haim Steinbach at Cable," *Art in America*, February 1986, p. 128.

and embracing commodification by using branding methods in their art and personas. As we have seen, one of the earliest artists to achieve such a brand-like presence was Andy Warhol (see fig. 10). His position within the newly mediatized system of the 1960s made him a star long before the profession of artist was co-opted as an integral part of the urban lifestyle. Following Warhol, a younger generation of artists began to focus intently on the representation of their personas. Ever since, successful artists have routinely taken flight on the "twin engines of branding knowledge, both as consummate image managers, and as managers of their own brand."[40]

In the early 1980s, Ashley Bickerton created a brand name, "SUSIE," for his artistic productions (see pp. 56–57). What began as the subject of a single painting later became a virtual trademark that served as a subversive artistic signature. "By choosing a phonetically casual, female first name, that whole agenda is thrown into some discursive light," wrote the art historian Abigail Solomon-Godeau. "In a sense it becomes the artist's *name brand*, but it also becomes the name brand. It breaks down the individual creator and they are no more Bickertons than they are Susies."[41] The artist also investigated the function of the work of art beyond its exhibition in a gallery. Bickerton saw his works as utilitarian products made specifically to be lifted, shipped, stored, and hung. Their installation streamlined via built-in brackets and soft covers, his works became object lessons on the subject of art and commodity (see p. 183). In 1987, inspired by the sight of surfboards covered with sponsorship decals, he began to sell ad space on his works:

> What better place for a Marlboro logo than in the lower right-hand corner of a rugged, hulking Richard Serra monolith? Or how about a pale-toned Cinzano logo discreetly placed on the elegant white surface of a Robert Ryman, just below the top right bracket? That was it. I would sell off portions of the face of the painting to various "tony" clients, who would have to pay a set fee in trade. I found eight buyers, including a fashion designer, two galleries, and a German bank, all of whom readily agreed to the terms. . . . All I ever really needed was their commitment to make the piece legit.[42]

Bickerton described these logo works as ways of seeing himself through the products he used, here mirroring the capitalist illusion of choice that triggers consumerism as a form of pure self-expression.

Although branding did not reach a fever pitch until the mid-1980s, the Canadian art collective General Idea was a precursor to Bickerton as far as self-branding and commercialized artistic production were concerned (see fig. 11). Between 1971 and 1987, AA Bronson, Felix Partz, and Jorge Zontal built a complex, self-referential body of work that internalized and commented on the art world and its commercial practices. *The Boutique from the 1984 Miss General Idea Pavilion*, which the artists staged in multiple forms and venues, was a retrospective of their works and editions presented on a desk shaped like a dollar sign (see p. 102). In its first appearances, with sales staff on site, the work represented a bona fide offer to sell editions of the artists' work, and copies of their magazine, *FILE*, for cash. Placed within an exhibition, this gift shop turned shopping into an art experience, anticipating Keith Haring's Pop Shop (which opened in 1986) and the scenarios of "relational aesthetics" that would follow nearly two decades later. General Idea's stance was as serious as it was tongue-in-cheek, poking fun at the commercialization of art and the self-branding of artists.

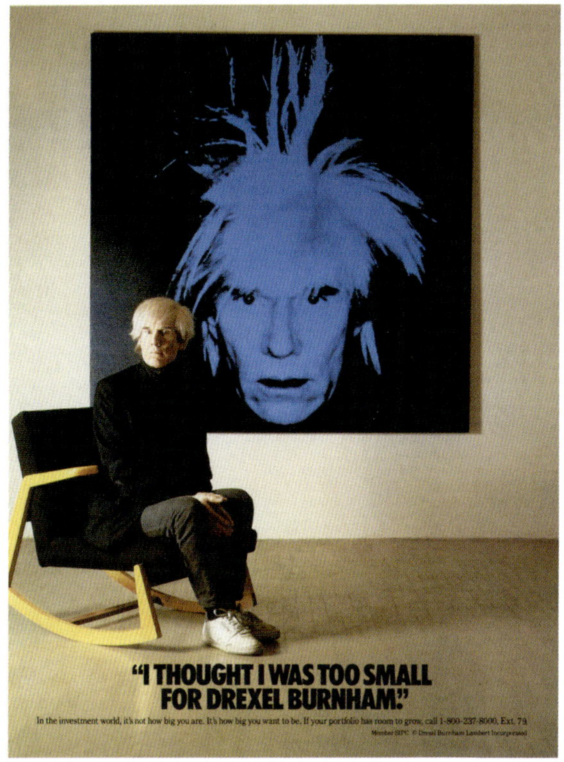

Fig. 10 Drexel Burnham Lambert advertisement, 1985 (ran 1985–87). The Andy Warhol Museum, Pittsburgh; Founding Collection, Contribution The Andy Warhol Foundation for the Visual Arts, Inc. (T185)

General Idea's and Ashley Bickerton's independent self-commercializing activities quickly became a general trend, as echoed in David Robbins's *Talent* (1986) (see p. 98–99). The work consists of eighteen framed black-and-white head shots, each portraying a member of the circle of artists that dominated the downtown New York art scene in 1986—a year that marked an important turning point in that scene. In October, the legendary Sonnabend Gallery in Soho presented an exhibition of four artists—Bickerton, Peter Halley, Jeff Koons, and Meyer Vaisman—who had previously shown with International With

40 Jonathan E. Schroeder, "The Artist and the Brand," *European Journal of Marketing* 39, no. 11/12 (2005), p. 1293.

41 Abigail Solomon-Godeau, "Bickerton's 'Bickertons' in the Realm of the Fetish," in Fredi Fischli and Niels Olsen, eds., *Ashley Bickerton: Susie* (Zurich: Edition Patrick Frey, 2014), p. 115.

42 Kara Vander Weg, ed., *Ashley Bickerton* (London: Other Criteria, 2015), p. 82.

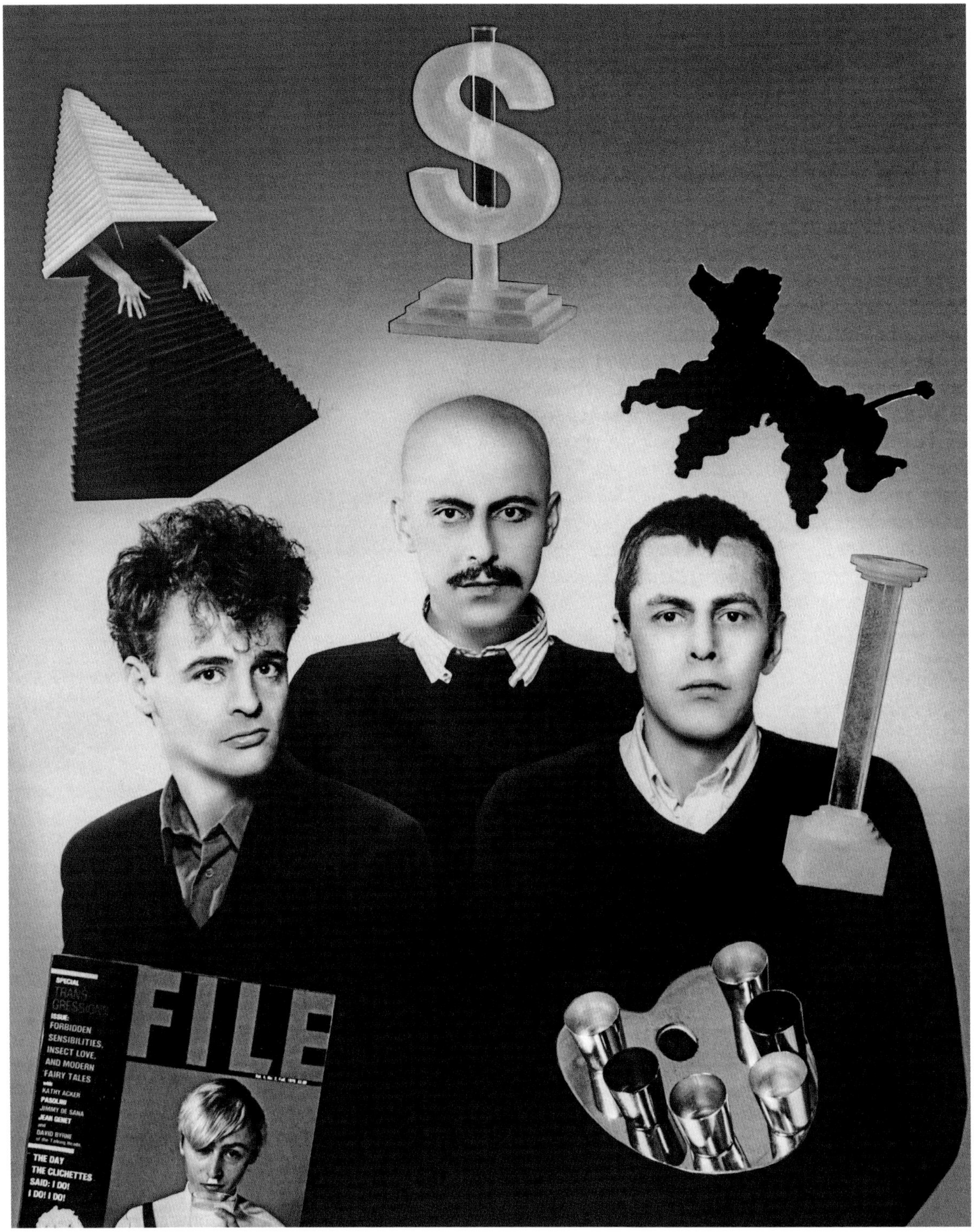

Fig. 11 **General Idea. *Self-portrait with Objects*, 1982. Gelatin silver print. National Gallery of Canada, Ottawa, CMCP Collection, Purchased 1985**

Monument, the artist-run gallery spearheaded by Vaisman in the East Village. The powerful, successful Ileana Sonnabend now represented the "Hot Four," as *New York* magazine dubbed them; each had been quite strategic in how he managed his connections and brokered his deals. The four self-made and (literally, in Bickerton's case) self-branded artists, with that show, fulfilled their soaring dreams of success and reinforced the strong brands that were inextricably linked with their "personas." As such, in *Talent*, Robbins portrayed Koons and Bickerton (and sixteen of their peers) as if they were television stars, conveying that, at the time, they operated simultaneously in two different contexts: in the art world, with intellectual, political, and moral standards and positions, and in the realm of pure entertainment. To a certain extent, *Talent* was meant as a critique of the very capitalist culture that influenced the artists' practices,

43 Mehmet Odekon, *Booms and Busts: An Encyclopedia of Economic History from the First Stock Market Crash of 1792 to the Current Global Economic Crisis* (Abingdon-on-Thames: Routledge, 2015), p. 784.

44 Surprisingly, the blue-chip art market continued in full force until 1989; art had become a more trusted currency than securities. See Paul Ardenne and Michel Vale, "The Art Market in the 1980s," *International Journal of Political Economy* 25, no. 2 (Summer 1995), pp. 100–128.

45 Krzysztof Wodiczko, *Critical Vehicles: Writings, Projects, Interviews* (Cambridge, MA: MIT Press, 1999), p. 79.

46 David Deitcher, "What Does Silence Equal Now?" in Brian Wallis, Marianne Weems, and Philip Yenawine, eds., *Art Matters: How the Culture Wars Changed America* (New York: New York University Press, 1999), p. 102.

thus pointing to a crossroads for this generation of artists. Some of them, like Koons, became remarkably successful commercially, while others went on developing their work with greater or lesser degrees of exposure.

With the closing of both International With Monument in 1987 and Nature Morte in 1988, a story that began as a DIY movement ended firmly in the realm of business. Artists who created subversive cultural forms–many of which were "dangerously" close to actual commercial practices–were ultimately digested by a capitalist system that transformed them and their artistic production into creative capital.

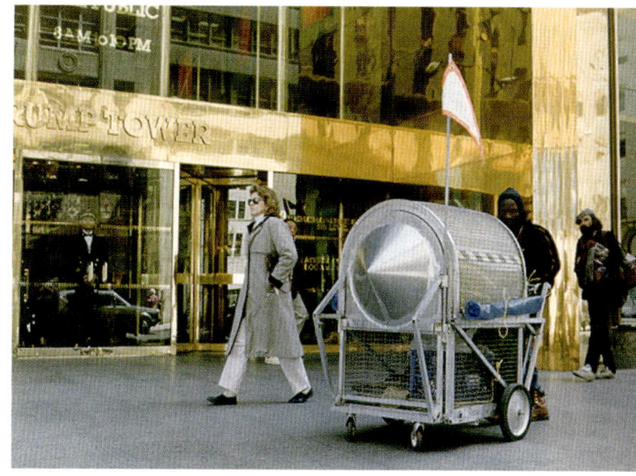

Fig. 12 Krzysztof Wodiczko. *Homeless Vehicle*, 1988–89. Aluminum, Lexan, plywood, plastic, fabric steel, rubber. Variant 3 pictured outside Trump Tower, New York

Commodity Signs and Social Change

The system at large would soon collapse under its weight. The stock market crash of 1987 ("Black Monday," as it came to be called) was the largest one-day market devaluation in history.[43] On October 19, 1987, the Dow Jones Average lost almost a quarter of its value, or $500 billion; the ensuing economic crisis hit New York hard.[44] An estimated 70,000 people were homeless in New York during the winter of 1987–88.[45] With this population in mind, the Polish-born artist Krzysztof Wodiczko redesigned the archetypal grocery shopping cart–traditionally used by homeless people to transport their possessions or collect cans for recycling–for greater functionality. With *Homeless Vehicle* (1988) **(see pp. 172–73)**, Wodiczko merged vehicle and sculpture, art and social work, community and museum, in a hybrid form that radically expanded what art imbued with commodity could accomplish. It is an early example of an artist's offering a service, even if for a limited time, to an underprivileged demographic, turning his work into a social and political statement **(see fig. 12)**.

The need to address social matters became even more urgent in the face of the AIDS epidemic. By the late 1980s, the disease had decimated communities around the country and the world, including New York's artistic community. Everyone was grieving; death seemed ubiquitous. In a remarkable extension and, in some ways, inversion of their 1980s evolution, strategies of commodity signification came to play a crucial role in addressing the urgent matters provoked by the AIDS crisis. William Olander, a curator at the New Museum and member of the activist group ACT UP (AIDS Coalition To Unleash Power), invited eleven artists–specifically, those who would later form the collective Gran Fury–to stage a beacon of hope in the museum's window during the month of July 1987.[46] The resulting neon work, *SILENCE = DEATH* **(see pp. 154–55)**, was a striking pink triangle placed above the eponymous text. It was at once eye-catching and irritatingly similar to a commercial logo. Its message, however, was as political as it was personal, because the lack of open discussion and education about the AIDS crisis was, ultimately, a great risk to society. In an age of consolidated, streamlined information, commercial forms became a medium through which even the most difficult topics could be discussed.

Compared with artists such as Gran Fury and Donald Moffett, who directly defied AIDS through words **(see p. 174–75)**, the Cuban-born American artist Felix Gonzalez-Torres opted for a more allegorical approach. His *"Untitled" (Perfect Lovers)* **(see pp. 156–57)** consists of a pair of identical store-bought wall clocks hanging side by side, running in sync. One of them will inevitably stop ticking before the other, causing the "perfect lovers" to part. Gonzalez-Torres began the work in 1987 and dedicated it to his partner, Ross Laycock, in 1991, the year Laycock died from an AIDS-related illness. Despite the gravity of the situation, the work is at once playful and romantic, public and private, wholly material yet representative of an intangible reality. Gonzalez-Torres cross-pollinated elements of his own biography, political activism, and conceptual art in a way that transcended the mundane product of which his work consisted. *"Untitled" (Perfect Lovers)* achieved an additional layer of complexity in the gradual convergence of art and commodity.

Although the gold-rush mood of the mid-1980s faded in the face of such serious social issues, the commodity language that had developed–a language influenced at once by Pop art, Minimalism, conceptualism, and the culture at large–boldly remained. The hard lines separating art, politics, and commodities had been eradicated. The deconstructive heyday of the 1980s would further determine artistic practices worldwide: by the decade's close, the commodity had gained an entirely new and ineradicable presence in art. Its potential had been explored and its properties tested; new conceptual ground had been cleared, upon which future generations would build their practices.

1979–82
DIY

1979

February
Twenty-nine-year-old **Julian Schnabel** has an extremely successful solo show at Mary Boone Gallery on West Broadway in Soho (in the same building as the legendary Leo Castelli Gallery), followed by another in October. His Neo-Expressionist broken-plate paintings create a stir and open up a new market for contemporary art.

March
Writer Susan Morgan and painter Thomas Lawson found ***REALLIFE Magazine*** to cover new and overlooked art from contemporary artists' points of view. The first issue contains the seminal article "Collage and the Problem of Representation: Sherrie Levine's New Work."

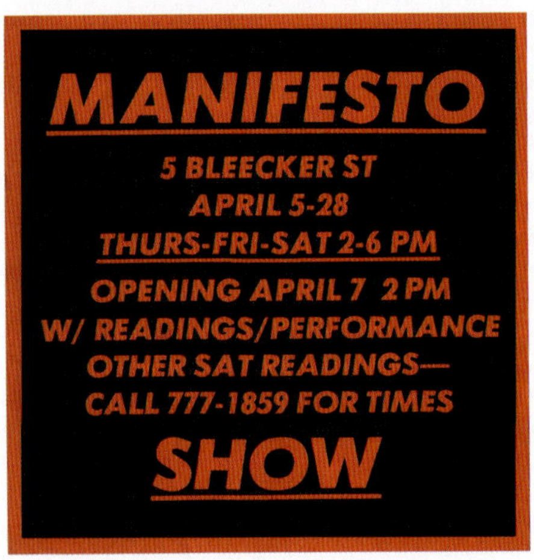

Jenny Holzer/Coleen Fitzgibbon. *Manifesto Show* poster, 1979

April
Jenny Holzer presents her *Inflammatory Essays* at the *Manifesto Show*, organized by herself and **Coleen Fitzgibbon**, both members of the artists' group Collaborative Projects (or Colab; see January 1980). Holzer: "There were manifestos in the window; printed tirades on the right-hand side of the room; visual manifestos—things that looked more like art—on the left; a platform for shouting in the middle; and we blasted speeches from a loud-speaker outside."

May
East Village Eye, a monthly newspaper devoted to avant-garde culture, is founded. Walter Robinson, a member of Colab, designs the back cover of the second (June) issue, in which both his work and Jenny Holzer's are discussed. The *Eye*, which ends its run in 1987, is a key player in creating the East Village scene.

June
Richard Prince presents three works from his *Single Men* series at Three Lives & Co., a bookstore in Greenwich Village, placing his appropriated film stills in the context of a shop window. An artist's statement musing about the mysterious complacency of contemporary life, via the depicted figures, is distributed at the bookstore.

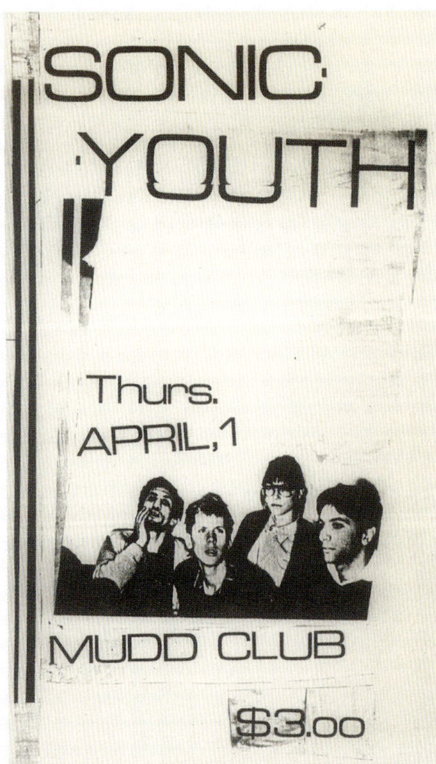

Poster for Sonic Youth concert at the Mudd Club, 1981

November
The Talking Heads song "Life During Wartime" enters the Billboard charts on November 3 and remains on the list for five weeks. The song features the lyric "This ain't no Mudd Club, or CBGB," referencing two underground music venues. The **Mudd Club**, founded the previous year in a Tribeca building owned by artist Ross Bleckner (77 White Street), gains notoriety as the Talking Heads, Sonic Youth, and Black Flag play to downtown punks. The No Wave and alternative scenes are nurtured here; from the beginning, performance art and other artist's programs are presented as well.

1980

Curator and artist Carole Ann Klonarides and producer Michael Owens launch **MICA-TV**, a collaborative video production company making video portraits of contemporary artists in the same manner and style in which the artists themselves work. The portraits borrow several formats from mainstream television, from interview to commercial.

Rosetta Brooks, a London-based writer, editor, and publisher, starts ***ZG***, a magazine for contemporary art and the avant-garde; she moves to New York in 1984 and continues to publish the magazine there. Each thematic issue features writings on and by artists and theorists, including Vito Acconci, Jean Baudrillard, Dara Birnbaum, and Peter Halley.

January
The Real Estate Show, an exhibition illegally staged by Colab in a vacant building on the Lower East Side (125 Delancey Street), sets the stage for the creation of the alternative space **ABC No Rio**, also founded in 1980 and still in existence today. **Colab**—a group of 50 or so artists working together to exhibit work wherever they can—is the first in a strong list of artists' collectives and collaboratives to establish alternative spaces on the Lower East Side and in the East Village.

May
Invited by Marcia Tucker, founding director of the New Museum, **Jeff Koons** shows

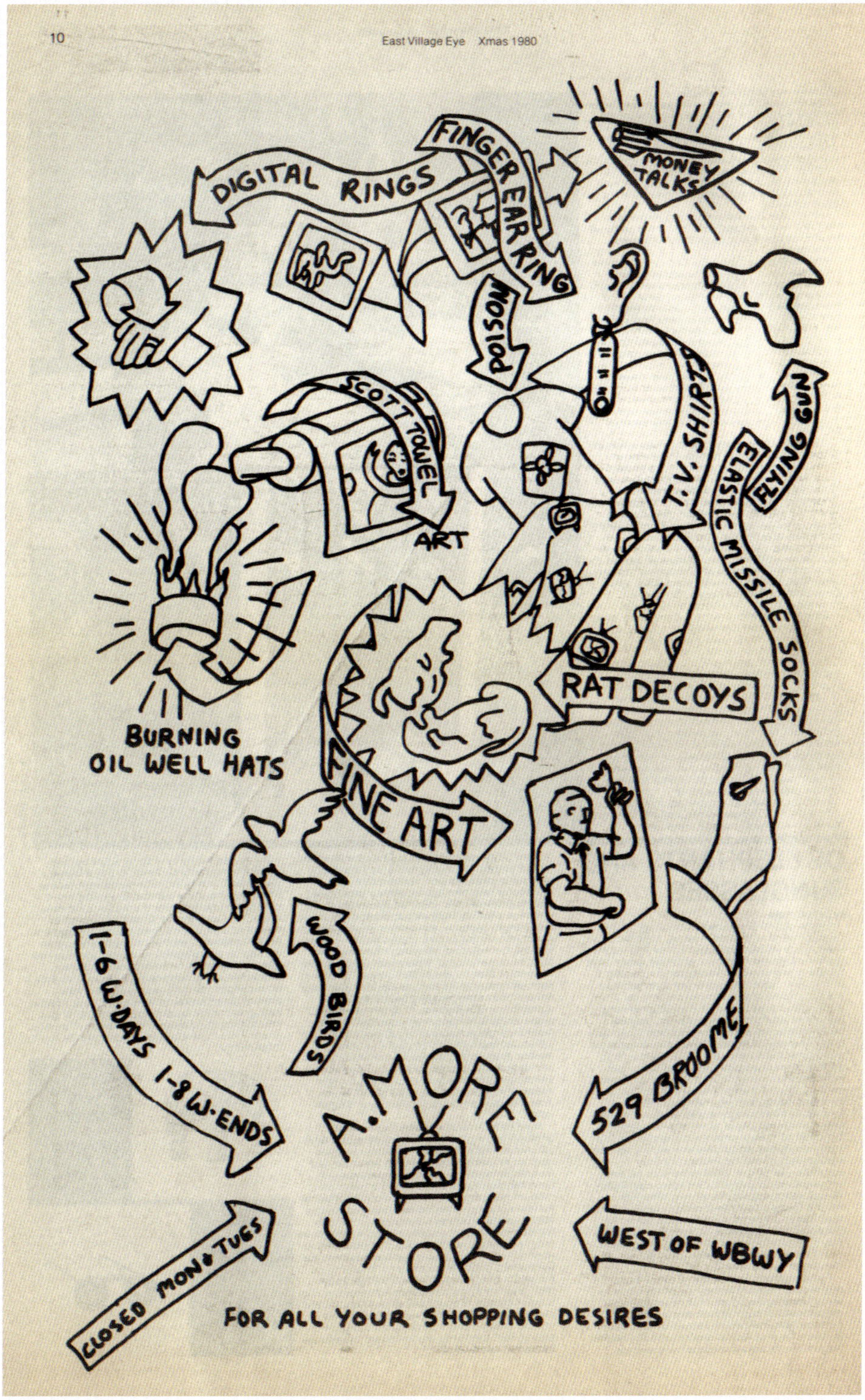

Advertisement for A. More Store, with drawing by Tom Otterness, 1980

in the museum's window at 65 Fifth Avenue in Greenwich Village. Three works consisting of vacuum cleaners and floor polishers mounted on fluorescent tubes are interrupted by a lightbox stating "THE NEW" in black letters on a red background.

Keith Haring begins organizing group shows at **Club 57**, located in the basement of a church at 57 St. Mark's Place in the East Village. A preamble to the alternative art scene in the East Village and Lower East Side, the club becomes a hotspot for artists and musicians.

June
Colab presents the *Times Square Show* in an abandoned building in Times Square (a district then dominated by sex-related businesses). The exhibition's gift shop, with cheap, artist-made objects for sale, inspires Colab's **A. More Store** around Christmastime. The pop-up store, selling inexpensive artist's editions, is organized by Ellen Cooper, Walter Robinson, and Kiki Smith at 529 Broome Street in Soho and runs in iterations until 1984, appearing at White Columns, Jack Tilton Gallery, Barbara Gladstone Gallery, and Printed Matter and including work by artists such as Barbara Kruger and Haim Steinbach. The group helps to popularize the concept of the art pop-up shop, which takes a different form later in the decade with Keith Haring's Pop Shop (see April 1986).

October
Group Material, a collective of artists and curators, holds its inaugural exhibition at 244 East 13th Street in the East Village. The gallery is one of the first in the East Village—then a rough neighborhood with cheap rent for emerging artists—and is quite engaged in the community. For the 1981 exhibition *The People's Choice (Arroz con Mango)*, members of Group Material go "door-to-door on their block . . . and [ask] each household to donate a valuable possession. . . . It wasn't so much that they wanted 'art,' as anything with 'sentimental, cultural value.'"[1] This activity parallels the burgeoning practices of artists Nancy Shaver and Haim Steinbach. Although the space lasts just one season, the collective keeps working together and organizes several more exhibitions outside the gallery space in unexpected places.

November
Janelle Reiring, previously of Leo Castelli Gallery, and Helene Winer, former director of Artists Space, open **Metro Pictures** on Greene Street in Soho. Metro's opening exhibition includes Sherrie Levine, Richard Prince, Cindy Sherman, and James Welling, representing the new theoretical developments in art. The year before, artist **Tony Shafrazi** (then infamous for his 1974 spray-painting of Picasso's *Guernica* at the Museum of Modern Art) had opened his namesake gallery on Mercer Street, also in Soho; Shafrazi goes on to make its reputation (alongside FUN Gallery and others like it; see September 1981) in contrast to the "serious," theory-heavy artists represented by Metro Pictures.

Ronald Reagan is elected the fortieth president of the United States.

1981

Run DMC, **Beastie Boys**, and **Sonic Youth** are all founded, each to gain notoriety and immense cultural traction in the coming years.

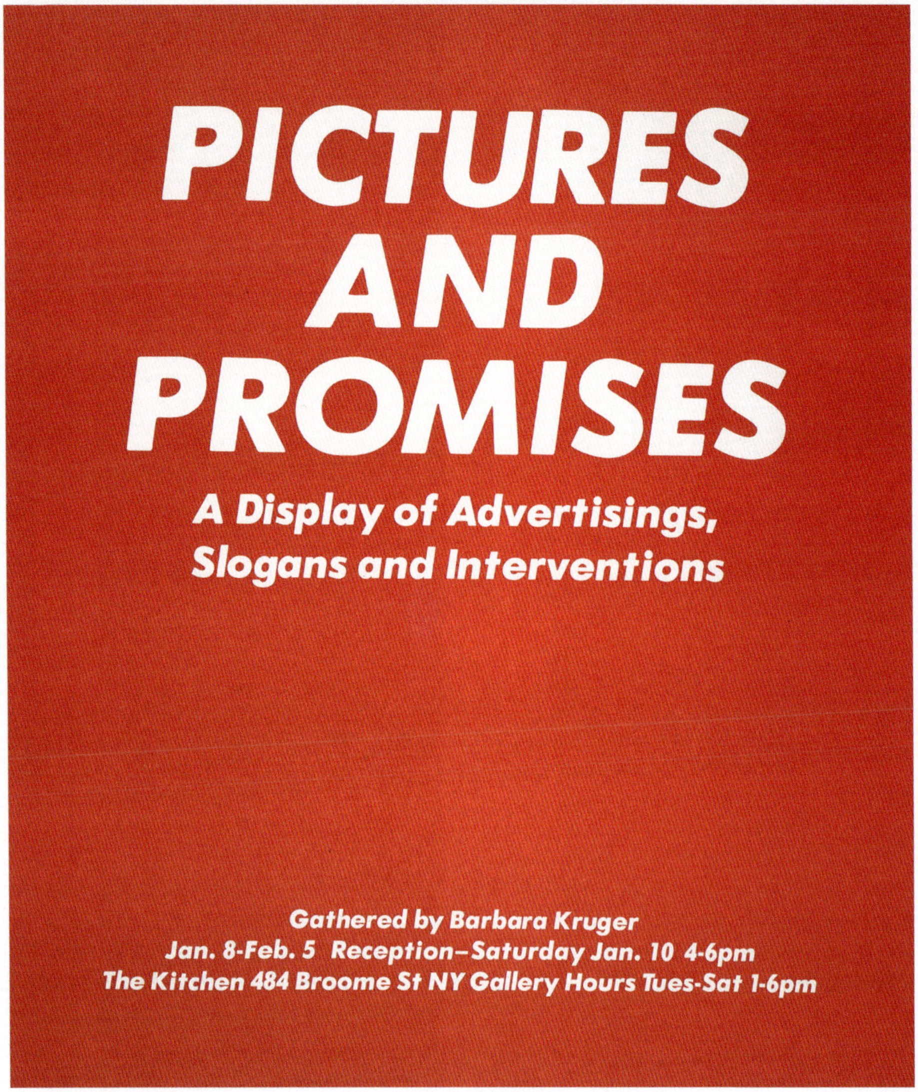

Barbara Kruger. *Pictures and Promises* poster, 1981

January
Barbara Kruger curates *Pictures and Promises* at the Kitchen in Soho, which includes work by Sherrie Levine, Matt Mullican, and Laurie Simmons, among others, as well as magazine spreads, advertisements, posters, and television commercials. The exhibition, by adding the word "Promises" to an allusion to the renowned "Pictures Generation," gets at the root of the desire summoned by commodities and their image.

February
Keith Haring curates his first show at the Mudd Club. The exhibition, titled *Lower Manhattan Drawing Show*, includes 99 artists and strays far from the official Soho gallery scene. Press release: "Many of them have shown their works outside of Soho at Fashion Moda, Group Material, ABC No Rio as well as the *Times Square Show*. They will now have the advantage of the convenience of Soho as well as a full length three week exhibition with gallery hours extending to as late as 2:00 am."[2]

April
The Japanese company **Nintendo** (originally a producer of playing cards) introduces Donkey Kong to North American markets; it eventually becomes one of the most important titles in the golden age of video arcade games.

August
MTV Music Television launches on Saturday, August 1, at 12:01 am EST with footage of a rocket launch and the words, "Ladies and gentlemen, rock 'n' roll." The iconic image of an astronaut standing on the moon with MTV's logo flickering on the flag in place of the Stars and Stripes is used as the station's original branding clip, played at the top of the hour between sets of music videos.

September
Bill Stelling and underground film star Patti Astor, who had met at the Mudd Club, open **FUN Gallery** at 229 East 11th Street. The gallery is the first to champion downtown graffiti art by the likes of Jean-Michel Basquiat and Keith Haring as well as one of the earliest to stake out ground in the up-and-coming East Village.

1982

January
Gay Men's Health Crisis (GMHC) is founded in response to what, later this year, the Centers for Disease Prevention and Control will officially name **AIDS** (Acquired Immune Deficiency Syndrome). GMHC cofounder Larry Kramer soon leaves the group in frustration, telling the *New York Times*: "Everything, everything, is too little, too late. By our silence we have helped murder each other."[3] This sentiment later takes shape in Gran Fury's 1989 project *Kissing Doesn't Kill: Greed And Indifference Do*, which appears on the sides of public buses and intentionally mimics popular ads by the Benetton clothing company.

February
Ingrid Sischy, editor in chief of ***Artforum*** since 1979, features a model wearing a dress designed by Issey Miyake on the magazine's cover. The issue avoids contemporary art as much as possible, featuring articles not only on fashion but on music, advertising, and news photography, and causes a stir in the art world.

March
Artist and dealer Gracie Mansion (born Joanne Mayhew Young) opens **Gracie Mansion Gallery** in the bathroom of her apartment. A bastion of the East Village art scene, Gracie Mansion shows group and solo exhibitions of her friends who are underrepresented in the mainstream art world. She later moves her operation to 15 St. Mark's Place, then to 337 East 10th Street, both in the East Village.

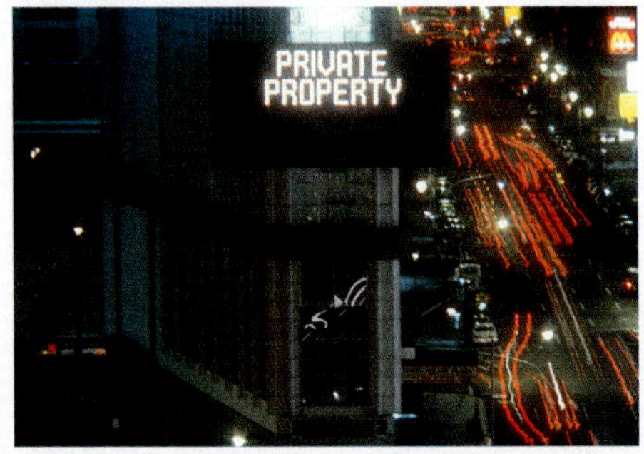

Installation view, Jenny Holzer's *Messages to the Public*, Times Square, New York, 1982

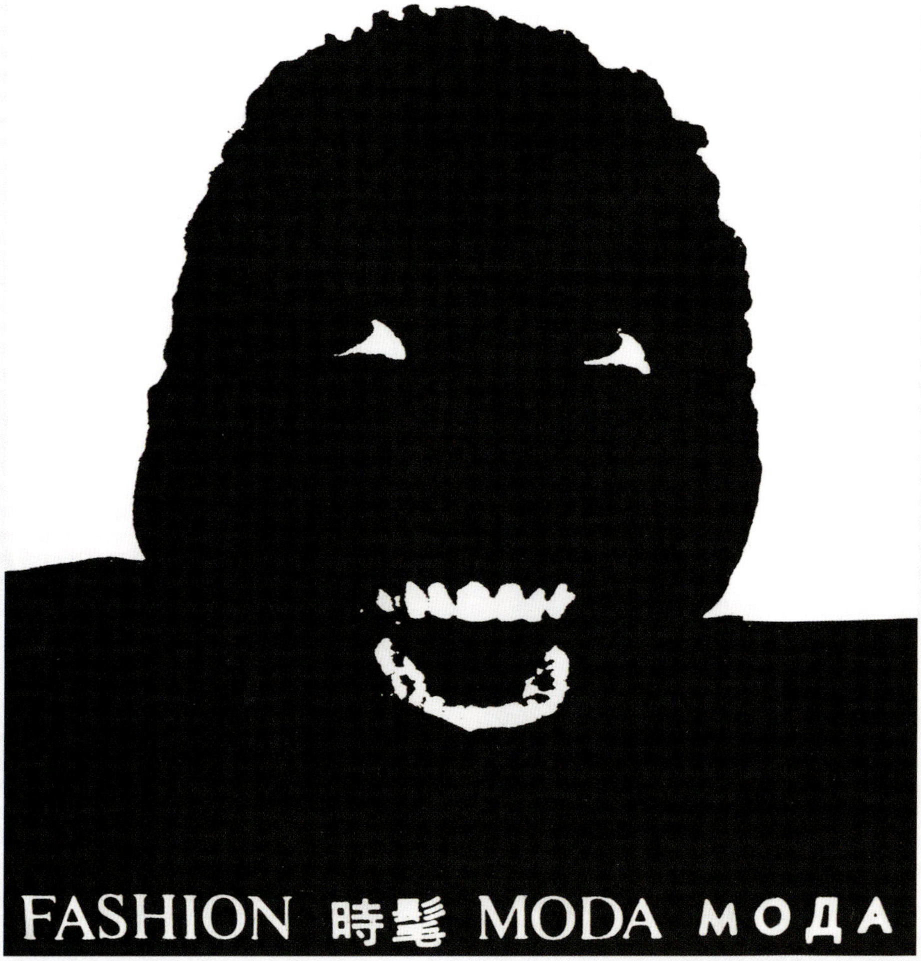

Poster for Fashion Moda designed by Stefan Eins, with photograph of work by John Ahearn, 1980

March
The first iteration of **Jenny Holzer**'s *Truisms* series using LED lights goes on view in Times Square. The public exhibition builds on her text-based work and further establishes her as an artist using commercial visual vocabularies. Holzer, along with Group Material, contrives the mode of using public advertising venues as presentation spaces for art.

April
Art dealer **Mary Boone** (the first two artists she represents are Julian Schnabel and David Salle) is featured on the cover of *New York* magazine and dubbed the "New Queen of the Art Scene."[4]

May
Alan Barrows and artist Dean Savard open **Civilian Warfare** in the former ice cream shop Savard had been using as a studio at 526 East 11th Street. At the time, the gallery represents many of the pair's friends clamoring for attention—including **David Wojnarowicz**—and is part of the emerging trend of artist-run commercial art spaces in the East Village.

Artists Alan Belcher and Peter Nagy open **Gallery Nature Morte** at 204 East 10th Street in the East Village. The gallery, whose program is influenced by the artists and theorists of the Pictures Generation, arguably launches the careers of Gretchen Bender, David Robbins, Julia Wachtel, and others.

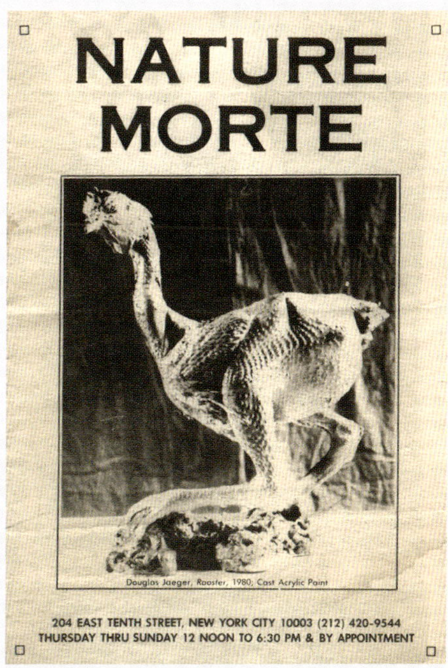

Advertisement for Gallery Nature Morte's inaugural group exhibition, 1982

June
Fashion Moda (in collaboration with Jenny Holzer) shows at documenta 7 in Kassel, Germany, establishing itself internationally as a pioneer of the so-called low end of art and commerce. In 1978, after running a gallery space/art shop out of his studio at 3 Mercer Street in Soho, artist Stefan Eins had opened Fashion Moda in the South Bronx—a site of experimentation by both artists and local community members, who frequently were the subjects of, contributed to, and even organized exhibitions there.

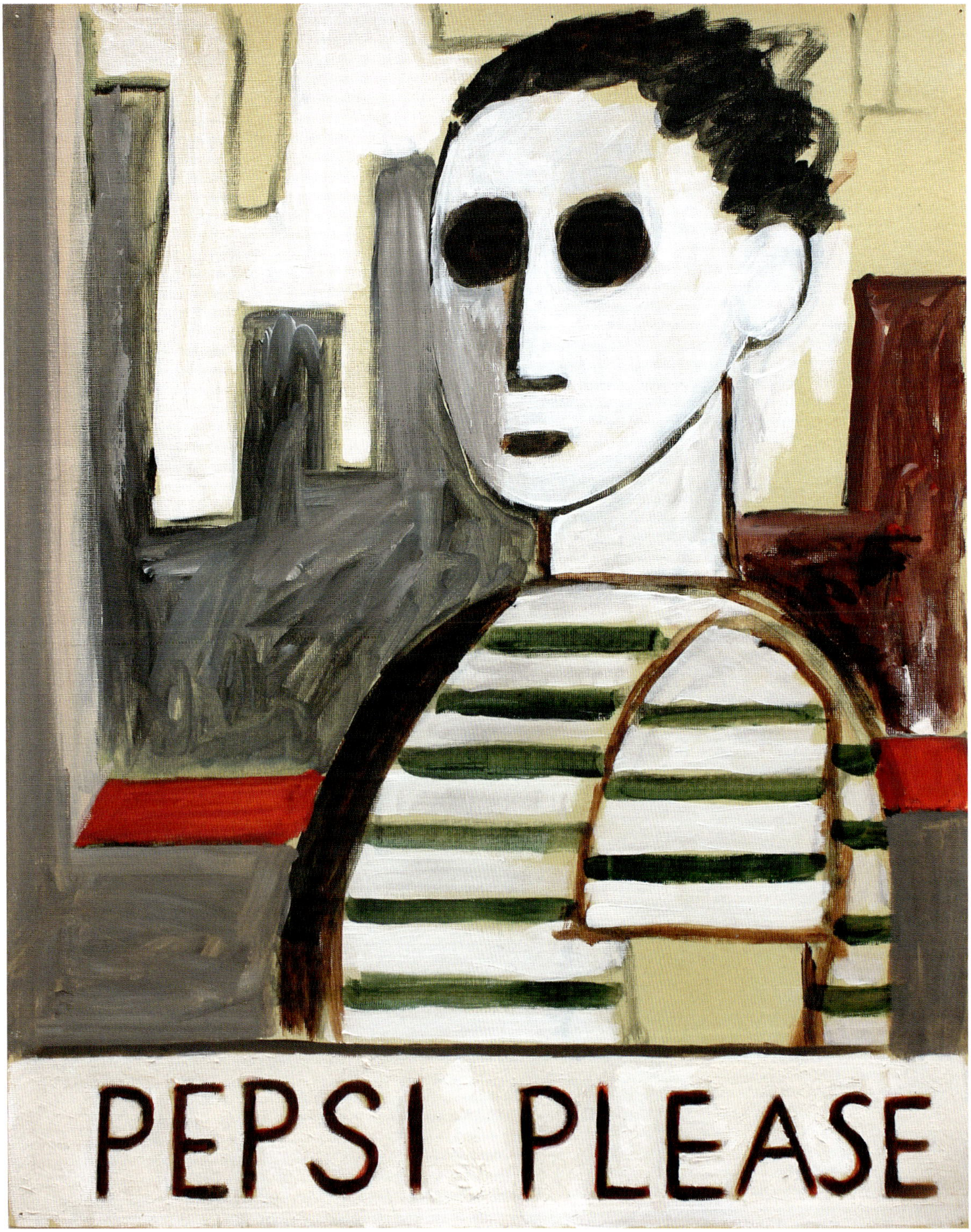

Peter Halley. ***Pepsi Please***, 1980. Acrylic on Canvasette, 20 × 16 in. (50.8 × 40.6 cm). Collection of the artist

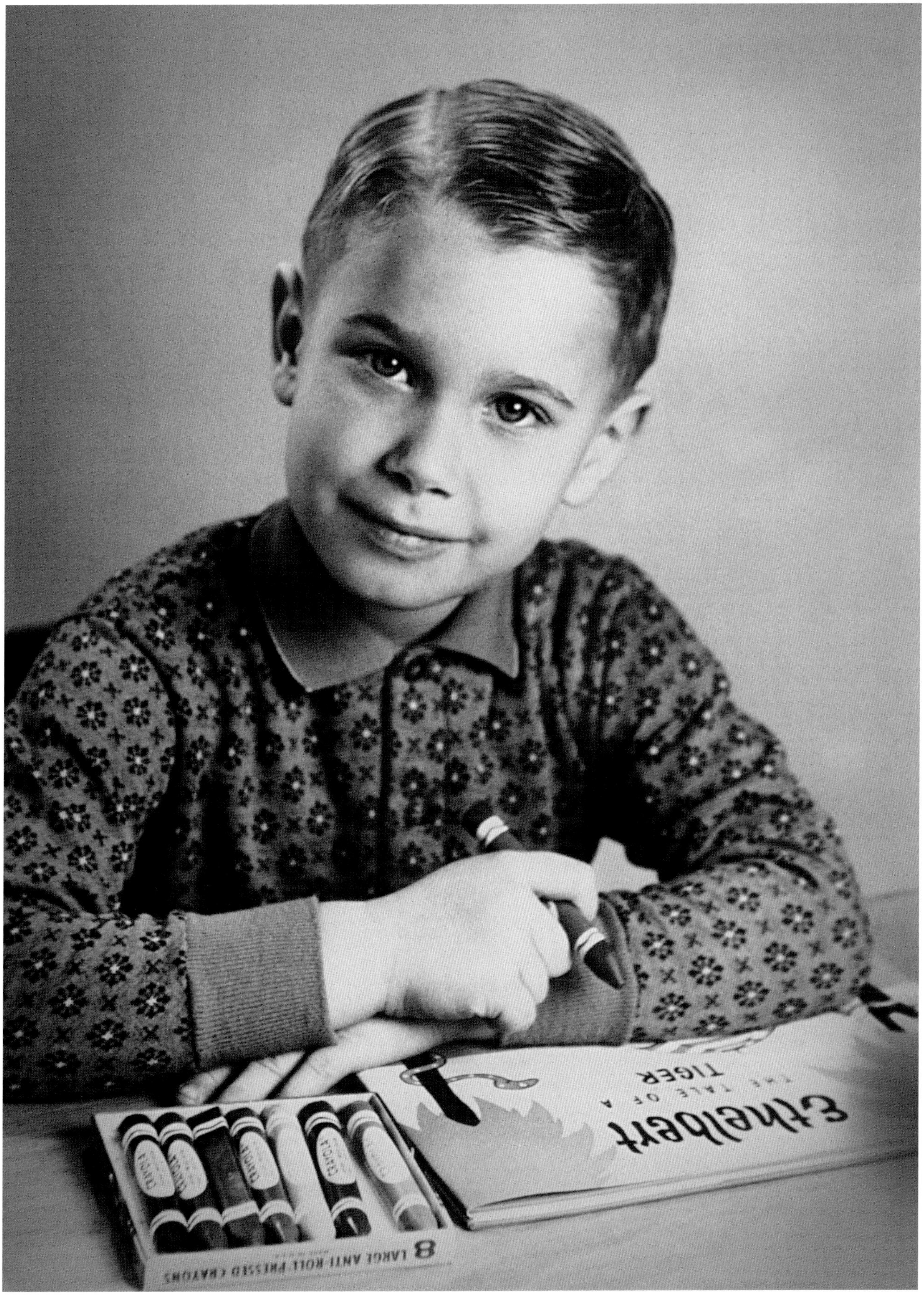

Jeff Koons. ***The New Jeff Koons***, 1980. Duratrans, fluorescent lightbox, 42 × 32 × 8 in. (106.7 × 81.3 × 20.3 cm). Private collection, New York

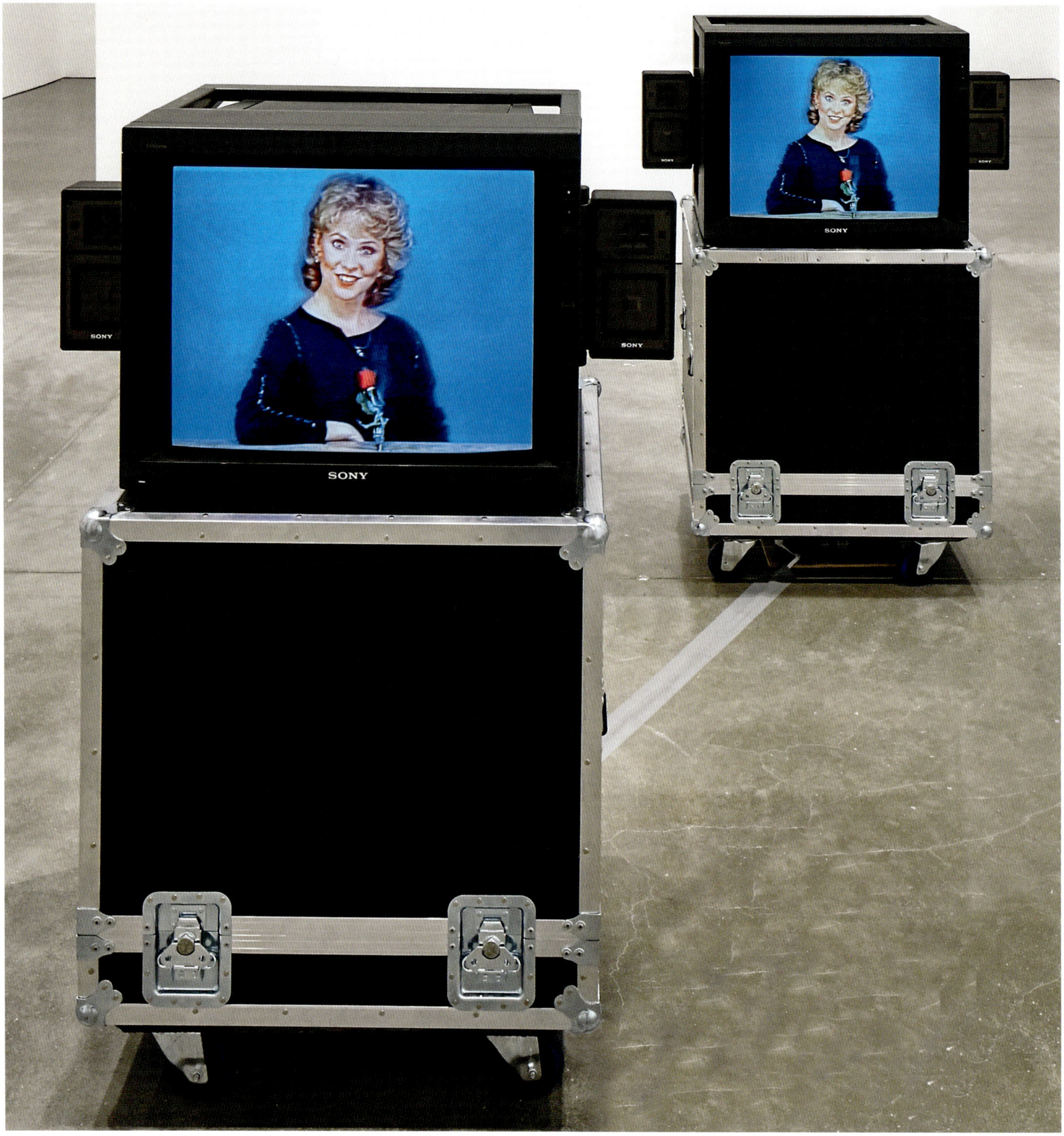

Dara Birnbaum. *Kiss the Girls: Make Them Cry*, 1979. Two-channel video, color, stereo, 6:26 min. loop.
Courtesy of the artist and Marian Goodman Gallery

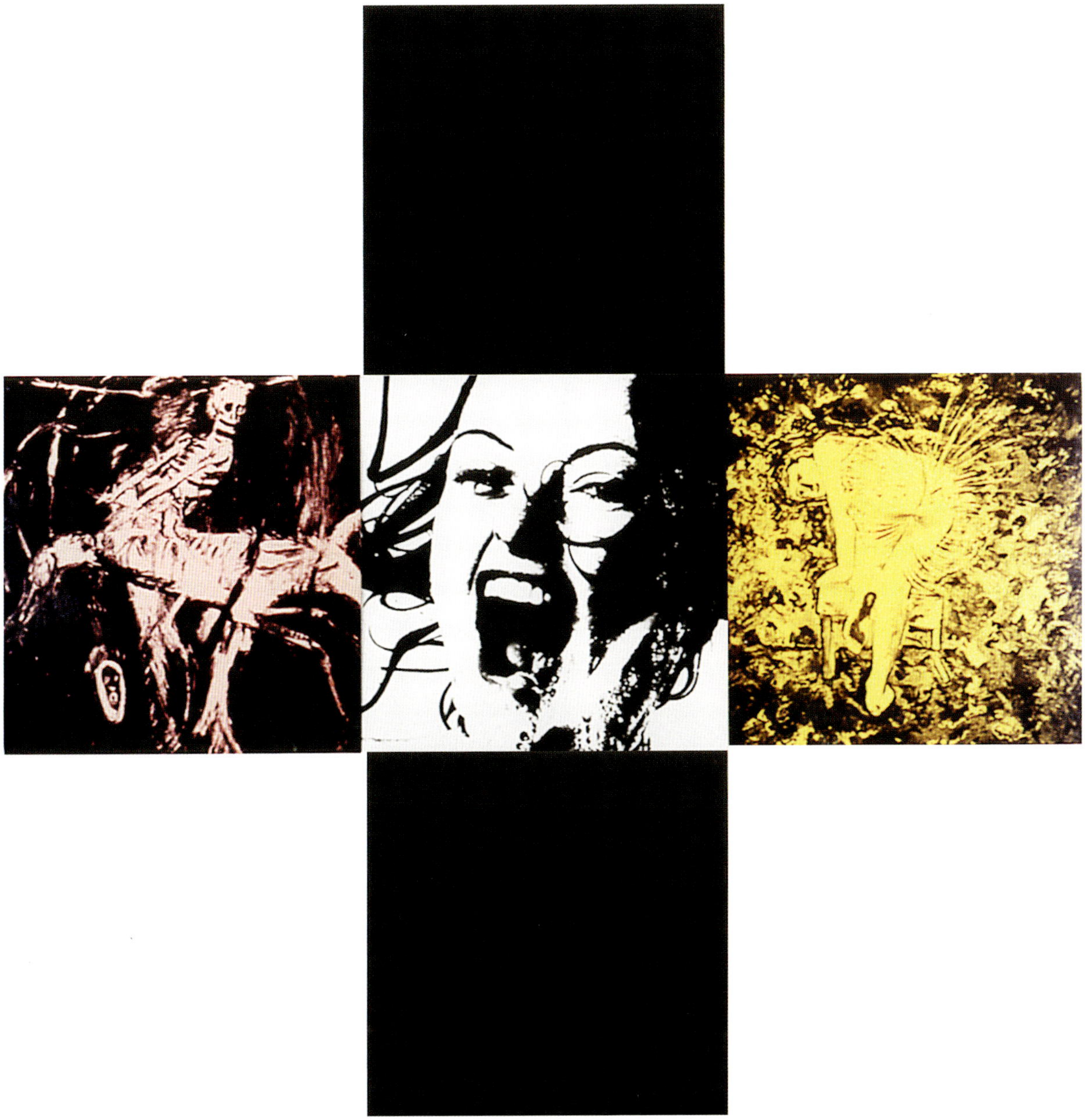

Gretchen Bender. ***Untitled (The Pleasure Is Back***), 1982. Photographic silkscreen on enamel sign tin (5 parts), overall 72 × 72 in. (182.9 × 182.9 cm). Courtesy of the Gretchen Bender Estate and OSMOS

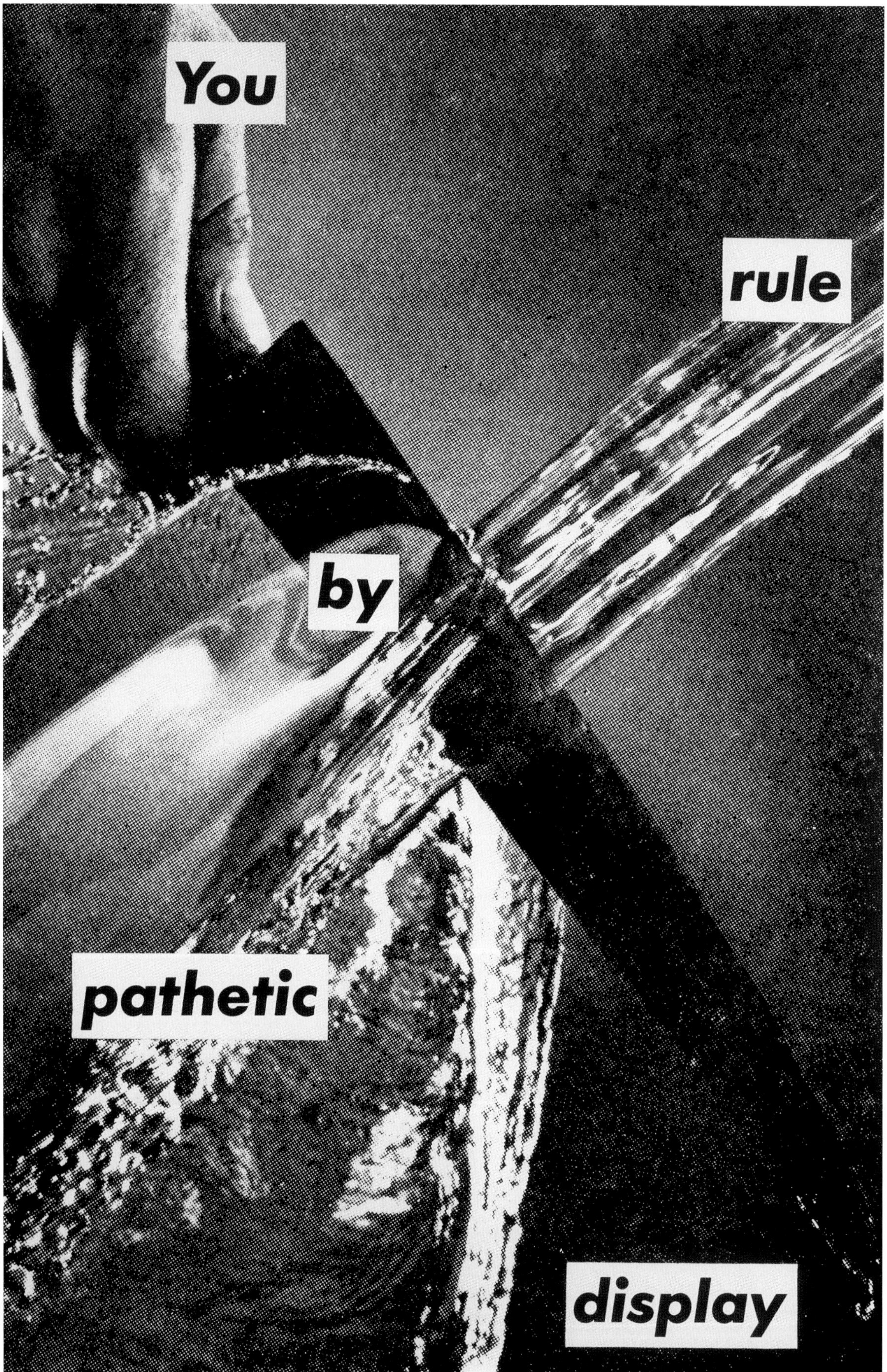

Barbara Kruger. ***Untitled (You Rule by Pathetic Display)***, 1982. Offset lithograph and silkscreen, 73 × 49 in. (185.4 × 124.5 cm). Krannert Art Museum, University of Illinois at Urbana-Champaign, Museum Purchase

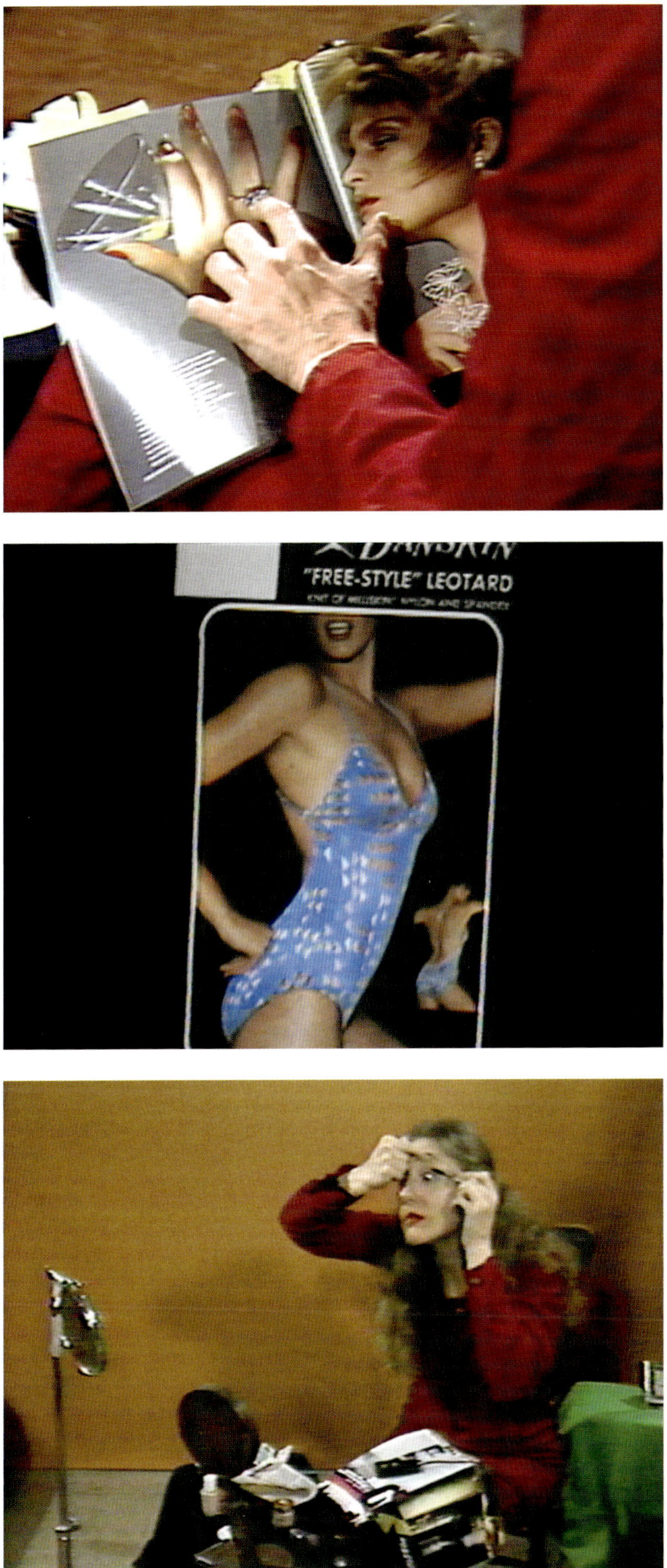

Martha Rosler. Stills from ***Martha Rosler Reads "Vogue,"*** 1982. Video, color, sound, 25:22 min.
Courtesy of Electronic Arts Intermix (EAI), New York

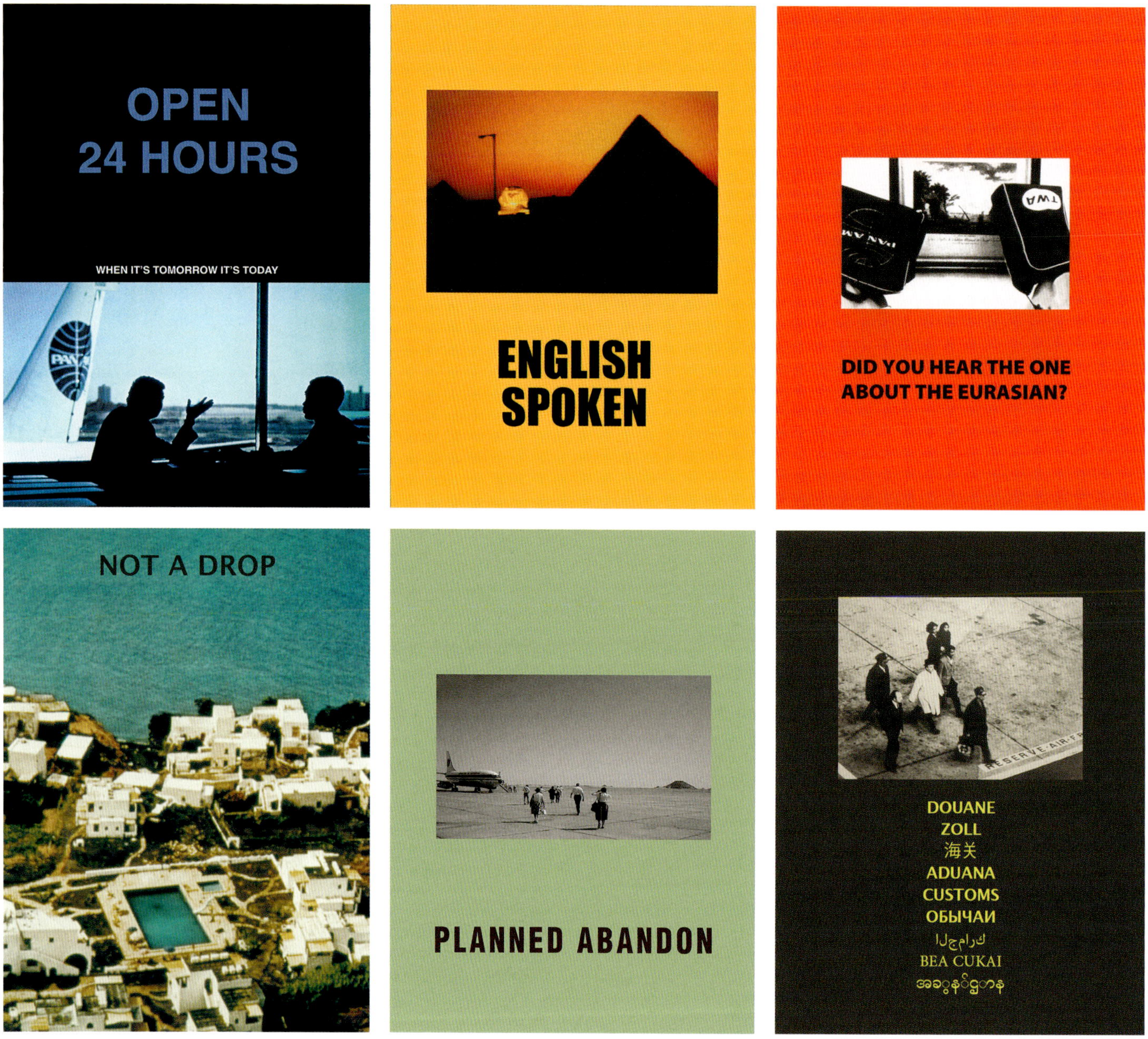

Barbara Bloom. *Planned Abandon* (installation detail), 1981. Wall mural, backdrop paper, information table, poster rack with fake travel posters, dimensions variable. Courtesy of the artist and David Lewis, New York

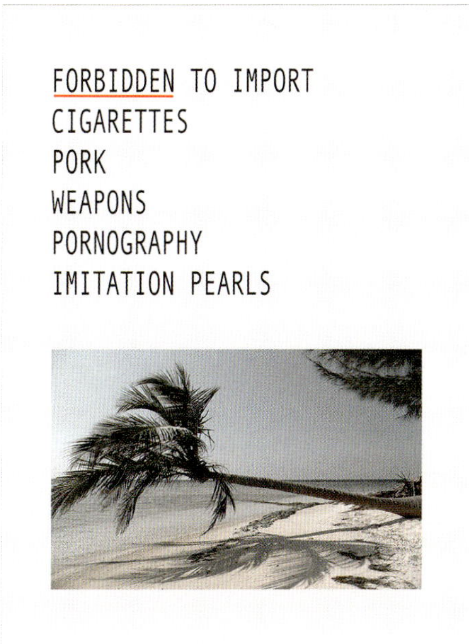
FORBIDDEN TO IMPORT
CIGARETTES
PORK
WEAPONS
PORNOGRAPHY
IMITATION PEARLS

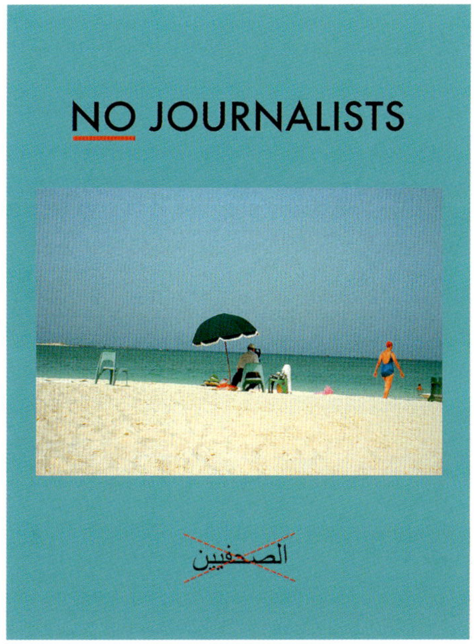
NO JOURNALISTS
الصحفيين

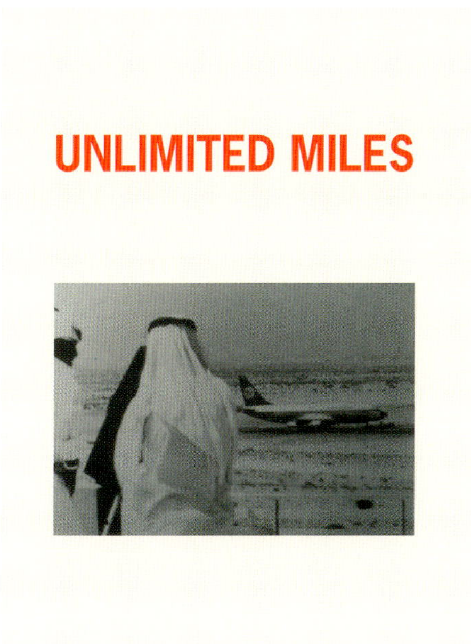
UNLIMITED MILES

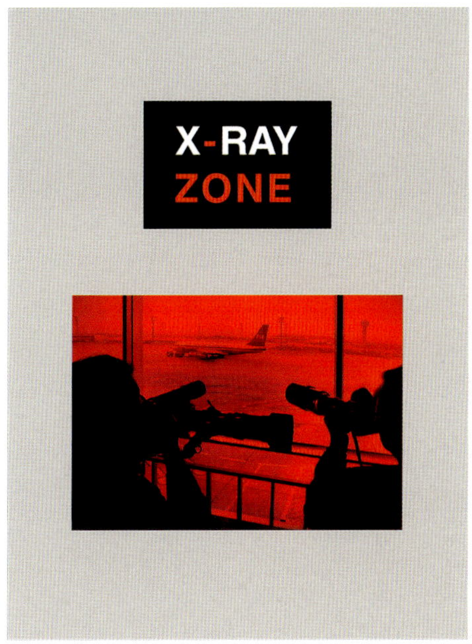
X-RAY
ZONE

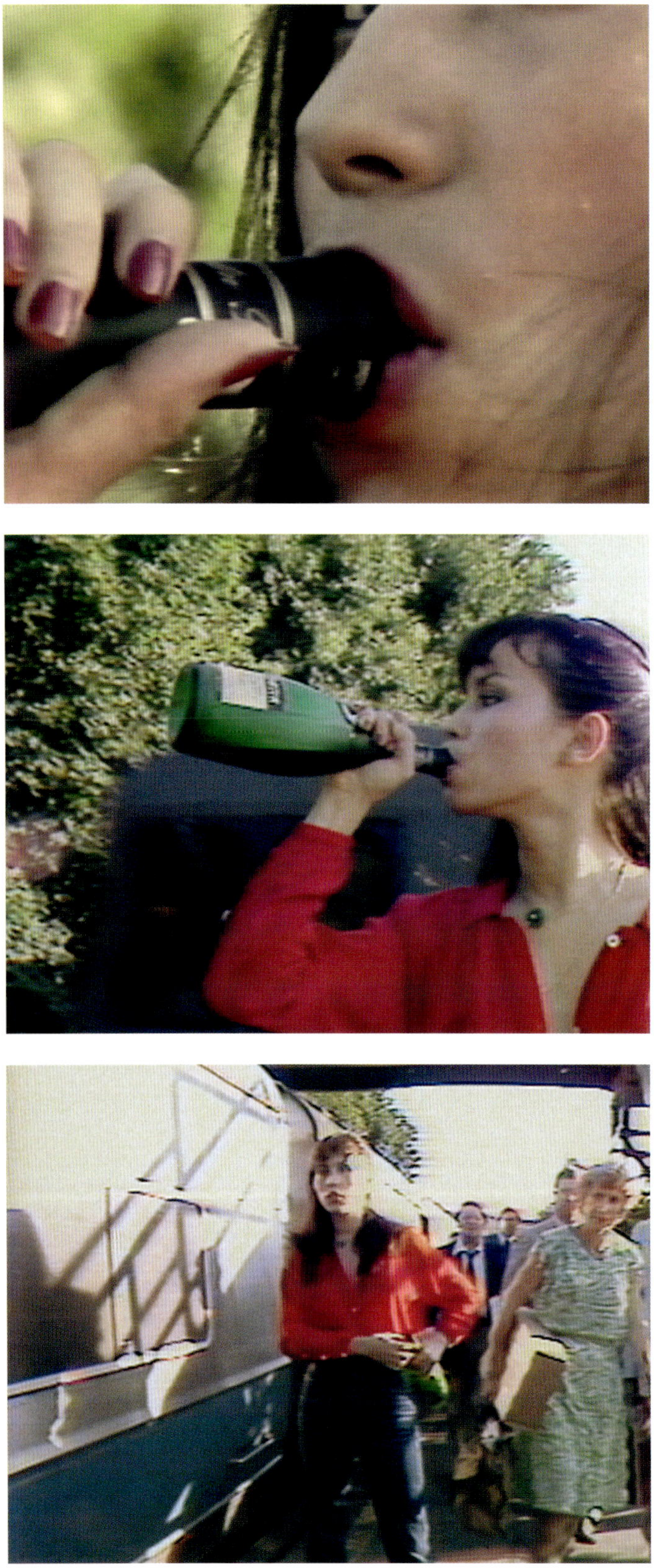

Dara Birnbaum. Stills from ***Rémy/Grand Central: Trains and Boats and Planes***, 1980. Video, color, sound, 4:18 min. Courtesy of the artist and Electronic Arts Intermix (EAI), New York

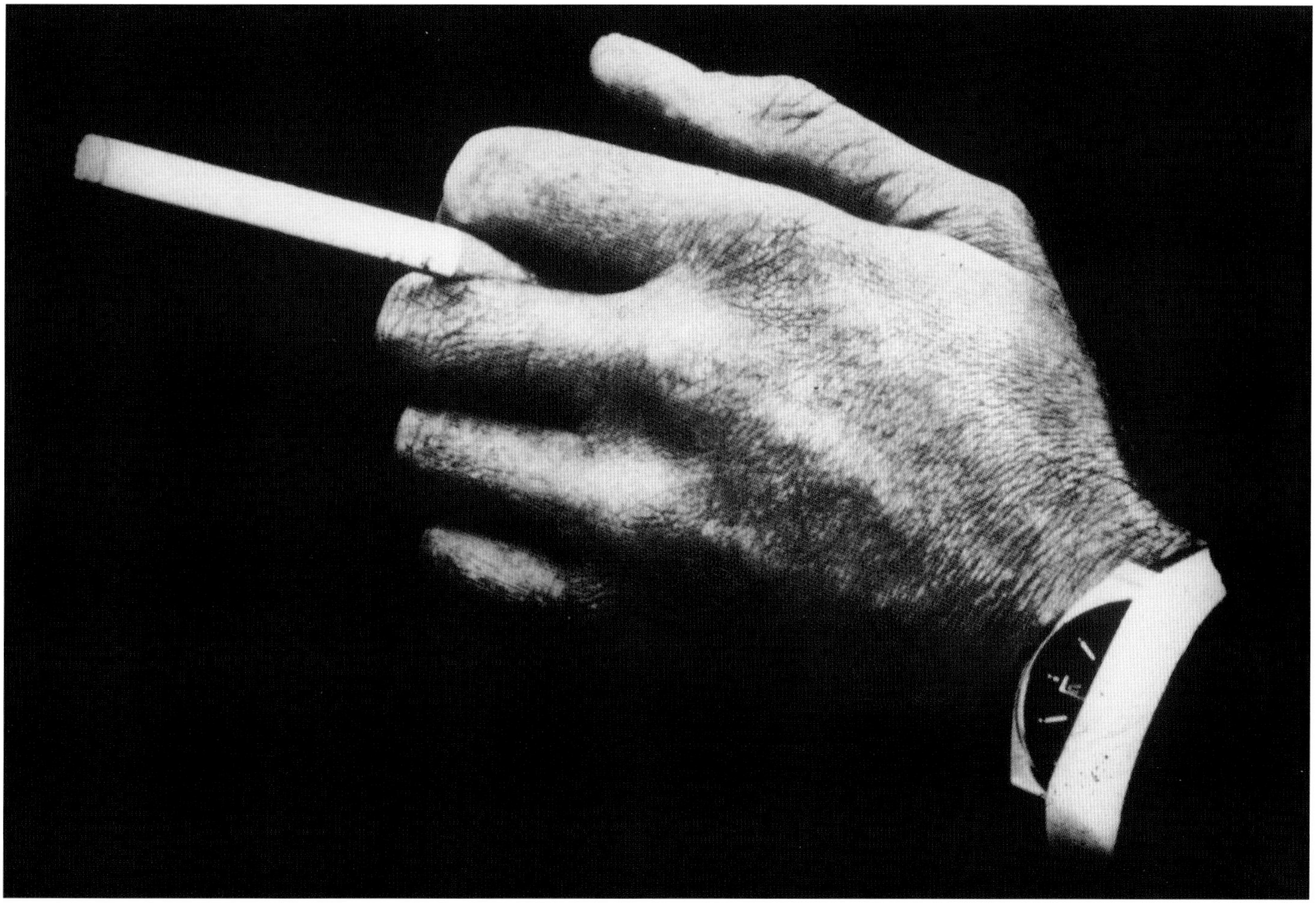

Richard Prince. ***Untitled (Hand with cigarette and watch)***, 1980. Chromogenic print, sheet 39 15⁄16 × 60 in. (101.4 × 152.4 cm), mount 39 15⁄16 × 60 × 1⁄4 in. (101.4 × 152.4 × 0.6 cm). Whitney Museum of American Art, New York, Promised gift of Thea Westreich Wagner and Ethan Wagner

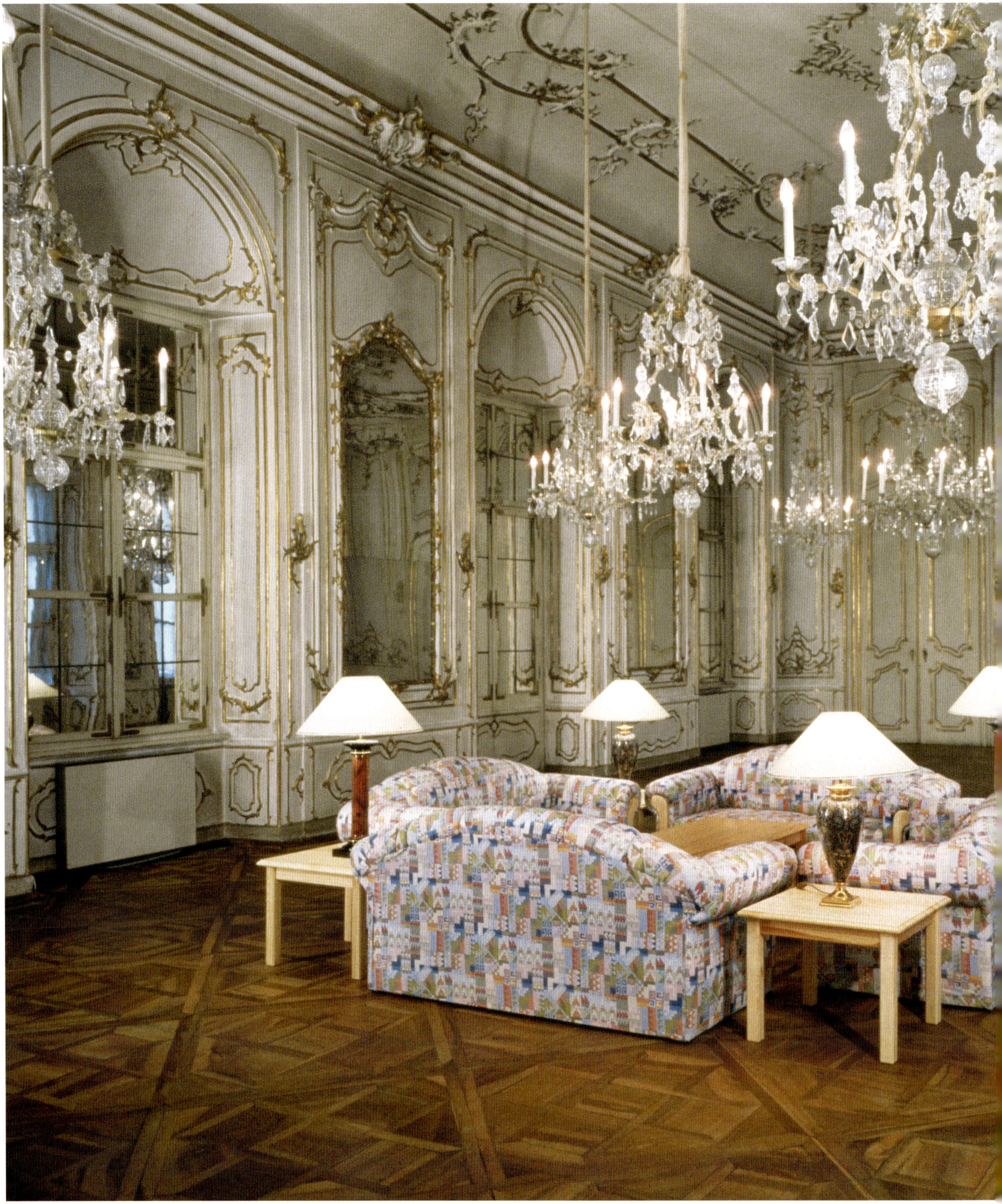

Ken Lum. *Untitled Furniture Sculpture*, 1980–present. Couches, side tables, table lamps, dimensions variable. Courtesy of the artist

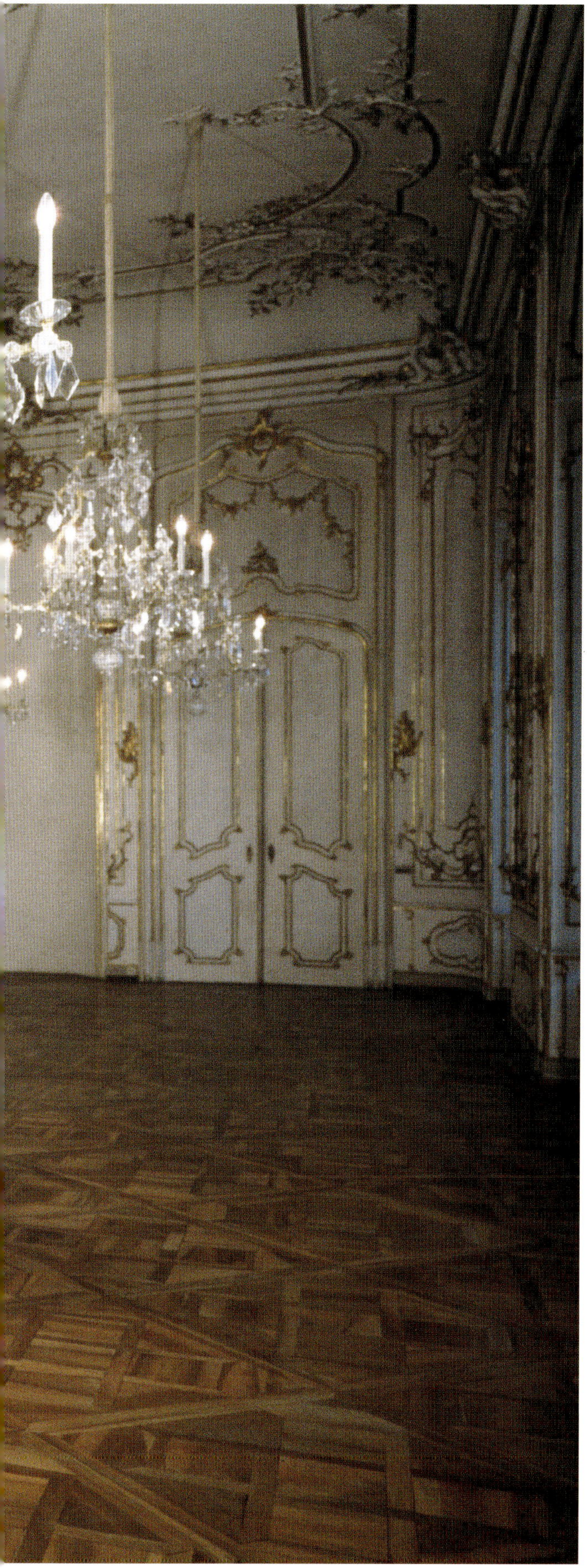

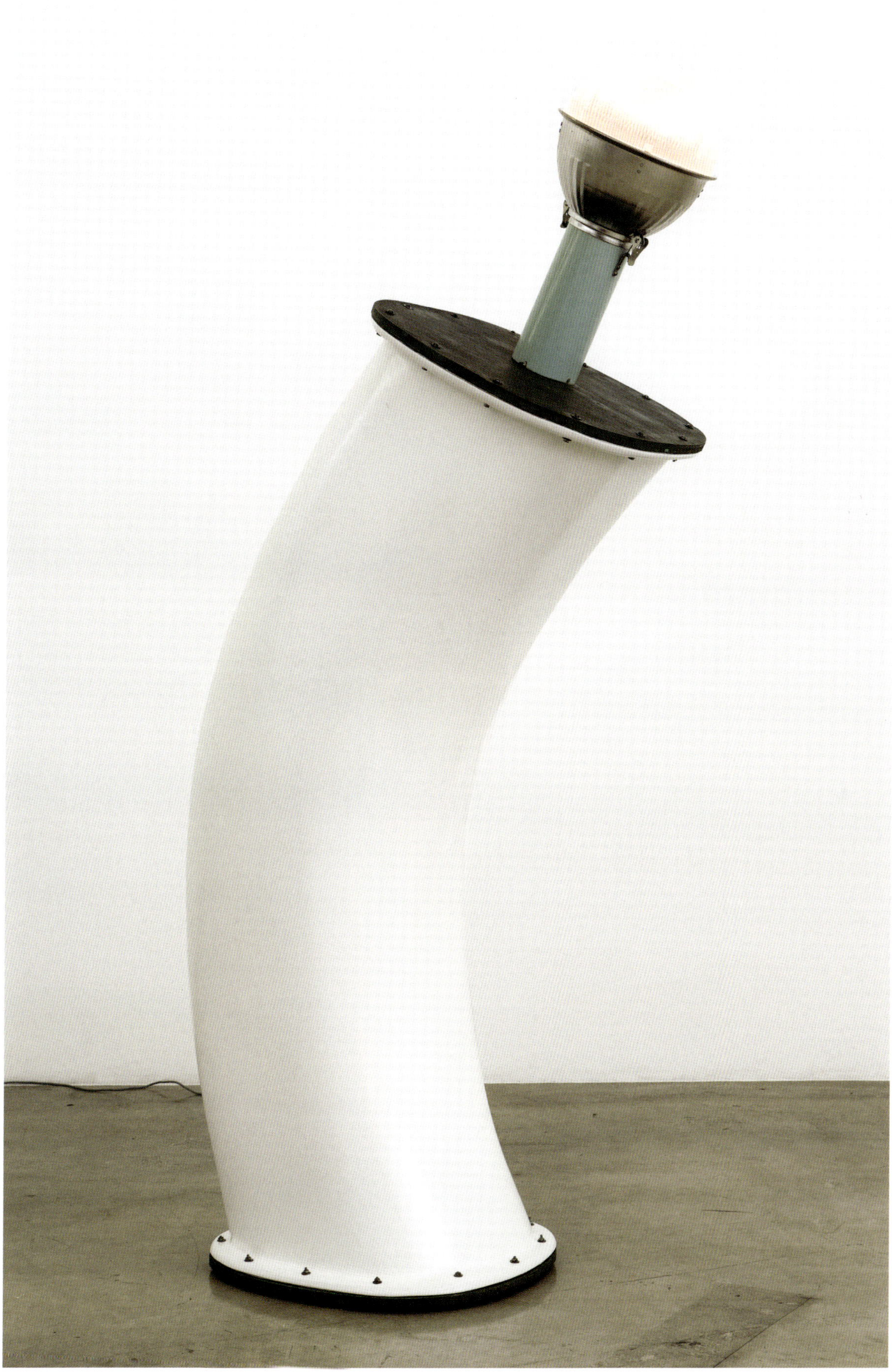

R. M. Fischer. ***Elbow Macaroni Lamp***, 1979. Multimedia lamp, 93 × 26 × 42 in. (236.2 × 66 × 106.7 cm). Rubell Family Collection, Miami

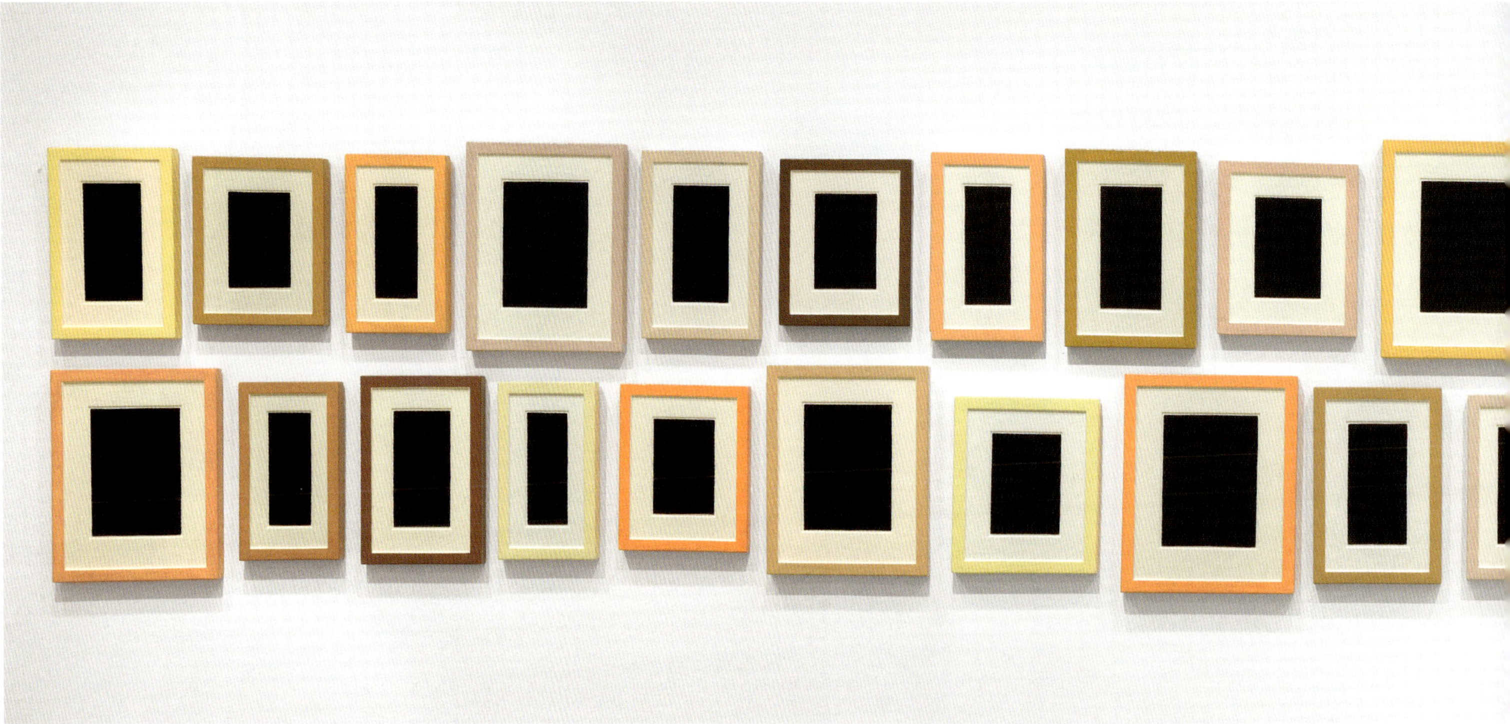

Allan McCollum. *40 Plaster Surrogates*, 1982–90. Enamel on Hydrocal, overall dimensions variable. Hirshhorn Museum and Sculpture Garden, Smithsonian Institution, Washington, DC, Joseph H. Hirshhorn Purchase Fund, 1990

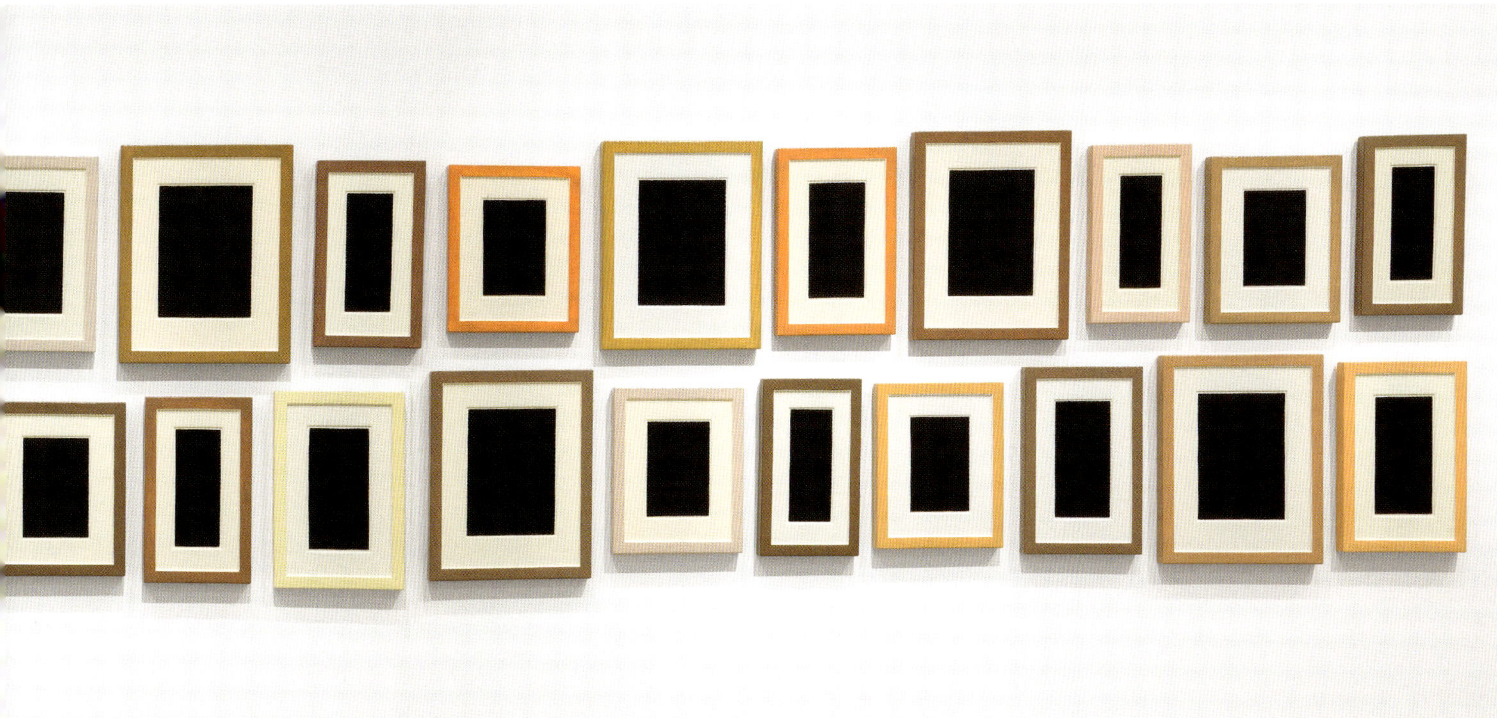

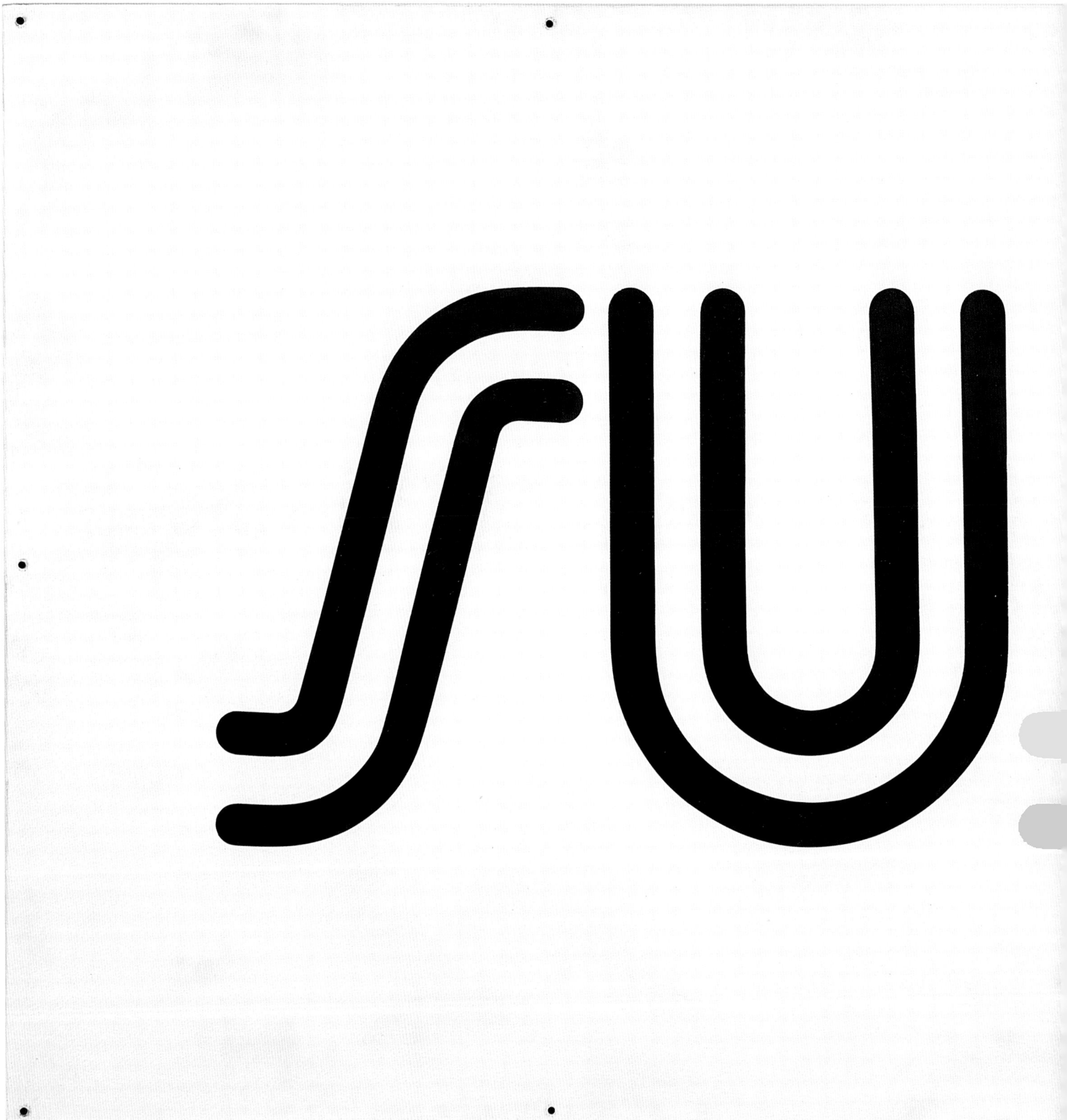

Ashley Bickerton. *Susie*, 1982. Polymer and latex paint on Masonite, 48 × 96 in. (121.9 × 243.8 cm). Courtesy of the artist and Lehmann Maupin, New York and Hong Kong

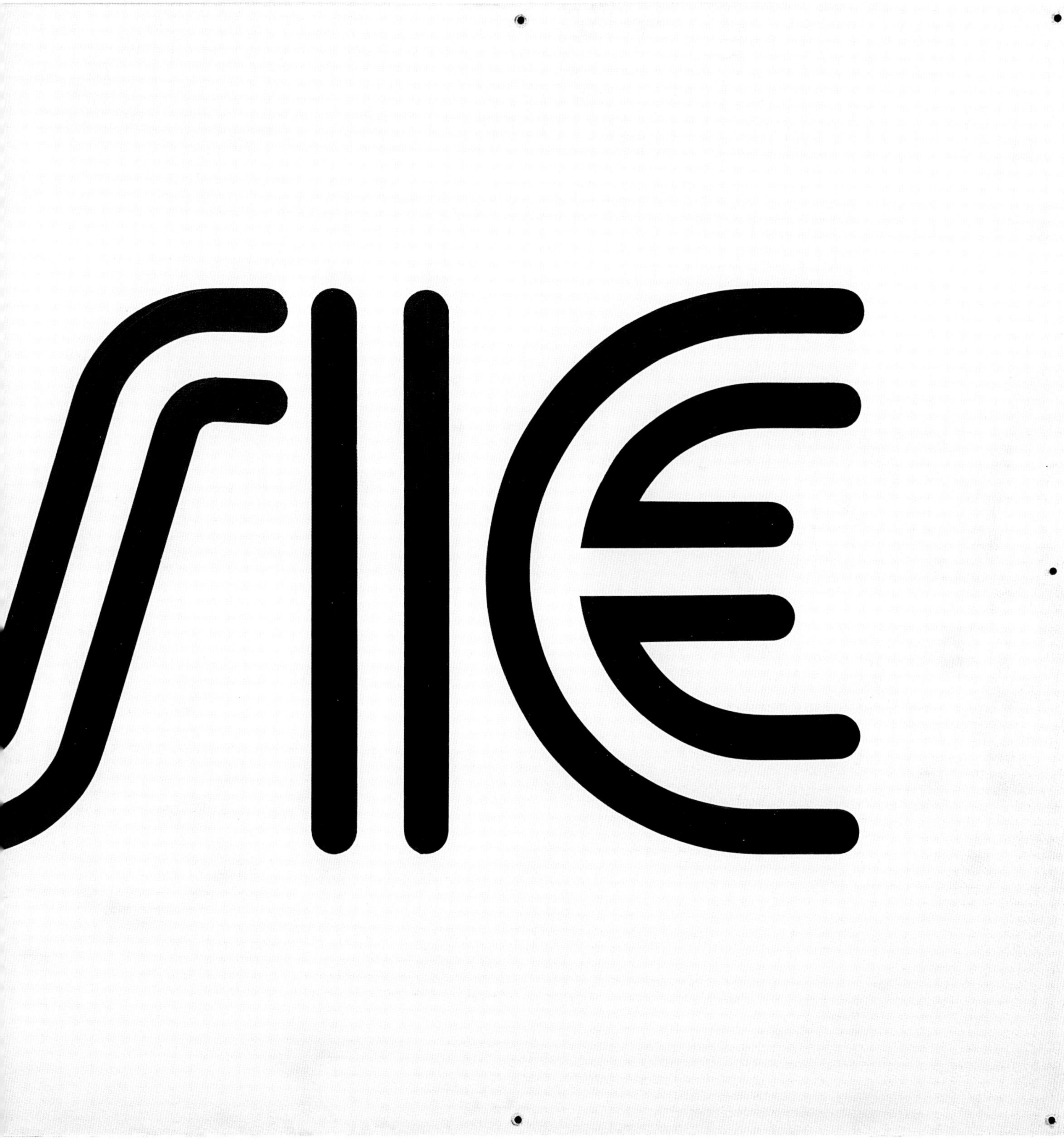

THE END OF THE U.S.A.

ALL YOU RICH FUCKERS SEE THE BEGINNING OF THE END AND TAKE WHAT YOU CAN WHILE YOU CAN. YOU IMAGINE THAT YOU WILL GET AWAY, BUT YOU'VE SHIT IN YOUR OWN BED AND YOU'RE THE ONE TO SLEEP IN IT. WHY SHOULD EVERYONE ELSE STAY BEHIND AND SMELL YOUR STINKING COWARDICE? HERE'S A MESSAGE TO YOU—SPACE TRAVEL IS UNCERTAIN AND ANY REFUGE OF YOURS CAN BE BLOWN OFF THE MAP. THERE'S NO OTHER PLACE FOR YOU TO GO. KNOW THAT YOUR FUTURE IS WITH US SO DON'T GIVE US MORE REASONS TO HATE YOU.

Jenny Holzer. ***The End of the U.S.A.***, from ***The Inflammatory Essays***, 1979–82. Offset lithograph on colored paper, 17 × 17 in. (43.2 × 43.2 cm). Tate, London

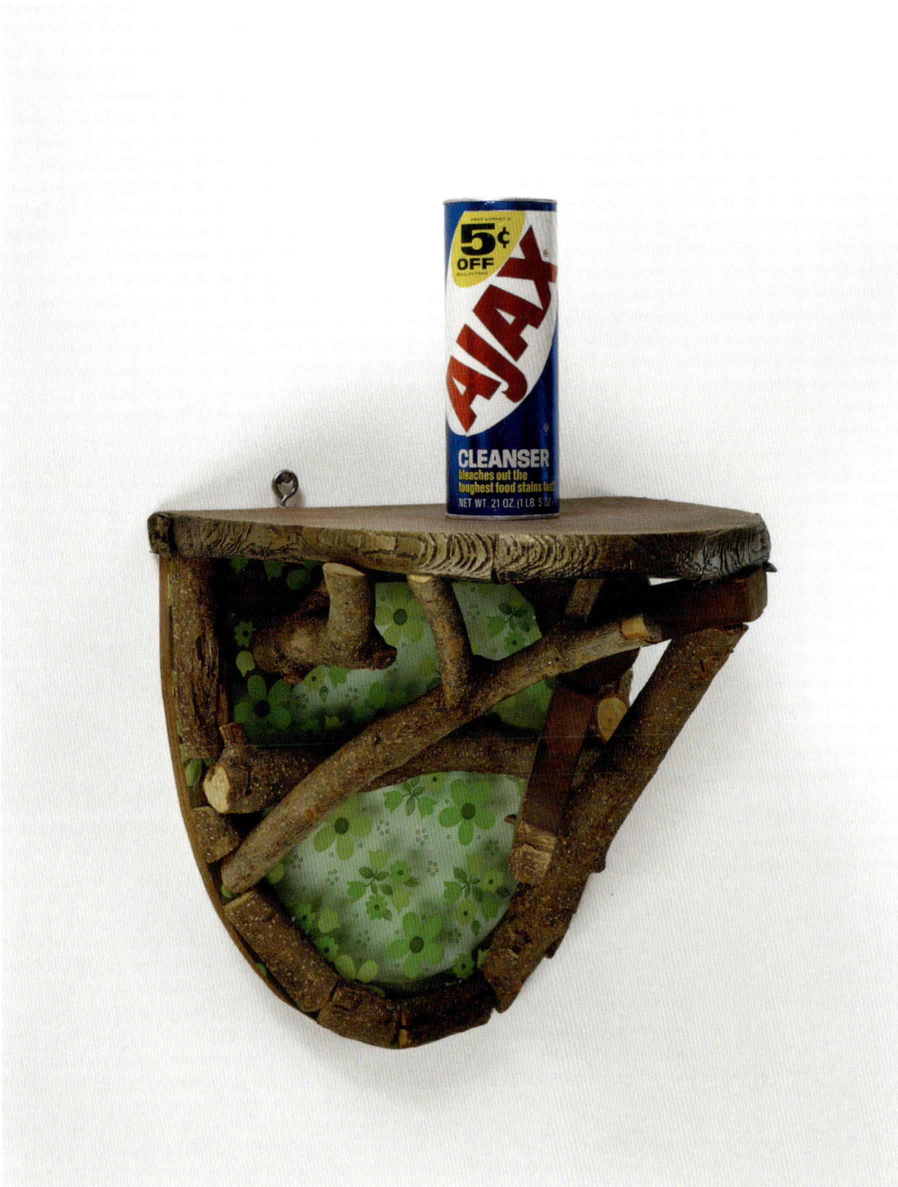

Haim Steinbach. *Shelf with Ajax*, 1981. Wood and plastic shelf, Ajax cleaner can, 22 × 14 × 14 in. (55.9 × 35.6 × 35.6 cm). Courtesy of the artist and Tanya Bonakdar Gallery, New York

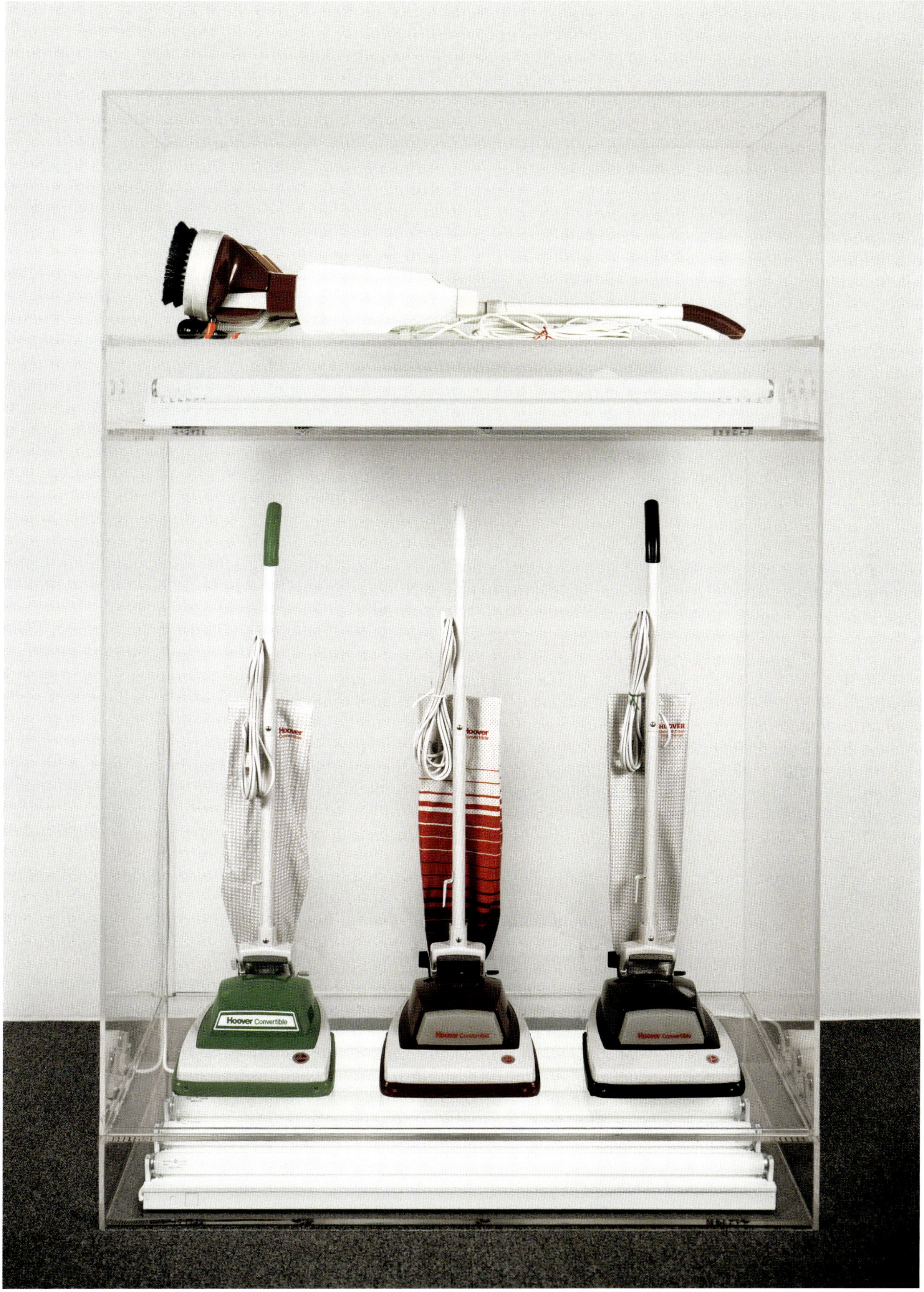

Jeff Koons. *New Hoover Convertibles, Green, Red, Brown, New Hoover Deluxe Shampoo Polishers, Yellow, Brown Doubledecker*, 1981. Three vacuum cleaners, two shampoo polishers, acrylic, fluorescent lights, overall 83 × 54 × 28 in. (210.8 × 137.2 × 71.1 cm). Glenstone, Potomac, Maryland

Pleasure/Function
Aesthetic Services circa 1980

Leah Pires

Someone hands you a business card with the heading THE OFFICES OF FEND, FITZGIBBON, HOLZER, NADIN, PRINCE & WINTERS inked on sensible, round-edged gray cardstock **(fig. 1)**. OUR CONSULTATION INCLUDES A REVIEW OF YOUR NEEDS AND SUGGESTIONS FOR REALISTIC ACTION, it promises. At first glance, the serif typeface and litany of surnames conveys a no-nonsense reliability; it seems likely that the card will connect you to a lawyer or an accountant. But this assumption is quickly undercut by an additional slogan: PRACTICAL ESTHETIC SERVICES ADAPTABLE TO CLIENT SITUATION. These offices, in fact, belong to a consulting firm cofounded by the artists Peter Fend, Coleen Fitzgibbon, Jenny Holzer, Peter Nadin, Richard Prince, and Robin Winters. In the fall of 1979, the members of this New York-based group set out to sell "art-based thought and practice to non-art clients," steering away from the art world per se.[1] They adopted a "real-world mode," feeling that it was the most viable method for making art in the 1980s—and they were not alone.[2]

A number of artists working in downtown Manhattan during this time expressed the desire to make art collaboratively and to move their artistic practices into "real life." Of course, this notion had been a leitmotif of avant-garde art since the early twentieth century, but the social, economic, and political climate in the United States at the end of the 1970s accounted for several new developments. Earlier attempts to push art into life had yielded limited results, but now it was the realm of commerce that began seeking cues from art and artists to an unprecedented degree. Artists became the ideal archetypes for a vast population of managers, entrepreneurs, and freelancers whose "immaterial labor" helped to propel the new economy.[3] The French sociologists Luc Boltanski and Eve Chiapello have identified the protagonist of this new paradigm as a hybrid figure:

> Is not the neo-manager, like the artist, a creative figure, a person of intuition, invention, contacts, chance encounters . . . ? Like the artist, is he not freed of the burdens of possession and the constraints of hierarchical attachments, of the signs of power—office or tie—and also, consequently, of the hypocrisies of bourgeois morality? Conversely, however, is not today's artist, even today's intellectual or researcher, likewise a network creature in search of producers, the realization of whose projects demands costly, heterogeneous and complex arrangements, an ability to arrive at an understanding with distant, multiple actors who hold very different positions . . . and whom he must interest, persuade, win over?[4]

Boltanski and Chiapello assert that, beginning in the 1980s, the business sector put strategies borrowed from art and the counterculture into practice. At the same moment, artists were appropriating images and roles from the realm of commerce with new zeal. Surely, the Offices of Fend, Fitzgibbon, Holzer, Nadin, Prince & Winters could not have anticipated how pervasive its offer of "practical esthetic services adaptable to client situation" would become in the labor economy of the twenty-first century.

Following the Second World War, widespread transformations in the United States and Europe shifted economic activity first from the manufacturing of goods to the provision of services and, later, to the management of information.[5] The work of artists indexed—and sometimes even anticipated—these changes. Artists' uniquely malleable job descriptions allowed them to adopt a shifting range of identities, which, at times, verged on the contradictory. For example, in the late 1950s, Frank Stella portrayed himself alternately as a humble house painter and as an "executive artist" in a pinstripe suit; around 1970, Robert Morris, a founding member of the Art Workers' Coalition, fashioned himself as both construction worker and boss man; and Andy Warhol famously dubbed his 1960s studio "The Factory" before rebranding it "The Office" in the mid-1970s.[6] As the art historian Caroline A. Jones has observed, Warhol's signature black turtleneck signaled a precisely calibrated dual coding: managerial, yet arty.[7]

1 Peter Fend, email message to author, March 26, 2016.

2 See Peter Fend, David Joselit, and Rachel Harrison, "A Conversation with Peter Fend," *October*, no. 125 (Summer 2008), p. 118.

3 See Michael Hardt and Antonio Negri, *Empire* (Cambridge, MA: Harvard University Press, 2000); Maurizio Lazzarato, *The Making of the Indebted Man: An Essay on the Neoliberal Condition*, trans. Joshua David Jordan (Los Angeles: Semiotext(e), 2012); Luc Boltanski and Eve Chiapello, *The New Spirit of Capitalism*, trans. Gregory Elliott (London and New York: Verso, 2005). The last was originally published as *Le nouvel esprit du capitalisme* (Paris: Éditions Gallimard, 1999).

4 Boltanski and Chiapello, *New Spirit of Capitalism*, p. 312.

5 See Helen Molesworth, ed., *Work Ethic*, exh. cat. (University Park, PA: Pennsylvania State University Press, 2003), p. 18.

6 For a detailed analysis of Stella's and Warhol's "industrial aesthetics," see Caroline A. Jones, *Machine in the Studio: Constructing the Postwar American Artist* (Chicago: University of Chicago Press, 1996), pp. 119, 197, 234, 238. On Warhol, see also Andy Warhol and Pat Hackett,

A similar look was cultivated by the conceptual artists represented by Seth Siegelaub.[8] A New York-based dealer of so-called dematerialized art, Siegelaub understood the importance of fostering artists' auras through publicity and events. He managed the public image of each member of his roster almost as an advertising executive would do.[9] A press photograph from 1969 **(fig. 2)** captures four artists in turtlenecks; the crossed arms of Robert Barry and Douglas Huebler seem downright uptight compared to the casual leans and free hands of Joseph Kosuth and Lawrence Weiner.[10] Conceptual art practices tended not to be anchored in physical objects, so documentation, contracts, and the artist's signature became paramount to establishing the "authenticity" of a work and facilitating its circulation.[11] Siegelaub's innovations in the display and circulation of conceptual art–his courting of the press and innovative use of printed publicity materials–constitute what the art historian Alexander Alberro has termed "the Siegelaub Idea." This approach paralleled innovations in product management and advertising in the 1960s; Siegelaub even developed art-based public relations programs for corporations.[12] Weiner likened Siegelaub to an advertising agency, "packaging and selling" his artists and their work. "He did have the best dishwashing liquid around," the artist wryly recalled.[13] By finding new ways to market and sell ideas, Siegelaub was a pioneer in both art and commerce.

Upon its emergence, conceptual art's uncoupling from the physical object represented a utopian attempt to create an anti-elitist, democratic form of expression that deprivileged the role of the artist. However, it failed to fulfill this aspiration, Alberro proposes, because dispensing with the singular art object did not forestall the commodification of conceptual art. On the contrary, its "dematerialized" properties eased its incorporation into the market. The art historian Benjamin Buchloh has described conceptual art as an "aesthetic of administration" whereby the administering of production and circulation becomes central to the work; moreover, he suggests that artists' attempts to evade commodification by supplanting object with idea in fact helped to pioneer, or at least portend, a new form of capitalism.[14] Boltanski and Chiapello, too, argue that the critiques of capitalism voiced by social movements in the late 1960s–namely, that it is stultifying and homogenizing–had, by the mid-1970s, been metabolized by the very same system. The demand that hierarchical, alienated labor be replaced by creative, fulfilling work simply gave rise to new forms of control. As the regimented eight-hour workday metamorphosed into the demand for perpetual availability and the ideal of self-management, work became at once more precarious and increasingly all-encompassing.[15]

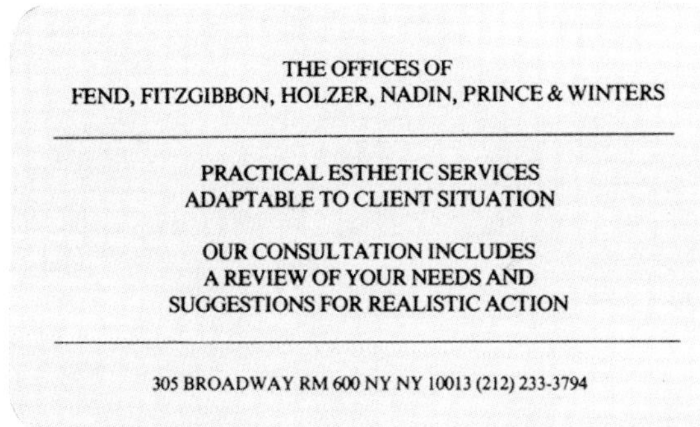

Fig. 1 Business card for the Offices of Fend, Fitzgibbon, Holzer, Nadin, Prince & Winters, 1979–81

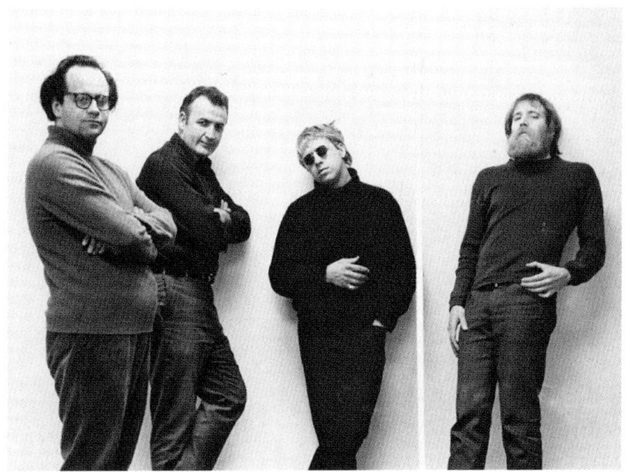

Fig. 2 Robert Barry, Douglas Huebler, Joseph Kosuth, and Lawrence Weiner, ca. 1969. Gelatin silver print (cut into two pieces). The Museum of Modern Art Archives, New York, Seth Siegelaub Archives, Gift of Seth Siegelaub and the Stichting Egress Foundation, Amsterdam

Amid these changes, the role of the artist in relation to American society underwent a parallel transformation. In 1981, the critic Craig Owens identified information as the medium of choice for many artists: "Power now resides with those who control the networks for the processing, retrieval, and transmission of information.... The artist no longer makes an object, but rather is involved in the transfer and processing of information."[16] Owens described artists' work in terms that more readily evoke that of a manager or an office clerk. What's more, he located power in the hands of those who control the *network*–the interconnection of people and things that constitutes both the art world and the realm of commerce. The paradigm shift initiated by conceptual art in the late 1960s now approached its apotheosis.

If Siegelaub was the first to understand the potency of an alliance between art and management, it was a group of artists working collaboratively in New York and Los Angeles between 1979 and 1982 who explored the breadth of its potential. In 1981, quick on the heels of the Offices, Louise Lawler and Sherrie Levine created an itinerant gallery and publicity apparatus called A Picture Is No Substitute for Anything. It is striking that these young artists believed that a consulting firm, on the one hand, and

Popism: The Warhol '60s (New York: Harper, 1987), pp. 262–63. Julia Bryan Wilson chronicles the ambivalent labor politics of Morris's work in *Art Workers: Radical Practice in the Vietnam War Era* (Berkeley, CA: University of California Press, 2009), pp. 83–126. Richard Meyer addresses Warhol's homoerotic appropriation of working-class masculinity in "Warhol's Clones," *Yale Journal of Criticism* 7, no. 1 (Spring 1994), pp. 79–109.

7 See Jones, *Machine in the Studio*, p. 240. The author offers a fascinating analysis of the gender hierarchies that implicitly governed Warhol's studio. Women were deliberately kept on the margins, rendering the gunshots fired by Valerie Solanas on June 3, 1968, a "founding moment for radical feminism's critique of patriarchal capitalism" (p. 248).

8 See Alexander Alberro, *Conceptual Art and the Politics of Publicity* (Cambridge, MA: MIT Press, 2004), p. 16.

9 The term "dematerialized" comes from Lucy Lippard, *Six Years: The Dematerialization of the Art Object from 1966 to 1972...* (New York: Praeger, 1973).

10 For an in-depth analysis of Kosuth's cultivation of his self-image and its relationship to Warhol, see Alberro, *Conceptual Art and the Politics of Publicity*, pp. 26–30.

11 See Alberro, *Conceptual Art and the Politics of Publicity*, pp. 4, 41.

12 Ibid., pp. 12–14, 118. In early 1967, Siegelaub and the businessman John W. "Jack" Wendler founded Image. Art Programs for Industry, Inc. (the period after "Image" was intentional). As Alberro recounts, Image. acted as a "public relations specialist" for corporations seeking to forge closer ties with the

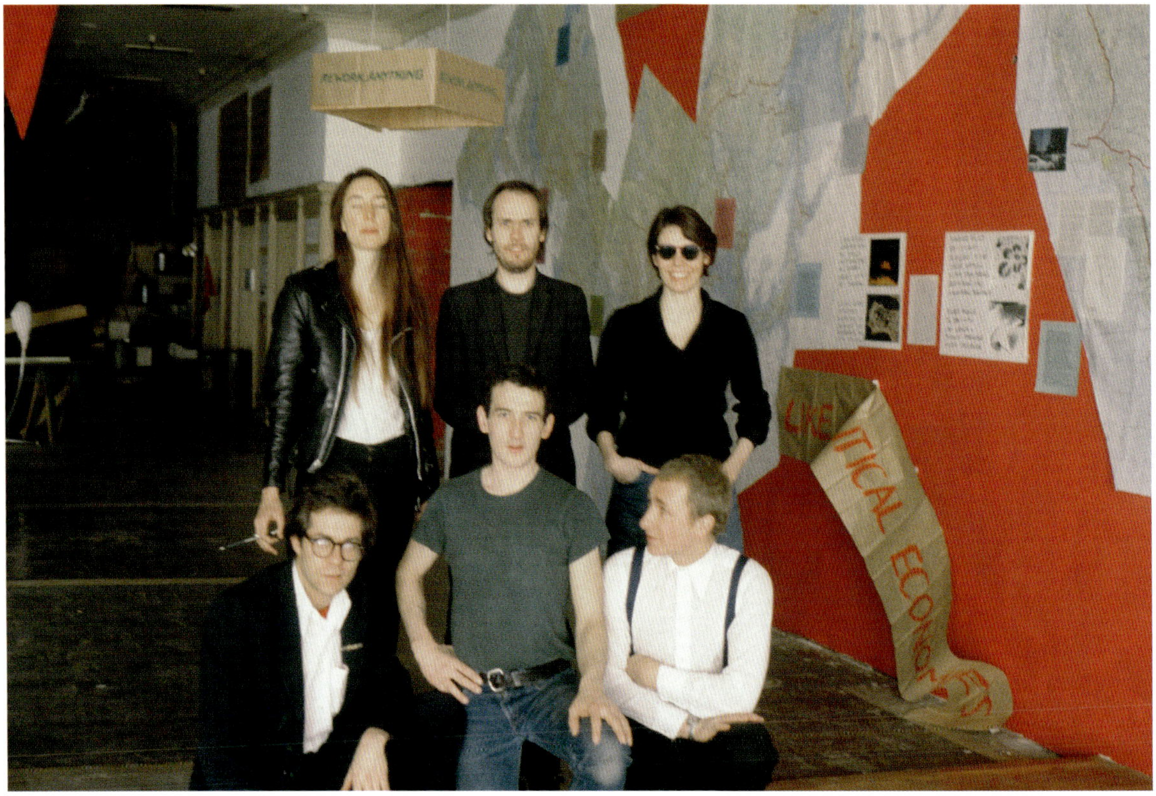

Fig. 3 **All six members of the Offices, Los Angeles, 1980. Top row: Jenny Holzer, Richard Prince, Coleen Fitzgibbon. Bottom row: Robin Winters, Peter Fend, Peter Nadin**

a quasi-gallery, on the other, were the best vehicles for their ideas at the time. Their efforts are significant not only because they prefigure artistic formations that came to define the 1980s but also for the insights they offer into the social and economic forces that have shaped life in the United States, and in a globalizing world, ever since.

Work for Yourself / Rework Anything

In the late 1970s, New York was in the throes of a financial crisis, and there were few opportunities for young artists to show their work at museums or commercial galleries. Yet there was no shortage of empty industrial buildings or of public funding for the arts, which fostered an efflorescence of artist-run, nonprofit, and "alternative" spaces in Lower Manhattan.[17] The artists under discussion here exhibited their work at such spaces, most often out of necessity but sometimes by choice.[18] In this climate, the prospect of an artist-run business venture such as the Offices must have been partly tongue-in-cheek. After all, its clientele was, at first, mostly imagined.

The Offices' founders met through Colab (short for Collaborative Projects), an artist-run collective that distributed grant funding to artists for group exhibitions, publications, television series, and other projects. Formed in 1977, Colab was characterized by its spirit of nonhierarchical egalitarianism: its leadership rotated regularly, and a committee voted on the allocation of funds.[19] All the members of the Offices, save Prince, were members of Colab. "The formation of a business partnership seemed to be a logical next step," Fend stated at the time.[20] From the outset, their idea was to offer services rather than produce object-based works.[21] The Offices "meant to deliver art as a form of consultation or service to non-art clients, certainly not collectors or museums," Fend elaborated. The founders reasoned that, as artists, they could sell aesthetic insights in the same way a lawyer would be consulted on matters of the law, and they modeled their operation on a law firm.[22] In October 1979, the group concretized its aims by issuing a manifesto-like statement. "The artist," it begins, "is an agency for the initiation of function." It articulates their intention to provide "professional artists [*sic*] alternatives to professional problems."[23] And, in declarative and occasionally cryptic terms, the statement calls for artists to reimagine their relationship to society and, more grandly, rethink the organization of society as a whole.

In February 1980, the Offices' ideas came to fruition in the collaborative exhibition *Pleasure/Function*, staged at 616 South Broadway in Los Angeles (**see fig. 3**).[24] The show's flyer (**fig. 4**) took the form of a multipanel comic strip featuring the phrases "Avoid Useless Work," "Rework Anything," and "Work for Yourself." The premise of the project reflected the artists' nascent conviction that there should be no

world of contemporary art. Its 1967 promotional pamphlet reads: "The art program is the medium through which you tell your story to the community. . . . [It is] designed to give you maximum return on your public relations dollar." Quoted in Alberro, *Conceptual Art and the Politics of Publicity*, p. 13.

13 Ibid., p. 5.

14 See Benjamin H. D. Buchloh, "Conceptual Art 1962–1969: From the Aesthetic of Administration to the Critique of Institutions," *October*, no. 55 (December 1990), pp. 128–29.

15 See Boltanski and Chiapello, *New Spirit of Capitalism*, p. 199.

16 Craig Owens et al., "Post-Modernism: A Symposium Presented by the Young Architects Circle, a Public Program of the Institute for Architecture and Urban Studies on March 30, 1981," *REALLIFE Magazine*, Summer 1981, p. 8.

17 See Julie Ault, ed., *Alternative Art, New York, 1965–1985: A Cultural Politics Book for the Social Text Collective* (New York: Drawing Center; Minneapolis: University of Minnesota Press, 2002); Lynne Cooke et al., *Mixed Use, Manhattan: Photography and Related Practices, 1970s to the Present*, exh. cat. (Madrid: Museo Nacional Centro de Arte Reina Sofía; Cambridge, MA: MIT Press, 2010).

18 "We believed we were the only audience for one another's work," Levine recalls. Sherrie Levine and Howard Singerman, "Sherrie Levine Talks to Howard Singerman (80s Then)," *Artforum* 41, no. 8 (April 2003), p. 190.

19 See Ault, *Alternative Art, New York*, pp. 48–49; David E. Little, "Colab Takes a Piece, History Takes It Back: Collectivity and New York Alternative Spaces," *Art Journal* 66, no. 1 (Spring 2007), p. 62.

"sharp bifurcation of work and play, of creation and recreation, of duty then leisure."[25] This imperative was put into practice at the site of the exhibition itself, a live/work space rented by the artist David Amico: it was hung with works of art by members of the Offices, but it doubled as their temporary living space and as the setting for a public event that sought to "transfer" the exhibition to the public. During the four-week run of the show, the artists also shared their views on a local call-in radio show and served as visiting artists at nearby colleges, cannily offering themselves as a "package deal." The exhibition functioned as an alibi for multifarious engagements with a wide variety of interlocutors.

Upon returning to New York, the Offices advertised a consulting portfolio in the March 1980 issue of *REALLIFE Magazine* **(see fig. 5)**. The heading, in all capital letters and italics, conveys a sense of urgency: WE ALL KNOW WHAT THE PROBLEMS ARE, BUT WHO NOW MEETS THEM DIRECTLY? Underneath, the text reads, in rather Potemkin fashion, "LOS ANGELES was our first client. From January 25 to February 25, we heard inquiries from and recommended changes for the Los Angeles region. We worked with these clients." Various local entities are then listed, such as a library, a radio station, universities, a marine development corporation, engineers, architects, and even a balloonist. The Offices claims to have advised on matters related to artistic practice, working conditions, infrastructure, and the environment. The list appears impressive, and deliberately so. It was meant to solicit new clients. But, reading between the lines, the advertisement doubles as a canny rebranding of the artists' visit to Los Angeles. The activities surrounding their exhibition at an informal artist-run space—a call-in radio show, some visiting-artist gigs, and a handful of conversations with local professionals—are artfully transformed into a formidable portfolio of work experience.

As a way of sharing its business acumen with new clients, the Offices assembled a dossier that compiled some of its insights. The dossier's contents evidence the artists' distinct voices while, at the same time, articulating their overarching aim—namely, the "functional rearrangement" of existing structures—under the banner of their signature letterhead. In the wake of *Pleasure/Function*, they managed to leverage their experience into a meeting with the International Labor Organization and perhaps even the United Nations (the participants' recollections vary).[26] Beyond that, the most concrete outcome of their work may have been their consultation for the artist-run space at 112 Greene Street, which, thanks to the Offices' rebranding, was known thereafter as White Columns. However, after just a few months of activity back in New York, the firm dissolved on account of internal disagreements about, among other things, whether to register as a nonprofit organization or a for-profit corporation.[27] The dispute speaks to the times.

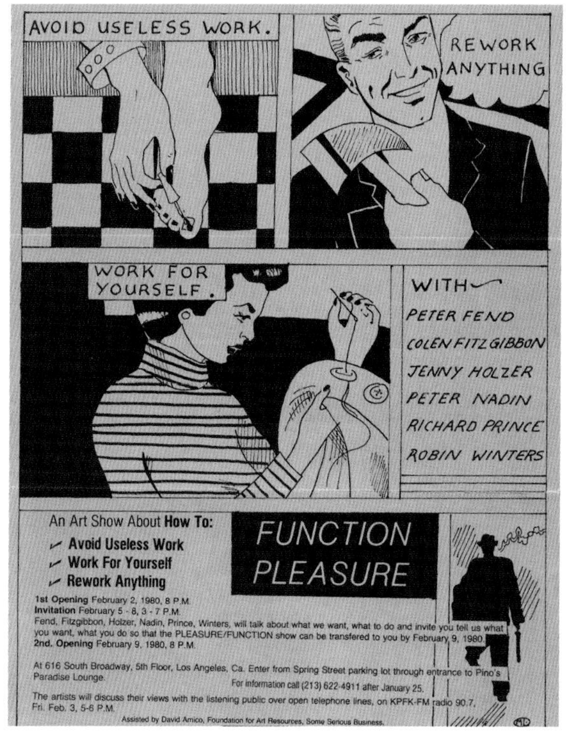

Fig. 4 Flyer for the Offices' exhibition *Pleasure/Function*, Los Angeles, 1980. Archives of American Art, Smithsonian Institution, Washington, DC, Foundation for Art Resources records, 1979–1983

Although the Offices' short lifespan and limited achievements could be seen as indications of failure, a longer view brings its significance into focus. The collective structure incubated the shared concerns of six individual artists—Fend, Fitzgibbon, Holzer, Nadin, Prince, and Winters—whose subsequent work brought those concerns to fruition in highly distinctive ways. Fend and Fitzgibbon, for example, founded the Ocean Earth Construction and Development Corporation, an independent satellite monitoring and analysis service that counted Holzer, Jonathan Crary, and Paul Sharits as three of its stakeholders.[28] More broadly, the Offices articulated a vision for artists' labor that went beyond Minimalism's apparent alliance with blue-collar fabricators and conceptualism's art of paperwork, forging a new identity for artists as entrepreneurs of ideas. This archetype circulated far beyond the art world as such—it became the key protagonist of a new labor paradigm.

His Gesture Moved Us to Tears

The year after the Offices folded, Louise Lawler and Sherrie Levine launched A Picture Is No Substitute for Anything—an umbrella for a sundry mix of events and exhibitions that took place in 1981 and 1982. Whereas the Offices had posed as a consulting firm, A Picture Is No Substitute for Anything simulated

20 The Offices of Fend, Fitzgibbon, Holzer, Nadin, Prince & Winters, "Pleasure/Function" (unpublished statement, n.d. [ca. 1980]), personal archive of David Amico, Los Angeles. The author of the document, which adopts a collective voice, is not cited, but it is written in Fend's penmanship.

21 Peter Nadin, interview by Gideon D'Arcangelo, November 27, 1992, Christopher D'Arcangelo Papers, Fales Archives and Special Collections, New York University, New York, Series IV, Subseries B, Box 6, Media ID 264.0028.

22 See The Offices, "Pleasure/Function" (n.d. [ca. 1980]); Jonathan Crary, "Peter Fend's Global Architecture," *Arts Magazine* 55, no. 10 (June 1981), pp. 152–53.

23 The lack of an apostrophe on "artists" is likely accidental but creates an intriguing ambiguity about whether the agency offers "professional artists' alternatives" or whether the founders, as artists, are being given an alternative to the problems of artistic professionalization by way of their service. (The former seems more likely.) The Offices of Fend, Fitzgibbon, Holzer, Nadin, Prince & Winters, "Pleasure/Function 1980" (unpublished statement, October 12, 1979), personal archive of Coleen Fitzgibbon.

24 616 South Broadway was a loft exhibition space run by the artist David Amico that had previously staged the exhibition *Individual and Collaborative Works by Nine Artists* (June 23–July 18, 1979), which included work by Holzer, Lawler, and Nadin.

25 The Offices of Fend, Fitzgibbon, Holzer, Nadin, Prince & Winters, "Pleasure/Function 1980" (press release, January 19, 1980), personal archive of David Amico.

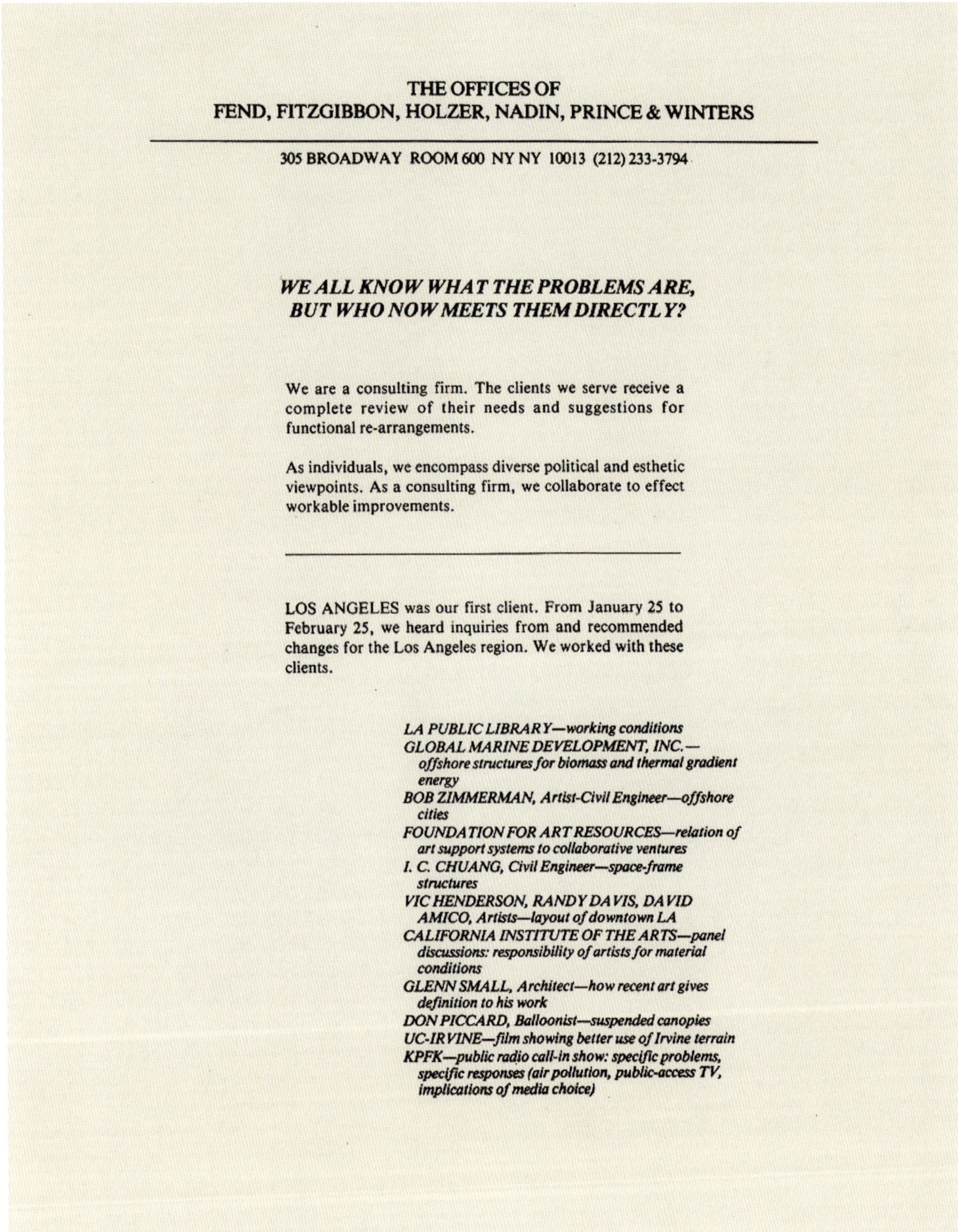

THE OFFICES OF
FEND, FITZGIBBON, HOLZER, NADIN, PRINCE & WINTERS

305 BROADWAY ROOM 600 NY NY 10013 (212) 233-3794

WE ALL KNOW WHAT THE PROBLEMS ARE, BUT WHO NOW MEETS THEM DIRECTLY?

We are a consulting firm. The clients we serve receive a complete review of their needs and suggestions for functional re-arrangements.

As individuals, we encompass diverse political and esthetic viewpoints. As a consulting firm, we collaborate to effect workable improvements.

LOS ANGELES was our first client. From January 25 to February 25, we heard inquiries from and recommended changes for the Los Angeles region. We worked with these clients.

LA PUBLIC LIBRARY—working conditions
GLOBAL MARINE DEVELOPMENT, INC.—offshore structures for biomass and thermal gradient energy
BOB ZIMMERMAN, Artist-Civil Engineer—offshore cities
FOUNDATION FOR ART RESOURCES—relation of art support systems to collaborative ventures
I. C. CHUANG, Civil Engineer—space-frame structures
VIC HENDERSON, RANDY DAVIS, DAVID AMICO, Artists—layout of downtown LA
CALIFORNIA INSTITUTE OF THE ARTS—panel discussions: responsibility of artists for material conditions
GLENN SMALL, Architect—how recent art gives definition to his work
DON PICCARD, Balloonist—suspended canopies
UC-IRVINE—film showing better use of Irvine terrain
KPFK—public radio call-in show: specific problems, specific responses (air pollution, public-access TV, implications of media choice)

Fig. 5 Advertisement for the Offices, *REALLIFE Magazine*, March 1980

a public relations apparatus. The catchphrase stemmed from a 1962 written exchange between the artist Carl Andre and the avant-garde filmmaker-photographer Hollis Frampton (published in 1981) wherein Frampton wagered that "a photograph is no substitute for anything."[29] Lawler and Levine adapted the expression, changing "photograph" to "picture"–a word with significant cachet at the time thanks to the 1977 exhibition *Pictures*, curated by Douglas Crimp at the nonprofit gallery Artists Space, then located in Tribeca.[30] The "pictures" sensibility, according to Crimp, was characterized by the appropriation of everyday images from mass media and popular culture by artists who recast their meanings through photography, film, and painting. This amounted to a radical reappraisal of originality and authorship and certainly loosened the structure of what an artistic practice could be. All told, Lawler

26 Fend recalls that Holzer "initiated our going to the UN. . . . She thought we could begin with the International Labour Organization. . . . We had a meeting in an ILO office near the UN Building; I don't think anything concrete came from it." Fend, Joselit, and Harrison, "Conversation with Peter Fend," p. 118. Fitzgibbon said more recently that the Offices "approached the UN to offer our 'function & pleasure' art services for their labor problems. (They did not accept.)" Coleen Fitzgibbon and P. Adams Sitney, "Coleen Fitzgibbon by P. Adams Sitney," *BOMB*, Spring 2013, p. 124.

27 See Fend, Joselit, and Harrison, "Conversation with Peter Fend," p. 119.

28 Ibid.

29 Carl Andre and Hollis Frampton, *12 Dialogues, 1962–1963*, ed. Benjamin Buchloh (Halifax and New York: Press of the Nova Scotia College of Art and Design and New York University Press, 1981), p. 21; Levine and Singerman, "Sherrie Levine Talks to Howard Singerman," p. 191.

30 The artists included in the exhibition, along with their peer group, came to be known as the "Pictures Generation." See Douglas Crimp, *Pictures: An Exhibition of the Work of Troy Brauntuch, Jack Goldstein, Sherrie Levine, Robert Longo, Philip Smith: Artists Space, September 24–October 29, 1977*, exh. cat. (New York: Committee for the Visual Arts, Inc., 1977). See also Douglas Eklund, *The Pictures Generation, 1974–1984*, exh. cat. (New York: The Metropolitan Museum of Art, 2009).

31 Henceforth referred to by the shortened "A Picture Is No Substitute."

32 Louise Lawler and Douglas Crimp, "Prominence Given, Authority Taken," *Grey Room*, no. 4 (Summer 2001), p. 79.

33 Levine and Singerman, "Sherrie Levine Talks to Howard Singerman," p. 190.

34 Eklund, *Pictures Generation*, p. 258.

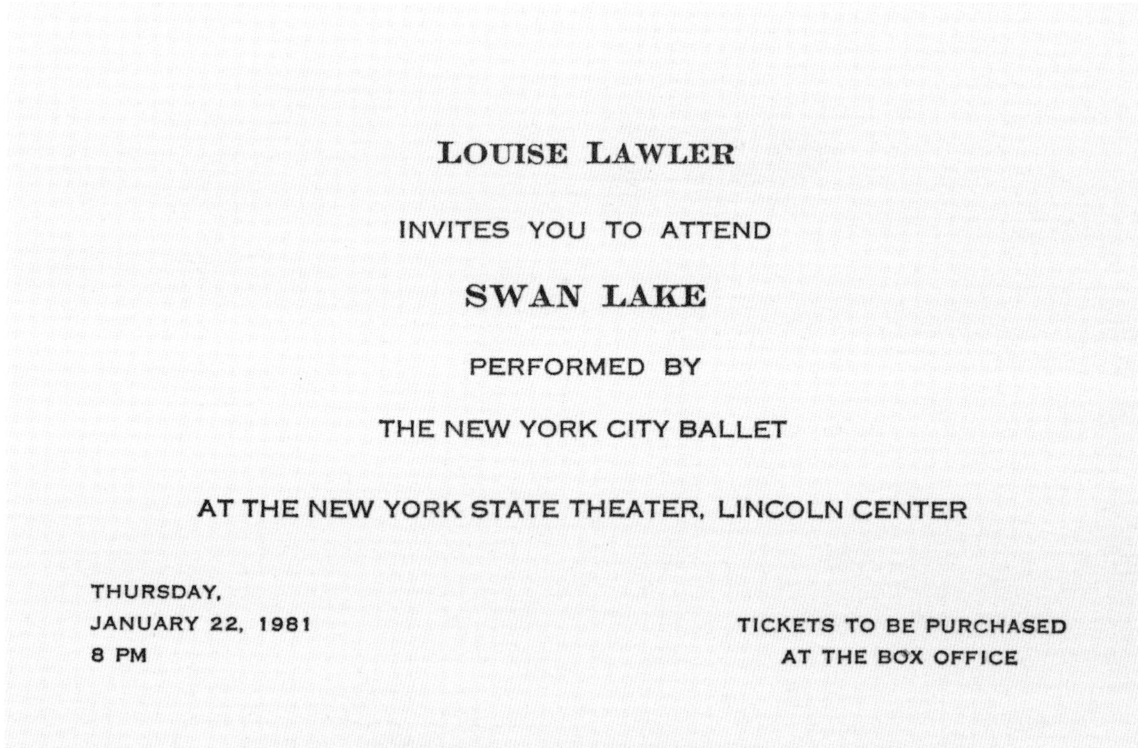

LOUISE LAWLER

INVITES YOU TO ATTEND

SWAN LAKE

PERFORMED BY

THE NEW YORK CITY BALLET

AT THE NEW YORK STATE THEATER, LINCOLN CENTER

THURSDAY,
JANUARY 22, 1981
8 PM

TICKETS TO BE PURCHASED
AT THE BOX OFFICE

Fig. 6 Louise Lawler's invitation to a performance of *Swan Lake*, 1981

and Levine may have spliced "pictures" into Frampton's phrase for the ambiguities the word now conjured. The result—A Picture Is No Substitute for Anything[31]—pointed to the inadequacy, or limits, of representation, a theme explored in Frampton's films as well as in Lawler and Levine's own art.

At a time when Lawler and Levine were working at the relative margins of the institutionally sanctioned art world, they became fascinated by the conventions and codes governing how art is circulated and displayed across different contexts. What distinguished a downtown artist-run space from, say, a gallery on East Fifty-Seventh Street, or a museum like the Modern? And what would it mean to scramble those codes? Through A Picture Is No Substitute, the artists made the secondary aspects of the art world—the drafting of guest lists, sending out of invitations, hosting of receptions—the main subject and substance of their work. They staged one-night salon-style events at informal venues that often contrasted starkly with the formal style of their letterpress announcements. Rather than appropriating and recontextualizing images, they recast situations and social cues.

Lawler recalled that A Picture Is No Substitute came into being "at a time when there wasn't much question about whether to show in a gallery—I mean, no one was asking us to show.... [D]eclaring our own gallery was also a way of showing that a gallery isn't just a showcase; *it's* also what's on display. We weren't being subsumed as part of a gallery; we *were* the gallery."[32] The self-initiated structure allowed the artists to pursue idiosyncratic lines of inquiry into the vagaries of niche contexts without having to justify or explain their choices to a curator or a dealer. "Our self-financed venture was a lot like Judy Garland and Mickey Rooney putting on a show in the backyard," Levine reminisced.[33] By imagining household names performing for a domestic audience, her analogy overlays the intimacy of a private home onto the hypervisibility of celebrity culture.

In January 1981, in a prefiguration of her collaborations with Levine, Lawler had mailed out invitations to a performance of *Swan Lake* at Lincoln Center for the Performing Arts in New York to a group of friends and colleagues **(see fig. 6)**. The heavy cream cardstock features an elegant typeface that reads:

LOUISE LAWLER
INVITES YOU TO ATTEND
SWAN LAKE
PERFORMED BY
THE NEW YORK CITY BALLET

The invitation's gentility is undermined by the caveat at the bottom: TICKETS TO BE PURCHASED AT THE BOX OFFICE. Lawler's unauthorized invitation had the effect of creating an audience within an audience; it generated a different frame for a public performance, perceptible only to the members of an art-world in-group. Lawler's invitees were invisibly embedded within the general public at Lincoln Center. As the curator Douglas Eklund has observed, "Lawler's gesture recast the quintessential uptown 'elitist' event as a conspiratorial, wittily invisible infiltration of a black-tie audience with double agents."[34] Two kinds of cultural capital abutted here: one, of downtown artists viewing the performance through the prism of a peer's invitation, and the other, of an uptown crowd habituated to an evening at the ballet.[35] The interplay of inclusion and exclusion was further complicated by the fact that the date Lawler had selected, Thursday, January 22, conflicted with a cocktail party hosted by the art dealer Janelle Reiring. The circumstances being what they were, almost none of Lawler's guests, save Levine and the artist Allan McCollum, attended the performance of *Swan Lake*.[36]

Through A Picture Is No Substitute, Lawler and Levine continued this sly line of inquiry into the politics of inclusion and exclusion implied by any invitation, whether to a public event, an artist's studio, or a private home. A few months later, they sent out handwritten invitations to an afternoon reception at the studio of the late Dimitry Merinoff, a little-known Russian American painter. Since his death in 1971, Merinoff's tiny studio near Union Square had been flawlessly preserved by his widow. The guests sipped Dubonnet and took in Merinoff's gestural, figurative paintings in the afternoon light. *Credo*, a painting then on view in his posthumous exhibition at Washburn Gallery on East Fifty-Seventh Street, bore a French inscription that translates as "I am myself the substance of my painting."[37] This gave voice to the notion that art might be an authentic expression of the self, a Romantic view of artistic creation that had been revived by Neo-Expressionist painters such as Francesco Clemente and Anselm Kiefer in the 1980s.[38] The agenda of such artists' dramatic, gestural, and emotive work contrasted starkly with Lawler and Levine's, whose subsequent activities reveal a deep skepticism toward the idea of a direct link between interiority and appearance.

For an exhibition at James Turcotte Gallery in Los Angeles in 1982, Lawler and Levine printed slick blue cards with the words *His gesture moved us to tears* in a bold, modern typeface (**fig. 7**). The cards' distribution and display were the sole content of the show. One card was mounted under glass on a gallery wall (**see fig. 8**); a stack of them rested on a small table nearby; and dozens more were distributed by mail to promote the exhibition. The declarative statement is purposefully vague. The pronouns chosen by the artists are general–*his*, *us*–yet suggest the gender of the actor as well as a "we" unified in their emotional response: tears. Are these tears of sadness, of joy, or, perhaps, even, crocodile tears? Levine called the show an "ode to neo-expressionism," meaning that "his gesture" could refer to paint on canvas.[39] But the action in question could also be that of a conceptual artist, whose dematerialized work–sometimes reduced to little more than a gesture–was deliber-

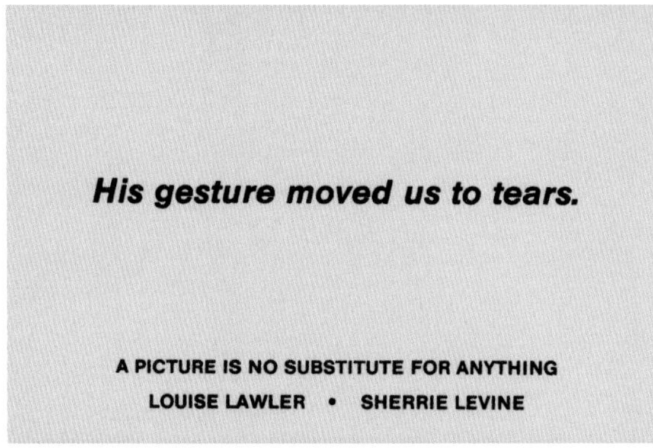

Fig. 7 Card produced for A Picture Is No Substitute for Anything's exhibition at James Turcotte Gallery, Los Angeles, 1982

ately drained of affect and materiality. Lawler and Levine's equally conceptual work eschewed this performance of neutrality in favor of printed matter laden with color, texture, and style. In light of these associations, the tears in question start to seem anything but earnest.

Under the aegis of their collaborative venture, Lawler and Levine also staged one-night exhibitions of their work at various informal venues, including Lawler's Tribeca loft. One such exhibition, which opened at midnight on Friday, January 1, 1982, marked the debut of a new series of works by Lawler. These were color photographs of works of art by Lawler's peers (including Levine, Holzer, Nadin, and McCollum) that she had set against vibrant backdrops and fashioned into idiosyncratic, jigsaw-like configurations (**see fig. 9**). The titles–*(Holzer, Nadin and Other Artists) Baby Blue*, for example–relegate the names of the artists to a curiously placed parenthetical, privileging instead the color that would otherwise seem to serve as a mere backdrop. The named and unnamed artists rotate depending on the piece. The works dissect and suture the codes and conventions that structure the display of art. Together, title and image invite examination of the hierarchies subtly signaled by placement: above or below, before or after, or entirely out of sight.

In November 1982, these works, and others like them, reappeared in Lawler's exhibition *Arrangements of Pictures* at Metro Pictures in Soho. The first room contained a group of works by the gallery's artists selected and arranged by Lawler (**see fig. 10**). The configuration was for sale for the combined price of the constituent works, plus a 10 percent fee that represented the "value added" by Lawler's aesthetic services. The larger back gallery featured an expanded series of her colorful still-life photographs featuring works by her peers (and now also by Warhol and Roy Lichtenstein). These were complemented by photographic tableaux of works of art hanging in collectors' homes and offices or installed in museums.[40] As the artist Andrea Fraser has observed, Lawler's work is constituted by the appropriation of *positions*:

35 The term "cultural capital" was introduced by the sociologist Pierre Bourdieu to describe the role played by taste, comportment, and cultural knowledge in organizing social relations. It appears in his writing beginning in 1973 and is elaborated in his essay "The Forms of Capital," in J. F. Richardson, ed., *Handbook of a Theory of Research in the Sociology of Education*, trans. Richard Nice (Westport, CT: Greenword Press, 1986), pp. 241-58.

36 See Eklund, *Pictures Generation*, p. 258.

37 Howard Singerman, *Art History, after Sherrie Levine* (Berkeley, CA: University of California Press, 2012), p. 29.

38 See Rosalyn Deutsche, "Representing Berlin," in *Evictions: Art and Spatial Politics* (Cambridge, MA: MIT Press, 1996), pp. 109-58; Benjamin H. D. Buchloh, "Figures of Authority, Ciphers of Regression: Notes on the Return of Representation in European Painting," *October*, no. 16 (Spring 1981), pp. 39-68.

39 Levine and Singerman, "Sherrie Levine Talks to Howard Singerman," p. 190.

40 Also hung in the back gallery were a color photograph taken from the upper tier of a sports stadium and a black-and-white image of a ballet performance taken from the balcony of the New York State Theater, Lincoln Center, on the night Lawler had attended *Swan Lake* in January 1981.

41 See Andrea Fraser, "In and Out of Place," *Art in America*, June 1985, p. 122. In 1988–89, Lawler collaborated with Fraser on the video "The Public Life of Art: The Museum."

42 See Peter Bürger, *Theory of the Avant-Garde*, trans. Michael Shaw (Minneapolis: University of Minnesota Press, 1984); Hal Foster, *The Return of the Real: The Avant-Garde at the End of the Century* (Cambridge, MA: MIT Press, 1996).

43 Peter Fend and Coleen Fitzgibbon, unpublished 2016 statement emailed to the author, March 30, 2016; Levine and Singerman, "Sherrie Levine Talks to Howard Singerman," p. 191. Levine went on to describe her idea that the art world was not the real world as "very naive, but attributable to our collective youth—a kind of Holden Caulfield hangover. Back then I often referred to Lawrence Weiner's statement about making art that directed us back to the real world."

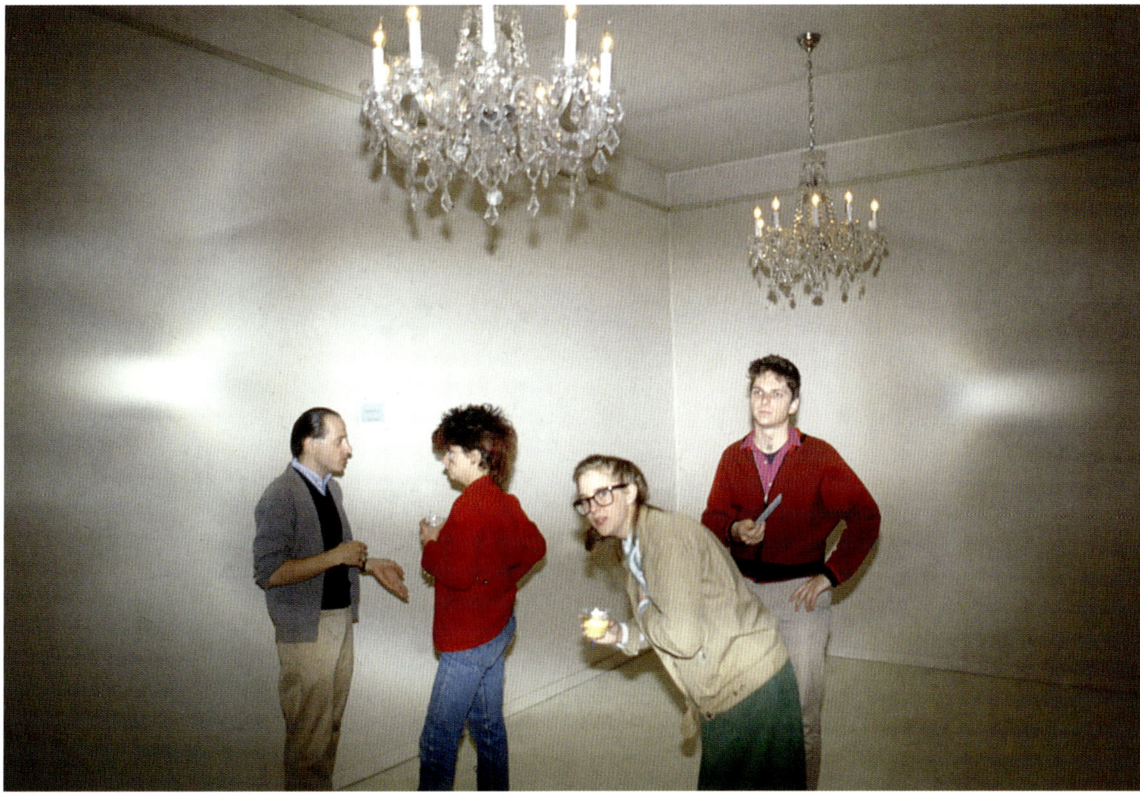

Fig. 8 Installation view with four unidentified visitors, James Turcotte Gallery, Los Angeles, 1982

here, she acts as a consultant, curator, and documentarian, while elsewhere she serves as a publicist, museum worker, graphic designer, or art director.[41] Her restless repositioning creates a parallax view, whereby familiar images are recast with new attributes depending on her angle of approach.

A Picture Is No Substitute offered an analysis of the artist in relation to her context that aligned with the Offices' inquiry into the roles artists might play in society at large. But Lawler and Levine did not share the latter's radical aim of transcending the realm of art entirely. Rather, like event planners or public relations agents, they reconfigured and manipulated social situations and publicity materials. Their primary product was immaterial: the cultivation of a public image. For the duration of its activity, A Picture Is No Substitute perched precariously on the fluctuating boundary of the officially sanctioned art world, as if caught in an existence between the "inside" and the "outside." Lawler and Levine's rearticulation of audiences and contexts hinged on their fluency in the art world's codes, coupled with their ability to hold those codes at arm's length. For a brief period in 1981 and 1982, they toed the line between "insiders" and "outsiders," making work that was most potent when it operated in the gap between the two.

Real Life

The multifaceted activities of the Offices and A Picture Is No Substitute attest to a shared preoccupation with what the artists collectively termed "real life"—a quasi-mythical realm that, for them, seemed to designate what lay beyond the "art world" (wherever that was). These artists, however, were hardly the first to be fascinated by the art/life distinction—a divide that could be understood as *the* structuring binary of the twentieth-century avant-gardes, subject to continual reformulation by artists who tested its elasticity, from the Soviet Productivists to the Art Workers' Coalition.[42] As for its status in the early 1980s, Fend has emphasized that "real-world outcomes were expected [by the Offices], not just art-image ones," while Levine recalled, "Real life . . . was a big concern of ours. I think it was a way of distancing ourselves from the art world. In those days I didn't think the art world was the real world."[43] The concept had such cachet at the time that it even lent its name to a periodical, *REALLIFE Magazine*, started by Thomas Lawson and Susan Morgan in New York in 1979 (and already the setting of the Offices' full-page advertisement in 1980). The cover of the fall 1981 issue, photographed and designed by Lawler, featured Levine's work exhibited in Lawler's loft earlier that year under the auspices of A Picture Is No Substitute **(figs. 11, 12)**. The image is purposefully cropped so that Levine's *After Eliot Porter* photographs are mostly out of view, underscored by the irregularly spaced words

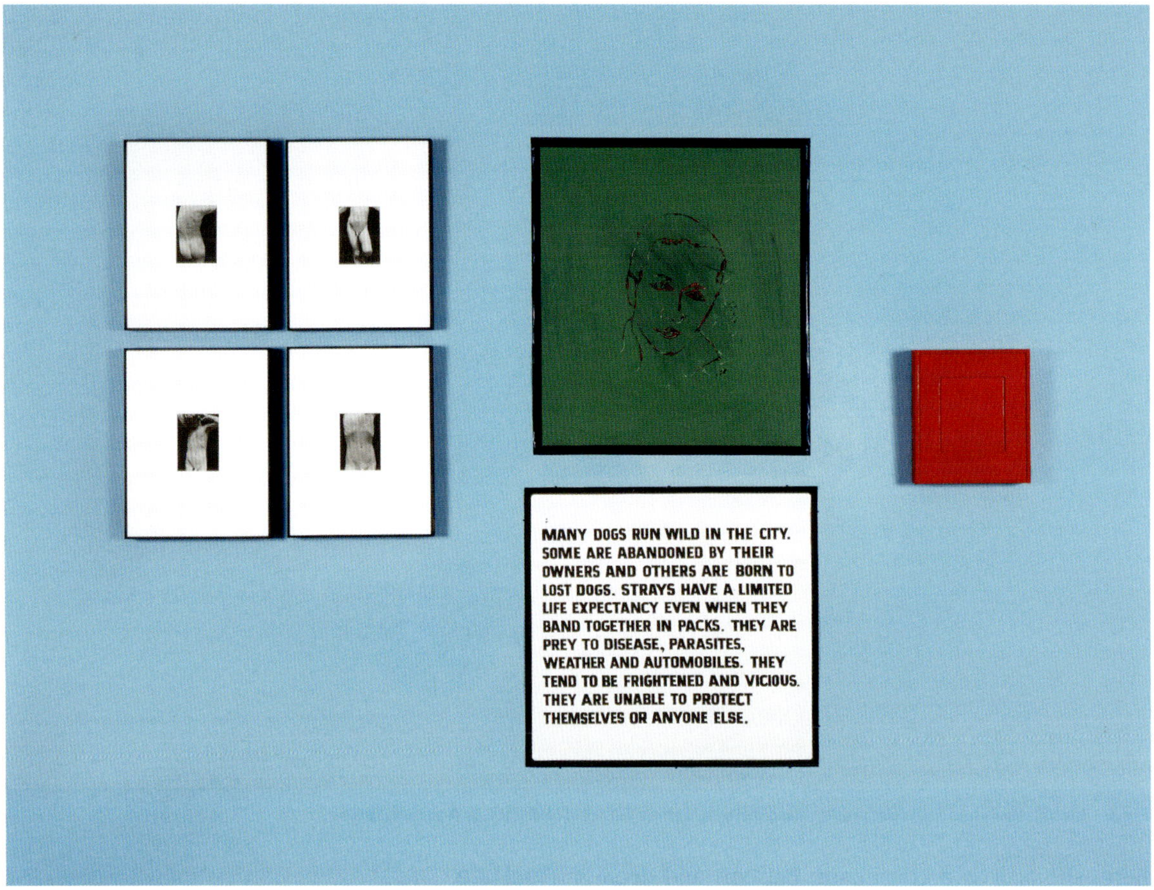

Fig. 9 Louise Lawler. ***(Holzer, Nadin and Other Artists) Baby Blue*****, 1981. Cibachrome**

"REALLIFE Magazine." A freestanding white wall and the distinctive black-and-white floor of Lawler's loft occupy the majority of the frame. The back cover offers a glimpse of the loft's living quarters, including Lawler's bed, whose frilly trim abuts the rough edges of the industrial space. Here, the live/work space printed recto/verso on the cover of an art magazine titled *REALLIFE* functions as a poignant metonym for the art/life binary probed by these artists.

At this same moment, the ascendancy of neoliberalism refashioned all realms of American life into a live/work space in which the boundaries between private and public became difficult to sustain. In this sense, the Offices' 1980 proposal to "Avoid Useless Work / Work for Yourself / Rework Anything"–implicit also in the contemporaneous activities of A Picture Is No Substitute–can be seen as a blueprint for the flexible, adaptable, creative work that came to define the post-Fordist information economy.[44] As the political theorist Wendy Brown has chronicled, this was also a time when financial institutions were deregulated in the service of a free-market economy, social services were diminished and privatized, and working conditions for the majority of Americans became increasingly precarious. The result was intensified inequality and economic havoc, heightened commercialization, and closer ties between corporations and the state.[45] The abiding significance of the Offices' and A Picture Is No Substitute's short-lived activities lies in their uncanny prescience: they were both symptom and diagnosis of their times.

The quintessential protagonist of this new labor paradigm was the artist-manager, often called the "project head" in 1990s management discourse. The term designates that freewheeling entrepreneurial type who has traded in his suit, desktop computer, and office hierarchy for jeans, a laptop, and a horizontal "team." The parallels between the "project head" and the Offices' image of the artist are striking: both are cast as charismatic, visionary leaders valued for their creativity, flexibility, and adaptability.[46] They excel at visual and verbal communication. They take on work on a short-term, "project" basis, likely juggling multiple gigs simultaneously. Public reputation and personal relationships are of paramount importance in securing work, which often develops informally and is framed as a mutually beneficial "collaboration" transcending conventional hierarchies.[47] These individuals favor fulfilling, "authentic" work that promises to lead to personal development and greater self-knowledge. For them, the line between business and personal relationships blurs: if you are your own boss, you are never at work, but never not working.[48]

Boltanski and Chiapello dub the result of this paradigm shift the "new spirit of capitalism." Their

44 The Italian theorists Maurizio Lazzarato, Christian Marazzi, and Franco "Bifo" Berardi coined the term "post-Fordism" to describe an economic system propelled by the exchange of immaterial goods and services (in contrast to the "Fordist" production-line model pioneered by the American industrialist Henry Ford).

45 See Wendy Brown, *Undoing the Demos: Neoliberalism's Stealth Revolution* (Cambridge, MA: MIT Press, 2015), p. 28.

46 "Today's productivity is increasingly determined by the capacity to respond to unforeseen and unforeseeable situations, *emergent situations*, those situations which make any sort of planning impracticable." Christian Marazzi, *Capital and Language: From the New Economy to the War Economy*, trans. Gregory Conti (Los Angeles: Semiotext(e), 2008), p. 51.

47 Artists have "portfolios of activities and resources containing different risks," which give "the individual organization of artistic work certain properties of a mini-firm." Pierre-Michel Menger, quoted in Boltanski and Chiapello, *New Spirit of Capitalism*, p. 312.

48 In *Late Capitalism*, the theorist Ernest Mandel suggests that the eponymous phenomenon is characterized by the logic of work's spreading to all areas of life. Ernest Mandel, *Late Capitalism*, trans. Joris De Bres (London: Verso, 1978), p. 387. See also Molesworth, *Work Ethic*, p. 38.

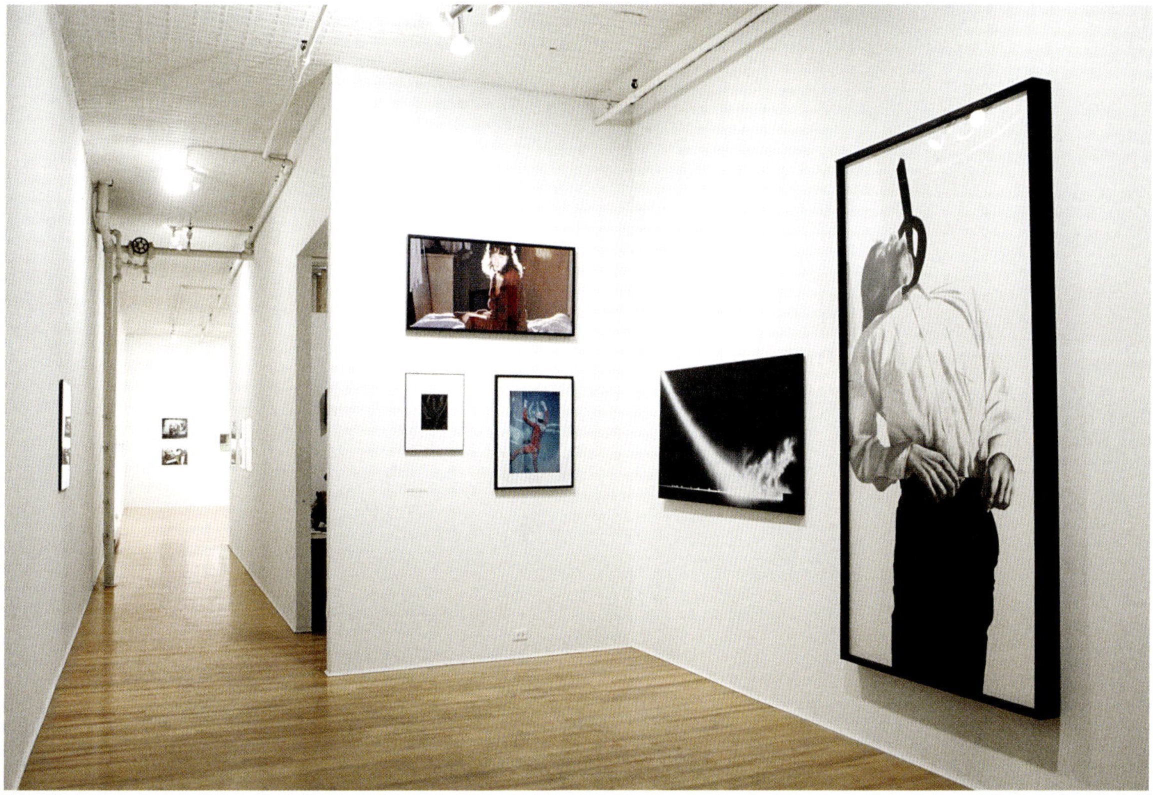

Fig. 10 Installation view, *Arrangements of Pictures*, Metro Pictures, New York, 1982

eponymous book offers the following explanation for the convergence of artistic practice and management discourse: "The qualities that are guarantees of success in this new spirit [of capitalism] . . . are taken directly from the repertoire of May '68."[49] In other words, the demands articulated by artists and intellectuals involved in the social movements of the late 1960s–demands that Boltanski and Chiapello term the "artistic critique" of capitalism and the economist Christian Marazzi calls the "cultural critique"–took aim at traditional modes of authority and paternalism, hierarchical modes of organization, prescribed tasks and stultifying work schedules, and the alienating effects of the division of labor.[50] This approach reflected the belief that greater autonomy, flexibility, personalization, and self-management could yield liberation and creative fulfillment.[51]

Yet from the present standpoint, it is clear that capitalism responded to these critiques simply by absorbing them. A rising tide of individualism and entrepreneurship, coupled with skepticism of government regulation and labor unions, had cemented this new paradigm by the late 1970s, leading to the growth of an increasingly vulnerable population working on freelance or short-term contracts.[52] At the same time, the support previously offered by social services decreased. Employers and the state called on workers to live with ever-greater risk.[53] As the sociologist Maurizio Lazzarato has observed, "The *work on the self* preached by management since the 1980s [has] become an injunction to *take upon oneself* the costs and risks of the economic and financial disaster."[54] This was hardly the freedom from alienated labor envisioned by the artists and intellectuals of May '68. Rather, it heralded the new regime of the never-ending workday.

As Michel Foucault proposed in his lectures at the Collège de France, Paris, in 1978-79, neoliberalism's quintessential move is the transformation of *all* relations into economic relations.[55] The neoliberal subject understands herself primarily in economic terms–as human capital, an "entrepreneur of the self."[56] Today, this mode has become axiomatic. The new labor economy is defined by self-management, investing in oneself, and building a "personal brand." Brown posits that "this figure of the human as an ensemble of entrepreneurial and investment capital is evident on every college and job application, every package of study strategies, every internship, every new exercise and diet program."[57] Those who work in so-called creative fields experience this phenomenon most acutely. In Brown's account, the *soixante-huitards*' call for authentic, individualized work and products found its counterpart in the capitalization of previously uncommodified spheres and practices: affect, emotion, and service.[58]

From this perspective, there seems to be no better model for the neoliberal paradigm–in both art and life–than the modes of artistic labor pioneered by the Offices and A Picture Is No Substitute. The two ventures were groundbreaking for their entrepreneurialization of the figure of the artist. Their efforts

49 Boltanski and Chiapello, *New Spirit of Capitalism*, p. 97. The terms "immaterial labor," "service economy," "neoliberalism," "the New Economy," and, again, "post-Fordism" have also been variously applied to this paradigm shift.

50 Boltanski and Chiapello, *New Spirit of Capitalism*, pp. 170, 199.

51 See Boltanski and Chiapello, *New Spirit of Capitalism*, p. 170; Marazzi, *Capital and Language*, p. 41.

52 See Thomas Borstelmann, *The 1970s: A New Global History from Civil Rights to Economic Inequality* (Princeton, NJ: Princeton University Press, 2013), p. 137. The new spirit of capitalism emerged "at the end of the crisis of the 1960s and 70s" and "continued and accelerated during the 1980s." Boltanski and Chiapello, *New Spirit of Capitalism*, p. 201.

53 See Borstelmann, *1970s*, p. 124; Lazzarato, *Making of the Indebted Man*, p. 106.

54 Lazzarato, *Making of the Indebted Man*, p. 9.

55 See Michel Foucault, *The Birth of Biopolitics: Lectures at the Collège de France, 1978-1979*, trans. Michel Senellart (New York: Palgrave Macmillan, 2011), p. 225; Brown, *Undoing the Demos*, pp. 31-32.

56 Lazzarato, *Making of the Indebted Man*, p. 91.

57 Brown, *Undoing the Demos*, p. 36.

58 Andrea Fraser has analyzed the counterpart to the service economy in the context of artists and institutions: the rise of project-based work as a form of "service provision." Andrea Fraser, "What's Intangible, Transitory, Mediating, Participatory, and Rendered in the Public Sphere?" *October*, no. 80 (Spring 1997), pp. 111-16.

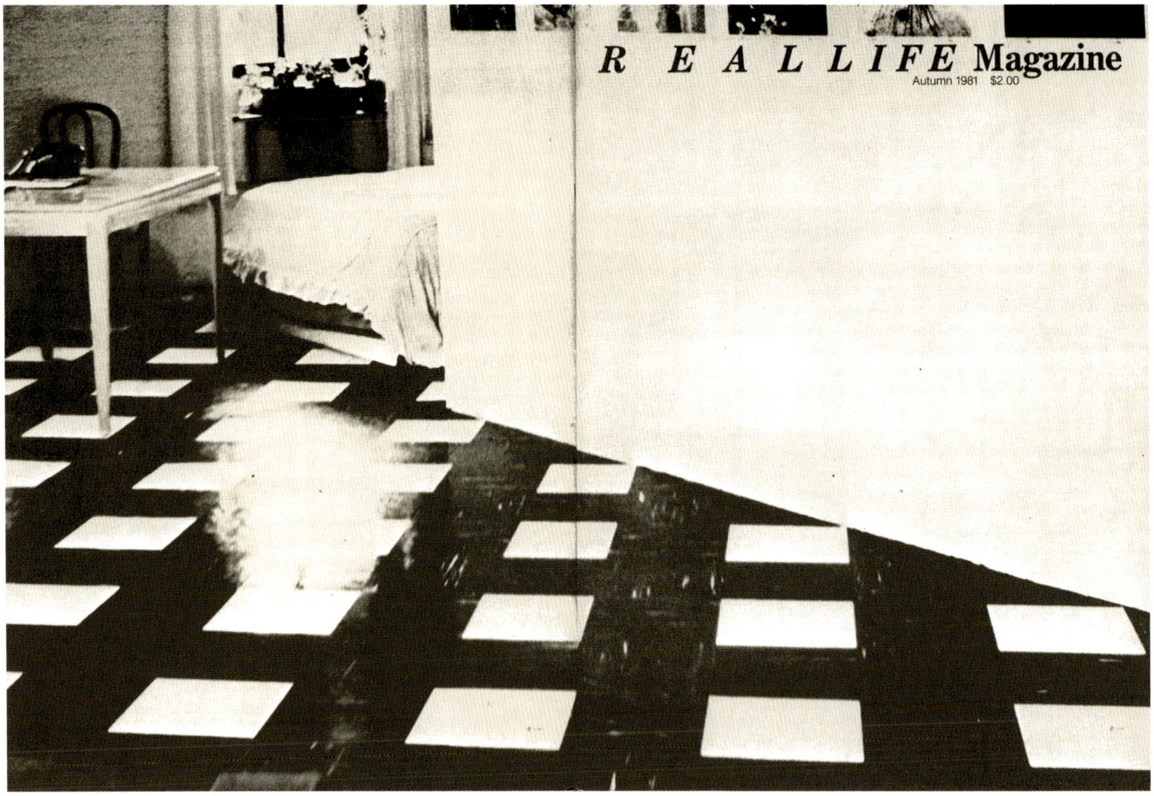

Fig. 11 Cover (front and back) of *REALLIFE Magazine* with photograph by Louise Lawler, Autumn 1981

moved beyond Warhol, who embraced the "factory" model so as to maximize production, and Siegelaub, who harnessed publicity to market art as pure idea: those precedents revised the criteria of what constituted a work of art but left intact the divide between producer and work. The members of the Offices and A Picture Is No Substitute aspired to eliminate that distinction by turning their *perspectives* and *actions* into the product itself. To do so, they forged new forms of collectivity and carved out contexts for their work beyond the gallery and museum system. The Offices pursued this rather directly, seeking to monetize its "aesthetic services" by working as a consultant for clients outside the art world. The mark of success in remaking artists' roles in society would have been participation in an economy beyond the art market. A Picture Is No Substitute took a more oblique approach, opting instead to manipulate the orthodoxies of viewership from within art's frame. Lawler and Levine's immaterial services–generating buzz, summoning an audience, constructing ambience–depended on their unique ability, as artists, to understand and manipulate cultural cues. Both projects signaled the paramount role that cultural capital, of which artists had long been the standard bearers, would soon assume in the broader economy.

The entrepreneurial efforts of the Offices and A Picture Is No Substitute unwittingly created a mold for the neoliberal subject at a time when the notions of autonomy, creativity, and adaptability still held utopian promise. In 1980, Fend imagined that artists' proclivity for self-organization would lay the groundwork for a new kind of economy: "Artists become model workers in a world run by non-workers.... The artists with experience in artist-run centers and artist-run exhibitions, magazines and film-video productions, now organized in The Offices, presage a society of worker-run ventures and productions–of worker-run economy."[59] Despite this foresight, he did not account for the extent to which this spirit of autonomy would be used against its advocates. The decades that followed witnessed the metabolization of the Offices' proposals about work into mainstream discourse and into the information economy of the twenty-first century. As such, these artists' vision for how artistic labor could function within society at large was absorbed into "real life" far more thoroughly than they could have imagined–though not necessarily on their terms or to their benefit.

The early 1980s also marked a turning point for Lawler's and Levine's work. The audience for their fly-by-night activities as A Picture Is No Substitute was largely composed of their peers. With the founding of the gallery Metro Pictures in November 1980 by Janelle Reiring and Helene Winer–former directors of Leo Castelli Gallery and the nonprofit Artists Space, respectively–the center of gravity shifted. A group of young artists (now known as the "Pictures Generation") who had previously orbited around Artists Space were thrust into greater visibility. "It definitely marks the death of the 60s," the critic Robert Pincus-Witten remarked of the gallery's

59 The Offices, "Pleasure/Function" (n.d. [ca. 1980]).

60 Robert Pincus-Witten, "Entries: Maximalism," in *Post-minimalism into Maximalism: American Art, 1966–1986* (Ann Arbor, MI: UMI Research Press, 1987), p. 268. The comment, written on November 12, 1980, is from Pincus-Witten's "diary" for *Arts* magazine. The entry was published in the February 1981 issue.

61 Levine and Singerman, "Sherrie Levine Talks to Howard Singerman," p. 190.

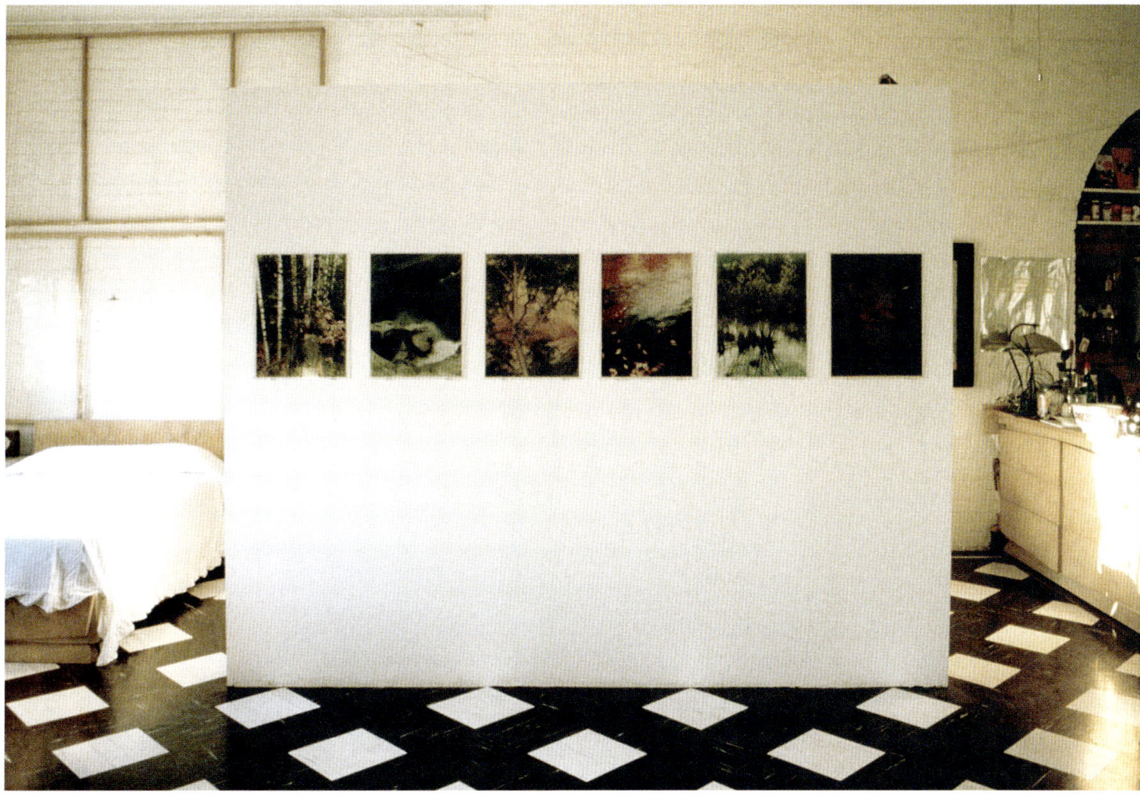

Fig. 12 Sherrie Levine. *After Eliot Porter*, 1981. Six color photographs. Installation view, Louise Lawler's loft, 407 Greenwich Street, New York, 1981

opening, signaling the larger symbolic significance of this shift from the nonprofit to the commercial sphere.[60] "By then, for me, the real party was over," Levine recalled. "Success is always crass. But so is failure."[61] Levine and Lawler would have solo exhibitions at the gallery in May-June 1981 (*Sherrie Levine*) and November-December 1982 (the aforementioned *Arrangements of Pictures*), respectively. Their short-lived collaborative venture dissolved in 1982. The idiosyncratic situational interventions they had staged as A Picture Is No Substitute were subsequently eclipsed by their photographic work, which was more easily circulated and displayed.

It would be easy to dismiss the Offices and A Picture Is No Substitute on account of their short lifespans and limited reach—or in light of the path down which the proposal to "Work for Yourself/ Rework Anything" seems to have led. But to do so would be to miss their prescience: the generation that encompasses Fend, Fitzgibbon, Holzer, Nadin, Prince, Winters, Lawler, and Levine was the first to work from the premise that no radical idea is beyond assimilation or recuperation. This realization does not invalidate the idea of resistance; it makes artists' continual reformulation of their critiques in response to shifting social, economic, and political conditions an even more crucial task. The lasting import of these practices resides not in the answers they offered but in the questions they posed. In the 1980 ad in *REALLIFE Magazine*, the Offices asked, WE ALL KNOW WHAT THE PROBLEMS ARE, BUT WHO NOW MEETS THEM DIRECTLY?—an appeal that resonates today as clearly and urgently as it did thirty-five years ago.

1983–86
The New Capital

1983

Semiotext(e), a publisher of critical theory housed at Columbia University, issues the first two volumes of its Foreign Agents series, Jean Baudrillard's *Simulations* and Gilles Deleuze and Félix Guattari's *On the Line*. Baudrillard's philosophy, first translated into English and introduced to American readers via Semiotext(e), quickly gains traction with artists working around commodities and the commodity image. The text is extremely influential on Peter Halley and his contemporaries, so much so that one of the labels used to describe them is "Simulationists."

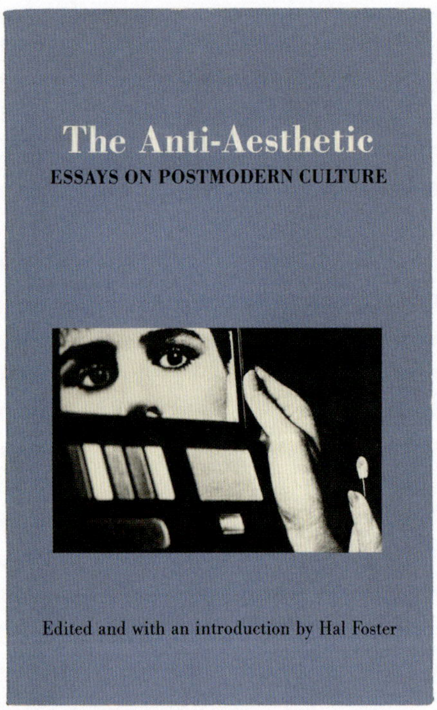

Cover of Hal Foster's *The Anti-Aesthetic* (Bay Press, 1983), with photograph by Richard Prince

Seattle's Bay Press publishes *The Anti-Aesthetic: Essays on Postmodern Culture*, edited by **Hal Foster**. Named a best book of the year by the East Village–based newspaper the *Village Voice*, the collection of essays is essential to understanding the developments in postmodernism of the 1980s and includes Jean Baudrillard's "The Ecstasy of Communication" and Fredric Jameson's "Postmodernism and Consumer Society."

Cable Gallery is founded in Soho by Clarissa Dalrymple and Nicole Klagsbrun to promote artists such as Ashley Bickerton, Haim Steinbach, and Christopher Wool.

Jenny Holzer prints an untitled series of text works on condom wrappers, addressing the AIDS crisis through what is, at this point, an extremely important commodity.

January
Peter Nagy and **Alan Belcher** of Gallery Nature Morte and **Dean Savard** of Civilian Warfare are interviewed by Jenny Dixon, director of the Public Art Fund, on PAF's WNYC radio initiative, *Artists in the City*. Dixon opens with the question "Why did you find that neighborhood [the East Village] particularly attractive for a gallery?" Nagy: "There are so many artists right now—our generation in particular—that can't live in Soho 'cause of the rent, so the East Village is basically the artists' neighborhood where the artists are living. . . . It's more of a support system for young artists so they can have a place to show on their way to Soho."[5] Meanwhile, Savard calls Civilian Warfare's programming and group shows "anti-Soho."

March
Metro Pictures and Leo Castelli Gallery present a two-venue solo exhibition of **Robert Longo**'s new work featuring *Corporate Wars: Wall of Influence* (1982), a large-scale wall relief with accompanying Minimalist forms that turns an ironic gaze toward Wall Street and corporate culture. The involvement of the commercially successful Castelli Gallery marks a significant turn in the artist's career, even as he mocks capitalism and business culture.

Dianne Benson commissions an advertising campaign for her Madison Avenue and Soho fashion boutiques from **Cindy Sherman** to run in *Interview* magazine. The artist photographs herself wearing false teeth and exaggerated makeup to critique and undermine the desire inherent in the glamorous clothing being advertised. Sherman goes on to produce similar work for designer Dorothée Bis in *Vogue Paris* in 1984.

May
Julian Schnabel's 1979 painting *Notre Dame* sells at Sotheby's in New York City for $93,500, almost twice the estimate. Schnabel, who commands the art market in the early part of the decade, demonstrates the new potential for money-making by artists.

June
The *New York Times* publishes an article titled "A Gallery Scene That Pioneers in New Territories." The article, featuring images of work by **Joel Otterson** and **David Wojnarowicz**, tracks the development of galleries and the art scene in the "gentrifying East Village." In December, the *Times* claims that "New Prosperity Brings Discord to the East Village," and in September 1984, it runs a feature titled "The Gentrification of the East Village."[6]

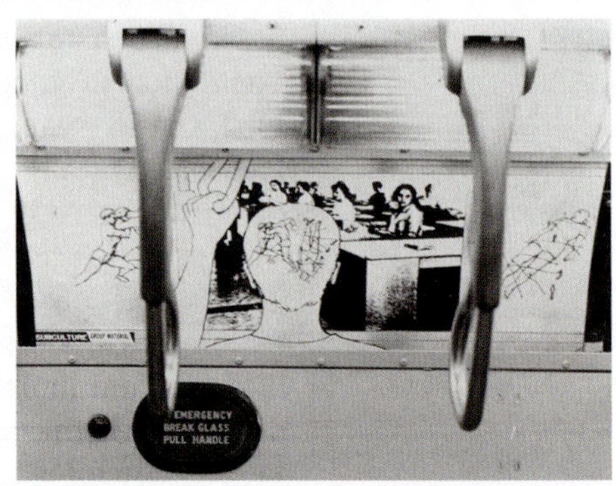

Janet Koenig and Gregory Sholette. Poster for Group Material's project *Subculture*, New York, 1983

September
Group Material rents advertising space in New York subway cars to present *Subculture*, an exhibition for which it has commissioned work from more than 100 artists, including Vito Acconci, Felix Gonzalez-Torres, Barbara Kruger, Haim Steinbach, Julia Wachtel, and Tom Warren.

Artist **Peter Halley** curates *Science Fiction* at John Weber Gallery, 142 Greene Street, in Soho. Included in the show is work by R. M. Fischer, Jeff Koons, Barbara Kruger, Richard Prince, and others, marking out the conceptual and aesthetic territories that would continue to define art and commodity.

1984

Oliver Wasow, Thomas Brazelton, and Karen Sylvester open **CASH/Newhouse Gallery** in a building on East 7th Street in the East Village. CASH/Newhouse, considered by *New York* magazine in 1987 to be one of the "conceptual galleries," helps to define the scene and the era. The gallery shows such artists as **Allan McCollum**, who had been working since the 1970s and, unlike his peers, had entered the East Village scene as a successful artist. At this point, he is also showing with Marian Goodman Gallery in Soho, where he had debuted his *Plaster Surrogates* in 1983.

Andrea Miller-Keller, curator at the Wadsworth Atheneum Museum of Art, introduces **Louise Lawler** to twentieth-century-art collectors Burton and Emily Tremaine. The couple were planning to sell their collection to establish a foundation; before the sale, Lawler photographs the installations of art presented in their home as decoration. This becomes an ongoing project of Lawler's: photographing art in collectors' homes, highlighting its status as a commodity. In 1991, 50 works from the Tremaine Collection ("one of the best collections of 20th-century art in the United States,"[7] including artists such as Robert Delaunay, Fernand Léger, Piet Mondrian, and Jasper Johns), are sold at Christie's.

International With Monument, a crucial artist-run East Village gallery, is started by artists Kent Klamen, Elizabeth Koury, and Meyer Vaisman. The gallery shows the first solo exhibitions of Peter Halley and Jeff Koons, who—along with Vaisman and fellow artist Ashley Bickerton—become rising stars showing at Sonnabend Gallery two years later (see October 1986).

January
In Tribeca, not-for-profit **Artists Space** puts on the exhibition *New Galleries of the Lower East Side*, featuring work by artists from 17 galleries, including CASH/Newhouse, Civilian Warfare, FUN, Gracie Mansion, International With Monument, Nature Morte, and P•P•O•W, and curated by Helene Winer, then a co-owner of Metro Pictures. Artist and critic Walter Robinson and critic Carlo McCormick note that "the East Village art explosion has been concocted of equal parts rampant careerism and internal esthetic necessity."[8]

June
A protest outside the **Museum of Modern Art** calls attention to the fact that only 19 artists of 169 included in *An International Survey of Painting and Sculpture* are women.[9] From this protest springs the activist group the **Guerrilla Girls** (see 1985), which develops a formal language based on corporate advertising to address inequalities in the contemporary art world.

Peter Halley publishes "The Crisis in Geometry," arguing for the importance of Baudrillard in relation to the work of Jeff Koons, Sherrie Levine, and others, in *Arts Magazine*. The essay influences the labeling of the group's aesthetic mode as "Neo-Geo," a term that is rejected by the artists as a marketing ploy.

October
Alan Belcher and **Peter Nagy** are photographed inside Nature Morte for a feature in the magazine *L'Uomo Vogue*. The photographs are taken during **Sherrie Levine**'s exhibition *1917*, which includes her works after Kazimir Malevich and Egon Schiele. The exhibition's title refers to the year of the Russian Revolution, also known as the October Revolution. ***October***, an important peer-reviewed journal that had started in 1976, similarly borrowed its title from the uprising.

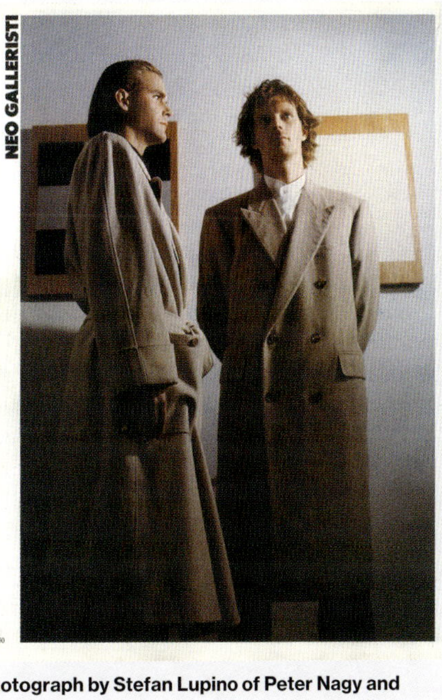

Photograph by Stefan Lupino of Peter Nagy and Alan Belcher at Sherrie Levine's exhibition *1917*, published in *L'Uomo Vogue*, December 1984

Allan McCollum and **Louise Lawler** collaborate on the installation *For Presentation and Display: Ideal Settings* at Diane Brown Gallery in Soho. More than 100 identical small objects made of Hydrocal are displayed on gray stands in the center of the room, illuminated by theatrical lighting. "$200.00" is projected onto the back wall of the gallery ("both the price of the commodity and the commodity itself," as the curator/critic Therese Lichtenstein notes in a December article in *Arts*).[10]

The exhibition *The East Village Scene* is mounted at the **ICA Philadelphia**. It is the first museum show to highlight the goings-on in the East Village at the time.

November
Ronald Reagan is re-elected president of the United States.

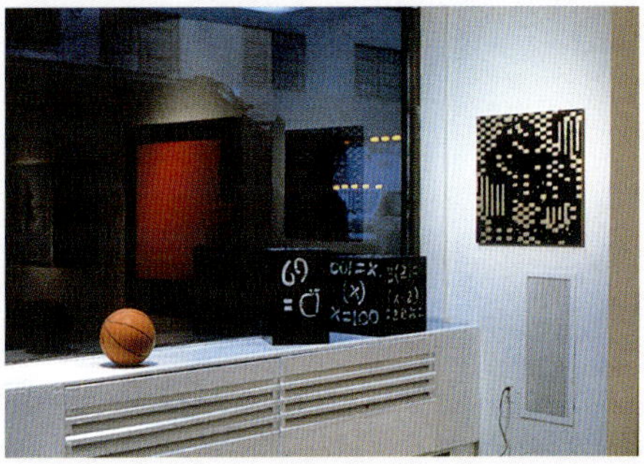

Installation view, *The New Capital*, White Columns, New York, 1984–85

December
The New Capital, curated by **Tricia Collins** and **Richard Milazzo**, opens at White Columns. The two key and controversial curators, with their writings and freelance exhibitions held in both commercial and gallery spaces, transform group shows into critical statements. They include many of the same artists in multiple exhibitions and continually contextualize their work, expanding the art of Jeff Koons, Peter Nagy, and others into theory.

1985

Never shown in New York, the exhibition ***Infotainment (18 Artists from New York)*** starts its international tour at Texas Gallery in Houston, including work by Gretchen Bender, Peter Halley, Steven Parrino, David Robbins, Haim Steinbach, and other artists associated with Nature Morte. The show's catalogue includes an essay by Robbins, who uses the phrase "the children of Barthes and Coca-Cola" (an update of Jean-Luc Godard's "the children of Marx and Coca-Cola") to describe the liberation inherent in deconstructing cultural codes.

Guerrilla Girls, a feminist activist art collective, is officially formed by seven anonymous women in response to the Museum of Modern Art's exhibition *An International Survey of Recent Painting and Sculpture* (see June 1984). By utilizing public spaces such as construction fences, walls, telephone poles, and billboards and foregoing individual identities by wearing gorilla masks, the collective successfully adapts (and continues to wield, at the time of this writing) branding and commercial methods to challenge dominant systems.

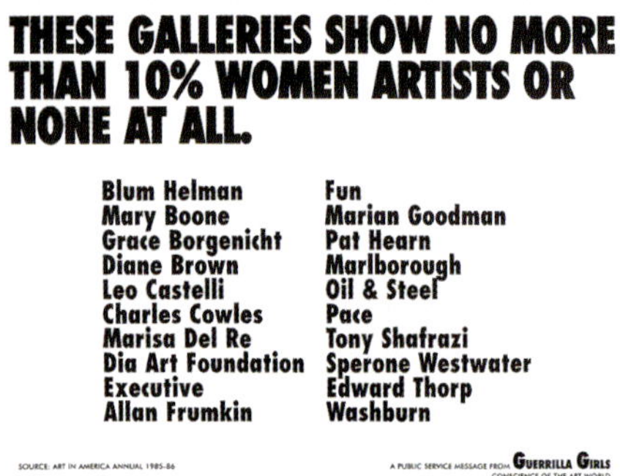

Poster by the Guerrilla Girls, 1985

MTV begins its ***Art Break*** series, in which artists such as Jean-Michel Basquiat, Dara Birnbaum, and Richard Prince present 20-second features, either new video works or montages of themselves at work and play. While sometimes thought of as having disrupted the mainstream with images of the avant-garde, the original *Art Breaks* are another testament to the open channels between art and the world of commerce.

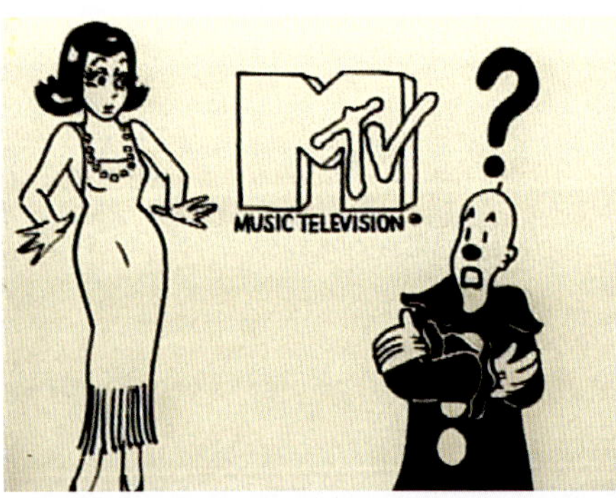

Dara Birnbaum. Still from MTV's *Art Break*, 1987

February
Production Re: Production, curated by **Bob Nickas**, opens with work by Gretchen Bender, Mike Bidlo, Louise Lawler, Philip Taaffe, and others at the now-defunct Gallery 345/Art for Social Change on Lafayette Street in Soho. The exhibition also includes work by artists of a previous generation, such as Jasper Johns, Andy Warhol, and Elaine Sturtevant; the pairings highlight art-historical appropriation as an established artistic practice.

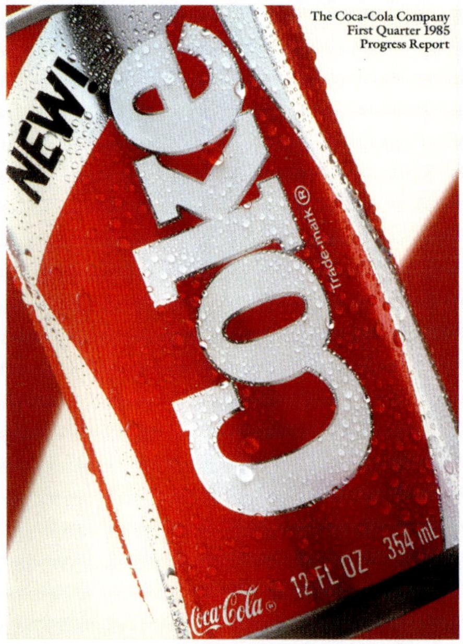

Cover of the Coca-Cola Company's first-quarter progress report, 1985

April
Coca-Cola launches **"New Coke"** in response to a decline in sales due, in part, to competition with Pepsi. The new formula is widely despised by the public. After only a few months on the market, "New Coke" is pulled and replaced by "classic" Coca-Cola, which, ironically, sparks a high point in sales for the company.

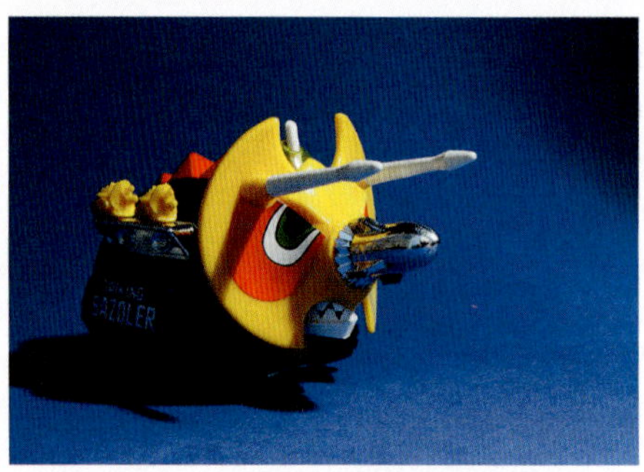

Louise Lawler. *Portrait (Blue)*, 1984

May
Louise Lawler's exhibition *Interesting* opens at Nature Morte. The press release describes the gallery as having been "altered to infer another kind of space, one that is redolent with the institutionalization of self interest, where money gets money."[11] New Museum curator Brian Wallis notes that the show suggests "ways in which the architecture and signage of the gallery—in relation to the artworks—could carry specific ideological meanings and cues."[12] The title is painted on the wall in green and white in the style of a logo, and two photographs of Japanese dinosaur toys are presented opposite a "long lacquered shelf like one might find in a bank machine vestibule."[13]

November
In his first solo show in New York, **Jeff Koons** presents his *Equilibrium* series at International With Monument. Both the basketballs hovering in tanks (previously shown as a stand-alone readymade in the group show *The New Capital*; see December 1984) and the bronze replicas of a lifeboat and other objects are highly ambitious productions that rely on professional manufacturing.

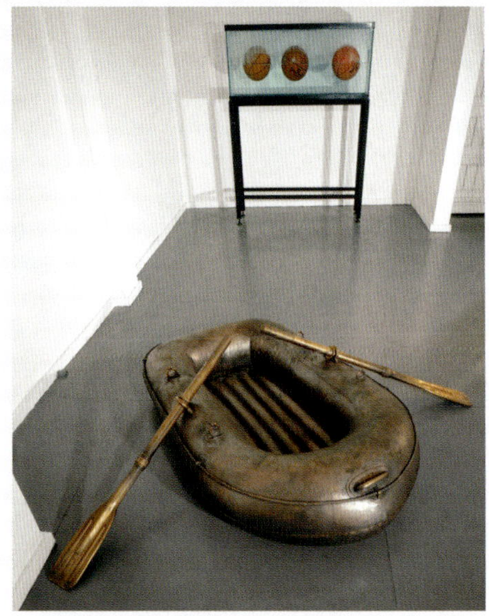

Installation view, Jeff Koons's *Equilibrium*, International With Monument, 1985

Alan Belcher's first solo show opens at Cable Gallery. The show, entitled *Made in New York*, contains bottles of fabric softener that the artist has rebranded with his own labels and 1980s catchwords.

1986

Absolut Vodka launches the **Absolut Art Collection**, an advertising campaign enlisting the likes of Andy Warhol and Julia Wachtel to create advertisements for the brand over the next several years.

April
Keith Haring opens his **Pop Shop** at 292 Lafayette Street in Soho, at which he sells a wide variety of small editions such as pins, T-shirts, and posters. The store is hugely popular and remains open until September 2005. Haring: "The Pop Shop makes my work accessible. It's about participation on a big level."[14]

May
Moderated by Peter Nagy, the important panel discussion **"From Criticism**

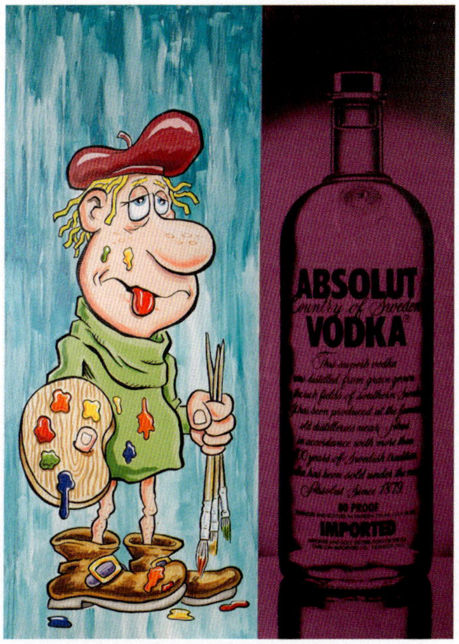

Julia Wachtel. *Absolut Wachtel*, 1989

to Complicity" among Ashley Bickerton, Peter Halley, Jeff Koons, Sherrie Levine, Haim Steinbach, and Philip Taaffe is held at Pat Hearn Gallery in the East Village. The transcript is published in the summer issue of *Flash Art*.

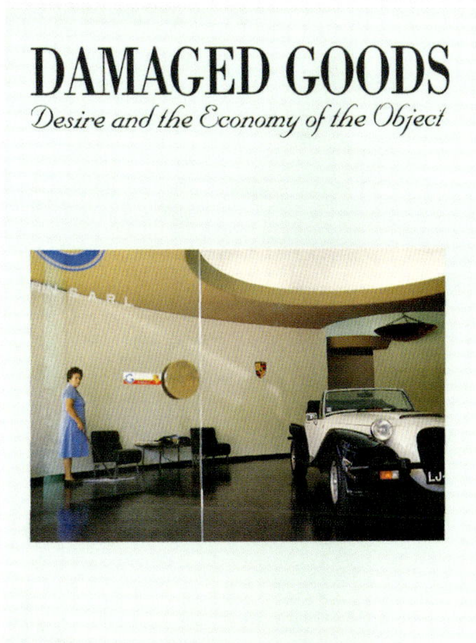

Cover of exhibition catalogue for *Damaged Goods*, New Museum of Contemporary Art, New York, 1986

June
Damaged Goods: Desire and the Economy of the Object opens at the New Museum, including work by Gretchen Bender, Barbara Bloom, Andrea Fraser, Jeff Koons, Justen Ladda, Louise Lawler, Ken Lum, Allan McCollum, Haim Steinbach, and others. Curator Brian Wallis notes in his essay: "The abstraction of the consumer object has been achieved through the spectacular effects of advertising, display, and presentation strategies which are directed more at motivating the viewer's desire for consumption than at demonstrating the utilitarian properties of the object. This exhibition seeks to raise some fundamental questions regarding the shifting state of economic and social exchange and to suggest ways in which the work of certain artists and critics have addressed these issues."[15]

September
Endgame: Reference and Simulation in Recent Painting and Sculpture, curated by Elisabeth Sussman, David Joselit, and Bob Riley, opens at the Institute of Contemporary Art, Boston. Included are works by Robert Gober, Sherrie Levine, Jeff Koons, Haim Steinbach, Philip Taaffe, and others. In the catalogue, Hal Foster writes of so-called mediated sculpture: "As it collapses art and commodity, it often replaces the lost aura of art with the false aura of commodity."[16]

Eleanor Hartney publishes the essay "Neo-Geo Storms New York" in *Art Examiner*. Although the label **"Neo-Geo"** gains traction in the media, many artists resent it.

When Attitudes Become Form, curated by **Bob Nickas** at Bess Cutler Gallery in Soho, includes work by Jennifer Bolande, Steven Parrino, Philip Taaffe, Julia Wachtel, and others. The exhibition, whose title Nickas appropriated from that of an exhibition organized by the famous curator Harald Szeeman at the Bern Kunsthalle in 1969, is a show of "works, concepts, processes, situations, and information [a list also appropriated by Nickas] that find correspondence from the late '60s and the late '80s."[17]

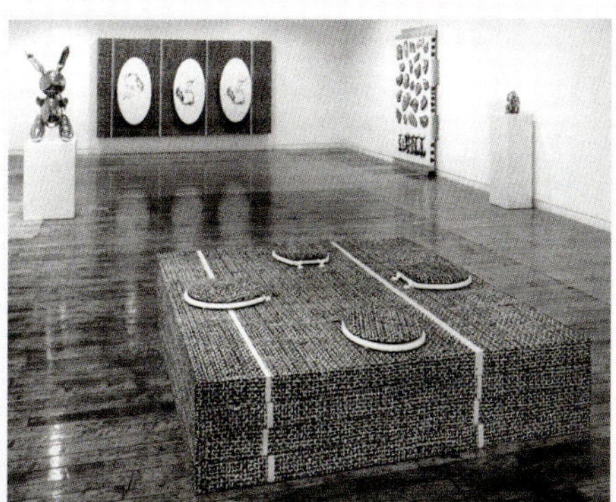

Installation view, *Ashley Bickerton, Peter Halley, Jeff Koons, Meyer Vaisman*, Sonnabend Gallery, New York, 1986

October
The exhibition of so-called Neo-Geo work by the "Hot Four" (Ashley Bickerton, Peter Halley, Jeff Koons, and Meyer Vaisman) at **Sonnabend Gallery** in Soho is one of the most hyped shows of the decade. The exhibition marks the beginning of the end of the East Village gallery scene, as the formerly subversive young artists began to get picked up by major galleries.

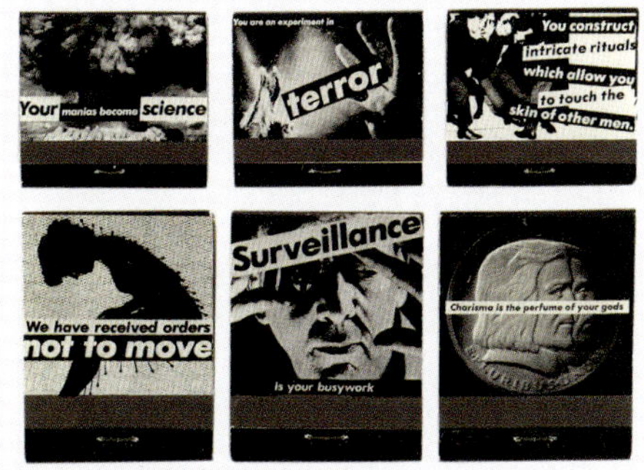

Barbara Kruger. Six matchbooks, 1986

November
Barbara Kruger prints some of her slogan-based works on matchbooks for sale at Colab's A. More Store at Barbara Gladstone Gallery in Soho. Three of the designs boldly read: "We have received orders not to move," "You construct intricate rituals which allow you to touch the skin of other men," and "Your manias become science."

Art and Its Double: A New York Perspective, curated by **Dan Cameron**—one of the first exhibitions of 1980s New York artists to be mounted in Europe—opens at Centre Cultural de la Fundació Caixa de Pensions, then travels to Madrid the following year.

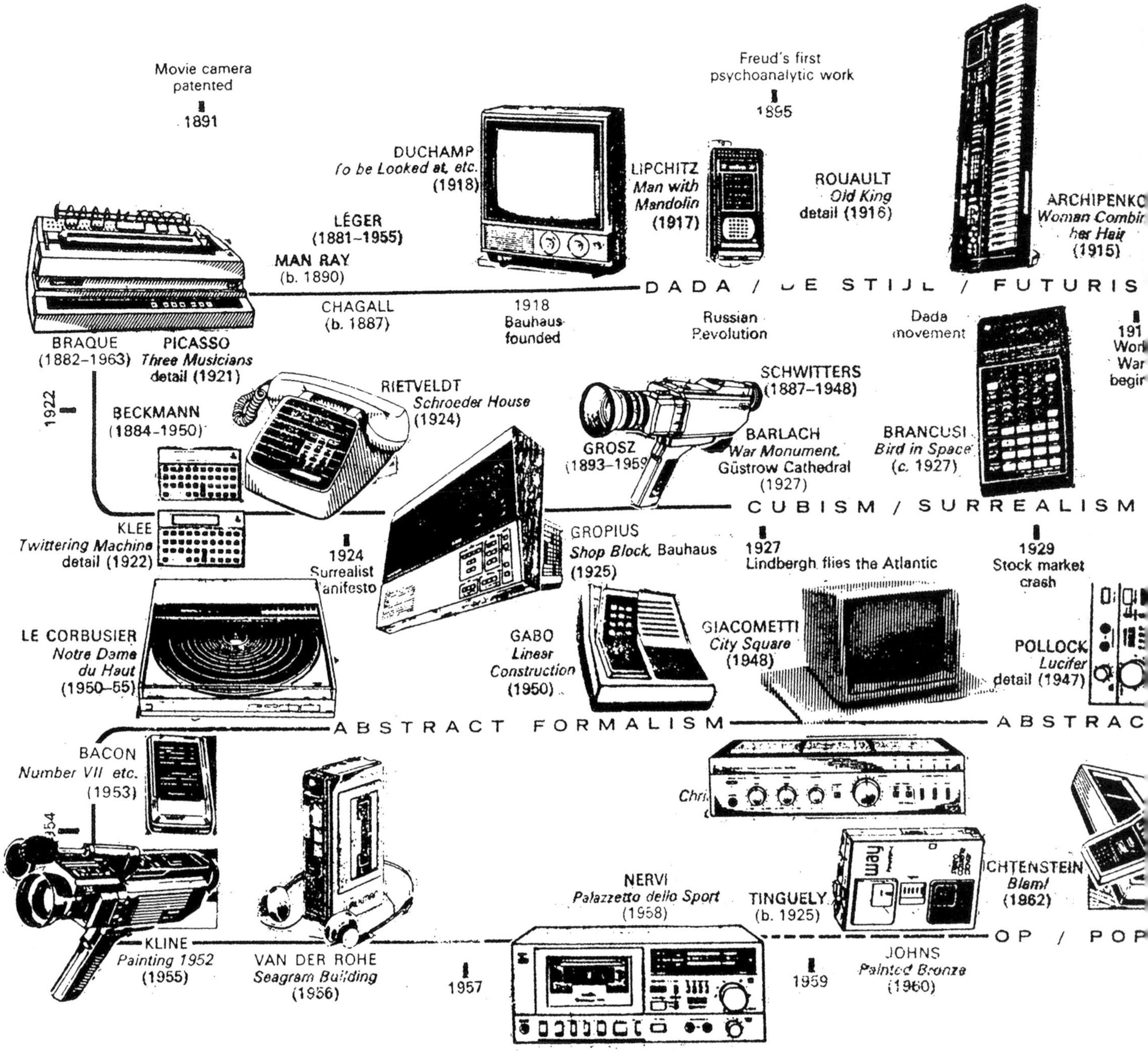

Peter Nagy. *Entertainment Erases History*, 1983. Black-and-white photocopy, dimensions variable.
Courtesy of the artist and Magenta Plains, New York

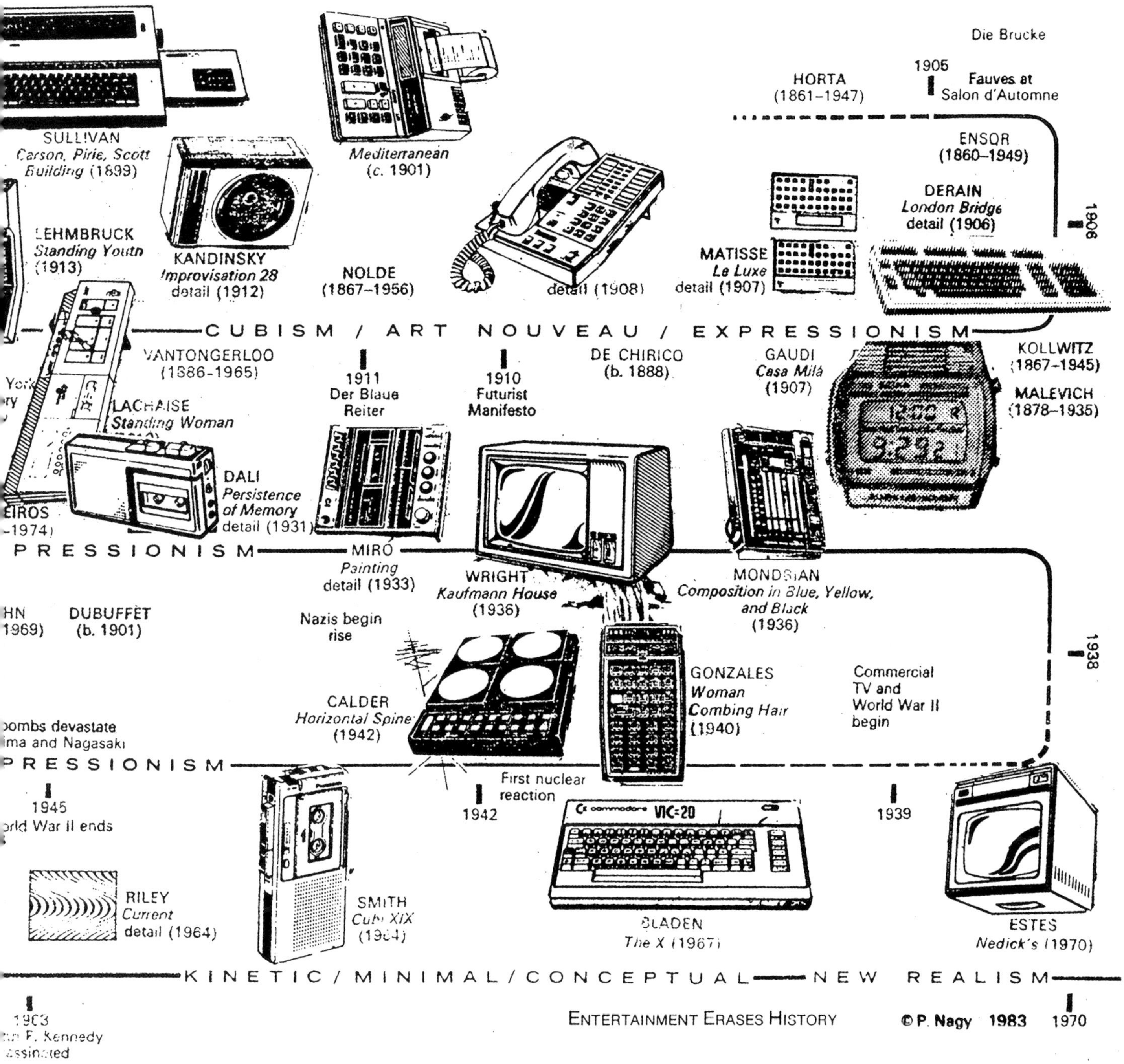

Die Brucke
1905
Fauves at Salon d'Automne
HORTA (1861–1947)
ENSOR (1860–1949)
DERAIN London Bridge detail (1906)
1906
SULLIVAN Carson, Pirie, Scott Building (1899)
Mediterranean (c. 1901)
LEHMBRUCK Standing Youth (1913)
KANDINSKY Improvisation 28 detail (1912)
NOLDE (1867–1956)
detail (1908)
MATISSE Le Luxe detail (1907)
CUBISM / ART NOUVEAU / EXPRESSIONISM
VANTONGERLOO (1886–1965)
1911 Der Blaue Reiter
1910 Futurist Manifesto
DE CHIRICO (b. 1888)
GAUDI Casa Milá (1907)
KOLLWITZ (1867–1945)
MALEVICH (1878–1935)
LACHAISE Standing Woman
DALI Persistence of Memory detail (1931)
EIROS -1974)
PRESSIONISM
MIRO Painting detail (1933)
WRIGHT Kaufmann House (1936)
MONDRIAN Composition in Blue, Yellow, and Black (1936)
HN 1969)
DUBUFFET (b. 1901)
Nazis begin rise
1938
GONZALES Woman Combing Hair (1940)
Commercial TV and World War II begin
CALDER Horizontal Spine (1942)
bombs devastate ima and Nagasaki
PRESSIONISM
1945 orld War II ends
First nuclear reaction
1942
VIC-20
1939
RILEY Current detail (1964)
SMITH Cubi XIX (1964)
BLADEN The X (1967)
ESTES Nedick's (1970)
KINETIC / MINIMAL / CONCEPTUAL — NEW REALISM
1963 John F. Kennedy assassinated
ENTERTAINMENT ERASES HISTORY
© P. Nagy 1983
1970

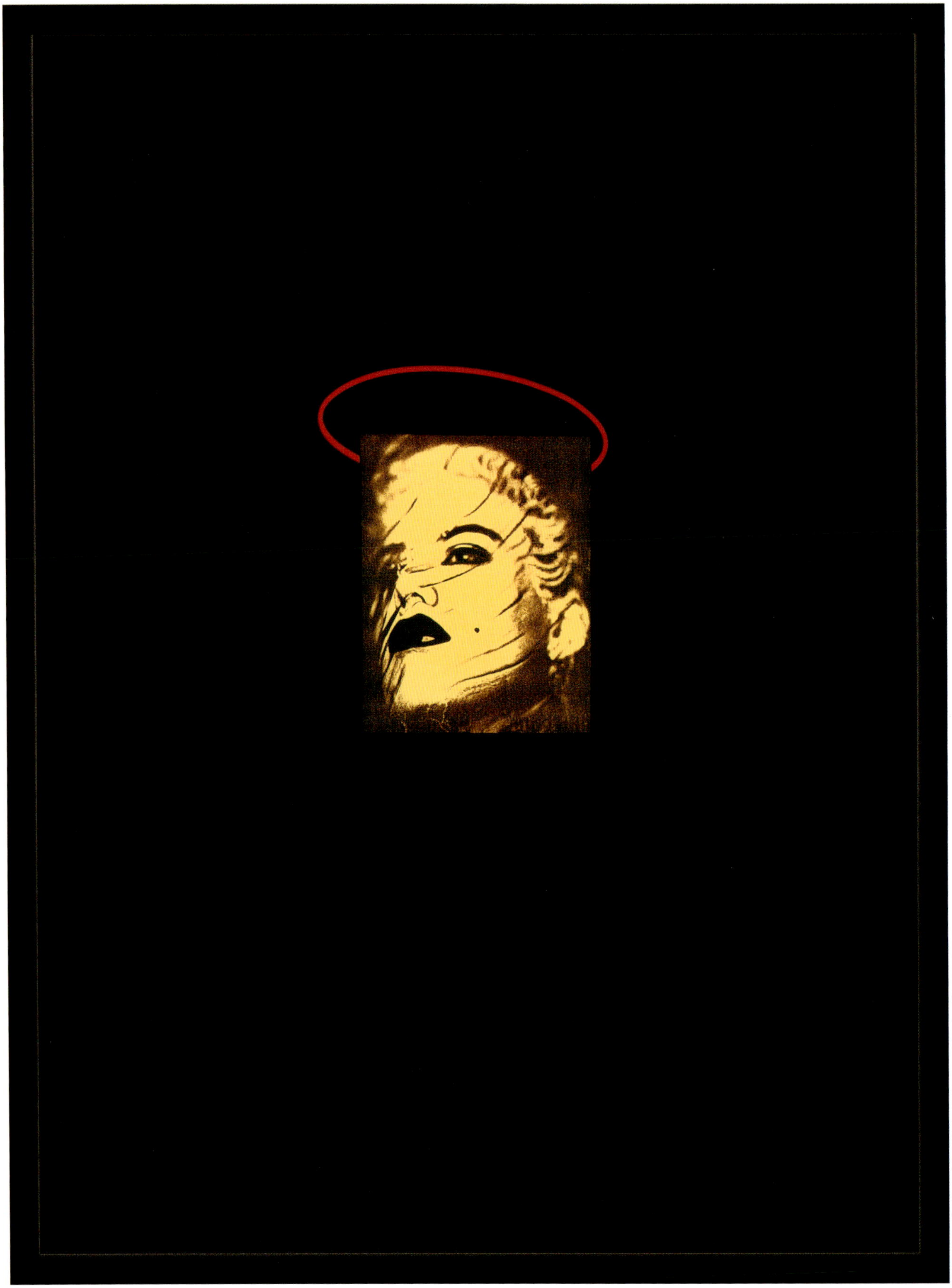

Sarah Charlesworth. ***Virgin***, 1986. Cibachrome with lacquered wood frame, 42 × 32 in. (106.7 × 81.3 cm). Courtesy of the Estate of Sarah Charlesworth and Maccarone, NY/LA

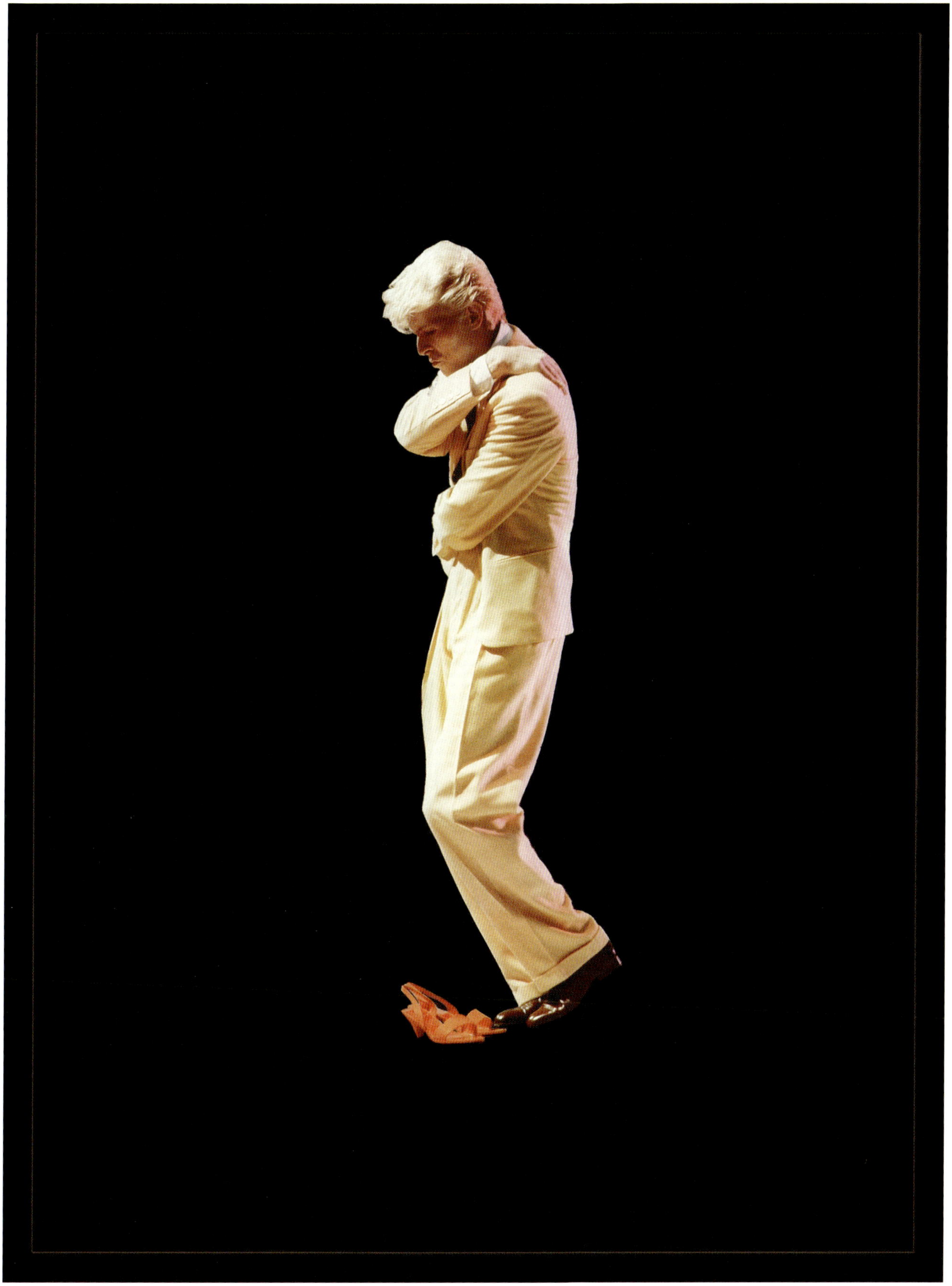

Sarah Charlesworth. ***Golden Boy***, 1983–84. Cibachrome with lacquered wood frame, 42 × 32 in. (106.7 × 81.3 cm). Courtesy of the Estate of Sarah Charlesworth and Maccarone, NY/LA

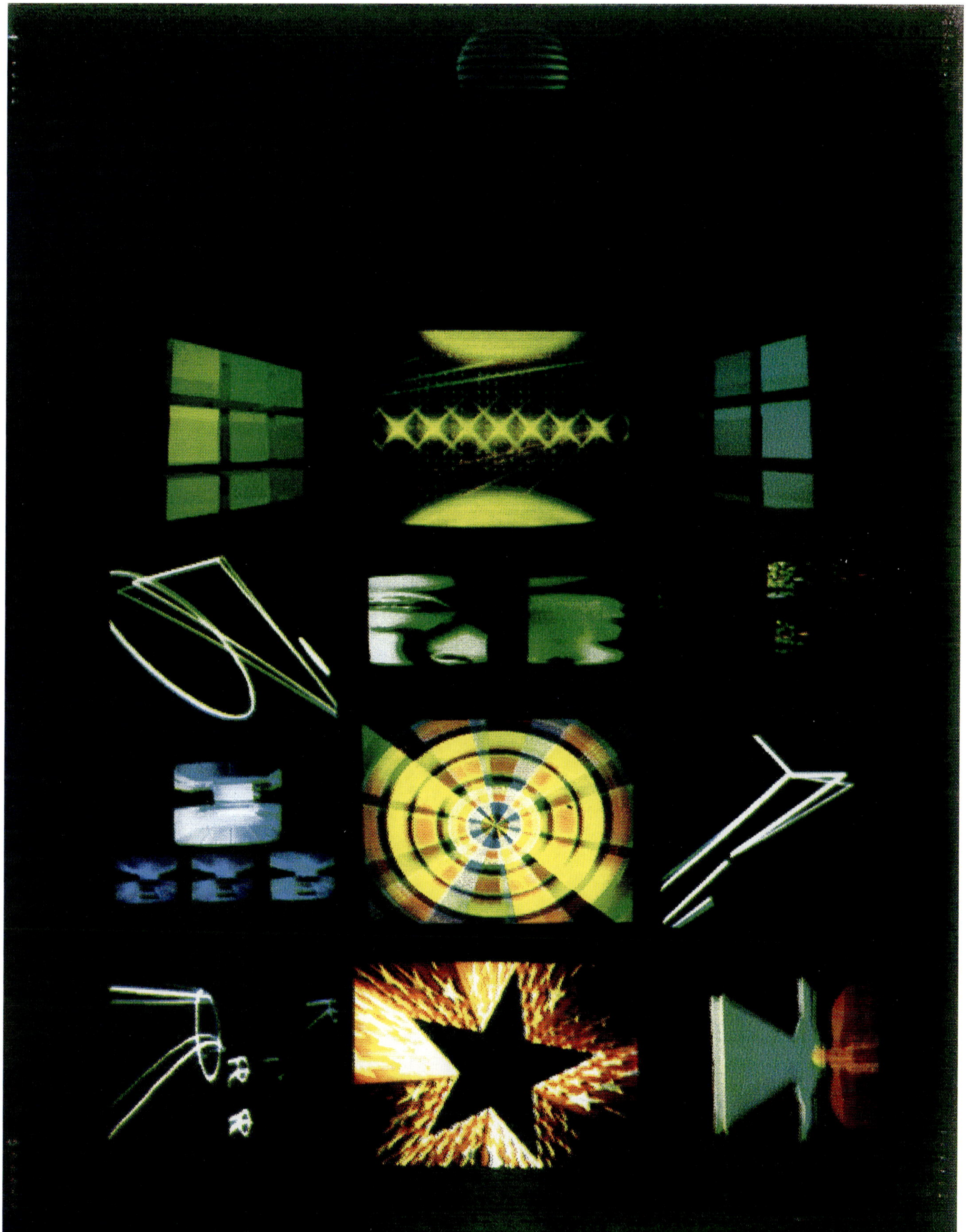

Gretchen Bender. *Dumping Core*, 1984. Four-channel video, color, sound, 13 min.; 13 monitors; dimensions variable. Courtesy of the Gretchen Bender Estate and OSMOS
Following spread: ***Dumping Core*** (detail)

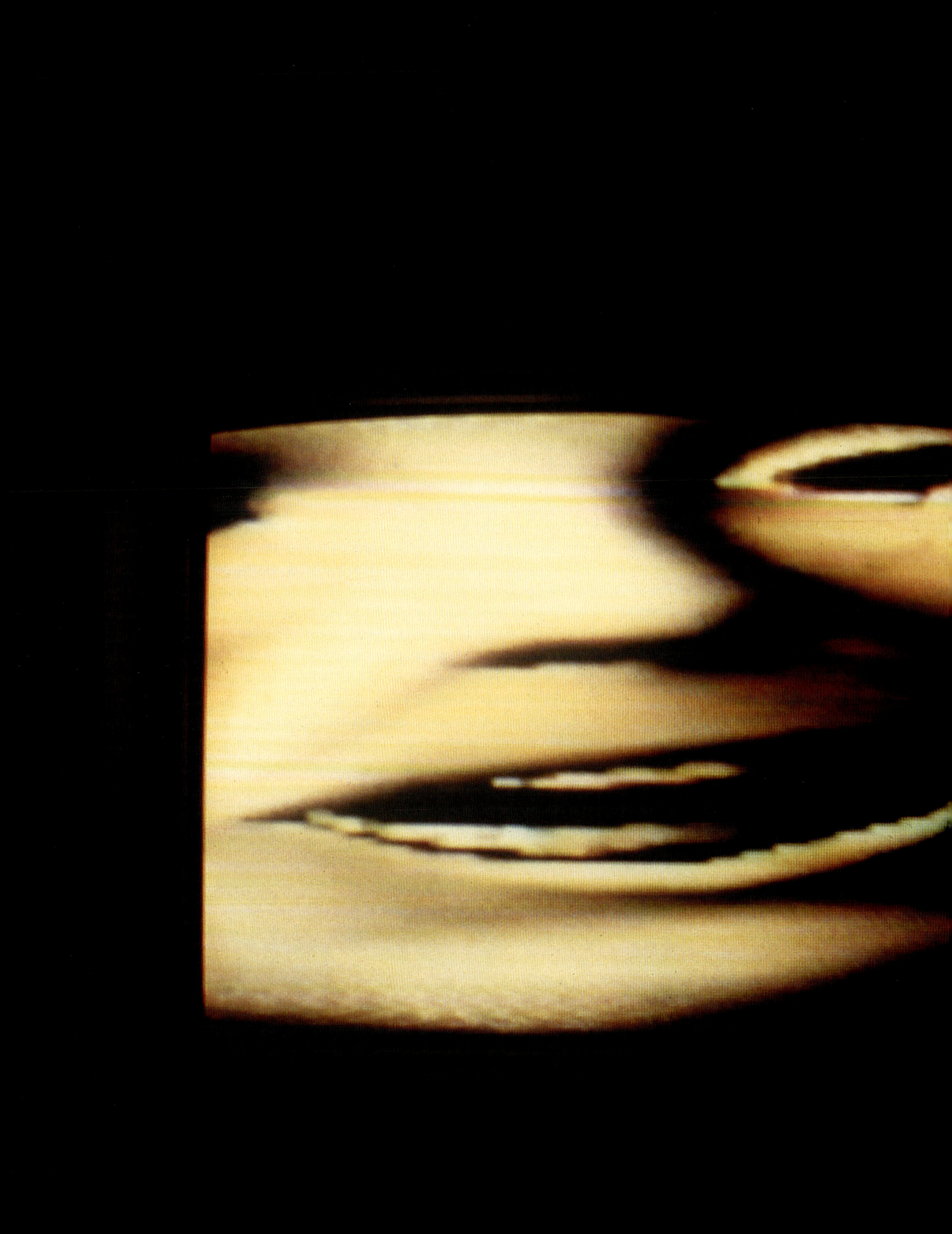

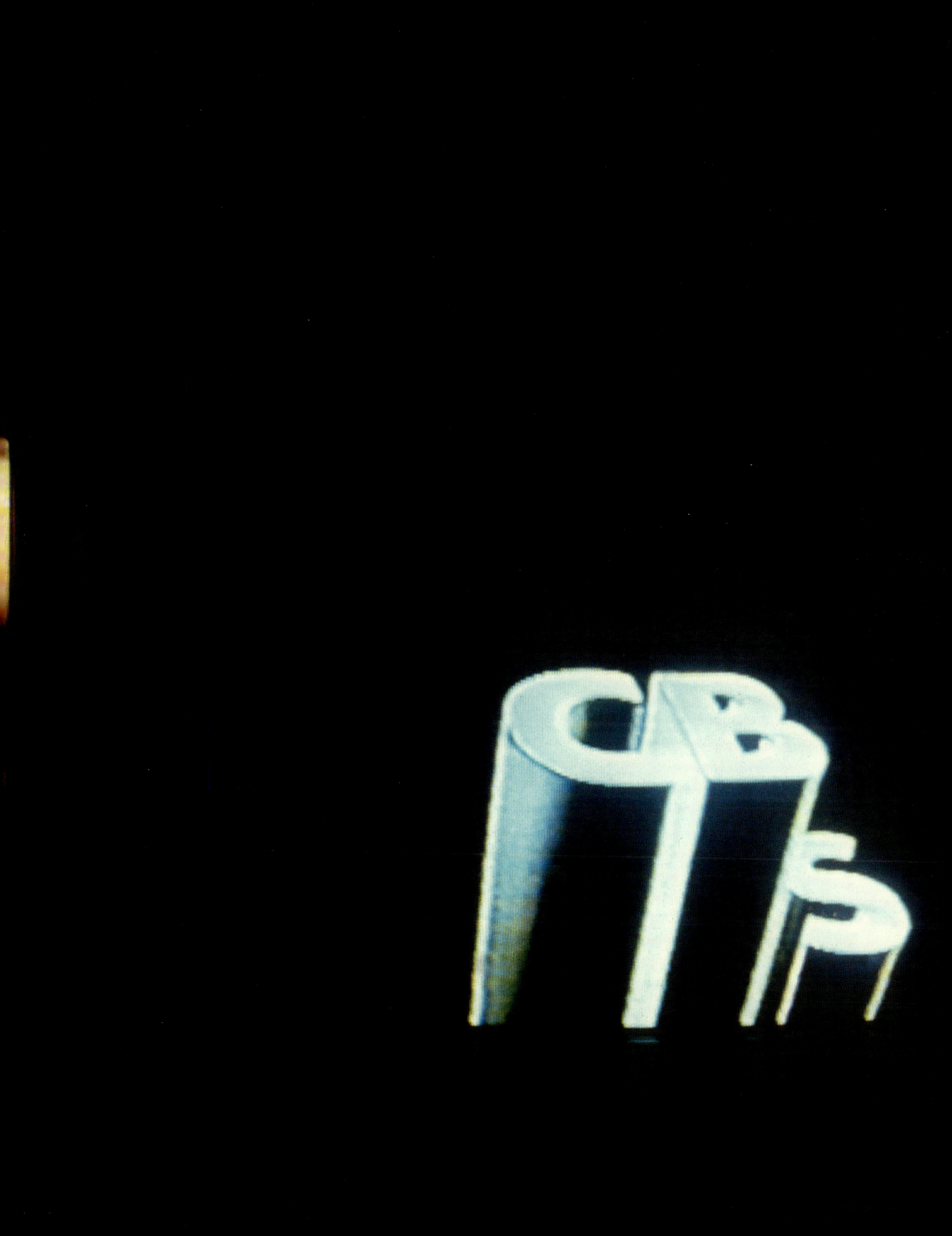
CBS

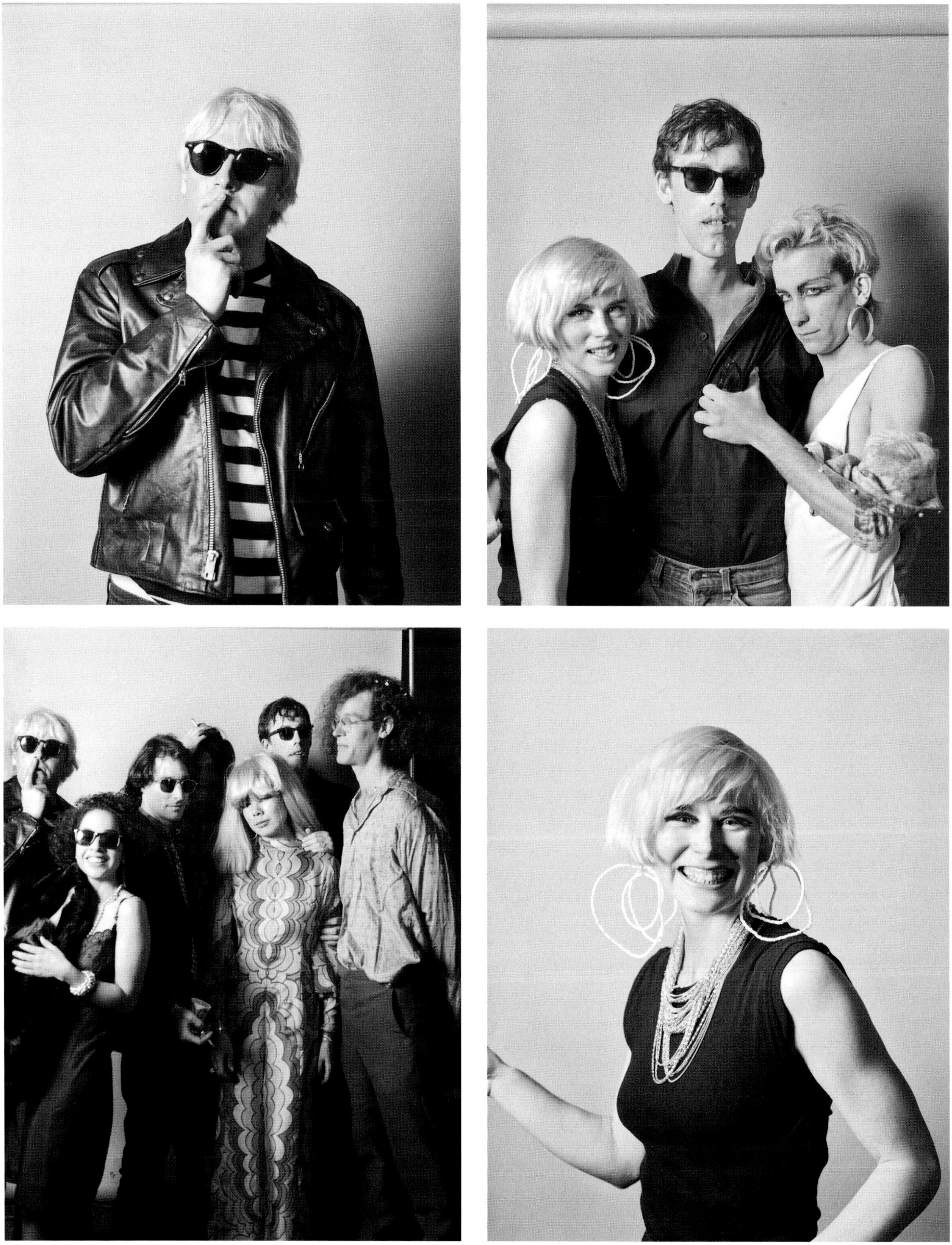

Mike Bidlo. ***Mike Bidlo Presents: The Factory at PS1***, 1984. Performance. Digital slide projection of photographs by Tom Warren. Tom Warren Portrait Studio

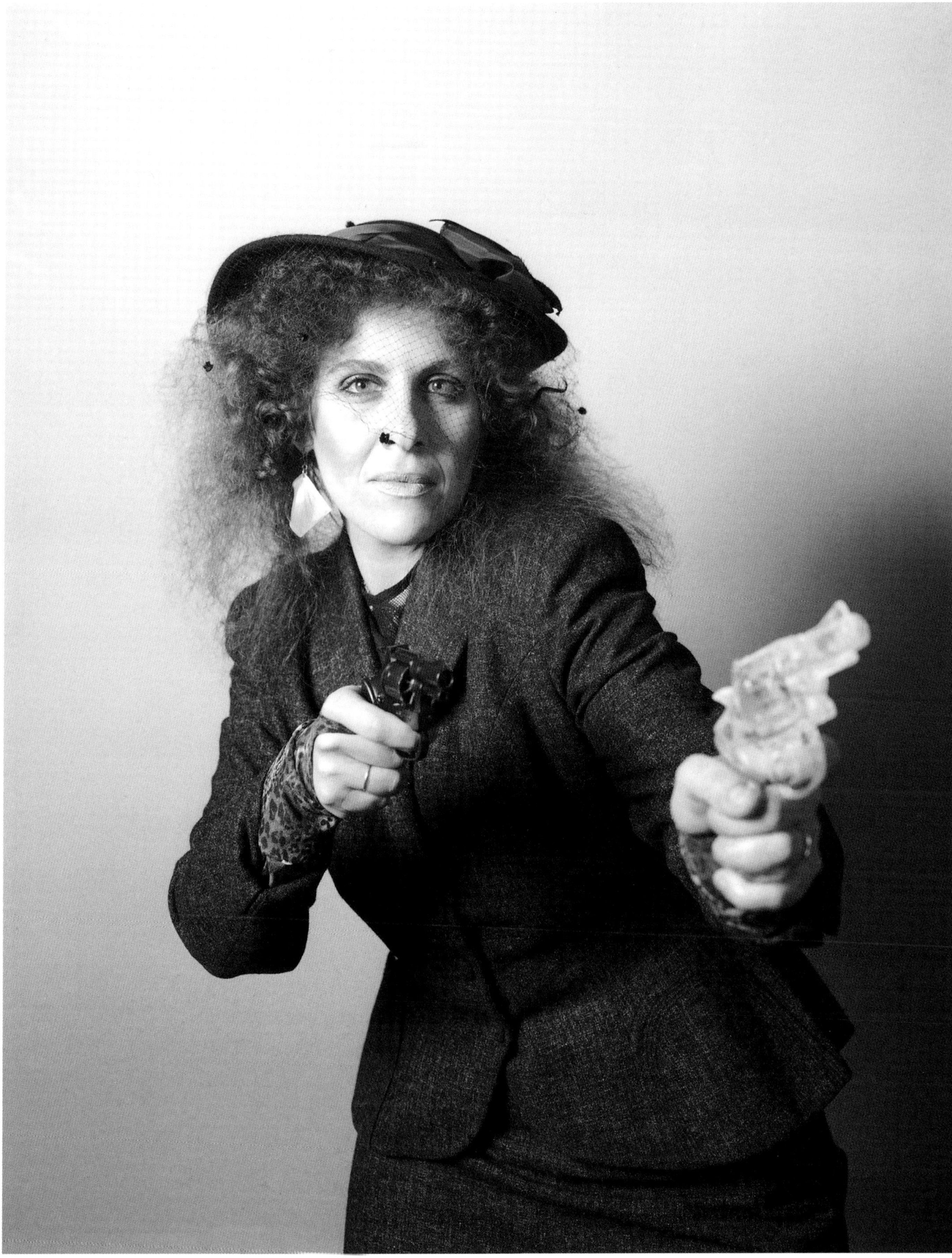

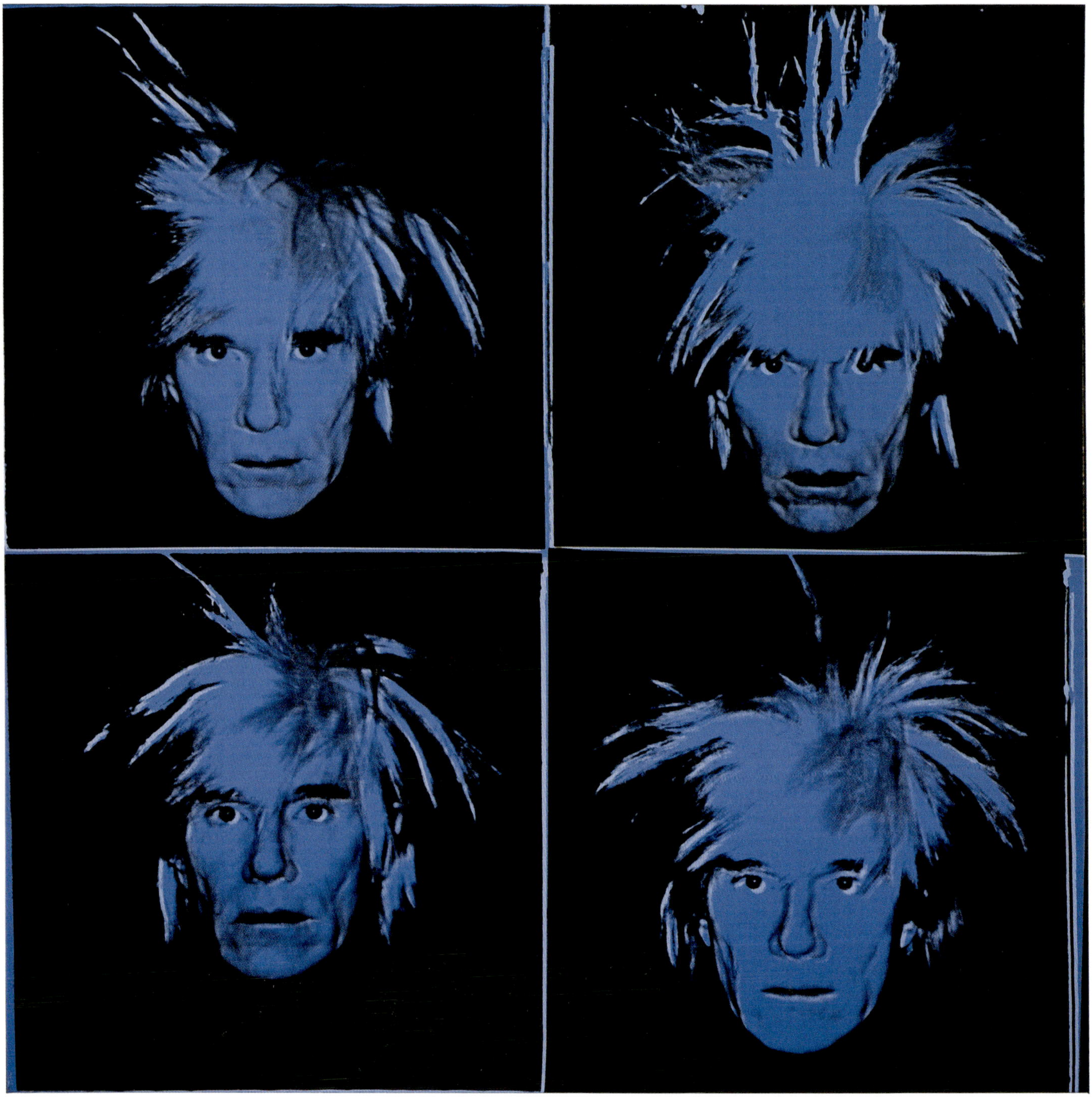

Andy Warhol. ***Self-Portrait***, 1986. Synthetic polymer and silkscreen ink on linen, 80 × 80¼ in. (203 × 203.4 cm). Hirshhorn Museum and Sculpture Garden, Smithsonian Institution, Washington, DC, Partial Gift of the Andy Warhol Foundation for the Visual Arts and Partial Purchase, Smithsonian Collections Acquisition Program and Joseph H. Hirshhorn Bequest

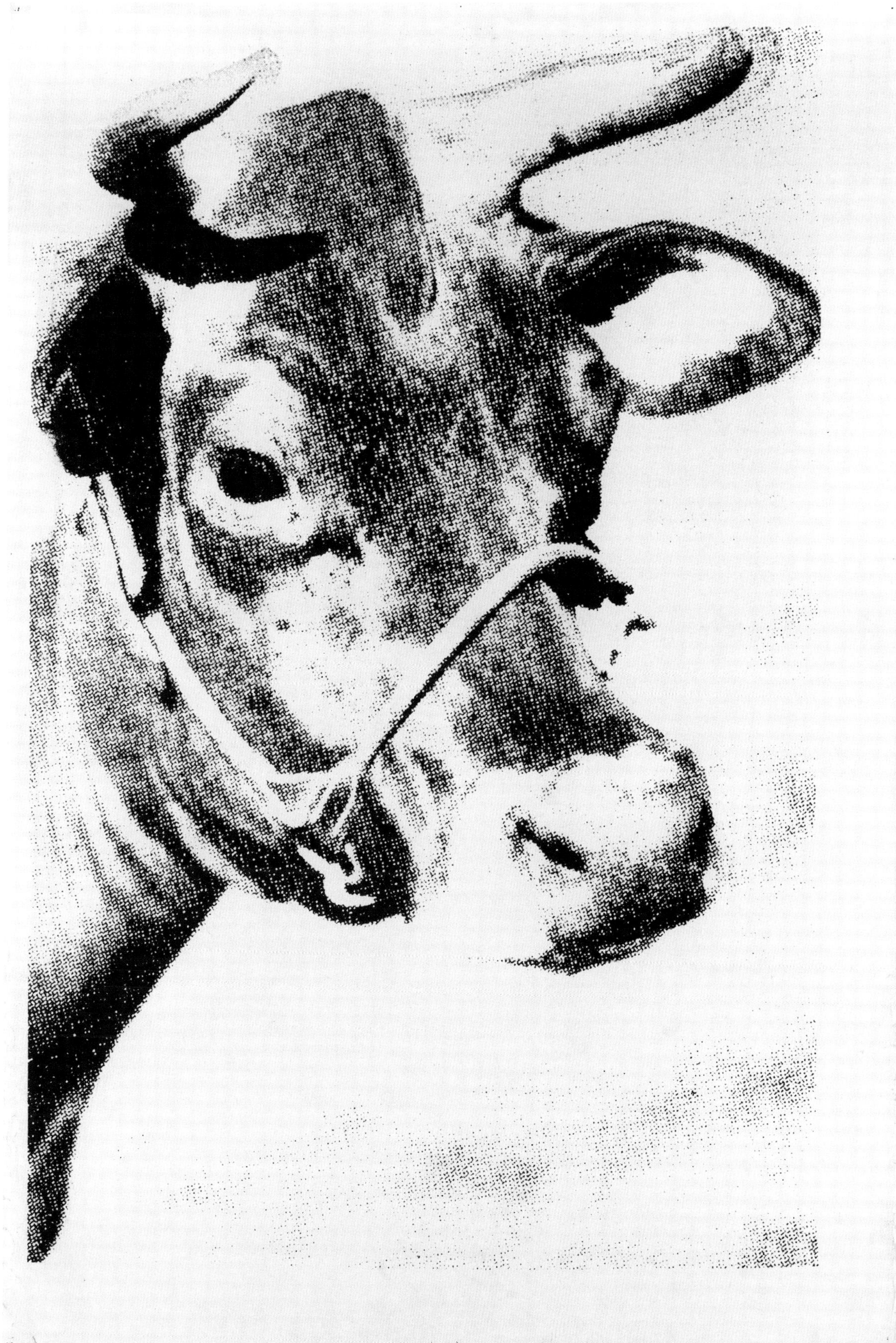

Mike Bidlo. ***Not Warhol (Cow Wallpaper, 1966***), 1984. Wallpaper repeat on adhesive vinyl, dimensions variable. Courtesy of Mike Bidlo and Galerie Bruno Bischofberger

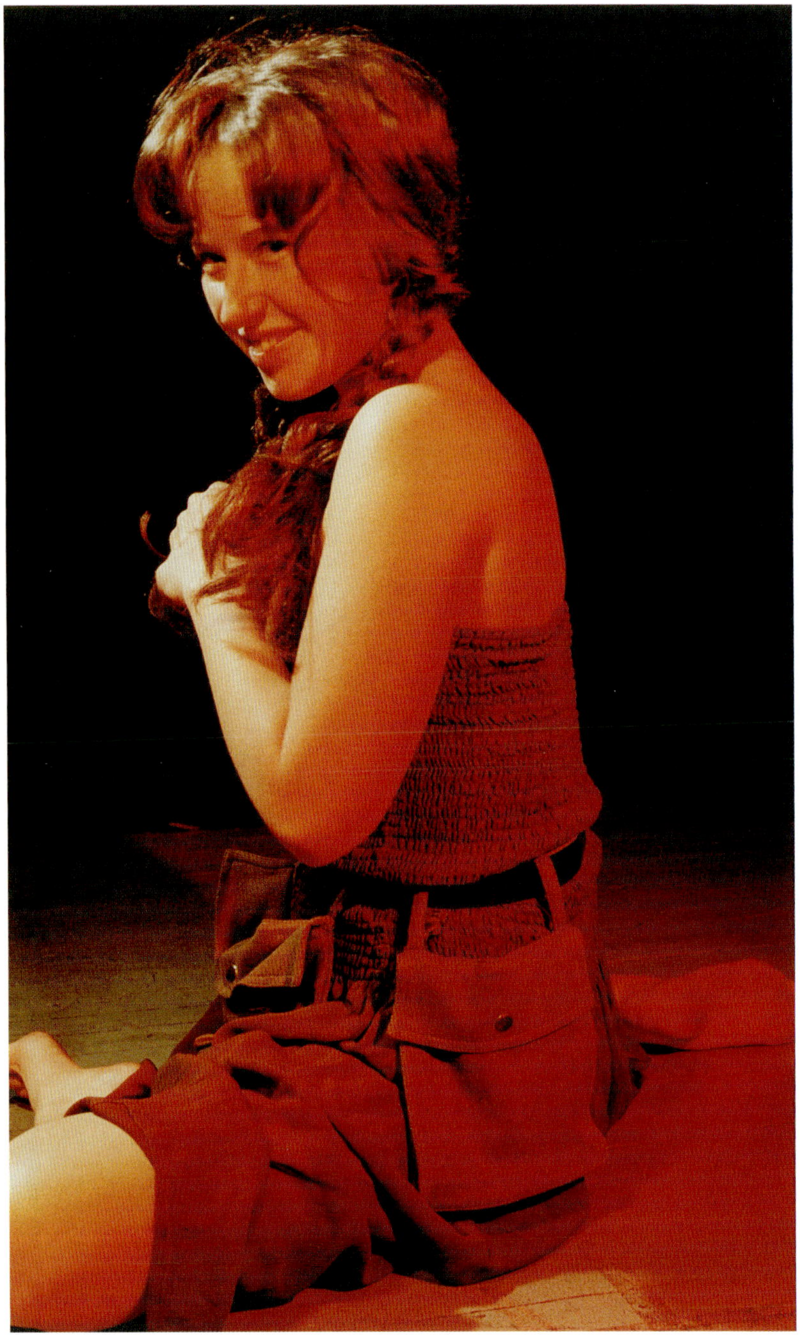

Cindy Sherman. *Untitled #121*, 1983. Chromogenic print, 40 × 27½ in. (101.5 × 69.8 cm). Hirshhorn Museum and Sculpture Garden, Smithsonian Institution, Washington, DC, Gift of Dr. William H. Goldiner, 1998

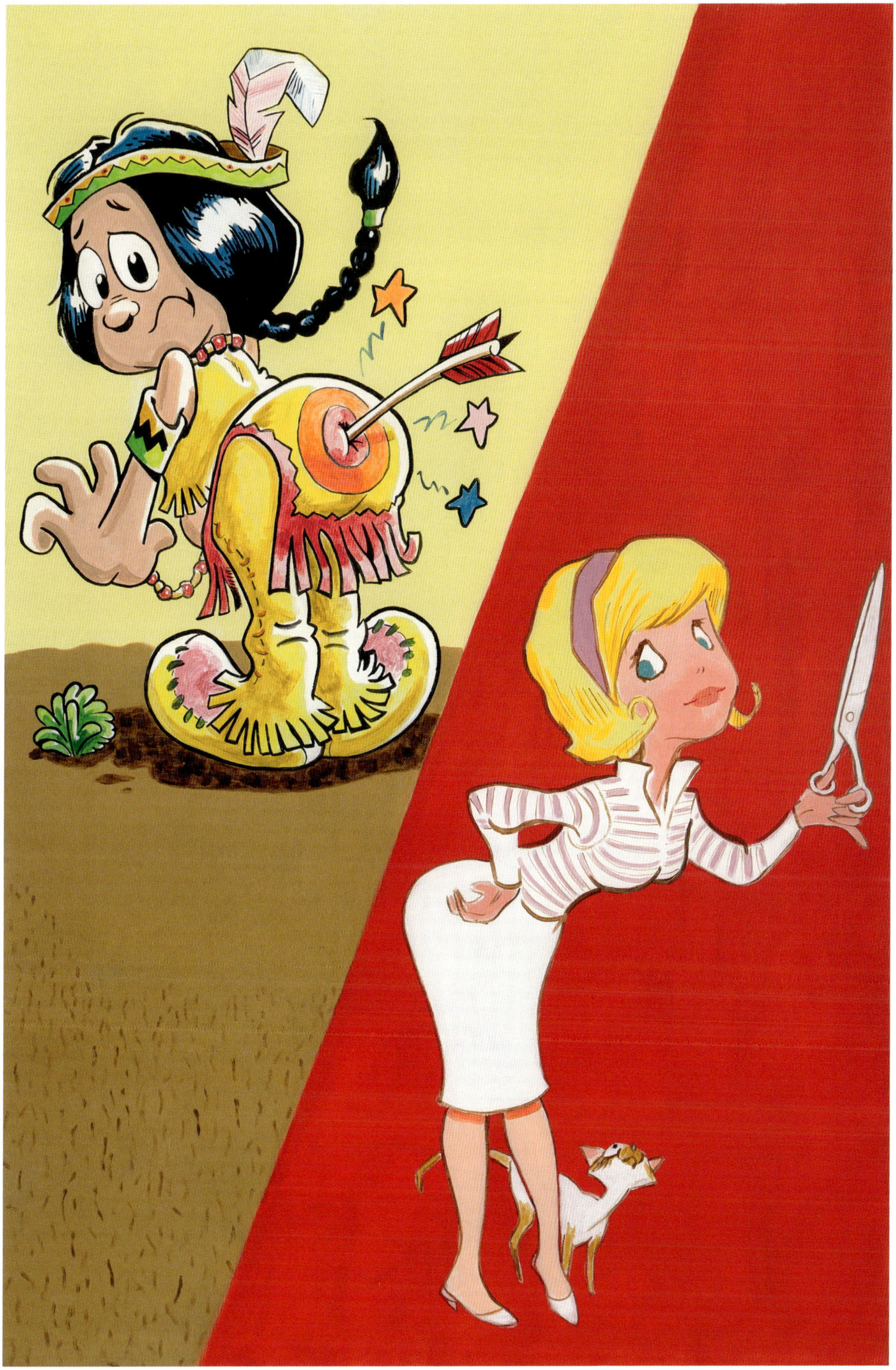

Julia Wachtel. *Love Thing*, 1983. Acrylic on canvas, 96 × 64 in. (243.8 × 162.6 cm).
Courtesy of the artist and Elizabeth Dee, New York

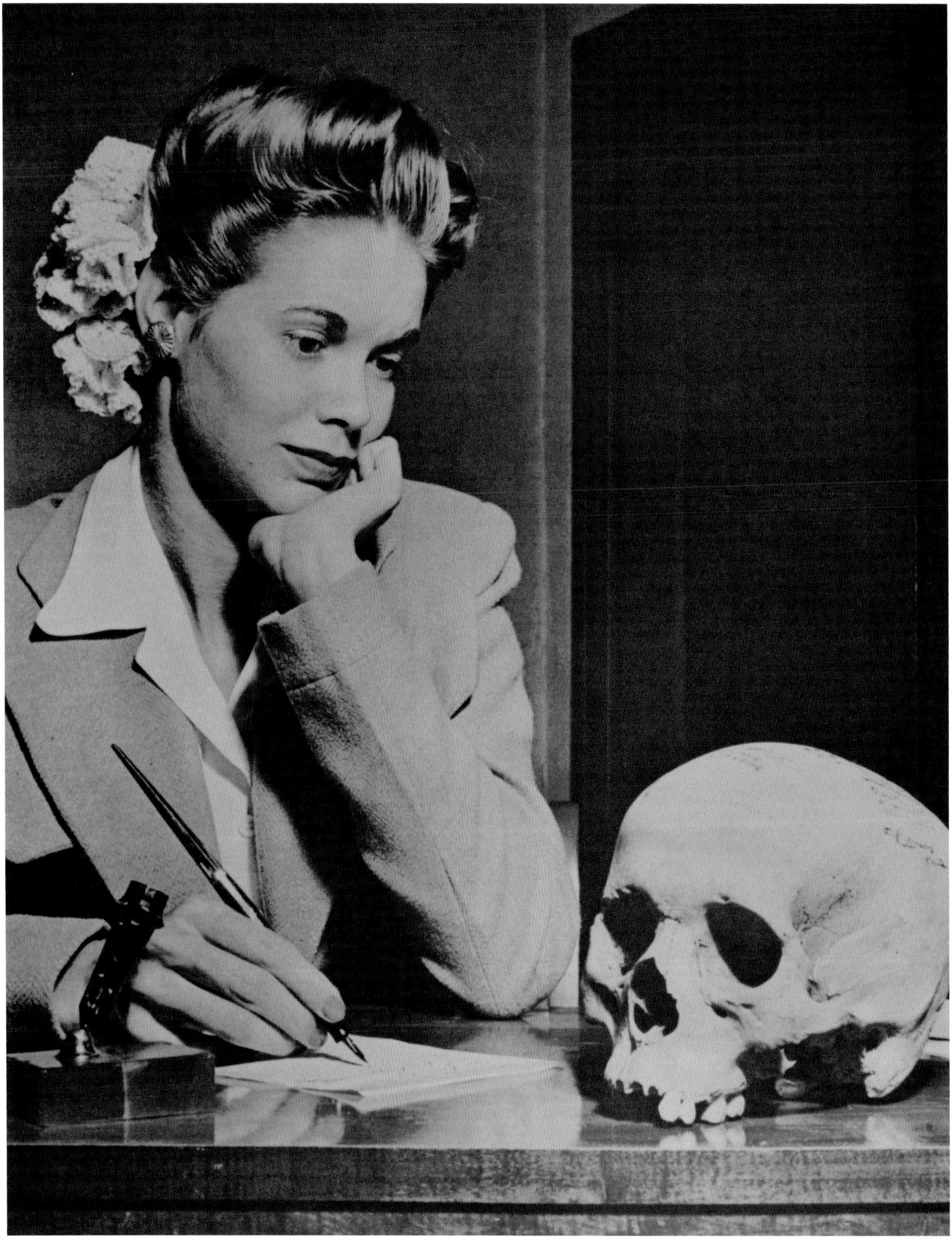

Annette Lemieux. *Courting Death*, 1985. Pigment print on Epson Luster paper, 48 × 38 in. (121.9 × 96.5 cm). Hirshhorn Museum and Sculpture Garden, Smithsonian Institution, Washington, DC

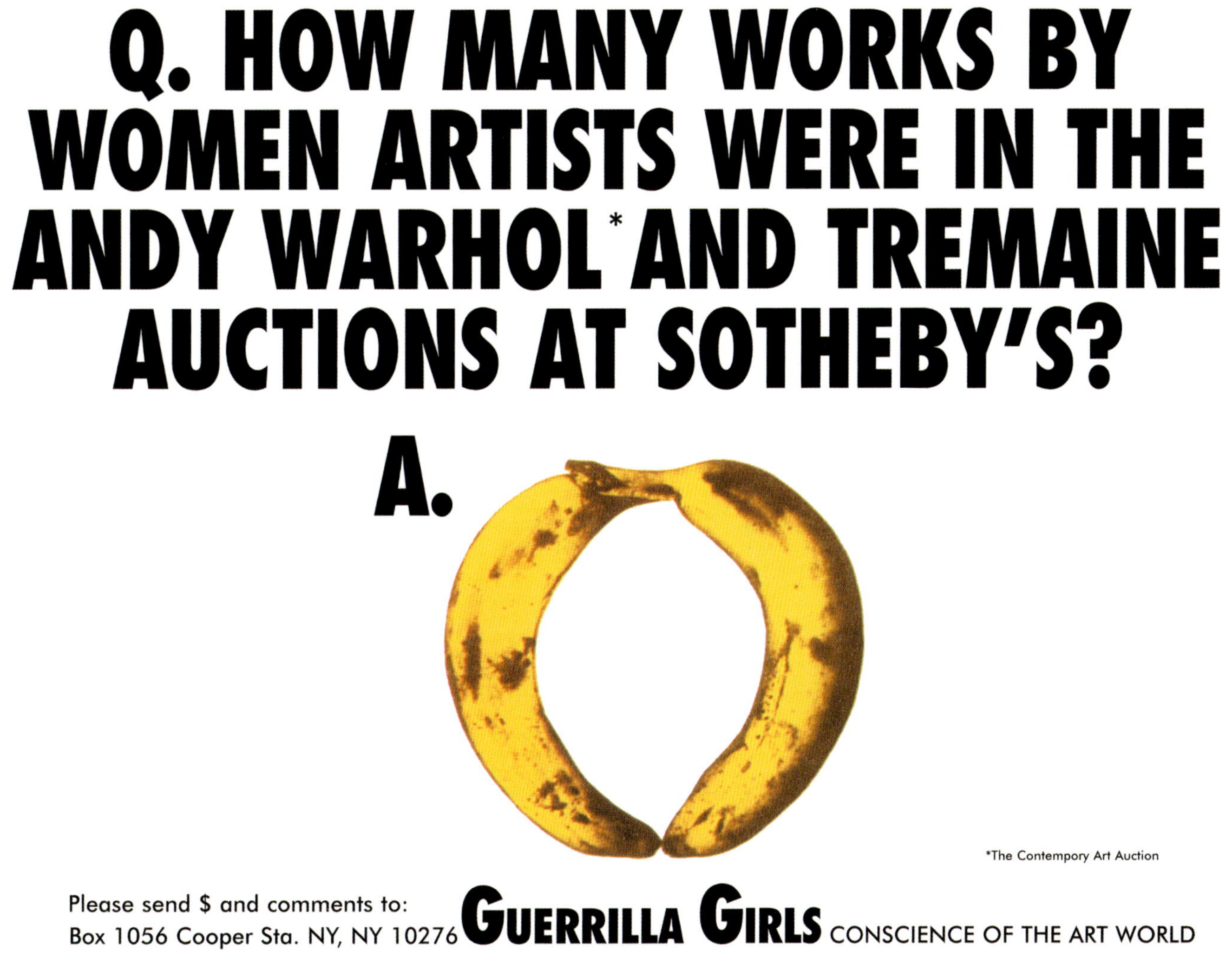

Guerrilla Girls. *Q. How Many Works by Women Artists Were in the Andy Warhol and Tremaine Auctions at Sotheby's?* 1989. Offset lithograph, 17 × 22 in. (43.2 × 55.9 cm). Courtesy of guerrillagirls.com

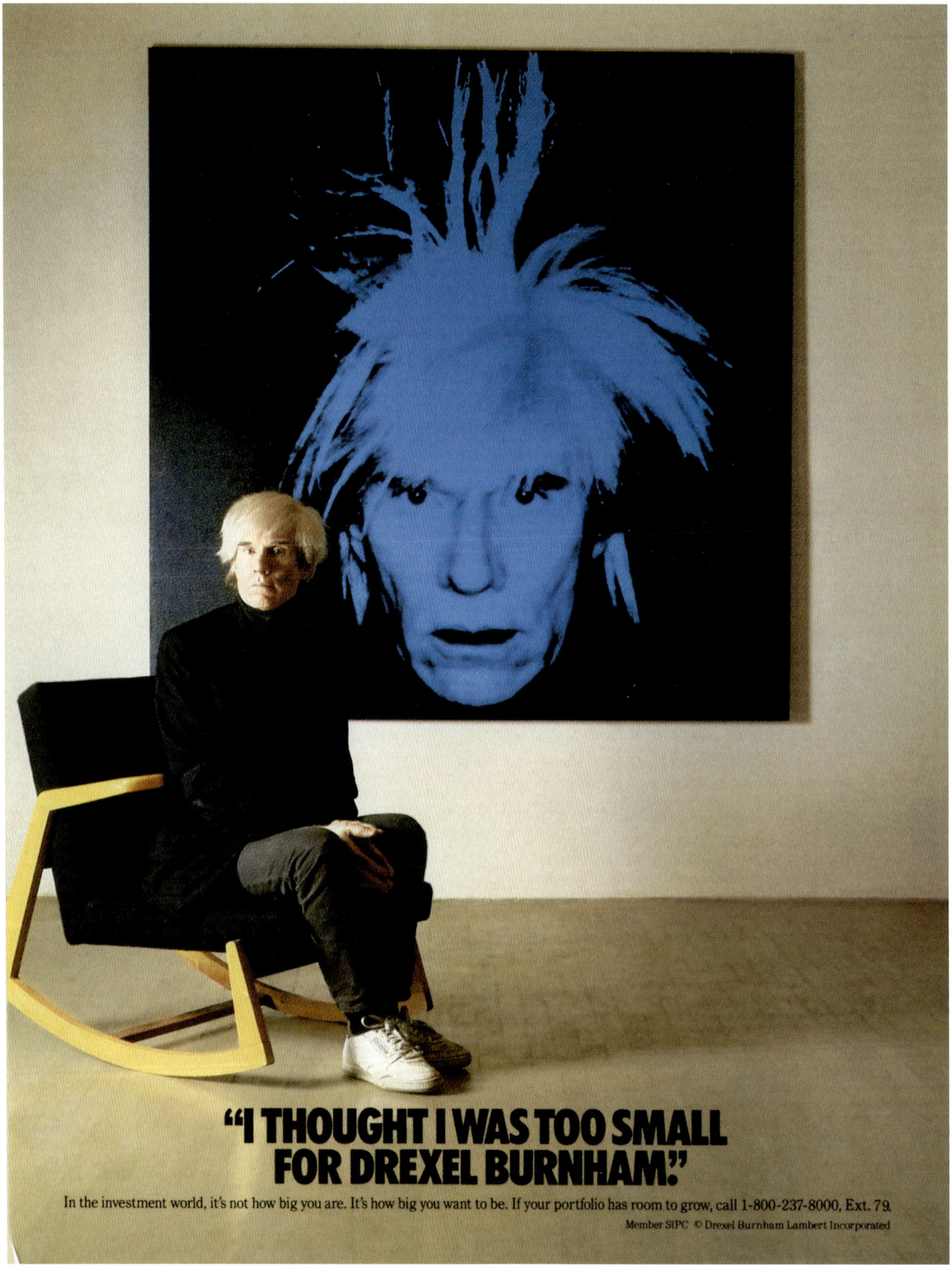

Drexel Burnham Lambert. Magazine advertisement featuring Andy Warhol, 1986. Published in *New York Times Magazine*, November 23, 1986

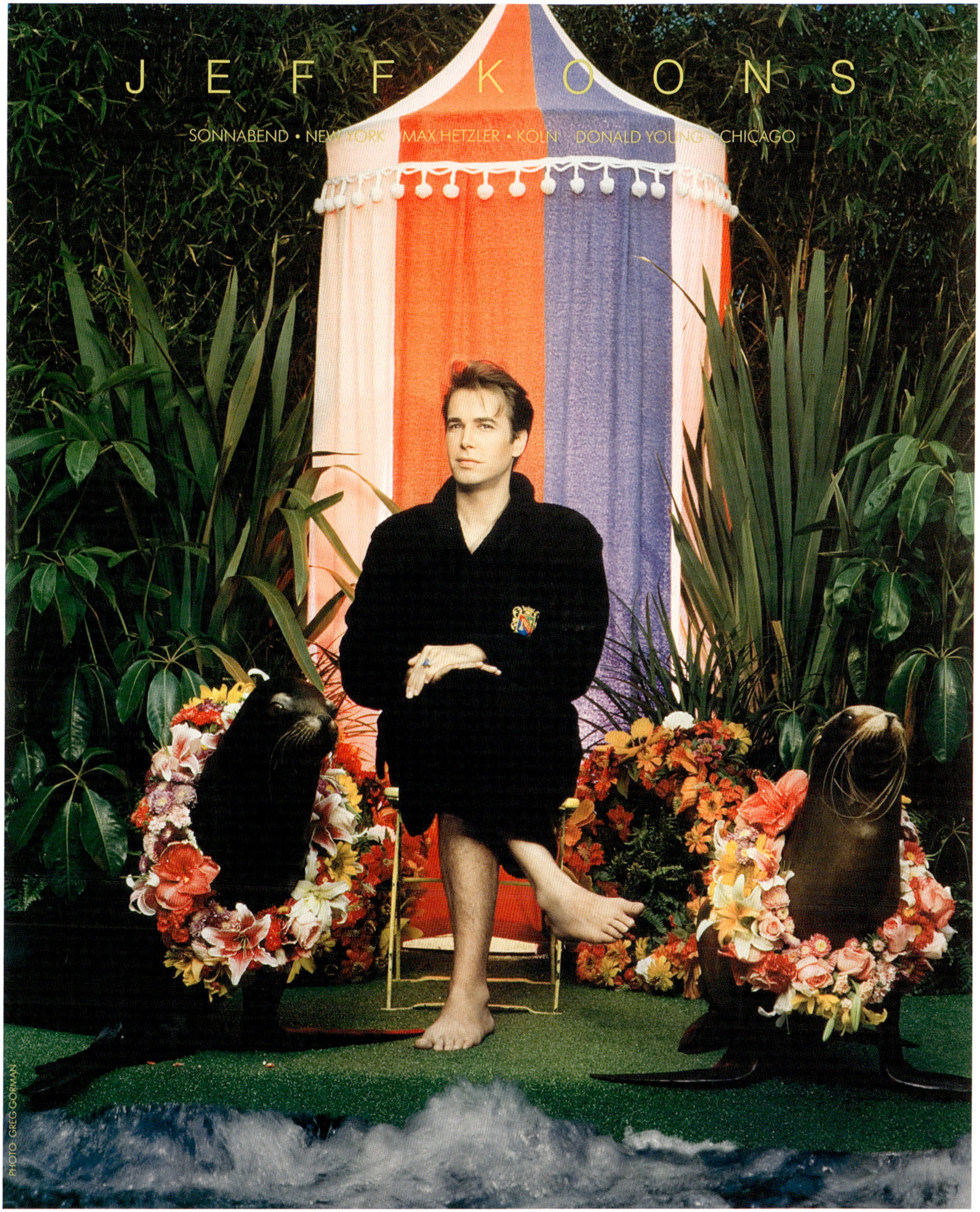

Jeff Koons. *Art Magazine Ad (Arts)*, 1988–89. Lithographic print, 45 × 37¼ in. (114.3 × 94.6 cm). Rubell Family Collection, Miami

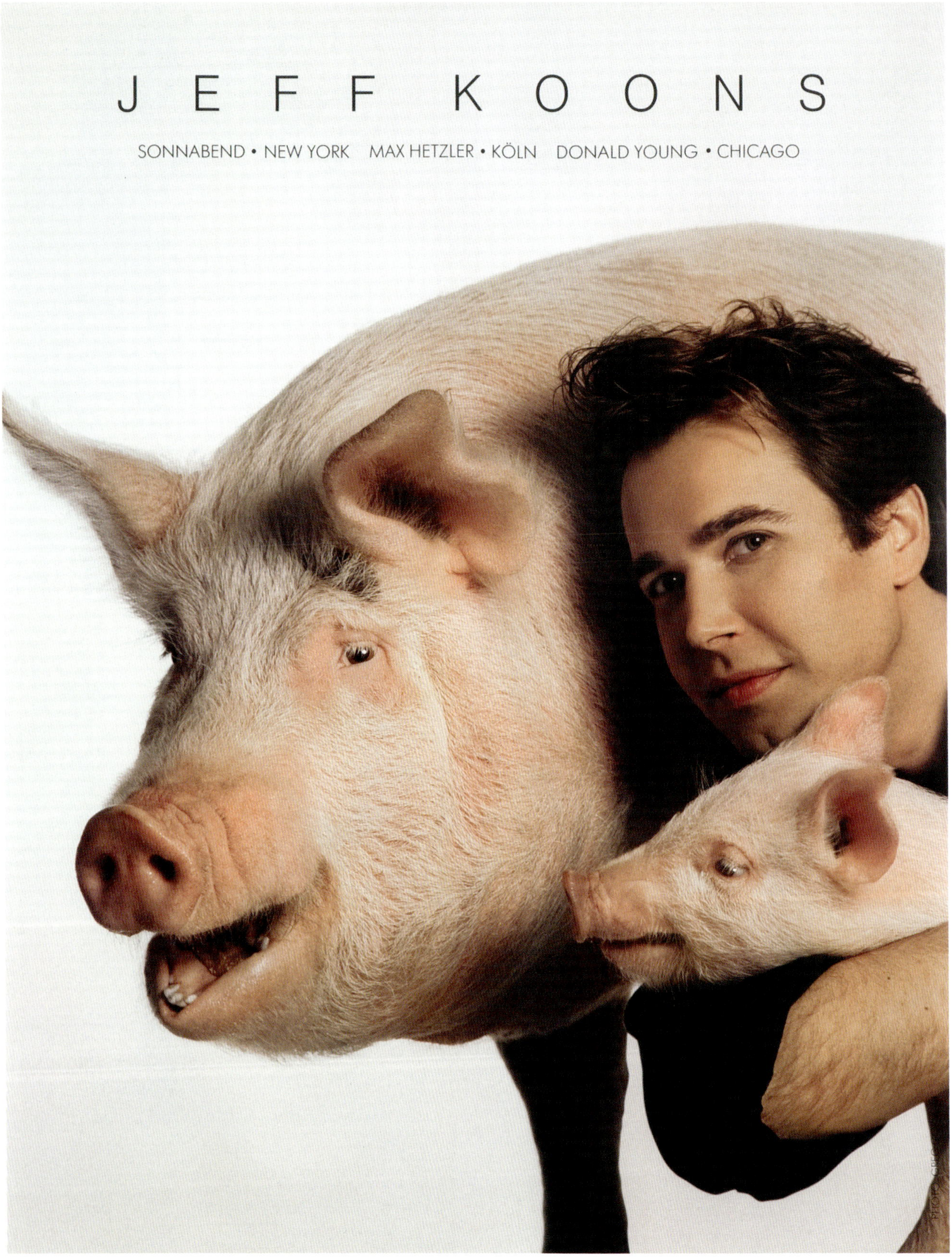

Jeff Koons. *Art Magazine Ad (Flash Art)*, 1988–89. Lithographic print, 45 × 37¼ in. (114.3 × 94.6 cm).
Rubell Family Collection, Miami

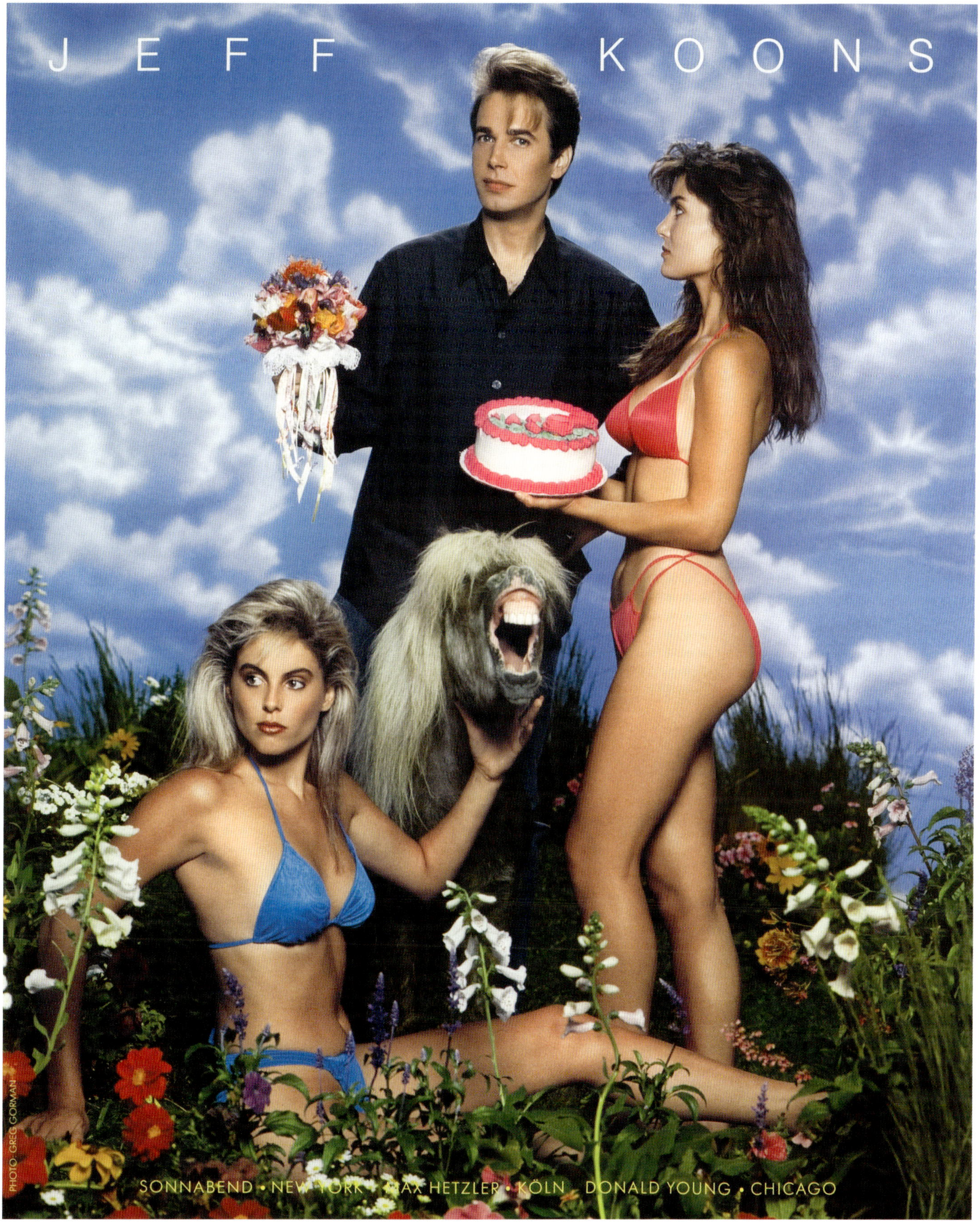

Jeff Koons. ***Art Magazine Ad (Art in America)***, 1988–89. Lithographic print, 45 × 37¼ in. (114.3 × 94.6 cm). Rubell Family Collection, Miami

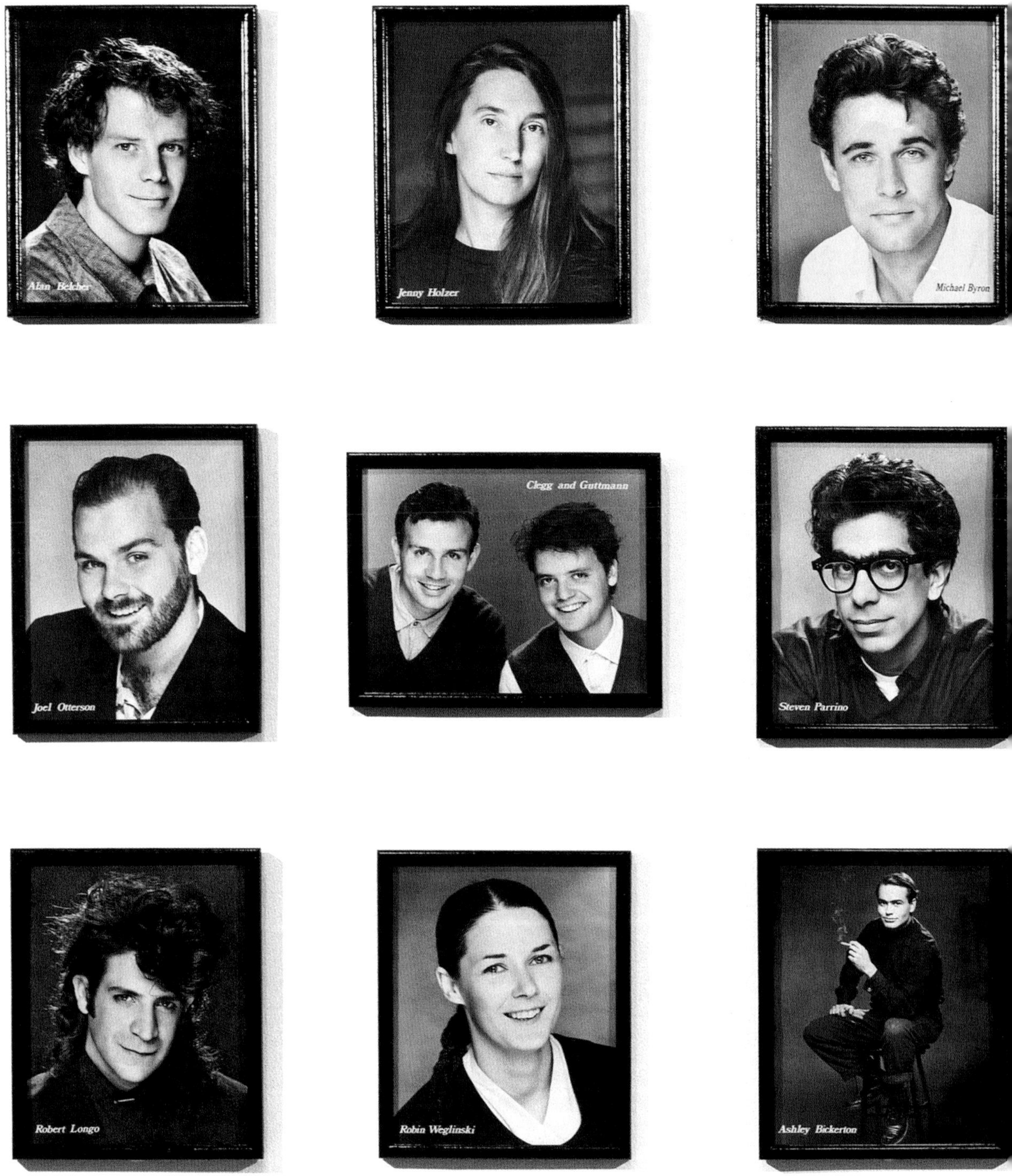

David Robbins. ***Talent***, 1986. Eighteen framed black-and-white photographs, each 11 × 9 in. (27.9 × 22.9 cm). Courtesy of Jessica R. Wolff and Stephen A. Wanta

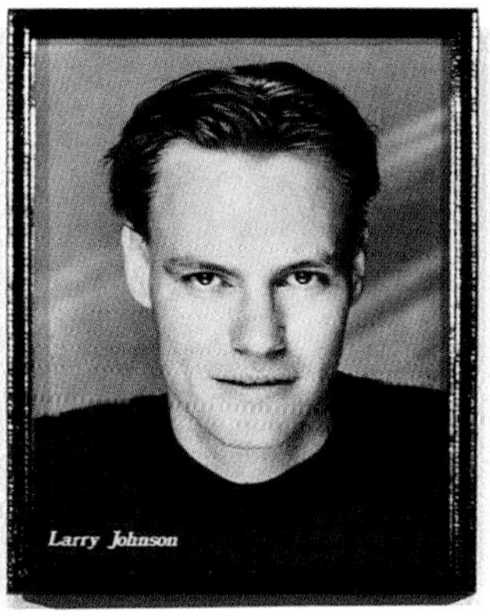
Larry Johnson

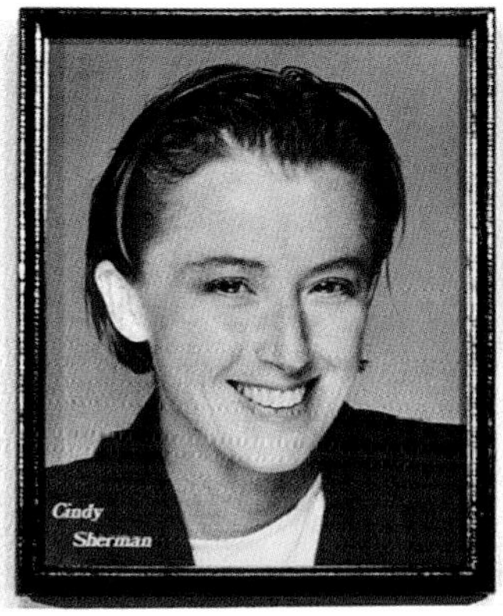
Cindy
Sherman

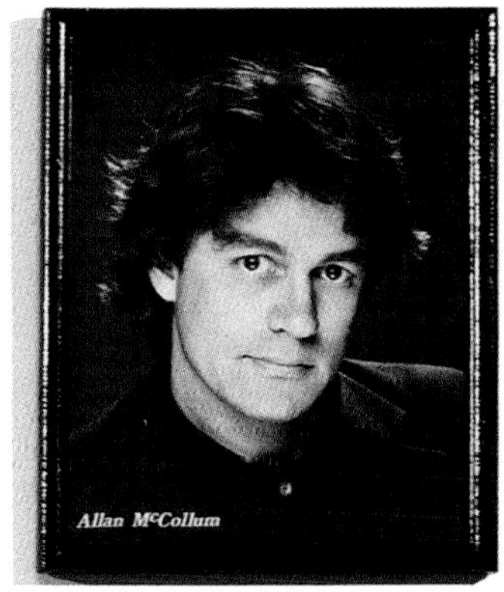
Allan McCollum

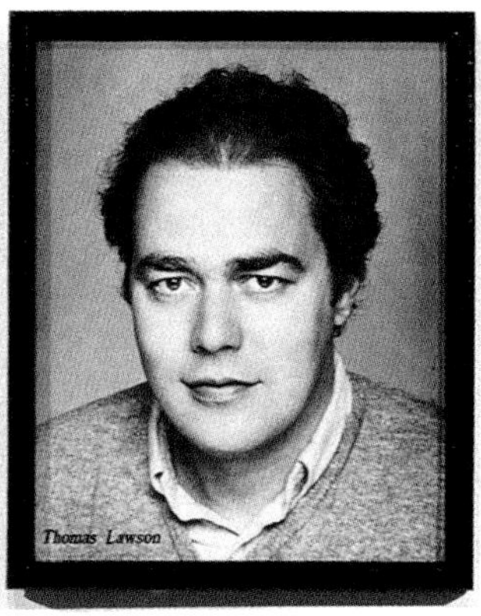
Thomas Lawson

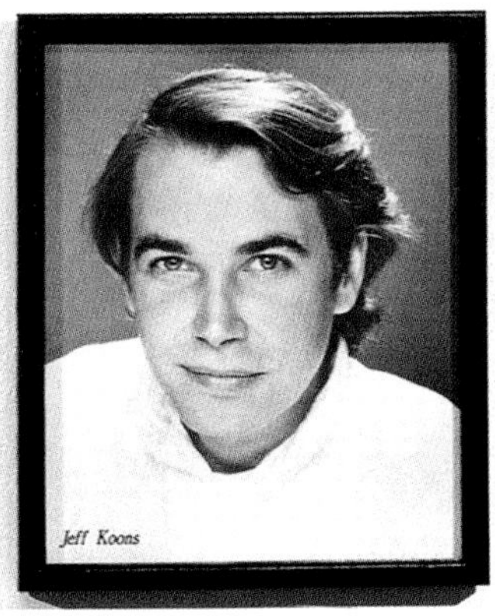
Jeff Koons

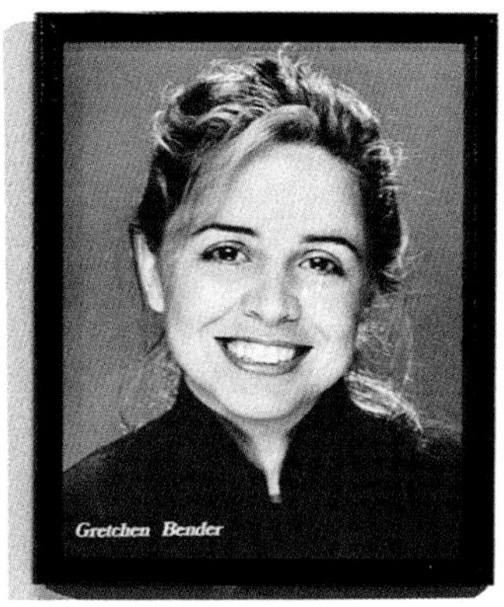
Gretchen Bender

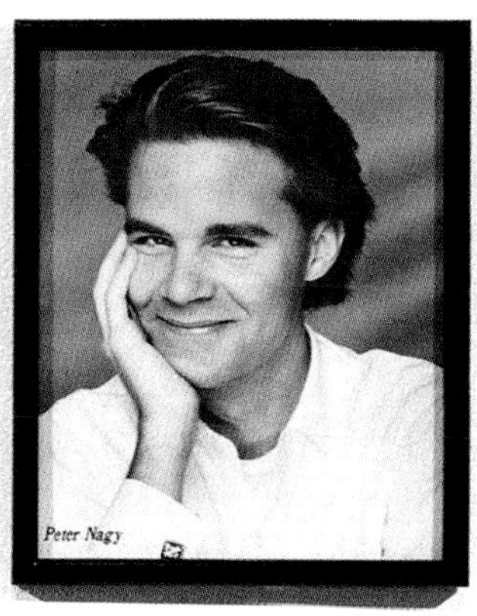
Peter Nagy

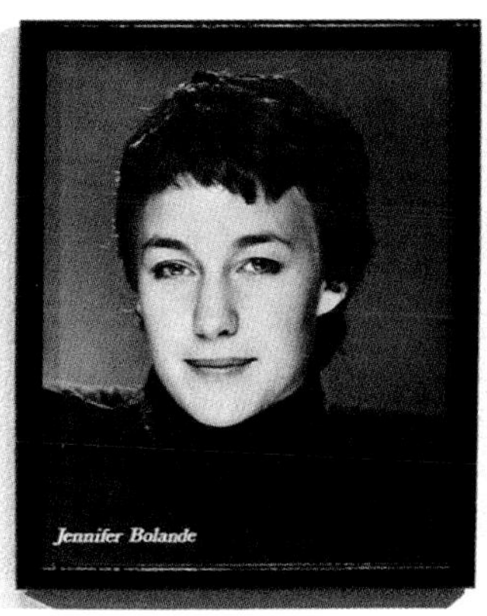
Jennifer Bolande

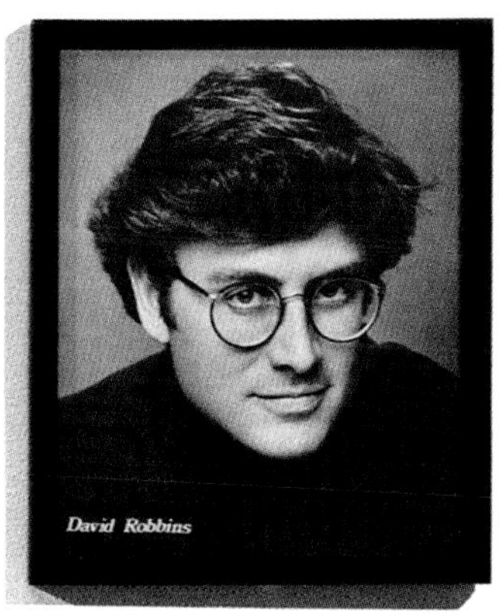
David Robbins

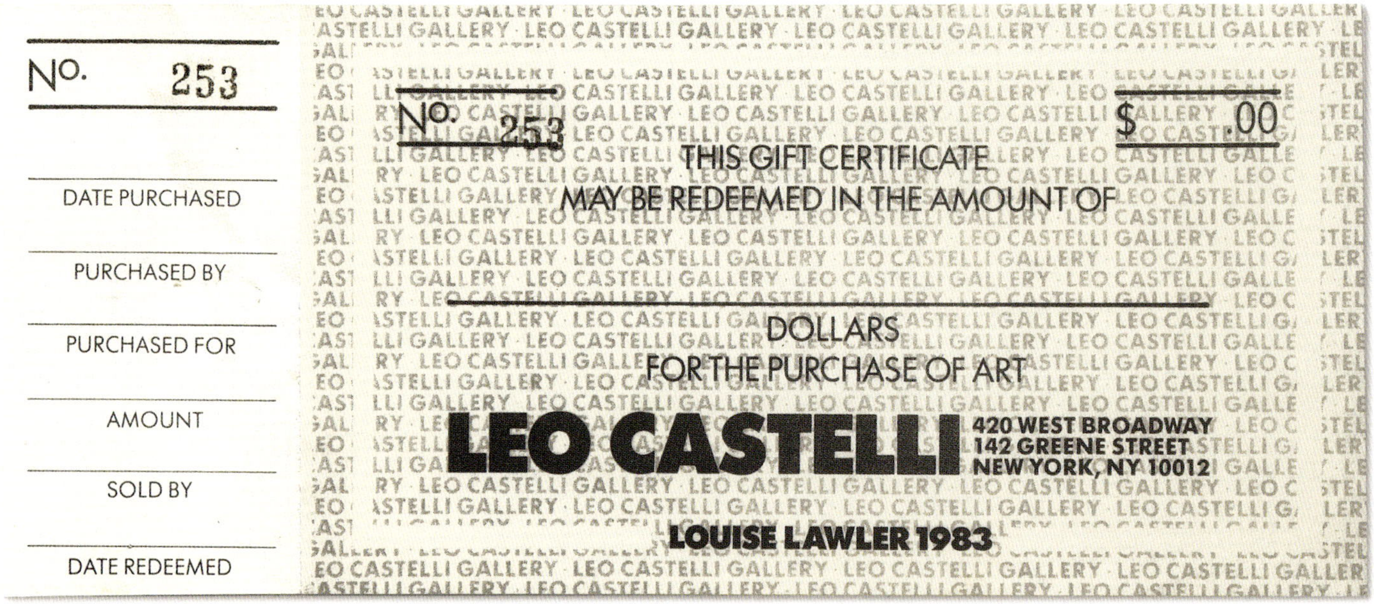

Louise Lawler. ***Gift Certificate for Leo Castelli Gallery, New York***, 1983. Printed matter, 3 9/16 × 6 1/2 in. (9 × 16.5 cm). Courtesy of the artist and Metro Pictures, New York

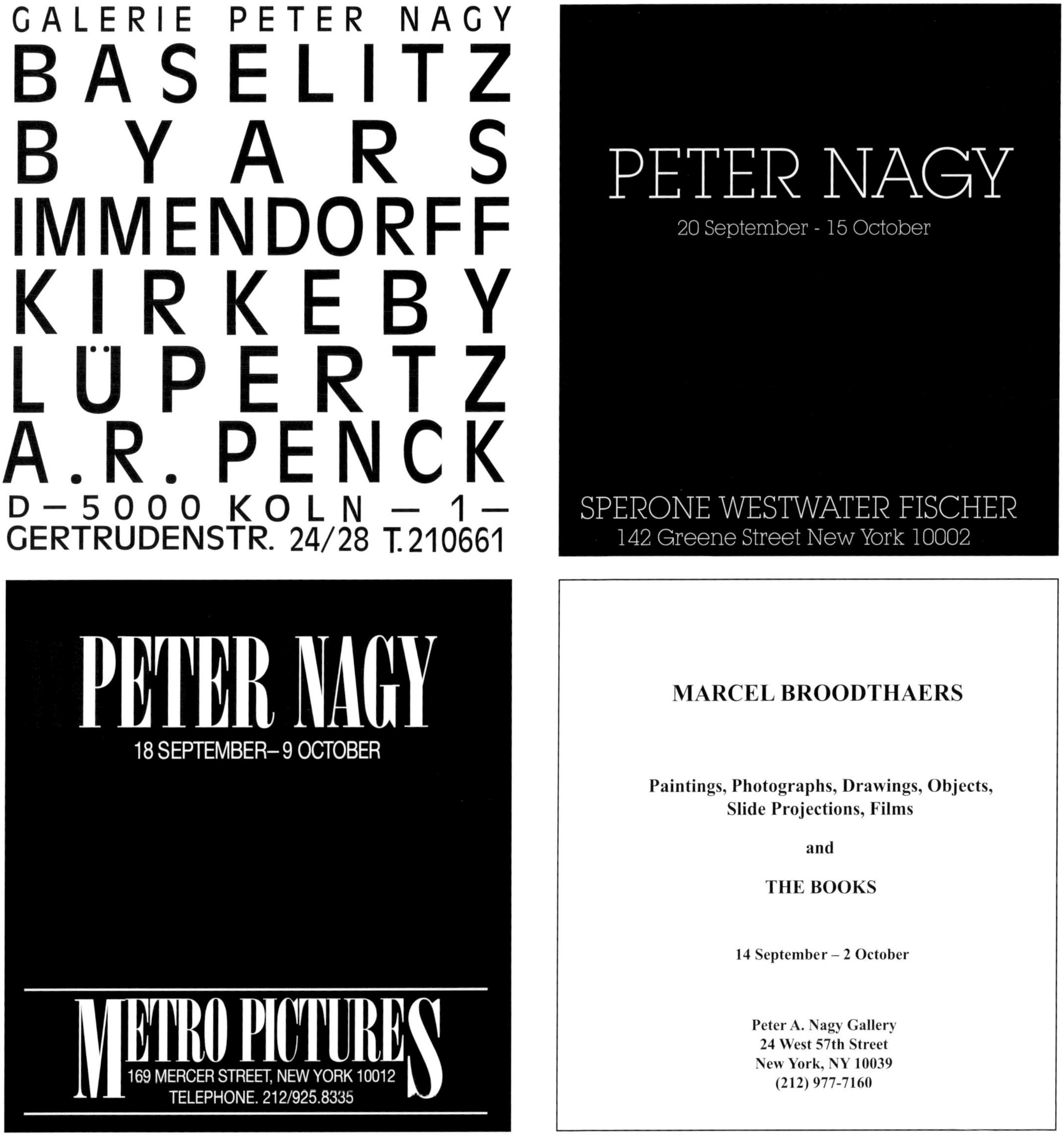

Peter Nagy. ***Adism***, 1983. Black-and-white photocopy, 10 × 10 in. (25.4 × 25.4 cm). Courtesy of the artist and Magenta Plains, New York

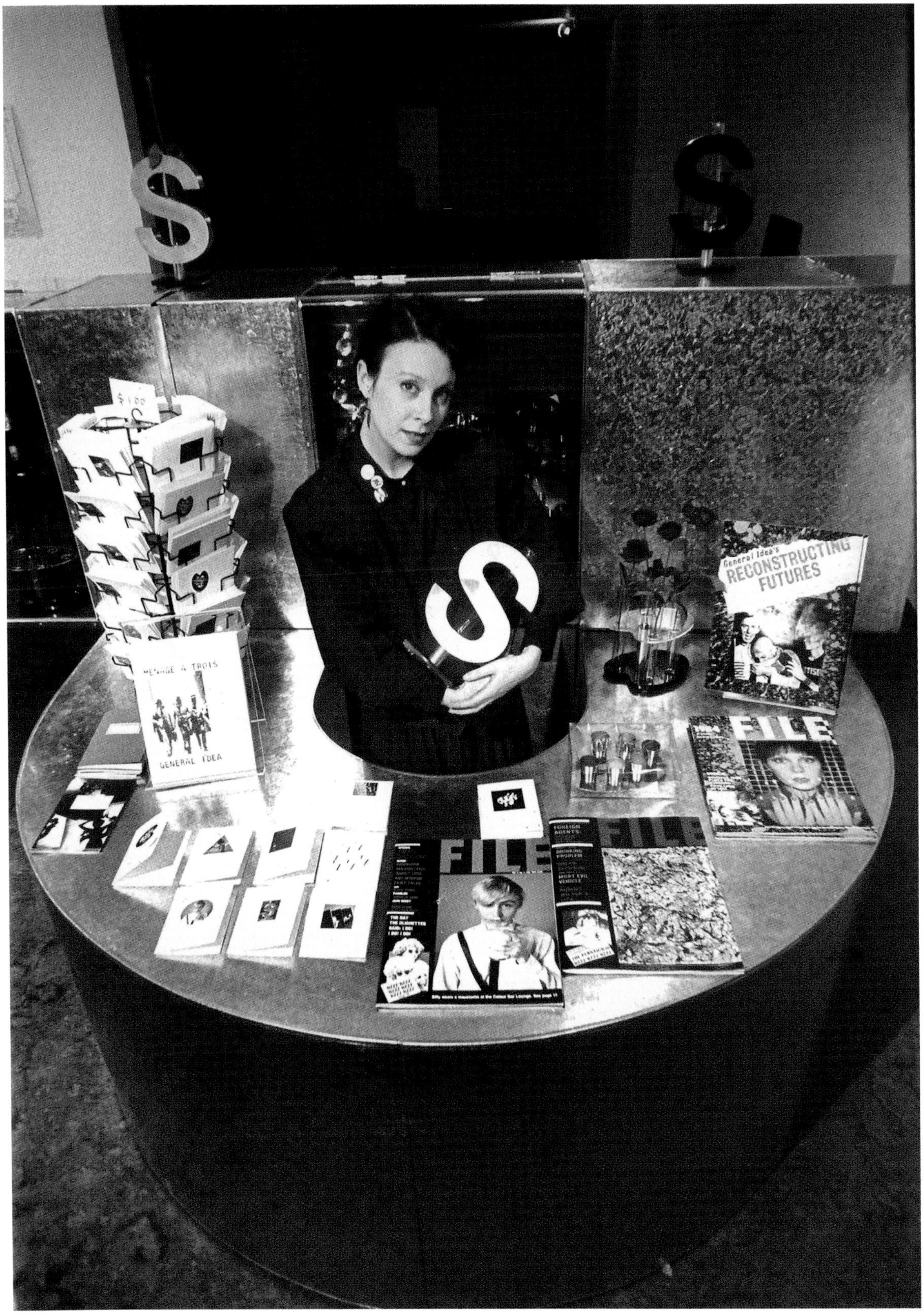

General Idea. ***Anya Presents Liquid Assets at the Boutique from the 1984 Miss General Idea Pavilion***, 1980. Gelatin silver print, 14 × 9⅞ in. (35.6 × 25.1 cm). Courtesy of Esther Schipper, Berlin

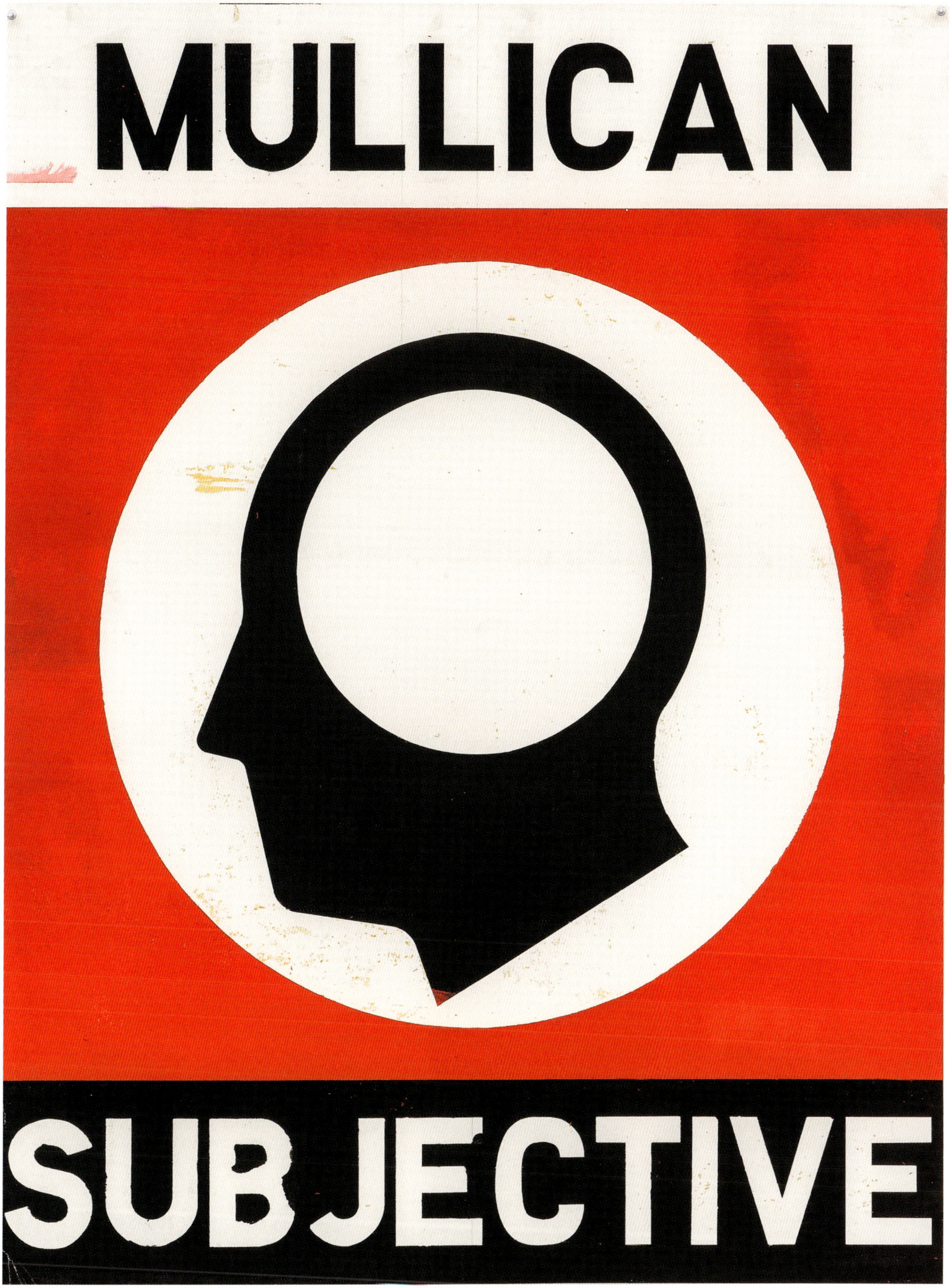

Matt Mullican. ***Untitled (Subjective)***, 1985. Lead paint on board, 50 × 38 1/16 in. (127 × 96.7 cm).
Courtesy of the artist, Mai 36 Galerie, and Peter Freeman, Inc.

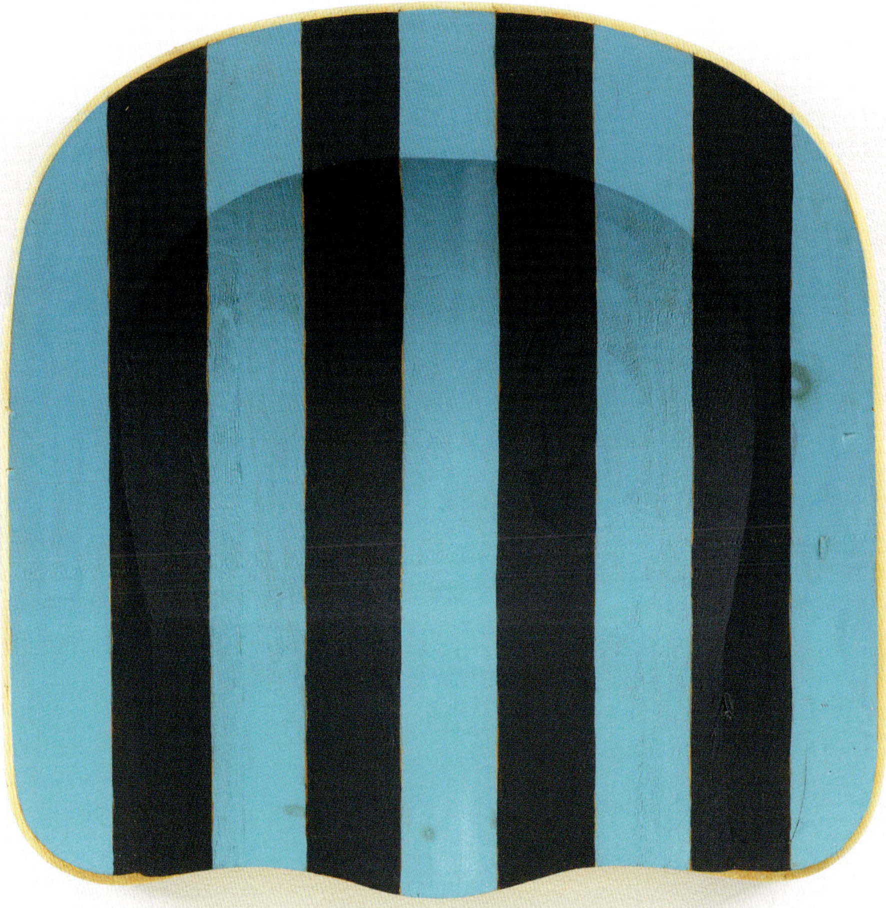

Sherrie Levine. ***Chair Seat: 5***, 1986. Casein and wax on wood, 18 × 18⅜ × 2¼ in. (45.7 × 46.7 × 5.7 cm).
Courtesy of the artist and David Zwirner, New York/London

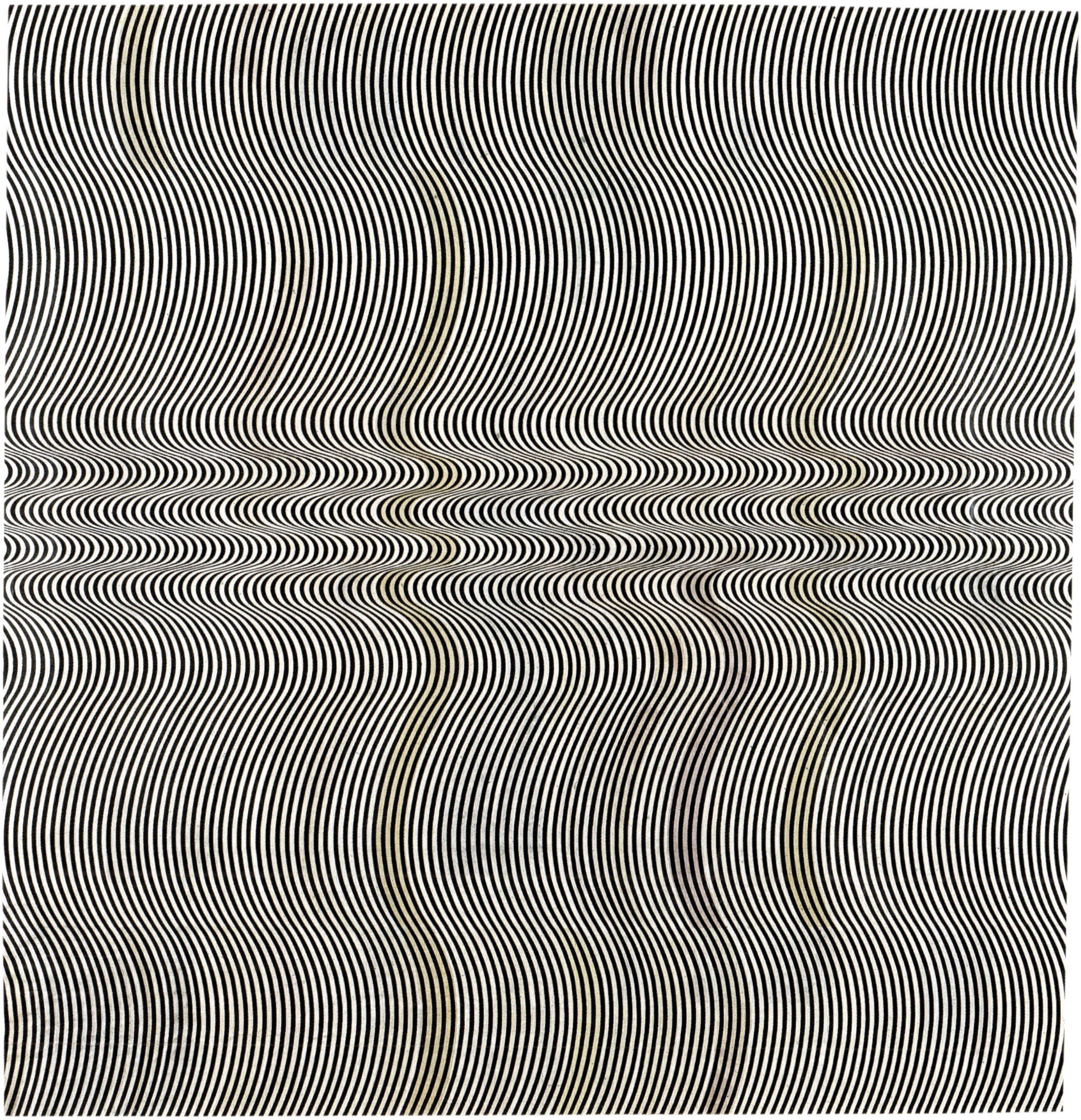

Philip Taaffe. ***Undercurrent***, 1984. Mixed media on canvas, 88 × 88 in. (223.5 × 223.5 cm).
Collection of the artist

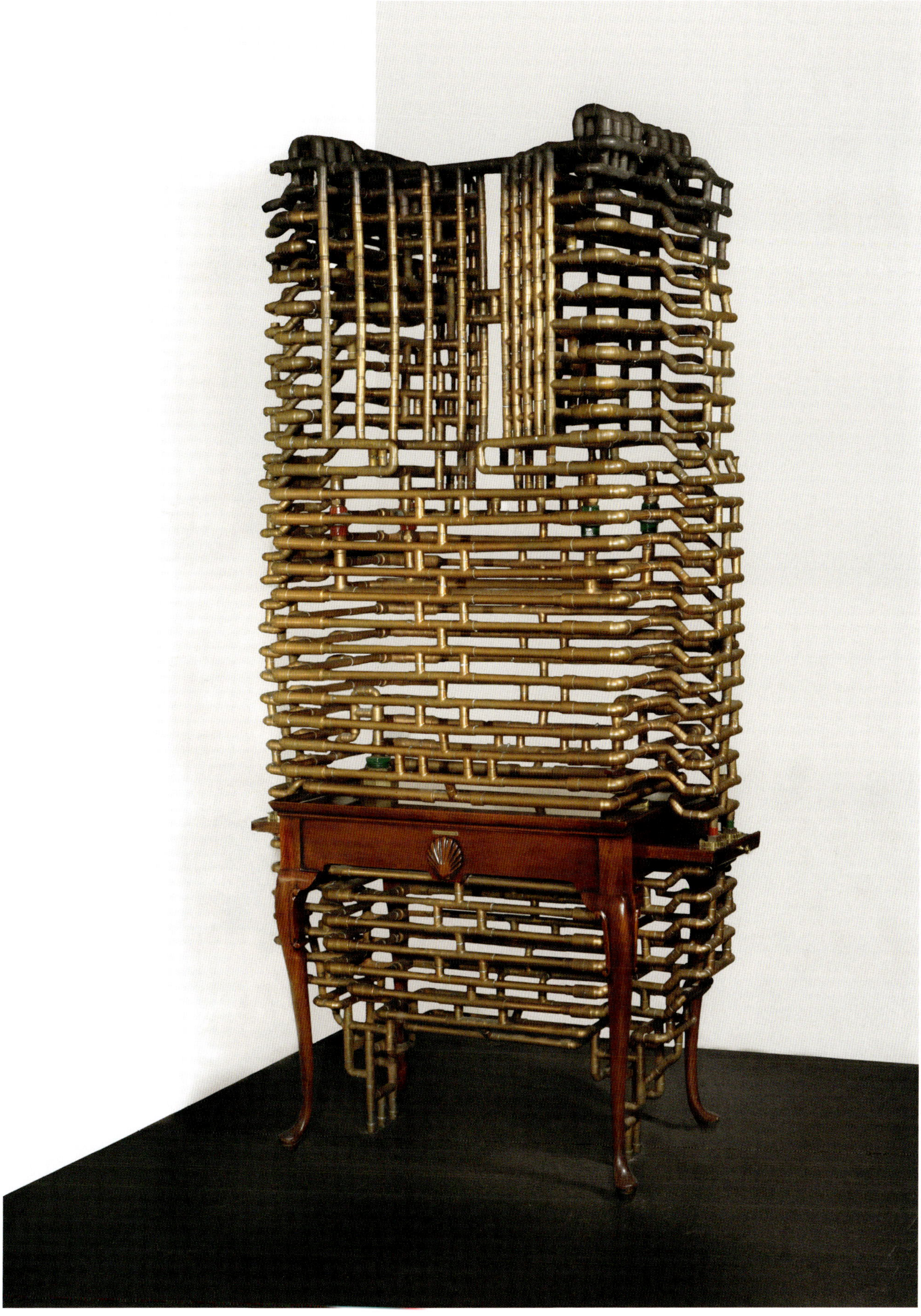

Joel Otterson. *Devil/Jesus*, 1986. Found table with copper pipes, 19 × 39 × 72 in. (48.3 × 99.1 × 182.9 cm). Ruth and William Ehrlich

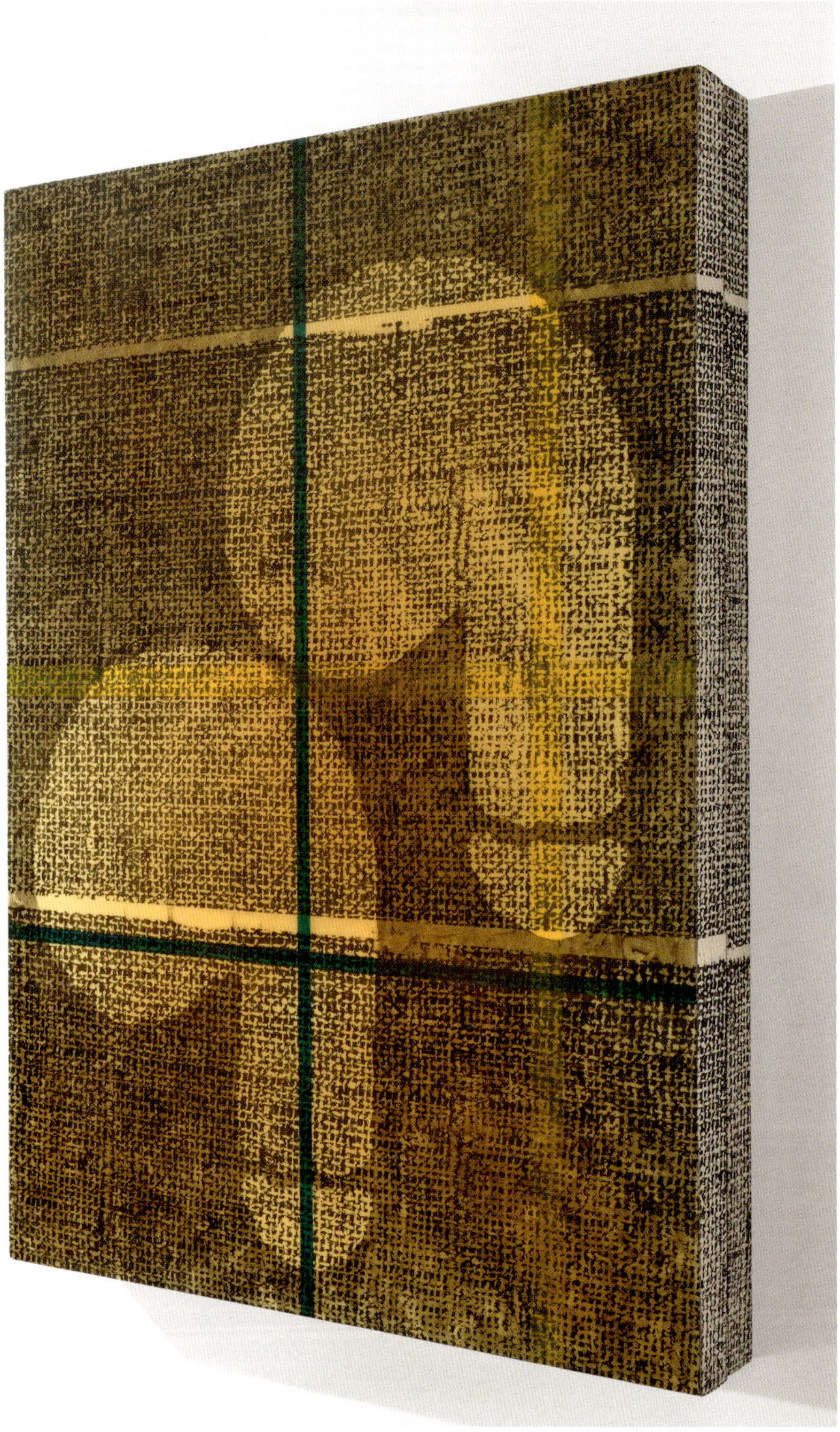

Meyer Vaisman. *The Stretch Painting*, 1986. Laminated process ink on canvas, 71½ × 51½ × 7½ in. (181.6 × 130.8 × 19 cm). Collection of B. Z. + Michael Schwartz

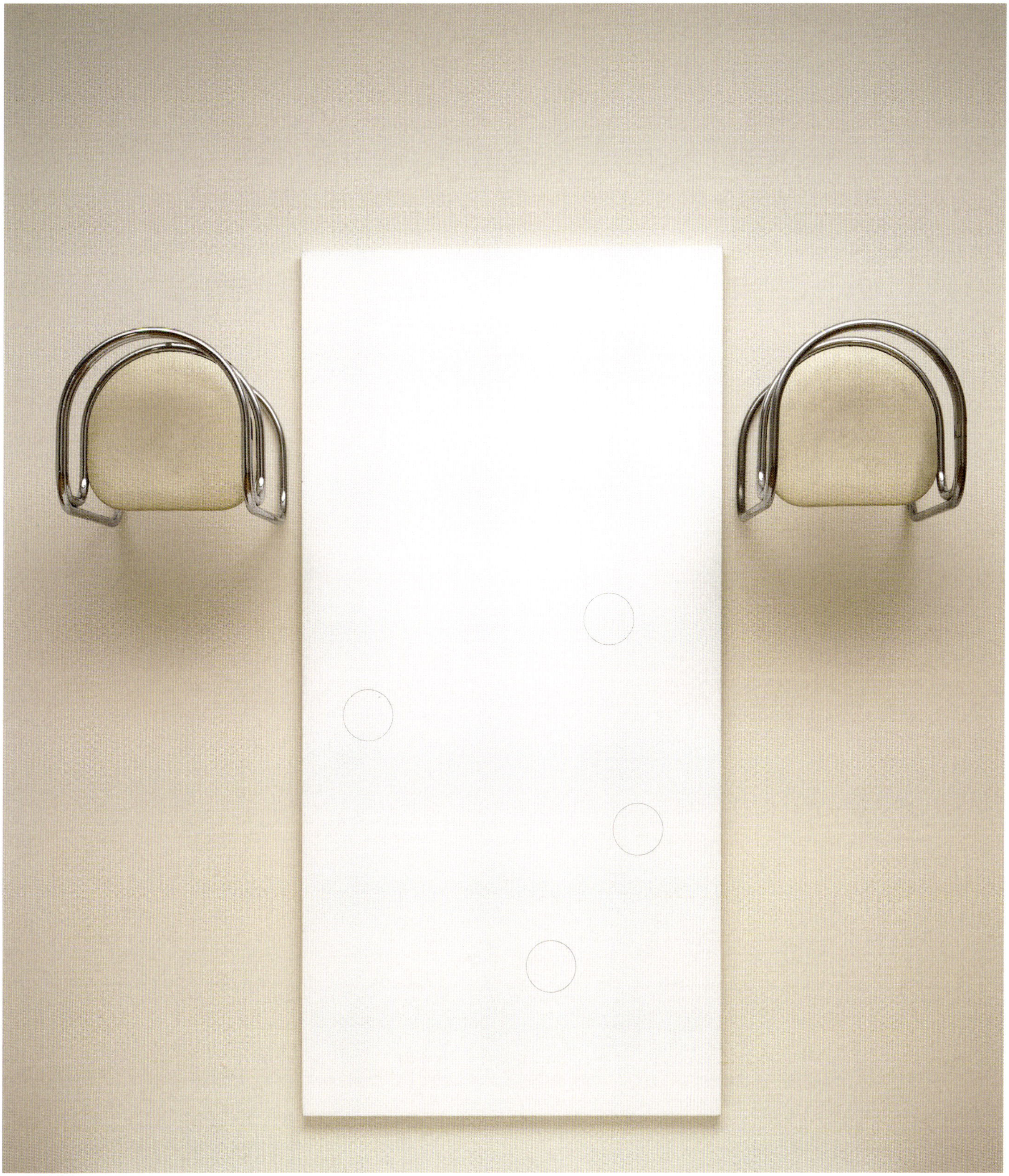

John M Armleder. ***Untitled***, 1986. Synthetic polymer paint and China ink on canvas, two chrome-and-vinyl chairs, canvas 8 ft. ¼ in. × 48⅛ in. (244.3 × 122.3 cm), each chair 18½ × 20 × 28 in. (47 × 50.8 × 71.1 cm). The Museum of Modern Art, New York, Gift of Raymond J. Learsy and Gabriella De Ferrari

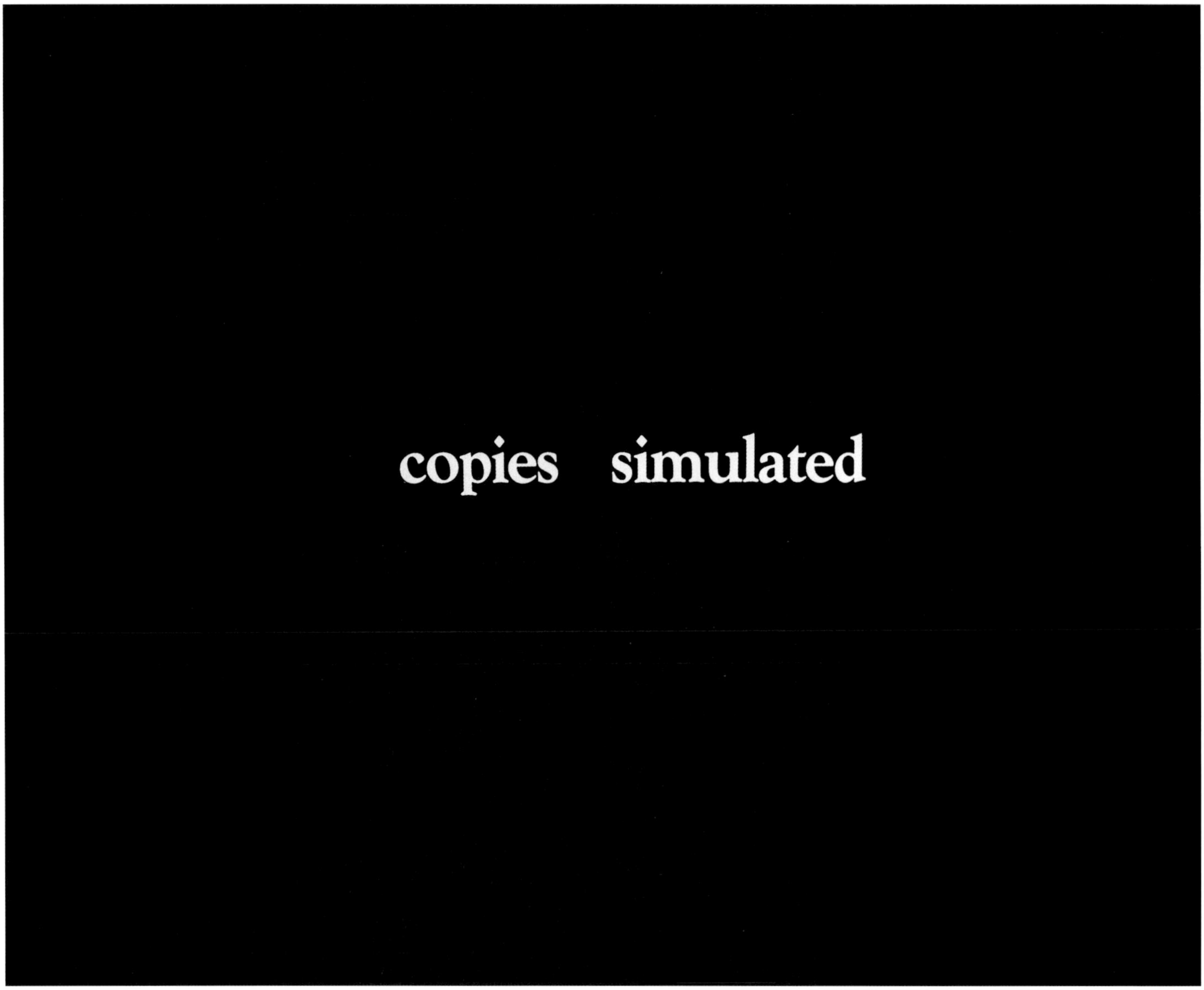

Peter Halley. *Copies Simulated*, 1984. Kodalith (photosensitive Mylar print), 17½ × 22¼ in. (44.5 × 56.5 cm). Ed. 2/2. Collection of the artist

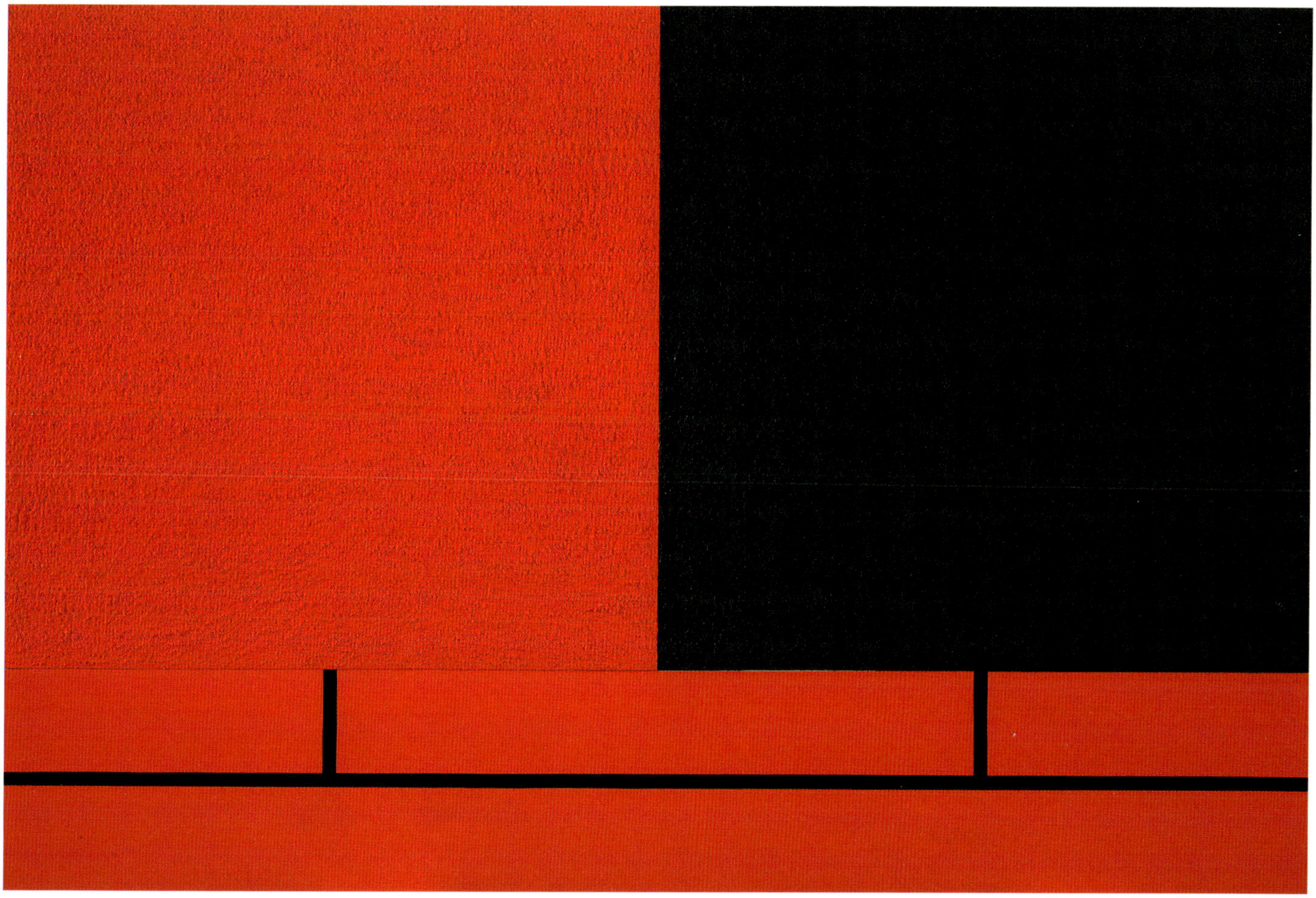

Peter Halley. ***Glowing and Burnt-Out Cells with Conduit***, 1981. Acrylic, Day-Glo acrylic, and Roll-A-Tex on canvas, 64 × 96 in. (162.6 × 243.8 cm). Collection of B. Z. + Michael Schwartz

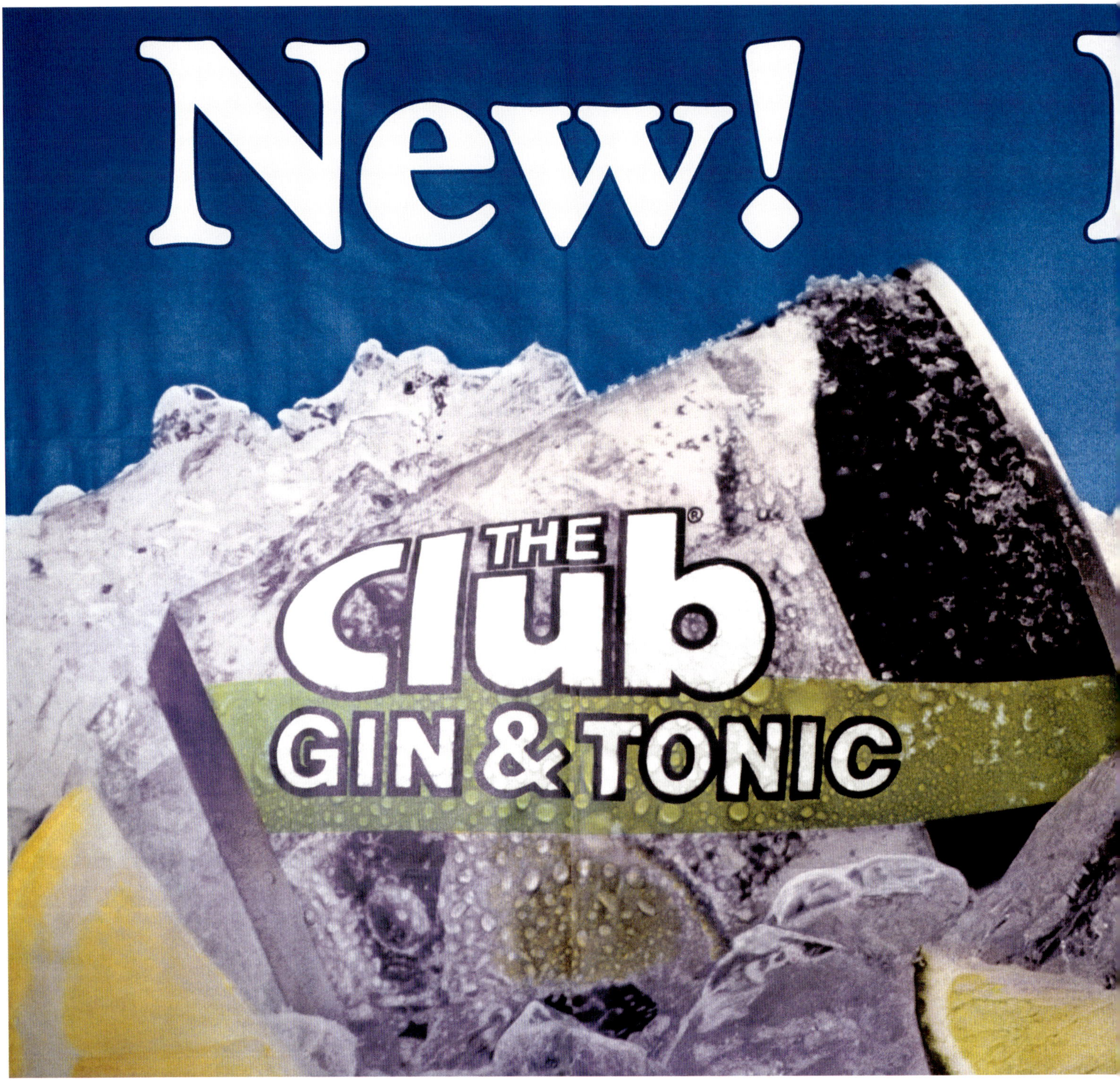

Jeff Koons. *New! New Too!* 1983. Lithographic billboard, mounted on cotton, 10 ft. 3 in. × 22 ft. 8 in. (312.4 × 690.9 cm). Private collection, New York

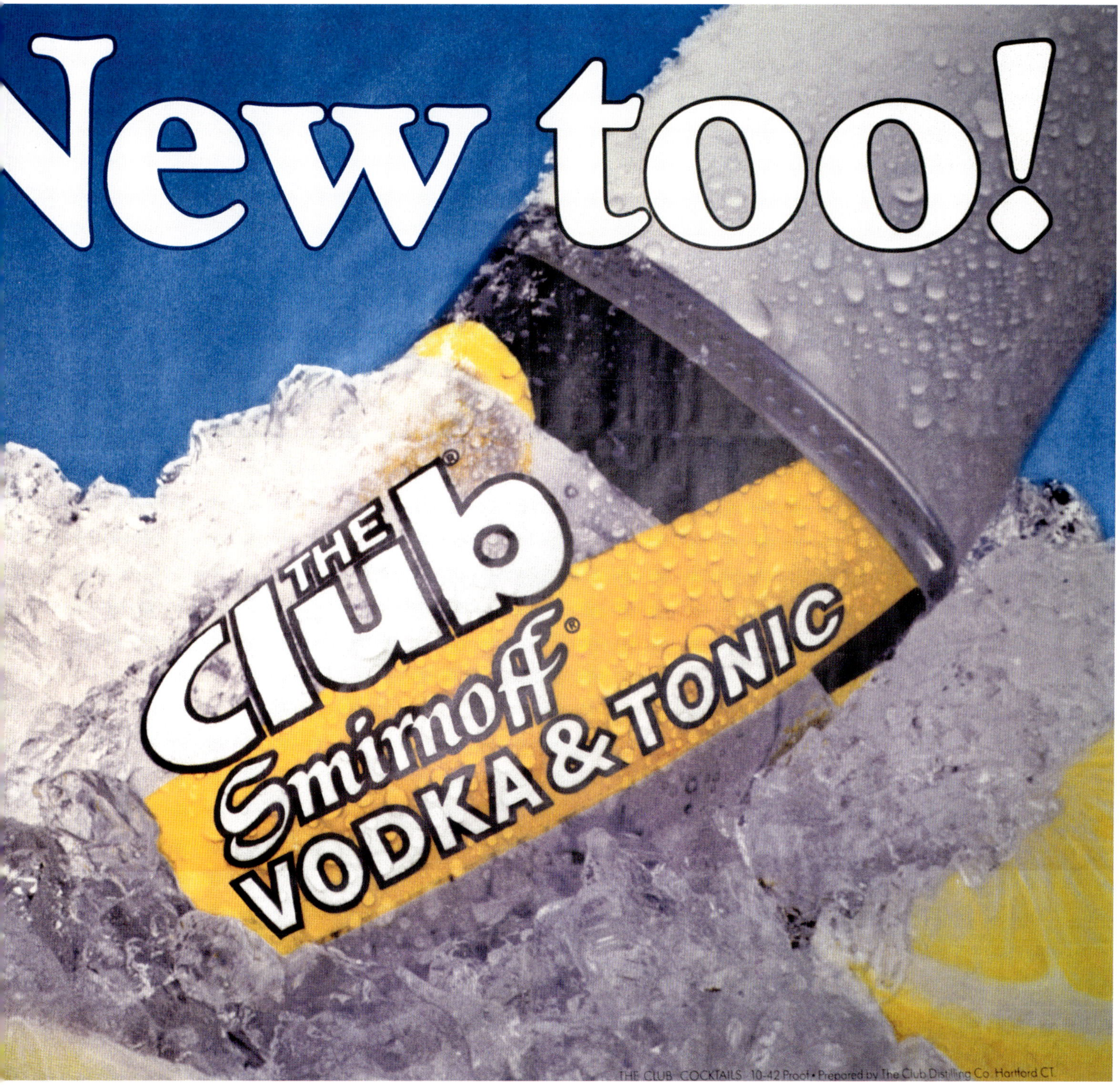
New too!
THE
Club®
Smirnoff®
VODKA & TONIC
THE CLUB COCKTAILS 10-42 Proof • Prepared by The Club Distilling Co. Hartford CT.

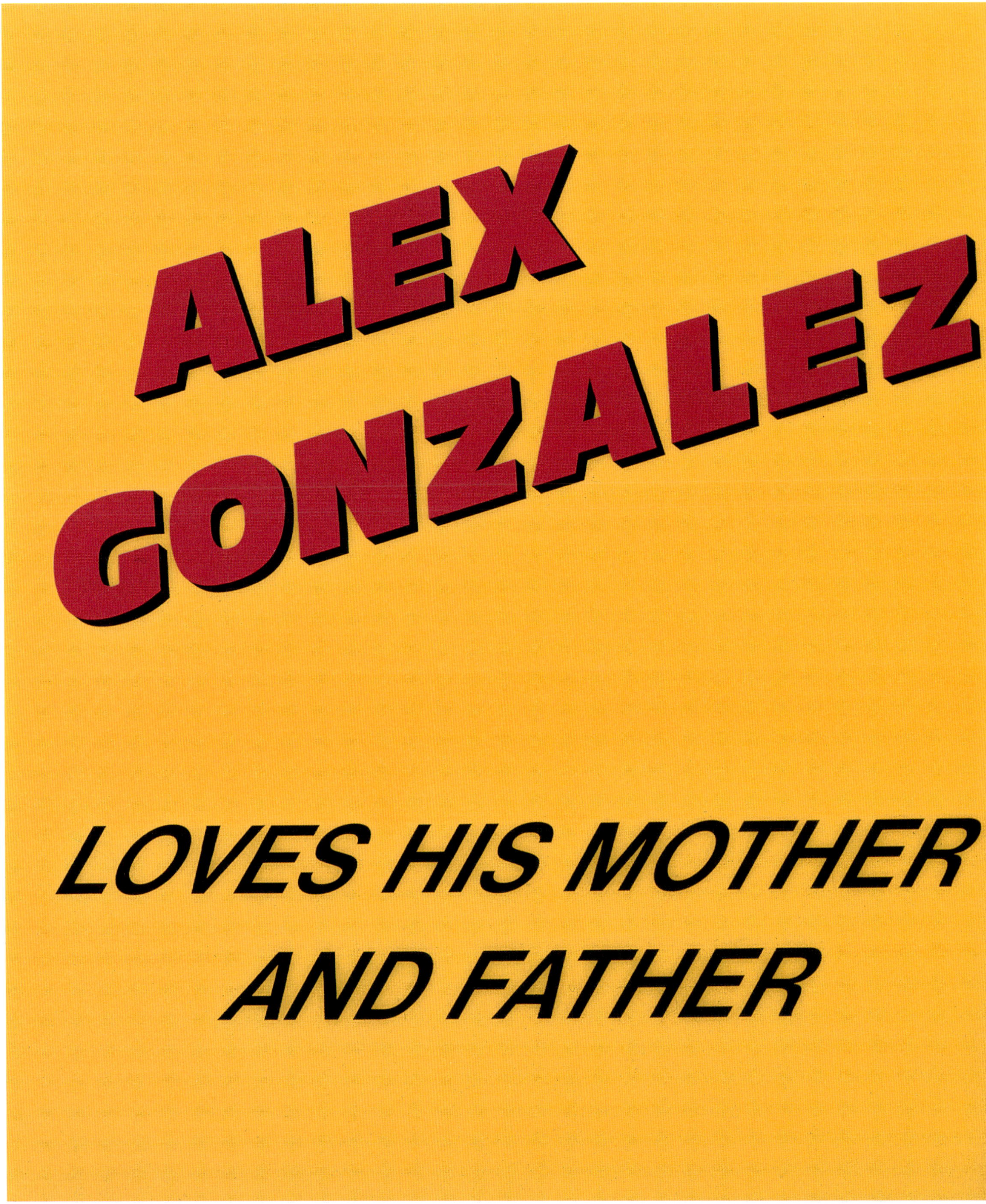

Ken Lum. ***Alex Gonzalez Loves His Mother and Father***, 1989. Chromogenic print on Sintra, mounted on acrylic with screenprinted ink text, 45⅞ × 80 × 2⅛ in. (116.5 × 203.3 × 5.5 cm). Courtesy of the artist

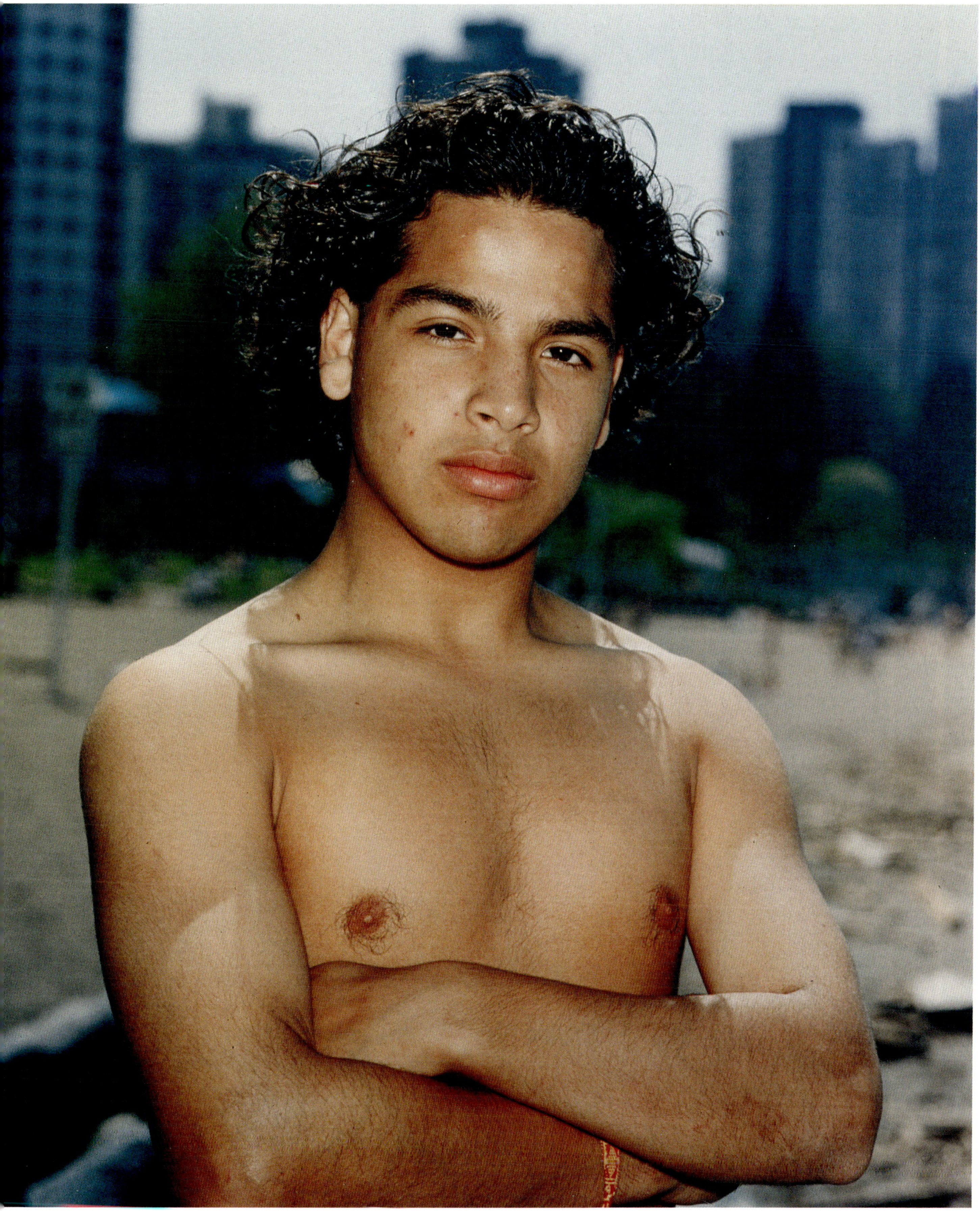

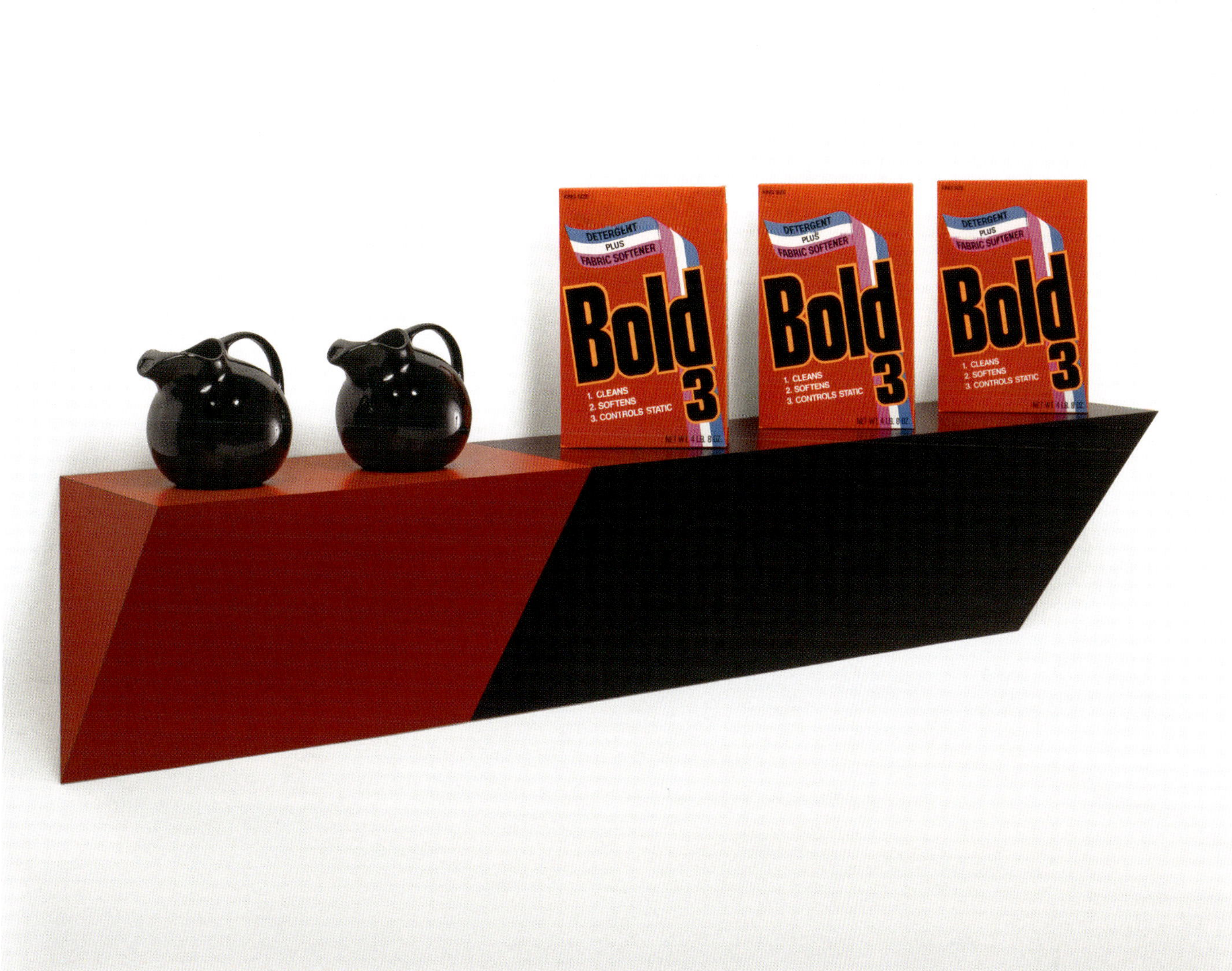

Haim Steinbach. ***supremely black***, 1985. Plastic-laminated wood shelf, two ceramic pitchers, three cardboard detergent boxes, 29 × 66 × 13 in. (73.7 × 167.6 × 33 cm). Ed. of 4. Courtesy of the artist; Tanya Bonakdar Gallery, New York; White Cube Gallery, London; and Galerie Laurent Godin, Paris

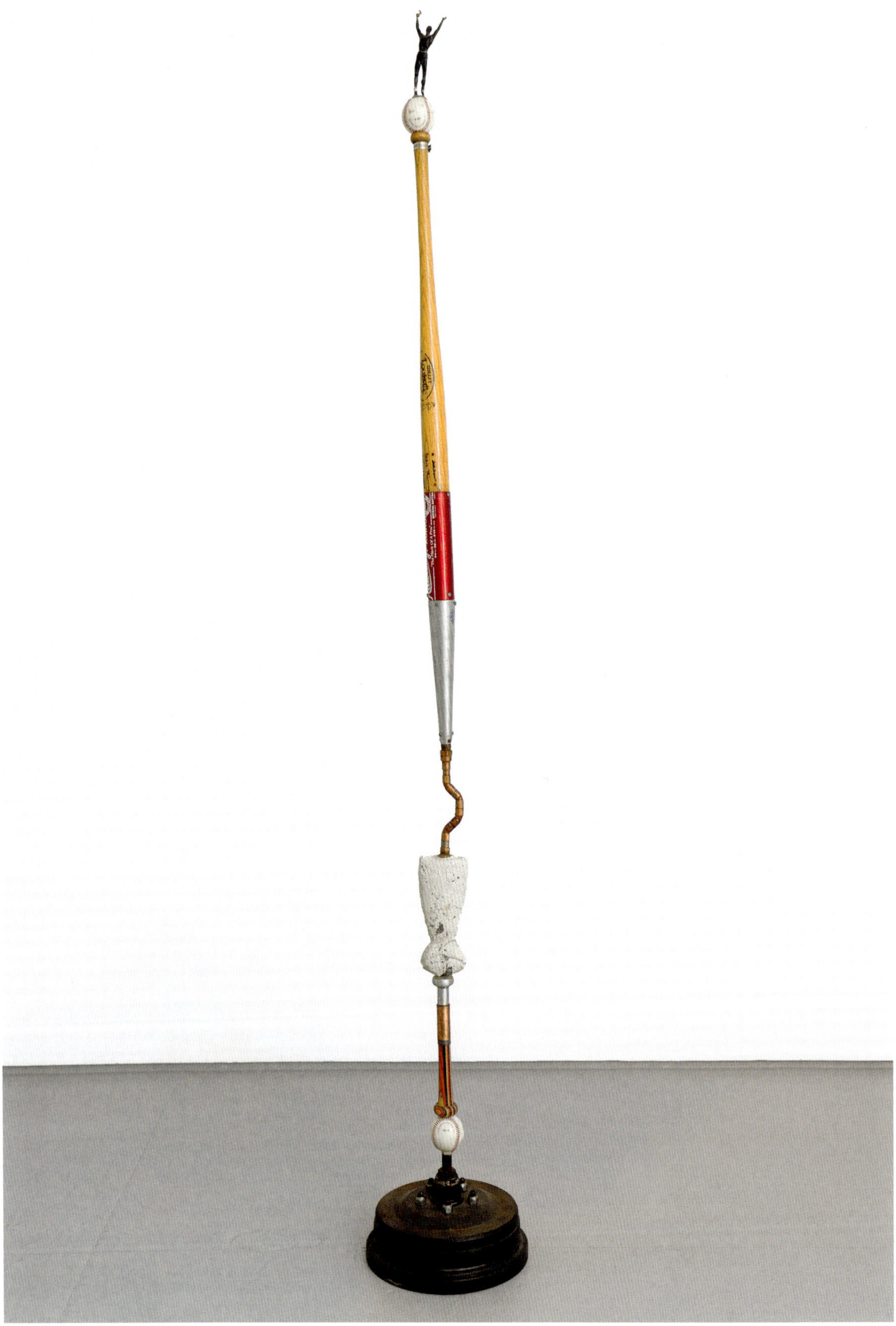

Joel Otterson. *Perfect Misuse*, 1985. Cast trophy figurine, baseballs, wood and aluminum baseball bats, copper piping, cast concrete, steel plates, 100 × 12 × 12 in. (254 × 30.5 × 30.5 cm). Courtesy of the artist and Elizabeth Dee, New York

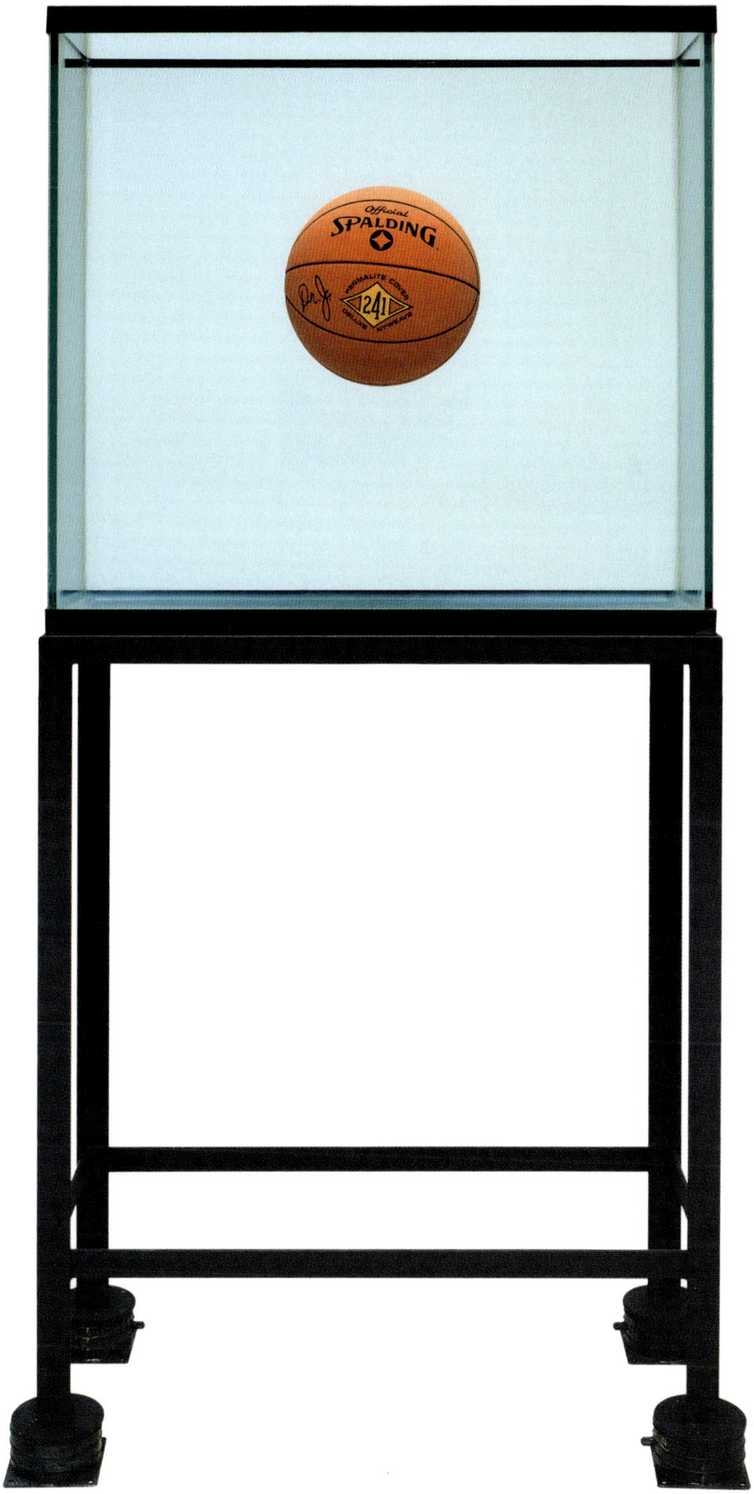

Jeff Koons. ***One Ball Total Equilibrium Tank (Spalding Dr. JK 241 Series)***, 1985. Glass, steel, sodium chloride reagent, distilled water, one basketball, 64¾ × 30¾ × 13¼ in. (164.5 × 78.1 × 33.7 cm). Ed. of 2

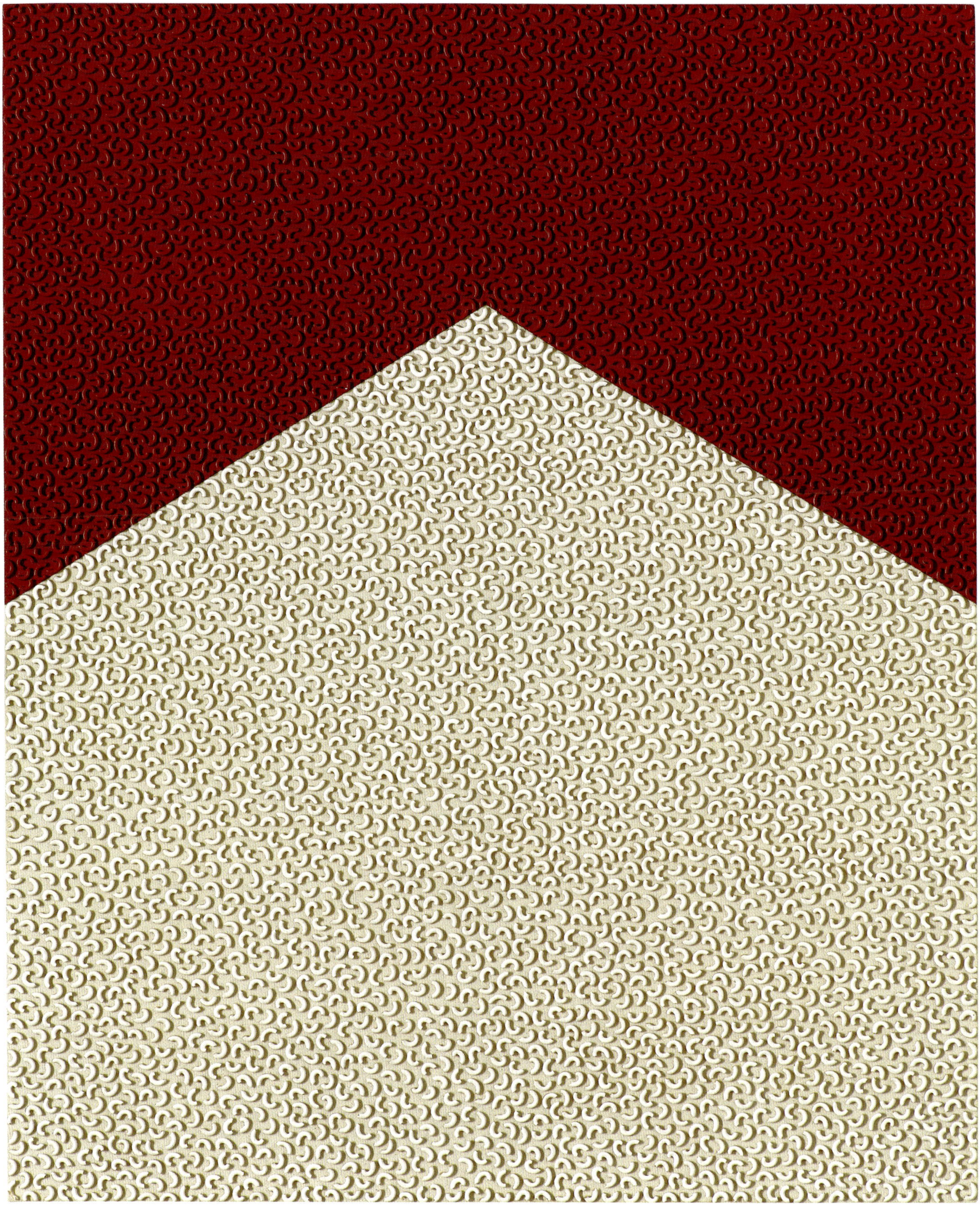

General Idea. *Sans titre (Marlboro)*, from the series ***Pasta Paintings***, 1986–87. Acrylic and dried pasta on canvas, 48 × 40⅛ in. (122 × 102 cm). MUDAM Luxembourg, Musée d'Art Moderne Grand-Duc Jean

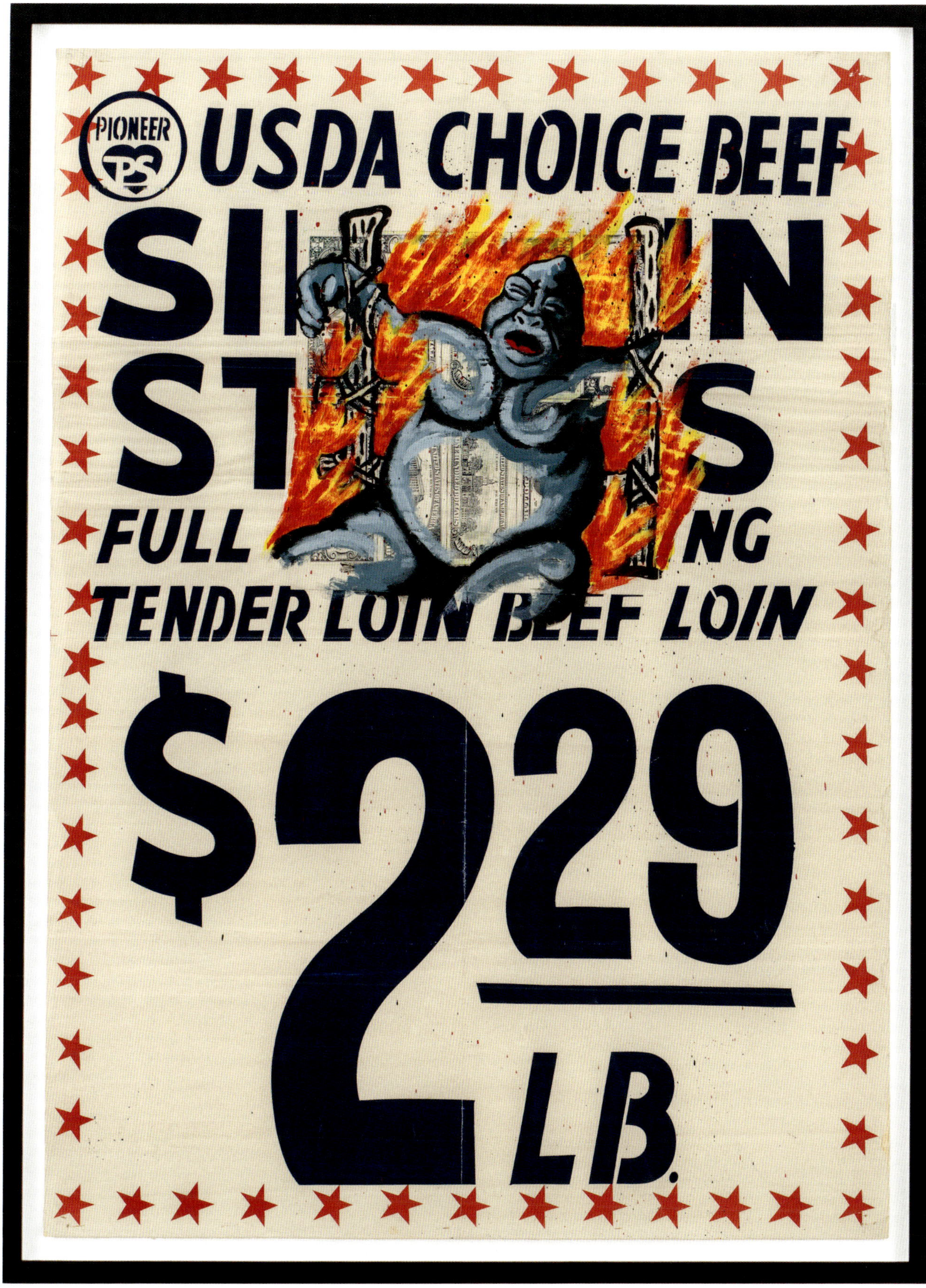

David Wojnarowicz. ***USDA Choice Beef***, 1985. Acrylic on found supermarket poster, 42 × 31½ in. (106.7 × 80 cm). Courtesy of the Estate of David Wojnarowicz and P•P•O•W, New York
Following spread: ***USDA Choice Beef*** (detail)

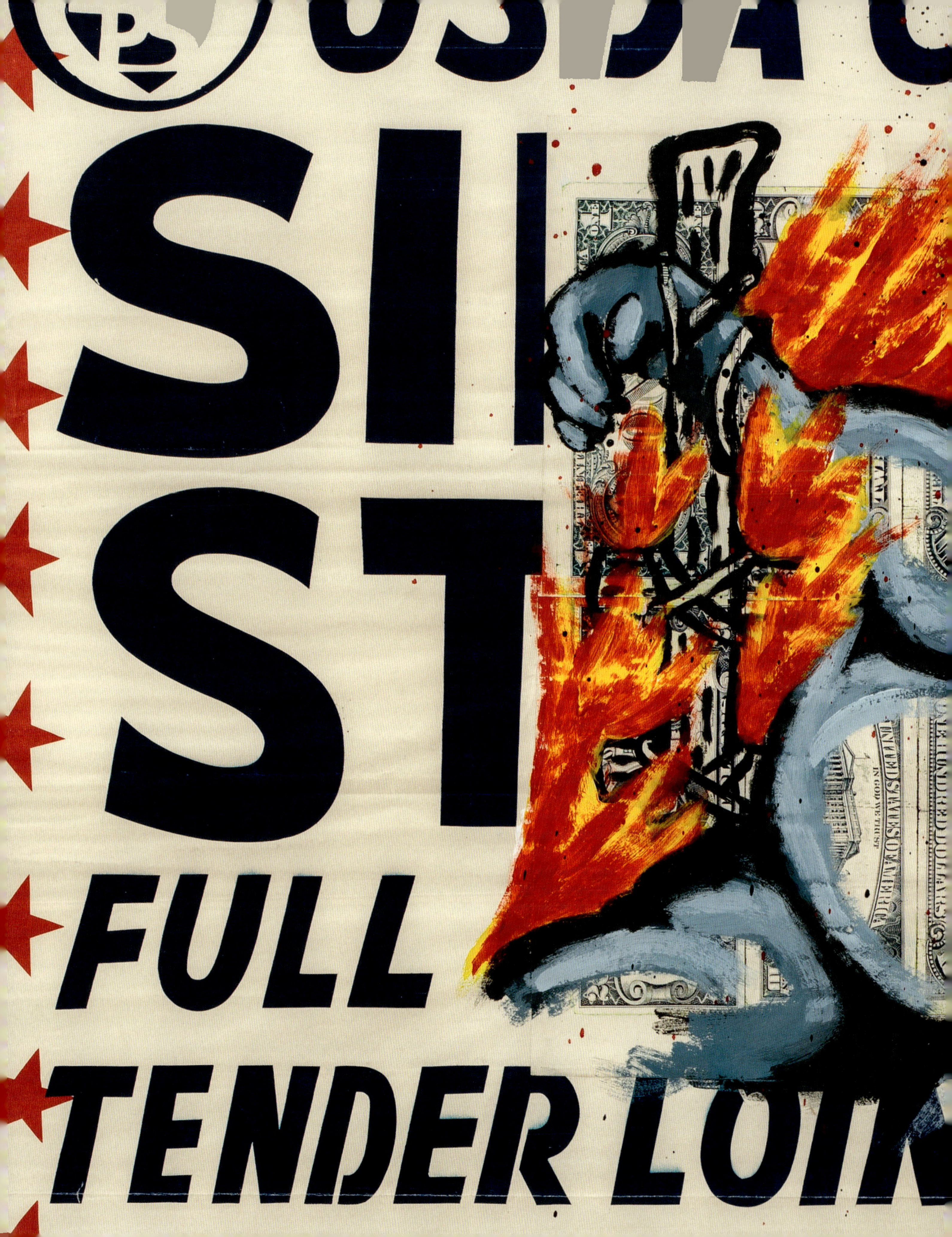
FULL
TENDER

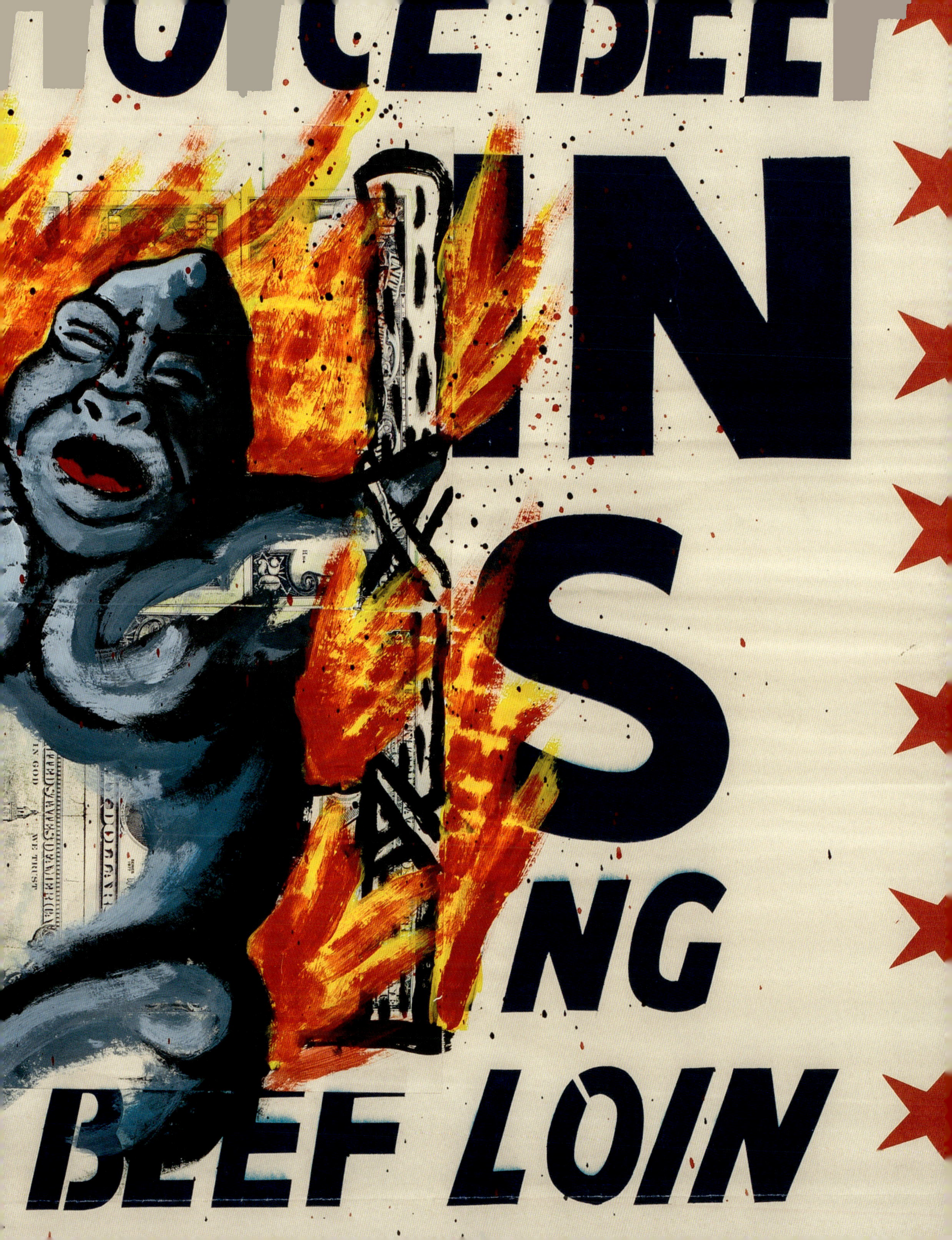
IN
S
NG
BEEF LOIN

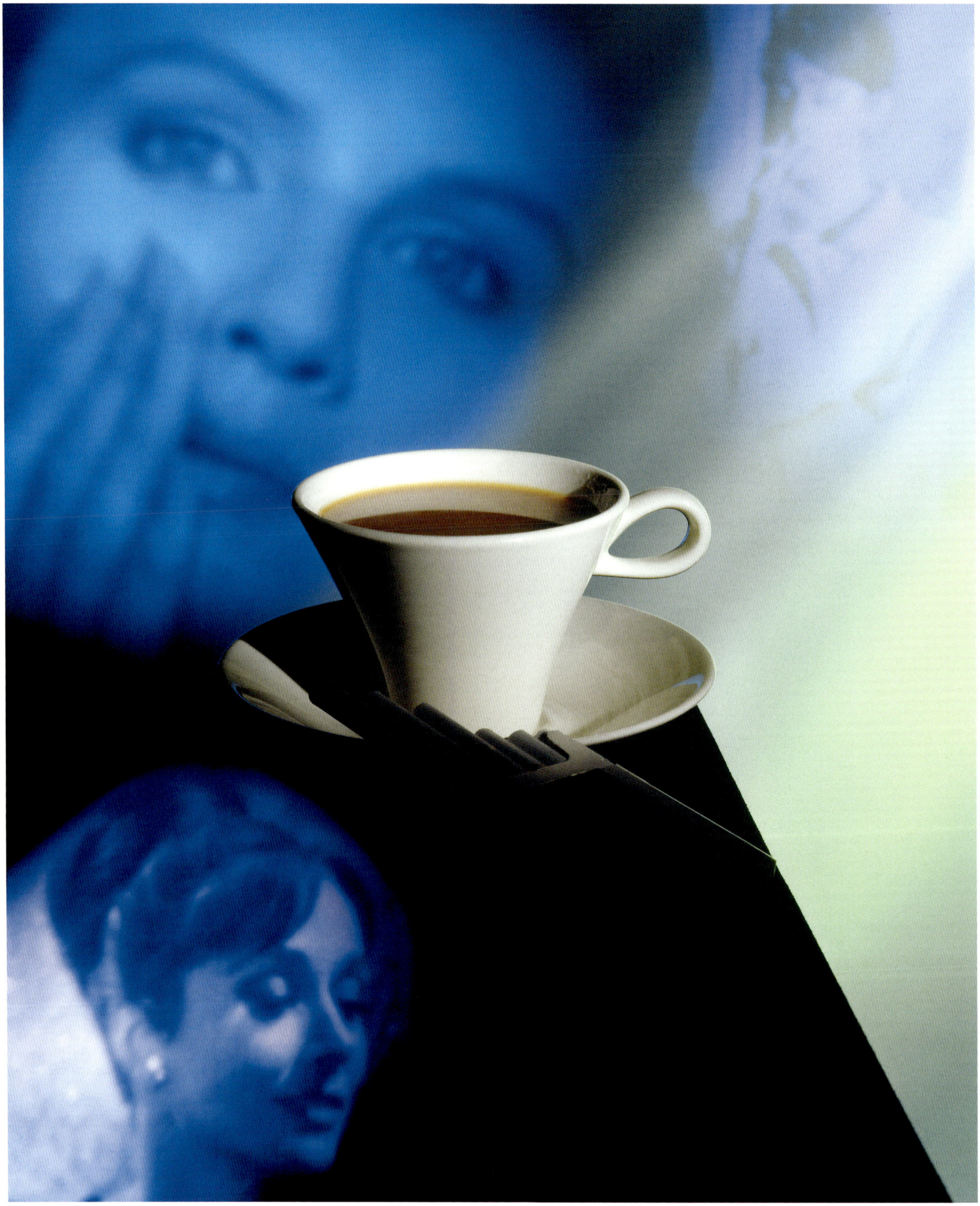

Frank Majore. *Four O'Clock*, 1985. Silver-dye bleach print, 24 × 20 in. (61 × 50.8 cm).
Collection of the artist

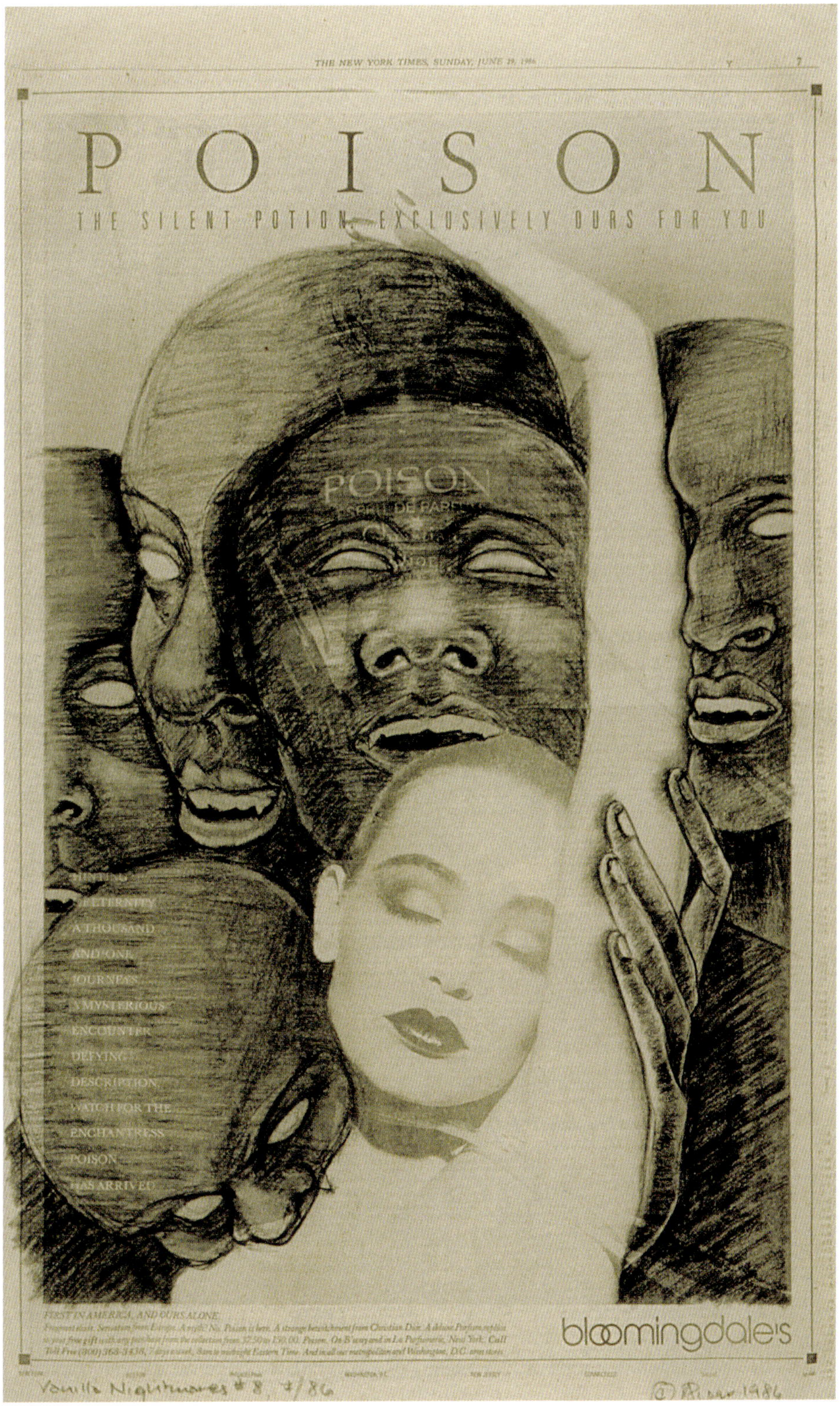

Adrian Piper. ***Vanilla Nightmares #8***, 1986. Charcoal on newspaper, 22 × 14 in. (55.9 × 35.6 cm).
Richard and Ellen Sandor Family Collections, LLC

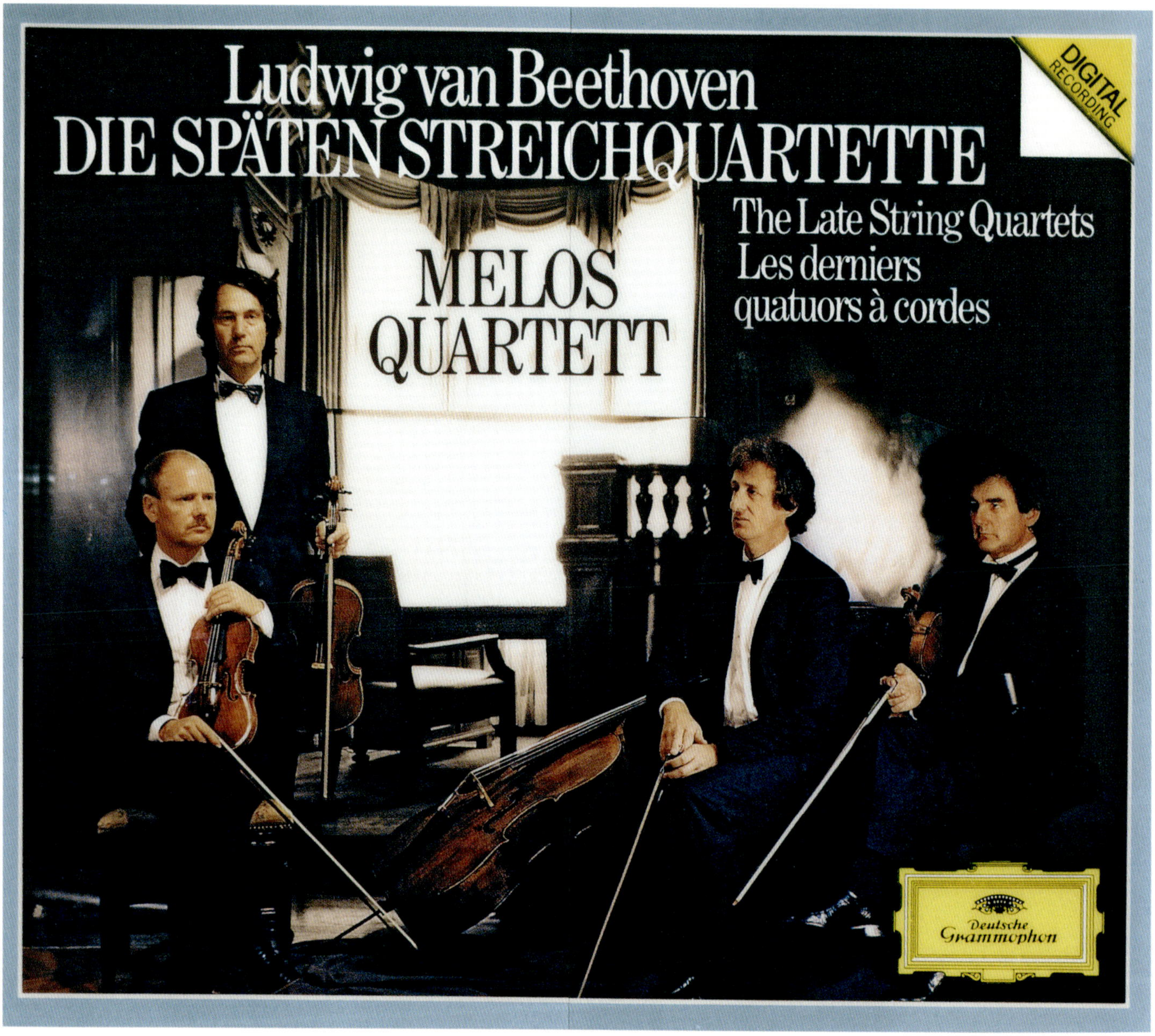

Clegg & Guttmann. ***Our Production, the Production of Others, 1986/2012, CD Cover Version II***, 1986/2012. Chromogenic print (2 panels), overall 91⁵⁄₁₆ × 105½ in. (231.9 × 268 cm). The Metropolitan Museum of Art, New York, Purchase, Vital Projects Fund Inc. Gift, through Joyce and Robert Menschel, 2013

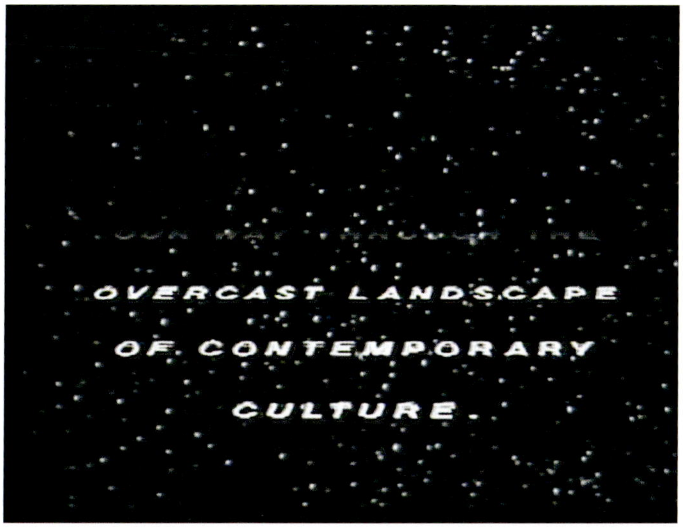

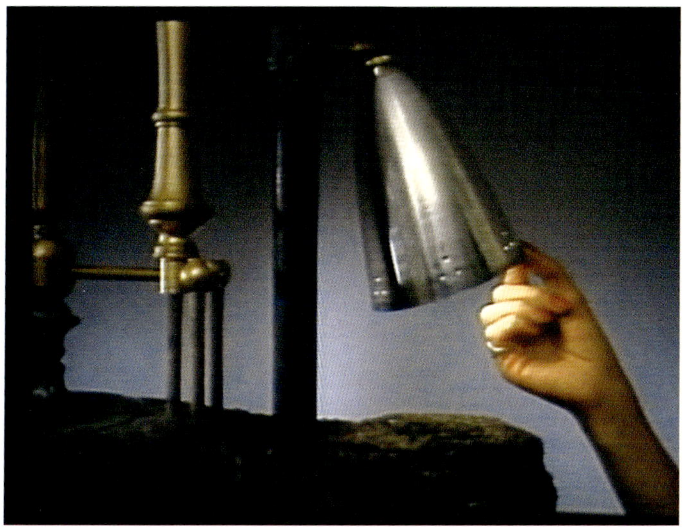

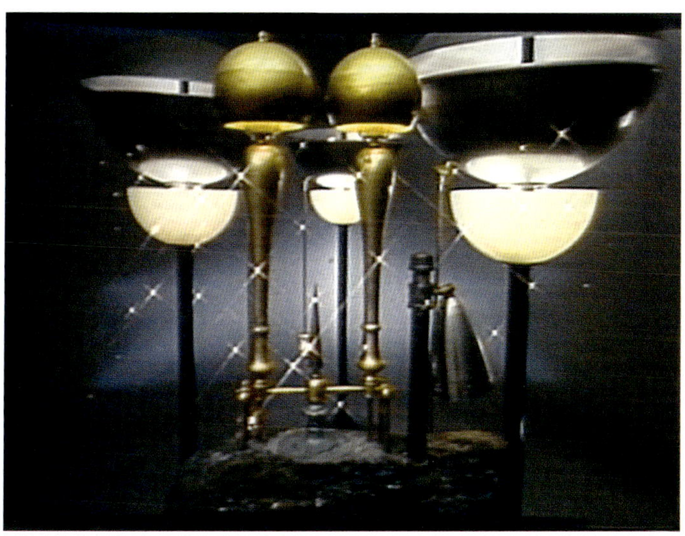

MICA-TV. Stills from ***R. M. Fischer: An Industrial***, 1983. Video, color, sound, 3:30 min.
Courtesy of Electronic Arts Intermix (EAI), New York

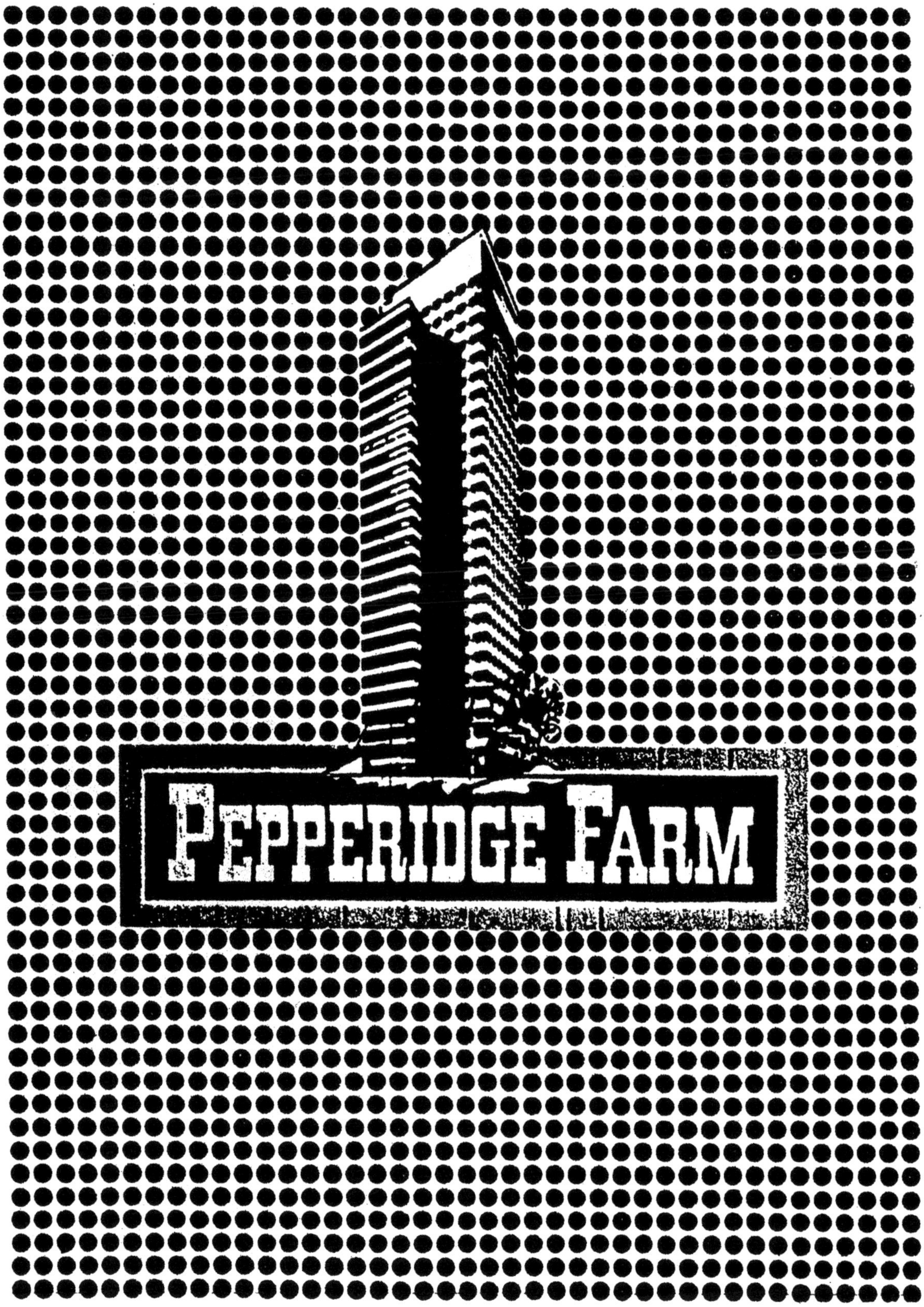

Peter Nagy. *EST Graduate*, 1983. Black-and-white photocopy, dimensions variable.
Courtesy of the artist and Magenta Plains, New York

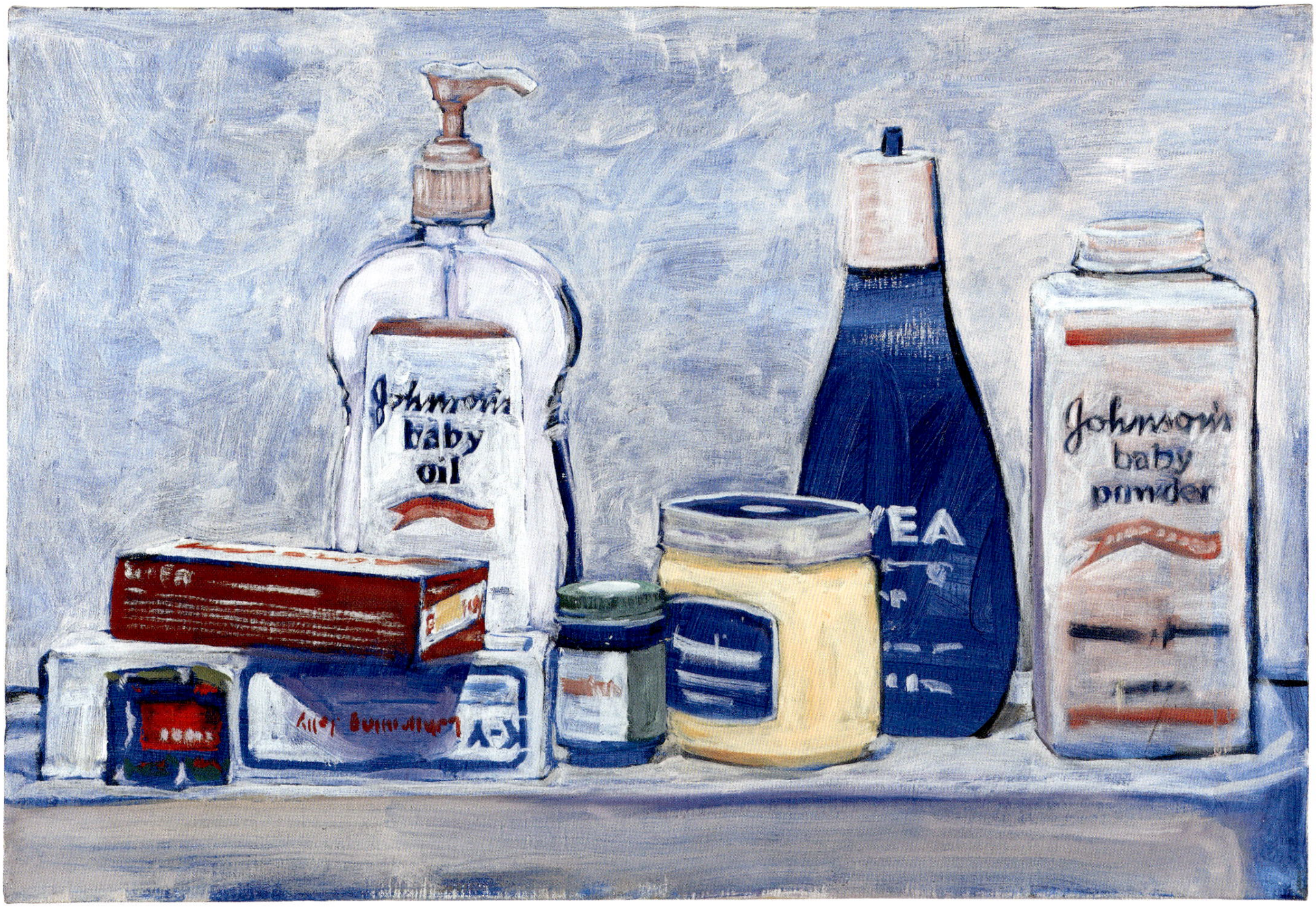

Walter Robinson. *Lube Landscape*, 1985. Acrylic on canvas, 24 × 36 in. (61 × 91.4 cm).
Collection of Gracie Mansion, New York

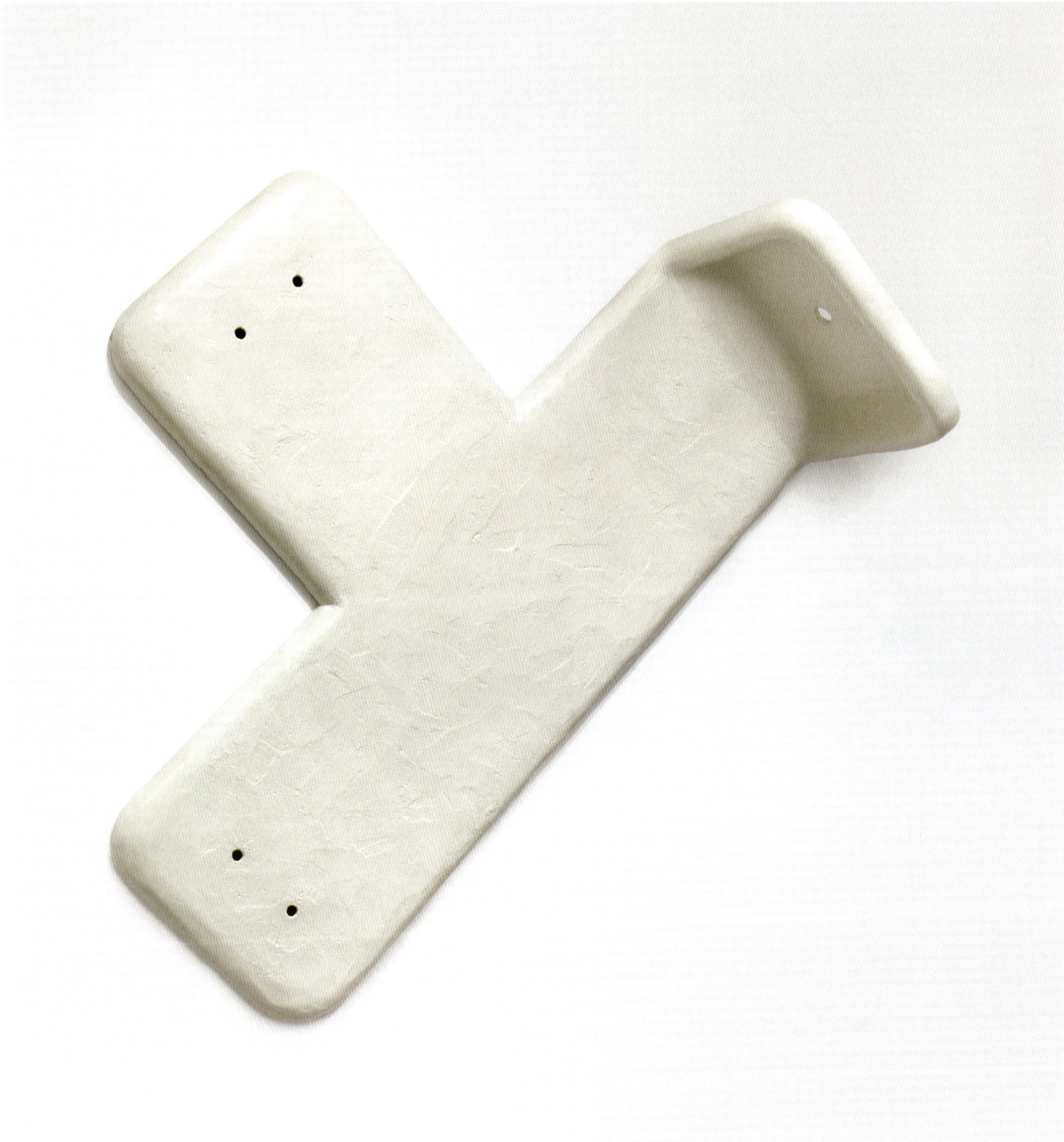

Robert Gober. *Three Parts of an X*, 1985. Plaster, wood, wire lath, steel, semigloss enamel paint, 82 × 82 × 26½ in. (208.3 × 208.3 × 67.3 cm). Hirshhorn Museum and Sculpture Garden, Smithsonian Institution, Washington, DC, Joseph H. Hirshhorn Purchase Fund, 1993

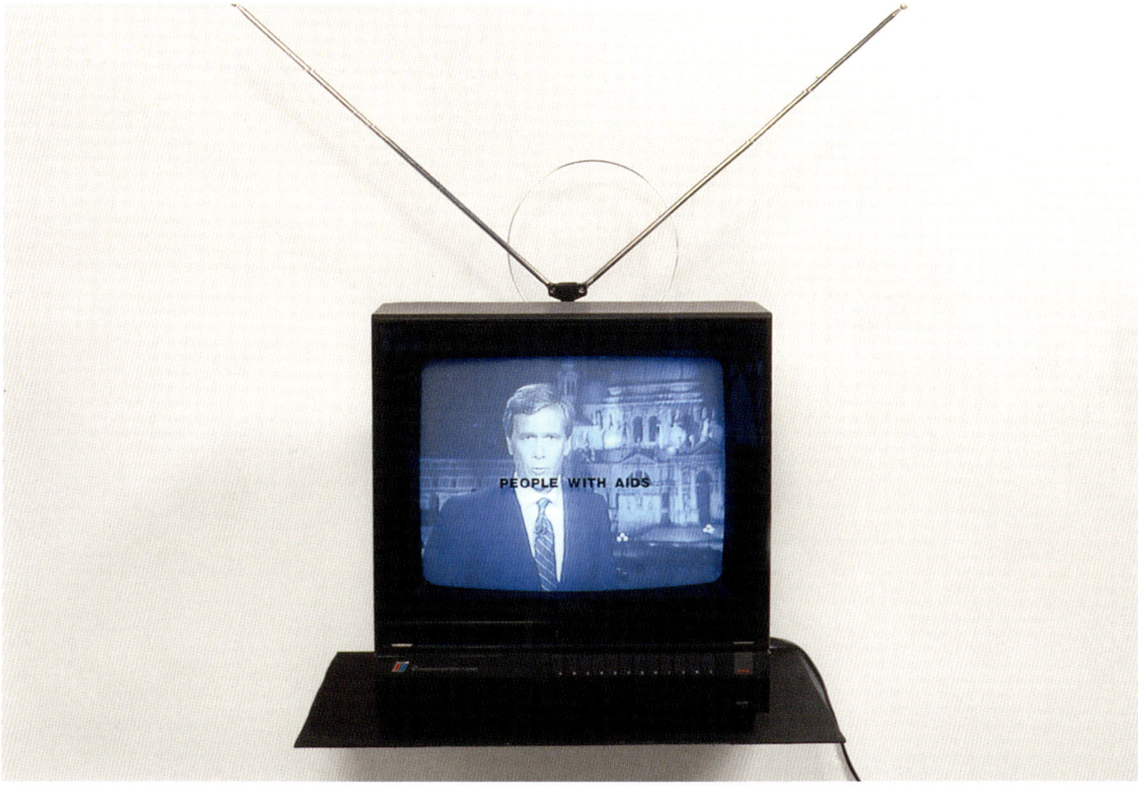

Gretchen Bender. ***Untitled (People with AIDS)***, 1986. Television with live broadcast, vinyl lettering, steel shelf, 20 × 15 × 15 in. (50.8 × 38.1 × 38.1 cm). Courtesy of the Gretchen Bender Estate and OSMOS

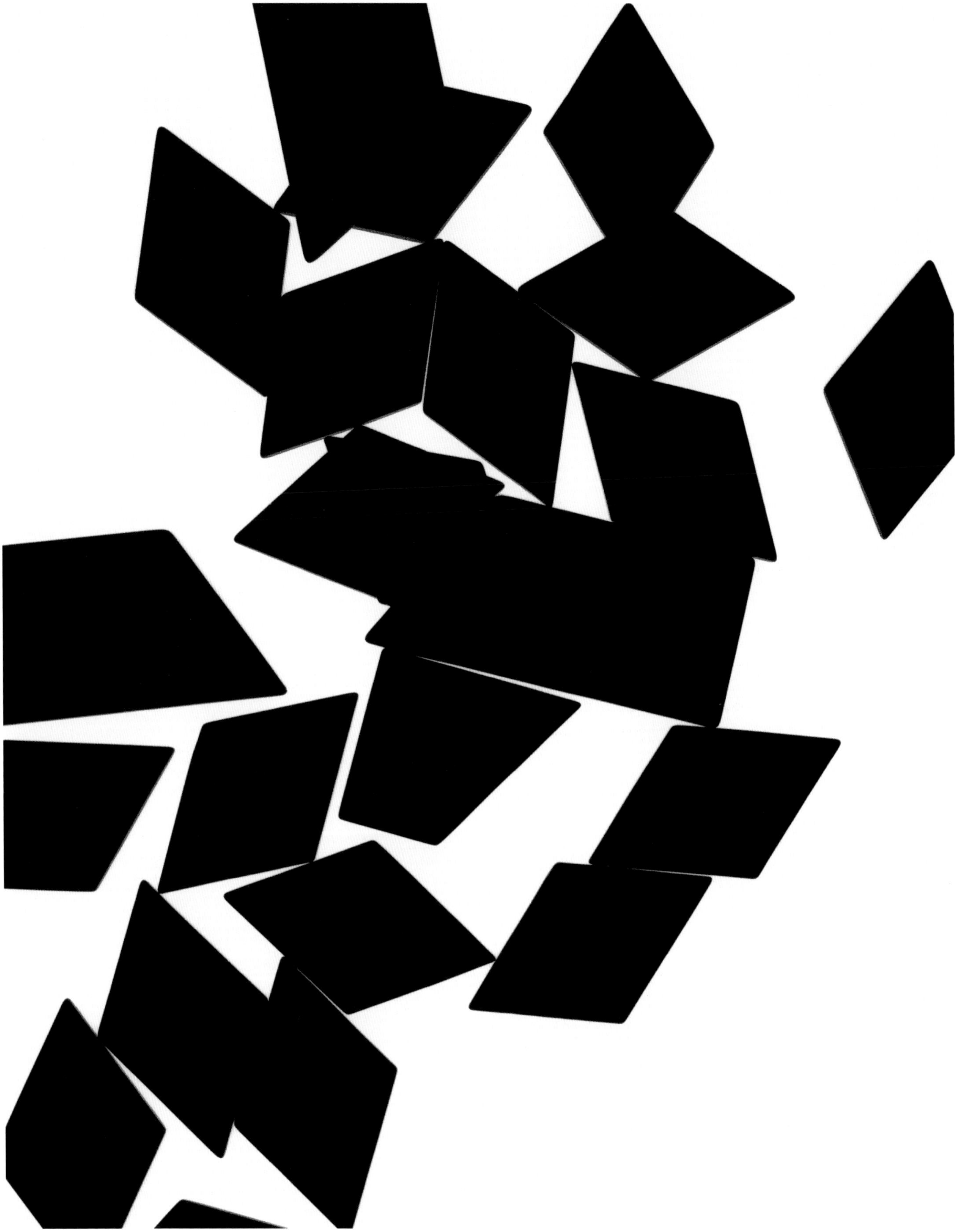

James Welling. ***Tile Photograph 1***, 1985. Vintage gelatin silver print, 20 × 16 in. (50.8 × 40.6 cm). Ed. of 3 with 2 artist's proofs. Courtesy of the artist and David Zwirner, New York/London

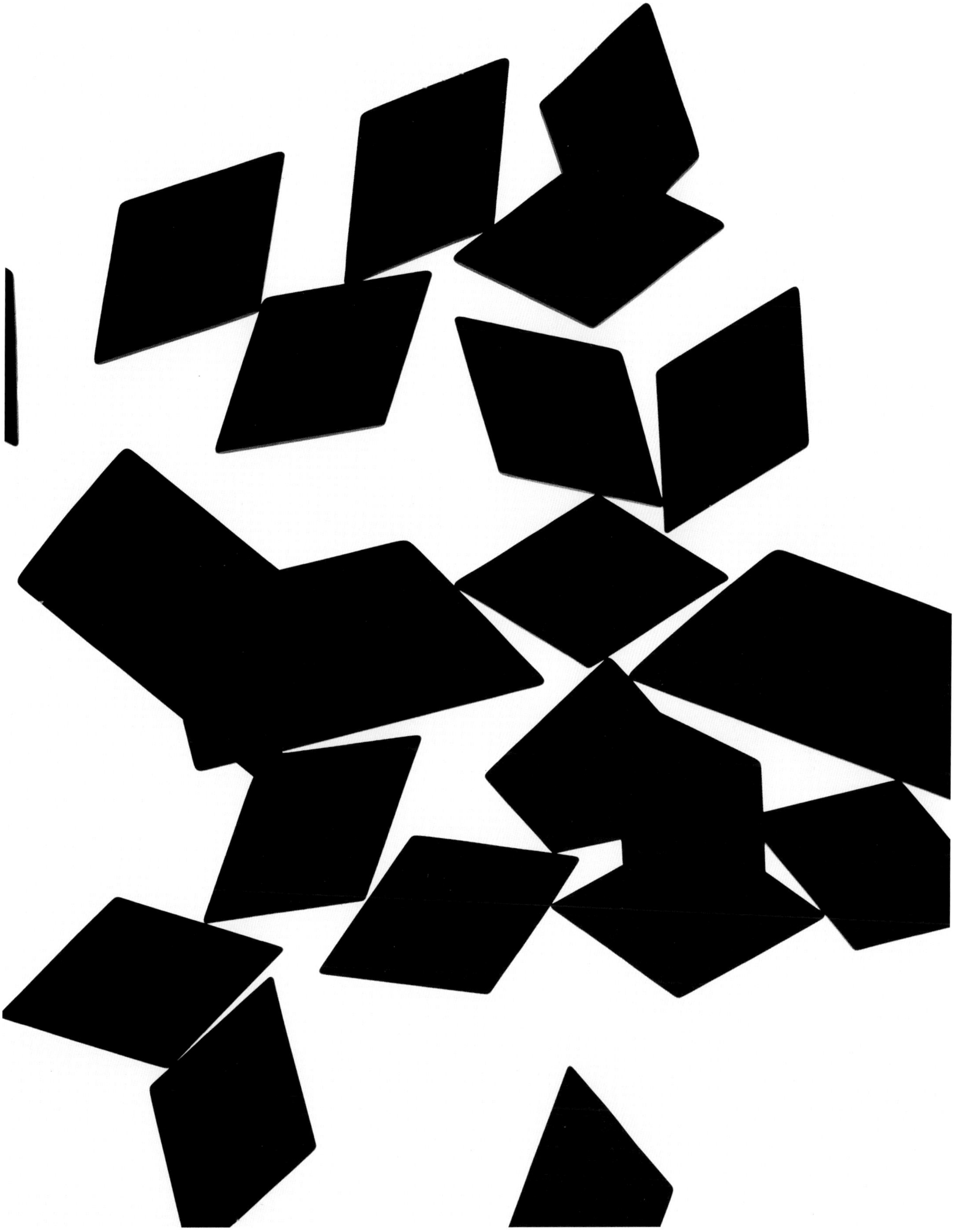

James Welling. ***Tile Photograph 4***, 1985. Vintage gelatin silver print, 20 × 16 in. (50.8 × 40.6 cm). Ed. of 3 with 2 artist's proofs. Courtesy of the artist and David Zwirner, New York/London

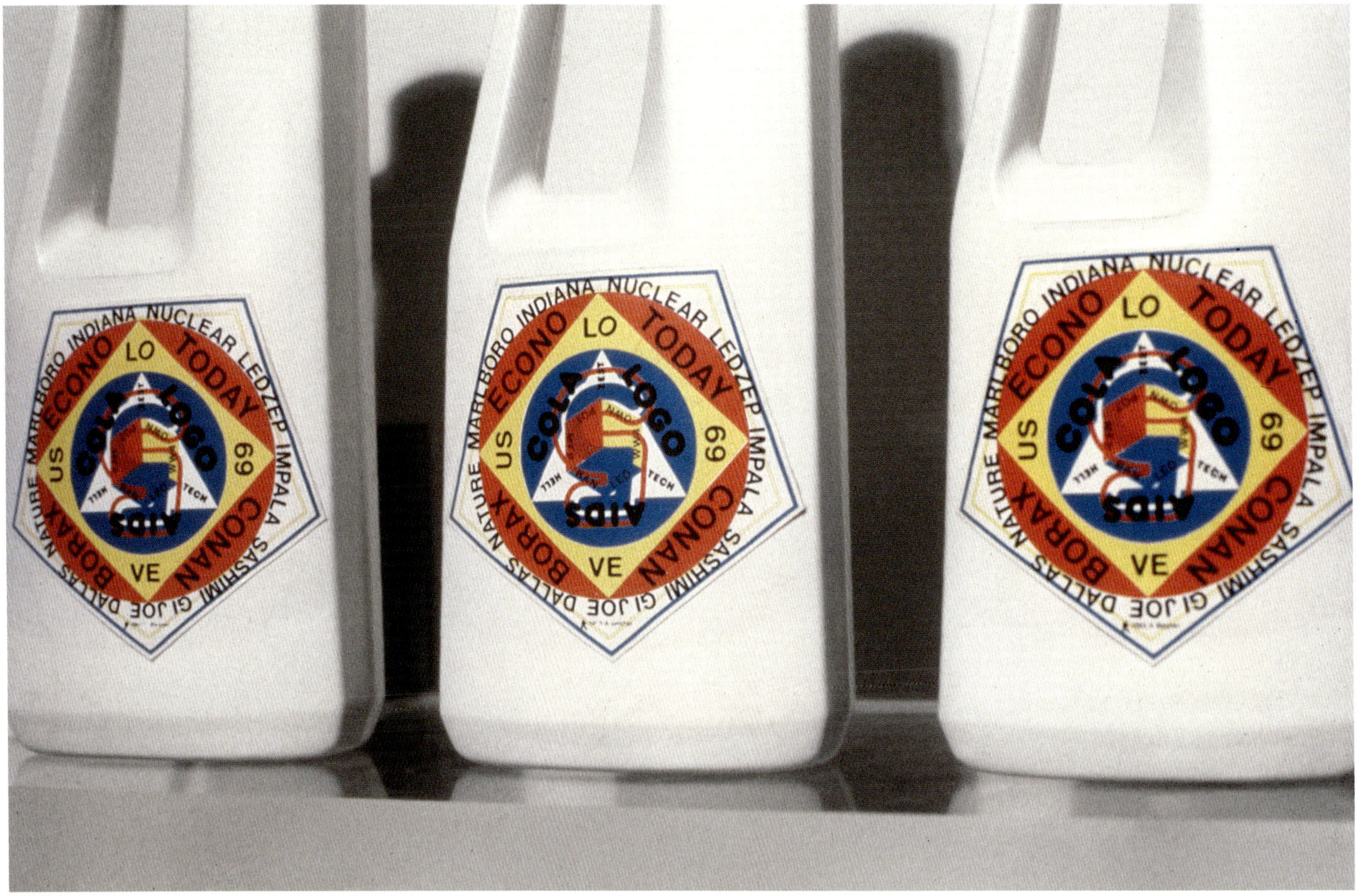

Alan Belcher. *$51.49*, 1983. Dye transfer prints on bottles of Solo fabric softener, each 8¾ × 3¾ × 1⅞ in. (22.2 × 9.5 × 4.8 cm), 16 fl. oz. (473.2 ml). Ed. of 12. Courtesy of the artist

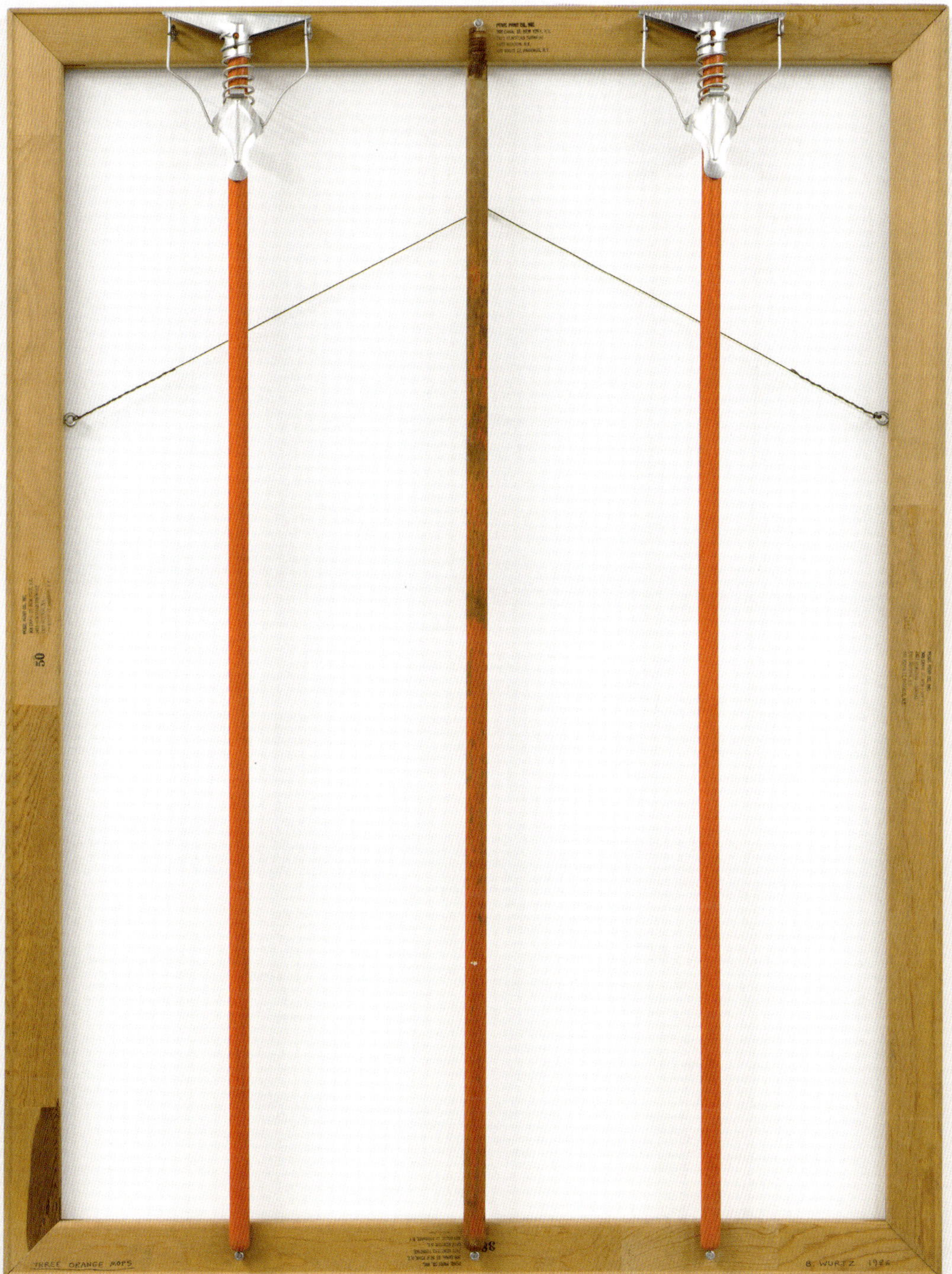

B. Wurtz. *Three Orange Mops*, 1986. Three mops, wood stretcher bars, 50 × 38 × 3 in. (127 × 96.5 × 7.6 cm). Courtesy of Martos Gallery, New York

Trading in Futures

Bob Nickas

Art is a commodity, art criticism is a commodity, the apple is a commodity, the air is a commodity, the ground under our feet is a commodity, God is very much a commodity. My emotions are a commodity, my desires the very locus of commodification. My last illness is a commodity (twenty-two days at so much a day), my grave is a commodity (and not inexpensive). Perhaps it is time, Levine suggests, to stop worrying about art-as-commodity.

So wrote Donald Barthelme in 1987 for the catalogue that accompanied Sherrie Levine's first exhibition with the Mary Boone/Michael Werner Gallery in New York that fall. Barthelme's essay remains one of the best on the artist, quite possibly on account of the fact that he was in no way an academic or an art historian. Rather, he was a master of short stories and fiction, a writer for whom authorship would never be considered elusive. On intimate terms with the sound of his own voice—not merely as a matter of style but as the very articulation of sensibility, of ideas and jokes made visible and playfully rigorous—Barthelme's wry sense of humor was always present, all of which he had in common with the artist. Where rhetoric and theory were concerned, neither had to bother with that sort of *baggage*, of the kind that circles endlessly unclaimed on an airport carousel or would have been, at that time, projected from a slide carousel in a darkened room: art history as bemusement park. In an art market *as serious as a circus*, the remaking of art becomes a veritable guided tour of the Lost and Found.[1] And what exists there, in no short supply? In a word: time. Works of art inevitably come to be seen as markers in time, a fact with which Sherrie Levine was, and is, well acquainted.

Long out of print, the catalogue for this 1987 exhibition is itself a valued commodity. Used copies can be found online for $200. When I remove the volume from my dusty shelf and turn its pages now, one reproduction stands out in greater relief than any other and always will, a testament to both the power of art and the persistence of regret—at the locus of desire. Made by Levine three years earlier and based on a Suprematist painting of the early 1920s by Ilya Chasnik, who had studied with Kazimir Malevich in Moscow, the image of a broad cross emerges from the catalogue page **(fig. 1)**.[2] This is a work I knew at the time it was originally made and shown at Gallery Nature Morte in the East Village, in 1984. The painting was key to an installation that included Levine's group of watercolors *After Egon Schiele* **(fig. 2)**—expressionistic, twisted figures, erotic, emaciated, and in various states of derangement, in stark contrast to the abstractions on view. In addition to the appropriated Chasnik, a hand-painted reproduction of a Malevich work, somewhat lyrical and decorative, completed the ensemble.

I recall the occasion of the show here not only for the particular orchestration of the works—exemplars of Expressionism and Suprematism standing in for 1980s Neo-Expressionism and Neo-Geo—but because I had wanted to buy, or, more accurately, had fantasized about buying, the Levine-Chasnik cross. Far more iconic than that uncharacteristic Malevich, its volume countered the Schiele figures in the undertone of their fragile agitation. As a young person recently moved to New York with no actual job, no reliable income, and having barely set out to become a critic and curator—neither of which would be in any way lucrative (which, with few exceptions, remains the case today)—there was no possibility for me to begin even a modest collection. Also to be considered: the question of whether or not the work would have been sold to me, as works were not so much sold then as *placed*, a strategy that only forestalled the inevitable: some would eventually come back on the market. Despite the lack of pretension encountered in most, though not all, of the East Village galleries, transactions were regulated by terms dating back a century at least. We can only imagine the difference between buying a work in Schiele's time and in Levine's. Would it be noticeable at all? Even if East Tenth and West Fifty-Seventh Streets could be thought to represent accessibility versus exclusivity—Nature Morte was around the corner

Epigraph: Donald Barthelme, "On the Level of Desire," in *Sherrie Levine*, exh. cat. (New York: Mary Boone/Michael Werner, 1987), p. 7.

1 The phrase is borrowed from a 1987 work by Louise Lawler, *As Serious as a Circus*.

2 Levine's choice to base a work of her own on one by Ilya Chasnik (also transliterated as Chashnik) is unexpected, particularly given the high art-historical standing of the artists she made reference to at the time, who, in addition to Malevich, included Constantin Brancusi, Vasily Kandinsky, Joan Miró, and, later, Marcel Duchamp and Man Ray. But exceptional works by Chasnik were exhibited in New York on a number of occasions between 1979 and 1983, and Levine may well have seen the artist's shows at the galleries of Rosa Esman and Leonard Hutton.

3 John Miller, "Morality and the Poetic," in Miriam Katzeff and Thomas Lawson, eds., *REALLIFE Magazine: Selected Writings and Projects 1979-1994* (New York: Primary Information, 2006), p. 176. Miller's text was originally published in a 1984 issue of *REALLIFE*.

from a bodega, while Marian Goodman was a stone's throw from Tiffany & Co.–galleries were, and are, based on a system that prevails no matter how mean or rarefied the streets. Some who opened galleries downtown had been trained uptown, or knew (and parodied) the protocols, while others who began in the East Village would eventually move on to Soho and greater ambition–from playing the part, as it were, to *being*. In fact, if galleries in the East Village were no more than small storefronts with battered trashcans on the sidewalk and passersby noisily rummaging through them–a fresh coat of paint lending respectability, as far as it goes–they would reveal just how contingent the system really is, how galleries, even more than the art they show, are fictions based on a well-staged suspension of disbelief. This would prove to be one of the more valuable, lasting lessons from a time that was, perhaps not coincidentally, marked by strategies of presentation and display, parody and appropriation, all of which fully engaged the legacy of Pop. Every subsequent generation, including today's, has dealt with the unfinished and, frankly, never-to-be-finished business of being *sold to*, where pictures are promises never meant to be kept, where someone always seems to know what we want before we do, and when something better suddenly appears, we don't want it anymore. Every product improving upon those that came before, and only just before, may be understood primarily as an advancement of obsolescence, rarely serendipitous.

If the objects of our affection are infinitely replaceable, this means one thing if we are considering a vacuum cleaner, for example–even one hermetically sealed inside an illuminated plexiglass box–and something else entirely if we regard another person, or ourselves, in this way. Convincing us to trade up for whatever is new and improved, bigger and better, is advertising's task, without necessarily acknowledging that desire and disaffection go hand in hand. Art, in its reflection, may plumb the very depths of these surface effects–a veneer not nearly as believable as the Formica on an Artschwager table–and their undertow. To this end, will the values and the absurdities, the very consciousness of society, be revealed? And what of the unconscious? Do most of us, upon waking, remember our dreams, or do we soon forget? We rise, passing from dream to reality, get dressed, and go to work, not sharing our dreams with anyone, if they are recalled; and when to share them is itself a valuable form of recollection. Is it possible, we still wonder, to be human in an increasingly inhuman world? Surprisingly enough, the art that poses this question is not always, on the face of it, readily identifiable as humanist.

The postmodernism associated with the art of Sherrie Levine and the writing of Donald Barthelme, each having stories to tell while at the same time undermining the very act of storytelling, can be con-

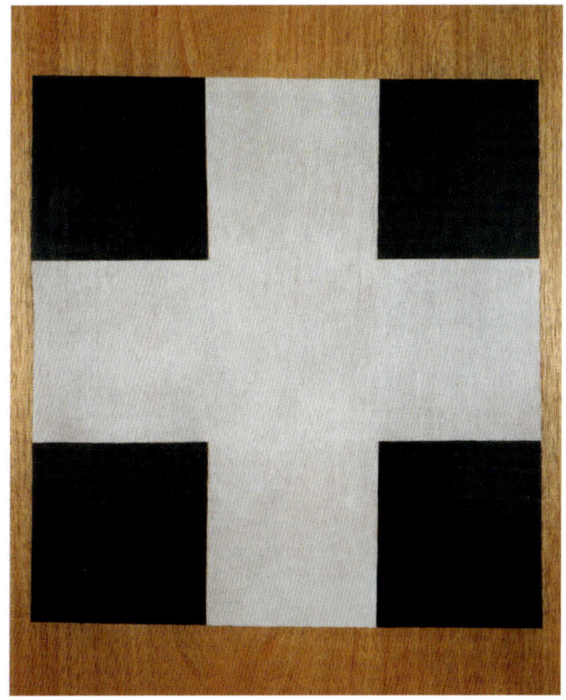

Fig. 1 Sherrie Levine. *After Chasnik*, 1984. Casein and wax on mahogany

sidered in terms of so much unfinished business. When in 1984 the artist and critic John Miller observed that "we are advised to trade in our old world of illusions for a new world of facts," he was not, as might be suspected, writing about "post-time." Rather, he was writing about modernism–specifically, how its scientific aspect served to circumvent the "ambiguous use value of art," how it "evinced a desire to see things without artifice, *to see things as they really are*." Continuing, he observed, "With the proclamation of Post Modernism (a transparent attempt to jump the gun historically) we see a movement no less culpable than its predecessor, but far more willing to skirt the dilemma of history. To derive criticism from this terminology is a typically academic inversion."[3]

In Barthelme's *At the End of the Mechanical Age*, published in 1976, roughly at the midpoint between the 1960s and the 1980s, he refers to "time periods within a period of time." Made in that moment, his formulation may be thought of as a fulcrum upon which these and other decades pivot, pointing to how–rather than finding ourselves at the end of the line, amid some sort of culmination and significant break–the story of art in our time appears more as a seesaw in slow motion than as a precipitous slide. Our "new world of facts" turns out to be an old world of illusions, repackaged. Chief among them is the notion that we have vanquished what came before, even as our very satisfaction reanimates its recognizable contours. As Miller remarked, "Dreams can foretell the future only as they reflect our wishes which, after all, mould it into 'a perfect likeness of the past.'" Or as Barthelme may have noticed, *the end is a commodity*.

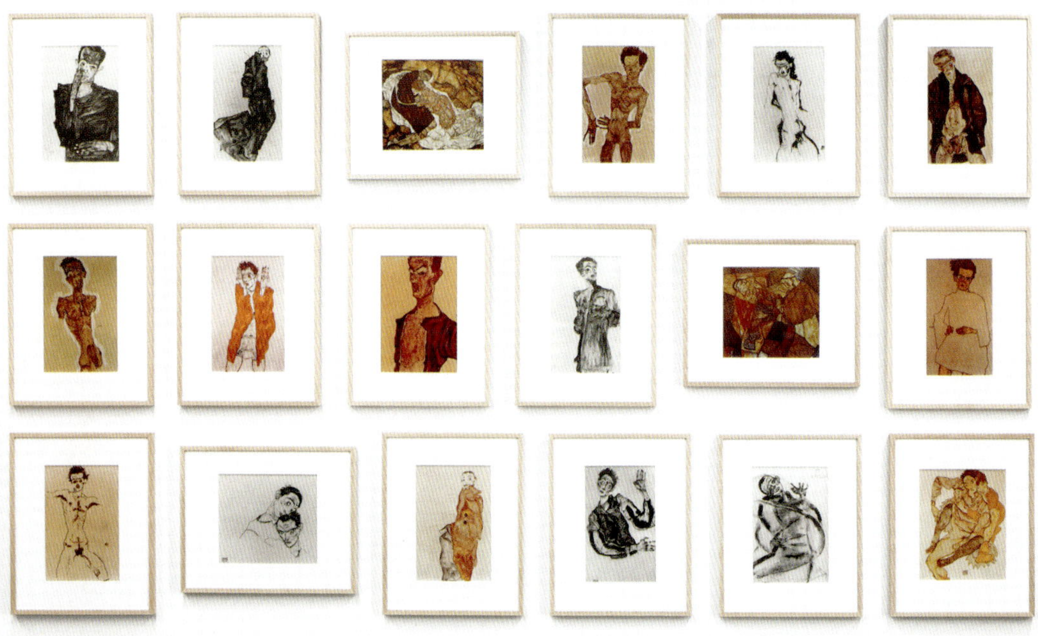

Fig. 2 Sherrie Levine. ***After Egon Schiele*****, 1982. Seven gelatin silver prints and eleven chromogenic prints. Art Institute of Chicago, Through prior bequest of Marion Livingston and prior gift of Emily Crane Chadbourne (2006.1)**

There is, at the risk of sounding facetious, a certainty that we can never be sure if we see things as they really are, let alone in their entirety. Even if all art is made at all times, it is neither possible nor necessarily advantageous for us to acknowledge or deal with it in its moment of creation or reception, because doing so results in a delimited view that allows us to identify only the more dominant tendencies, the repetitions, the copycat paradigms, or whatever in any moment is chosen to be illuminated, placed within the beacon of attention.

Accounting for reactionary turns–for instance, the valuation of and subsequent dispensing with craftsmanship, or the predictable fatigue that eventually greets whatever is on offer and has been consumed–we may propose that the age of mechanical reproduction was followed by a return to manual production, as if the body of art had a "retractable hand," which was followed by a renewed taste for mechanical reproduction, and so on. Andy Warhol, Neo-Pop's father figure, never wanted to be a machine (wasn't his silkscreening done by hand?). Rather, he strove to be human and, as a way to protect himself from rejection, feigned indifference. Having absorbed all that came before, Neo-Pop understood these contradictions. For, in the briefest of shorthand, a succession of periods in art may also be characterized as shifting focus from the individual to the culture, from inward to outward points of view: the Abstract Expressionist 1950s and the post-studio 1960s; the "individual mythologies" of the 1970s and the wider narrative of the 1980s; the identity politics of the 1990s and wherever we are now and wherever we may be headed, which is anyone's guess.[4] Art, having grown so large in recent years–already suffering from gigantism, more of it everywhere, and more co-opted than at any moment in history–is now, if not identity-less, then that much harder to discern, its defining features indistinct. Anything goes has won the day, if winning, in scare quotes, even matters in a game consisting almost entirely of extra innings.

The 1986 museum exhibition *Endgame: Reference and Simulation in Recent Painting and Sculpture*, which was at that time meant to be definitive, cleverly sat us before a chessboard, with Marcel Duchamp hovering above and a certain French philosopher, no longer au courant, voyeuristically not far off. Looking at the catalogue now, it's worth noting that the contributing writers, rather than the artists whose works were shown, are listed on the front cover **(fig. 3)**, a small clue to what awaits inside. In fact, the names of the artists are not even to be found on the title page.[5] Two of the essays go so far as to summarily dismiss the artists: Peter Halley and Philip Taaffe are referred to, awkwardly, as "manic mourners," and the mourning as "pathological." This is, quite possibly, the only instance of a museum's elevating artists by exhibiting their work while simultaneously allowing it to be undermined in print. The curator's essay, "The Last Picture Show," reminds us not so much of endgame strategies and appropriation as it does of Ad Reinhardt's black paintings and his remark "I'm merely making the last painting which anyone can make."[6] Since Reinhardt–or, as Reinhardt himself might have said, since Malevich–hasn't every painting been

4 "Individual Mythologies" was the theme of one section of Documenta 5. Organized by Harald Szeemann in 1972, the exhibition was criticized on both the left and the right, even by some of the participating artists, who protested that their works were used to illustrate "misguided sociological principles and categories of art history." See the letter published in the *Frankfurter Allgemeine Zeitung*, May 12, 1972.

5 *Endgame: Reference and Painting in Recent Sculpture*, organized by Elisabeth Sussman, David Joselit, and Bob Riley, was presented at the Institute of Contemporary Art, Boston, from September 25 through November 30, 1986. In addition to an essay by each of the curators, the catalogue features contributions by Yve-Alain Bois, Thomas Crow, and Hal Foster.

6 Bruce Glaser, "An Interview with Ad Reinhardt," *Art International*, Winter 1966–67, reprinted in Barbara Rose, ed., *Art-As-Art: The Selected Writings of Ad Reinhardt* (New York: Viking Press, 1975), p. 13.

penultimate, the next to last? A half century after Reinhardt, we look around, and what do we see? As one moment is passing and another is becoming, how does it feel to be in *the same moment*? In the present, of course, it is always too soon to tell, and yet it has been the present for quite a while now. Or has it been the future after all? Busying ourselves in the day-to-day, our world appearing to revolve around so much busywork, we had not even noticed its arrival. Futures and pasts, *time periods within a period of time*, which Barthelme himself could not have foreseen, are a vacuum of another sort entirely. It may be that the discourse of the 1980s allows for just this sort of reflection, demented though it seems.

Art and Its Double

November 1986: a lively dinner with Jeff Koons, the collectors Don and Mera Rubell, the critic Gary Indiana, and the editor and publisher of *Flash Art*, among many others gathered in a restaurant in Barcelona after the opening of Dan Cameron's exhibition *Art and Its Double* (see fig. 4). Intensely focused, speaking in a calm, measured tone–almost as if to children–Koons is explaining his work, and everyone appears rapt as he makes one claim after another, each more fanciful and hyperbolic, forging onward despite occasionally contradicting his own looping logic. Having made two mutually exclusive and rather grand claims for his work, he is interrupted midsentence by a writer at his side. Asked how it is that both claims are possible, Koons stops, seems to consider the question thoughtfully, a nanosecond of introspection, and then, his face brightening, picks up exactly where he'd left off, as if a tape that was playing had only momentarily been paused. A *Stepford Wives* moment to be sure, equally impressive and scary: the artist and his double, one and the same, trancelike, programmed, unshakable, determined to "make the sale."

Koons, who is often described as a former Wall Street commodities broker (although the accuracy of that has been questioned) and who once sold memberships at MoMA, was now signing up members of his own, selling himself. The more ambitious artists have always done this, but Koons was operating on a very different register, palpable and distant; it was, in a word, post-human. He delivered a monologue with near-religious conviction, and although art requires true believers as much as it needs skeptics–as Koons knows so well–reason clearly had no place at this table. Having been dismissed, perhaps that writer, possibly for the first time, felt excluded, not only from the conversation but from his own reason for being. Back in the mid-1980s, critics, curators, and art magazines were not yet irrelevant, at least not entirely. They had always served as

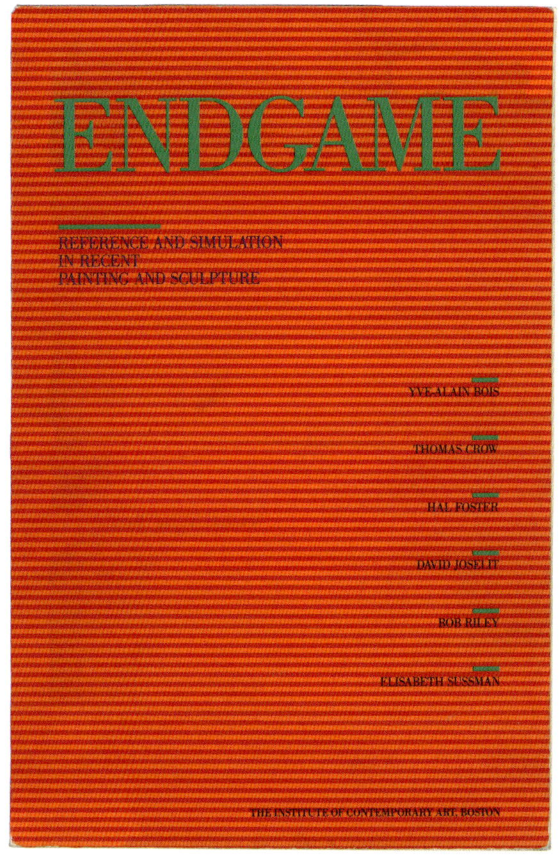

Fig. 3 Cover of exhibition catalogue for ***Endgame: Reference and Simulation in Recent Painting and Sculpture,*** published by Institute of Contemporary Art, Boston, and MIT Press, Cambridge, MA, 1986

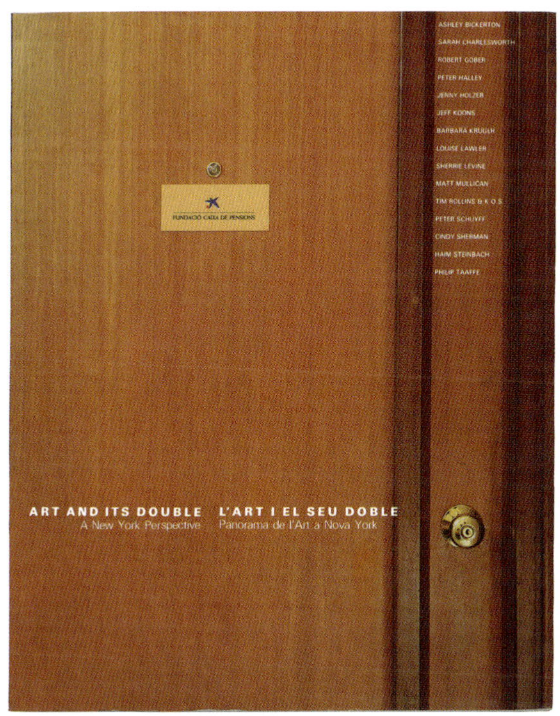

Fig. 4 Cover of exhibition catalogue for ***Art and Its Double: A New York Perspective,*** published by Fundació Caixa de Pensions, Barcelona, 1986

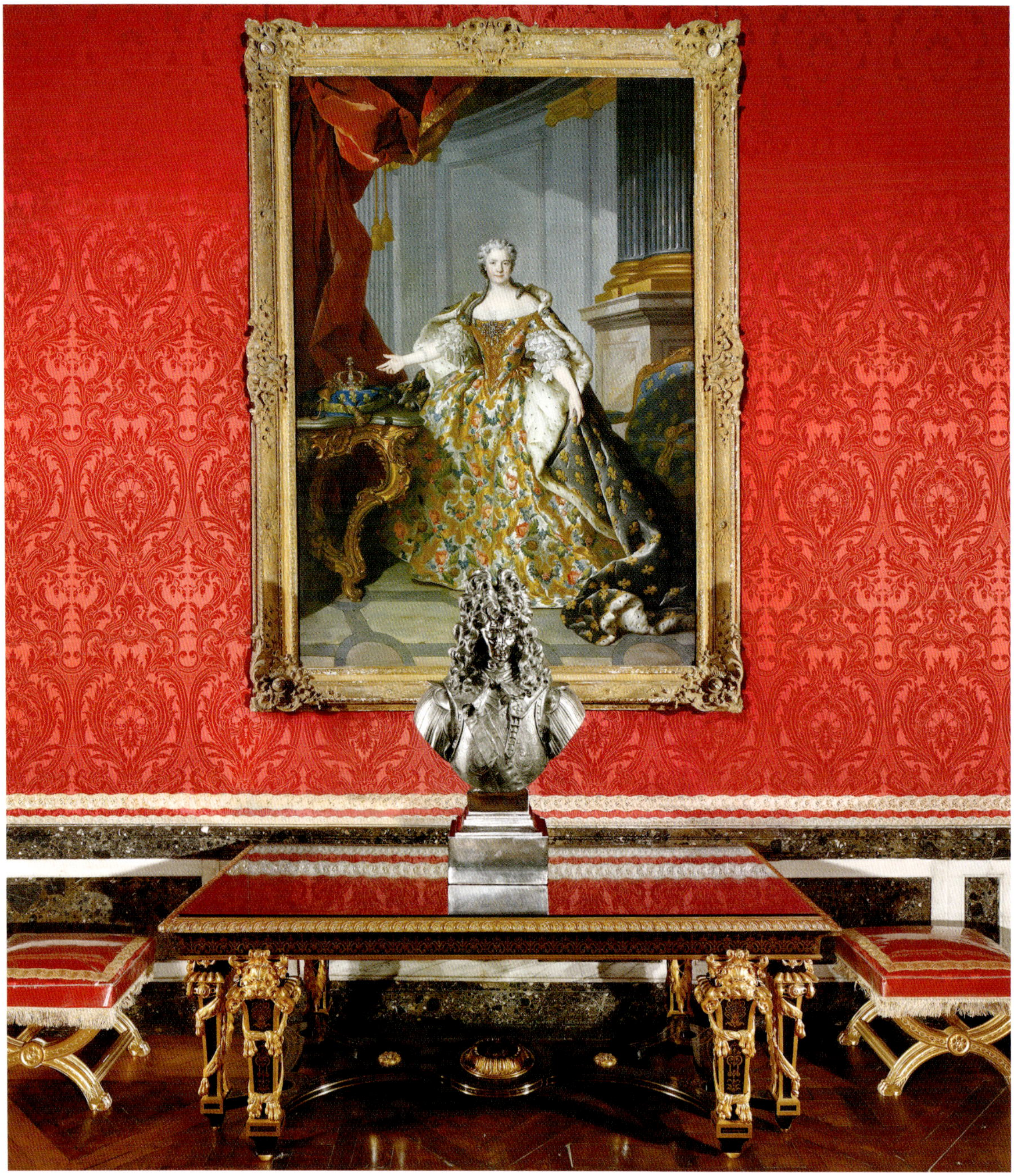

Fig. 5 Jeff Koons. *Louis XIV*, 1986. Stainless steel. Installation view before Louis Tocqué's 1740 portrait of Marie Leszczyńska, Queen of France, *Jeff Koons Versailles*, Château de Versailles, 2008–9

promoters and detractors of the new—since Pop, there had been no such thing as bad publicity—but what critic or curator wanted to be reduced to a publicist, though not nearly as well paid? Was that 1986 dinner a symbolic point of departure? For criticality, for the curator as the artist's defender, for the critic as art's barometer? And how do we take the temperature when it is tepid but claimed to be hot? Is art criticism a healthy skepticism, guarding against unbridled enthusiasm? And now? Is it good-bye to all that? The exhibition, *Art and Its Double*, was timely and well done. In his naming of it, Cameron's canny construction spoke volumes, accounting for both that period's appropriative gestures and the fluidity of roles: artists-as-critics, critics-as-curators, curators-as-collectors, collectors-as-dealers (Charles Saatchi had lent numerous works to the show), double agents one and all. If the art world can be thought to have become, from that point onward, a funhouse hall of mirrors, it is no wonder that Koons ended up at Versailles twenty years later.[7] There could be no greater backdrop for his crowning moment—his trophies and baubles, such as *Louis XIV* (1986) **(fig. 5)** and *Michael Jackson and Bubbles* (1988), merging almost imperceptibly with the ornate rooms of the palace.

7 Charles Saatchi, then known solely as a collector of contemporary art, had lent works by Robert Gober, Jeff Koons, Peter Schuyff, Haim Steinbach, and Philip Taaffe.

8 Jack Goldstein, "Untitled," in Yves Aupetitallot and Lionel Bovier, eds., *Jack Goldstein*, exh. cat. (Grenoble: Le Magasin-Centre National d'Art Contemporain, 2002), p. 88. Originally published in the catalogue for Documenta 7, 1982.

9 Originally published in 1970 by the New York Cultural Center, in association with Fairleigh Dickinson University, the booklet was reprinted by Edition Taube in 2011, at the initiative of John Beeson, who also edited it.

Where the curator-as-collector is concerned, whether real or imagined, had I been able to purchase just one work from each show seen and admired in those exhilarating days, or if my curatorial colleagues in museums had done so, entire galleries devoted to the decade would have been established long ago. But in large part, as has been revealed, theirs were *eyes wide shut*. The art of the 1980s, a period now entering into history, was passed over by most American museums in its time and in the years that followed—for a whole host of reasons, some obviously practical (prices rise and material becomes scarce), others moralistic (the work's value was dubious then, with doubts only recently lifting)—and is still to this very day. In this regard, we are reminded that American institutions were resistant to Pop when it first appeared in the 1960s, that the readymade was less an object of desire than one of derision, and that, with the conceptual art that followed in the late 1960s and early 1970s, the supposedly dematerialized object of art was resistant to being collected.

At first, Neo-Pop—quite possibly the only *neo* that made any sense in a time when the proliferation of such labels laid bare the marketing of "postmovement" art—would fare no better, nor would what was dismissed as "shopper's art." It is worth noting as well that to sell a photograph of a photograph in the early 1980s was potentially as difficult as trying to sell an original print by a photographer whose reputation had been established decades prior. (Oddly enough, what would jump-start the market for photographs in contemporary art were Cindy Sherman's black-and-white "stills" from nonexistent films that seemed to be from the past, works through which the artist Jack Goldstein's aphorism continues to resonate: "Art should be a trailer for the future."[8] But it is also the case that Koons's inkjet prints on canvas, the *Made in Heaven* faux-porn series, allowed photography to occupy a space of importance that painting had traditionally held.) A coming together of Neo-Pop, assisted readymades, object-type painting, object-type photography, camera works, and a Pop-inflected Minimalism (that actually manifested theatricality) would be filtered through an idea-driven, mischievous sensibility—a conceptualism made visible, often with an irreverent sense of humor. This was a heady mix, and it was not necessarily for everyone. Looking back now, what is to be admired in that moment is the openness and discernment of the collectors who did step forward, some of whom had lived through the 1960s and were able to identify parallels between the art and artists of that time and what followed twenty years later, the business unfinished.

Gene Schwartz stands out among them. A collector of Stella and Warhol, he had been, in the mid-1960s, one of the few enthusiastic supporters of the proto-appropriationist Elaine Sturtevant, and his openness to the work of Sherrie Levine and Philip Taaffe in the mid-1980s was no surprise. When he organized the exhibition *Post-Abstract Abstraction* at the Aldrich Museum of Contemporary Art in 1987, those artists were present, along with Peter Halley, Jeff Koons, Mark Stahl, Haim Steinbach, Meyer Vaisman, Julia Wachtel, and B. Wurtz (a particularly prescient inclusion). Seventeen years earlier, Schwartz had written what may be best described as a how-to-collect-art book that in many ways illuminates his enthusiasm. Published in 1970 but not well known until fairly recently, *Confessions of a Poor Collector: How to Build a Worthwhile Art Collection with the Least Possible Money* begins:

> A. The art of our time is possibly as great as that of any period in history.
> B. Therefore, to collect this art is to collect both greatness and immortality.
> C. Therefore, the only thing about this art, as any art, is the art itself. Not its monetary value, not its social prestige, not its public relations leverage, not the artists themselves, and not the fact that you collected them first. The only thing that counts—the only prize in the game—is who ends up with the paintings.[9]

Schwartz, who had established himself as a copywriter specializing in direct-mail advertising and had written the marketing classic *Breakthrough Advertising* (1966), goes on to detail his philosophy and the process of collecting in his *Confessions*. In sections such as "How to Get Started"—"You start by collecting *books* on works of art"—and "How to Let the Art World Itself Tell You What Paintings to Buy" (his use of "paintings" throughout the text is shorthand for "art"), he asserts that critics, artists, and curators, "all of whom have no money," are among the first to recognize which art will enter into history. Schwartz's observations made in 1970 were entirely resonant in the 1980s and, even factoring in market shifts across more than forty years, still echo to this day. He recommends, for example, that "every time an artist goes wild with anger about another artist, go see him. (This also holds with critics.)" His advice would have served anyone warily curious about Koons's work early on. Remembered by all who encountered him as ever smiling, friendly, and enthusiastic, Schwartz notes in the section "How to Pay the Dealer," "Most collectors practice being cool. They are so cool you can't imagine them going to bed with their own spouses. So, if you're a little warm, you'll stand out." In buying works without haggling over price or ever missing a payment, in expressing interest in older (and unsold) works that are in the gallery inventory or may have been in the dealer's home, he observes, "You help this dealer recognize you, like you, think of you as a resource person for tomorrow." But he also suggests: "Spend more money than you've got. It will make you work harder to earn it." Here, however, his advice collides with a disconcerting reality of the present. Today, more often than not, collectors buy art to be resold, and with the profit they hope to earn, they buy more. In all this buying and selling, they are not actually collecting but leveraging, and in using one artist's work to pay for that of another, they buy but do not pay for the art. Each artist pays for the next.

Gene Schwartz didn't live to see the turnaround time between owning and selling works of art whittled down to mere months, but he did witness the excess of the late 1980s and may have sensed the inevitability of this bad behavior. In a 1991 interview, he wryly remarked, "Collecting is the only socially commendable form of greed." As antiquated and naive as it may sound to the buyers and sellers of today–who would be incredulous to learn how much valuable art he and his wife, Barbara, gave away to museums–the advice offered in his little how-to book resounds still: "You have an opportunity to spend your lifetime with some of the most beautiful and ennobling works of man." Those collectors who embraced the art of their time, who held on to it and eventually donated it to institutions, offer an example for our own time. Works were not routinely bought to be auctioned off before the signature on the check had even dried. This is a phenomenon of the twenty-first century, and against it the so-called Big Bad Eighties do not seem to have been so predatorily speculative after all, bearing scant if any comparison to how professional and well oiled the present appears. As Barthelme himself might have said, *the past is a commodity*, and it may come back to haunt us in a way we never expected: as an indictment of the present.

Our Cross to Bear

The art of the mid- to late 1980s had its connections both to art history–to its supposed "rupture"–and to the larger culture, an increasingly image-driven world in which, pre-internet, artists continued to occupy a relevant position as producers and interrogators of visual information, while critics and curators remained essential to the framing of its reception. In a period before the art fair obsession, before works of art became props in a larger, alienating and desultory, spectacle, the gallery was still the stage on which art performed, and those who presented the art were themselves artists, individuals who had come from the worlds of film, theater, and performance (what was a well-cut suit on a younger gallery owner but establishment drag?). The exhibitions were a changing backdrop against which these individuals performed. In the East Village, there was still fun to be had. Peter Nagy, who opened Gallery Nature Morte with Alan Belcher in 1982 (both were artists who showed elsewhere), remarked that in the late 1970s, there were nightclubs, while in the early 1980s, galleries served as "dayclubs."[10]

In recognizing how many of these galleries were artist-run–the artist as art dealer, particularly someone "playing the part" as a mediator between artists and a public consisting of collectors, critics, and curators–one understood that the space between the studio and the gallery had, in a sense, been compressed and theatricalized, but without the art's losing its breadth or definition. In a time of appropriation, coincidentally enough, casting a skeptical eye on museums and out-of-date criticism revealed that institutions inevitably appropriate the meaning of what they are showing and what they own. Sherrie Levine's 1984 exhibition at Nature Morte had been titled *1917*, and so, in the year that had long represented future dread by way of George Orwell's *Nineteen Eighty-Four*, art, as it had always done, would allow us to time travel, using the past to magnify and examine the present.

Levine's painting *After Chasnik* had not sold at Nature Morte, neither to me nor to anyone else. It is possible that none of the works from the show found a home. Although one of the hallmarks of the 1980s was the *waiting list*–which was, whether written down or mentally held, a list of people who had signed on to be considered (or rather, deemed worthy enough!) for the privilege of buying something by an artist whose supply in no way matched demand–not every show had a line around the block. Nor would every collector be satisfied, as "flying standby" all too often meant not being sold to at all. As if it were only thirty years ago, I can recall being in a gallery on East Tenth Street (a storefront that later housed a dry-cleaning establishment called Le Pressing) and seeing the long faces of a couple who were told, "This work already has three reserves, all of them very, very, very strong." The painting in question made reference to a Dutch wife–an archaic sailor's term for a particular conjugal surrogate, with one or more greased holes at roughly crotch height. After furtive glances in the direction of the husband and the wife, then down to the greased holes, I quietly slipped out the door.[11]

Like many galleries in the East Village in the 1980s, Nature Morte was artist-centric, as opposed to those in nearby Soho and uptown that revolved around collectors. There were exceptions, however–notably, Cable Gallery and Metro Pictures, which had strong artist-critic-curator followings. In a time before the predominance of fairs, advisors, websites, Instagram, and works sent to auction barely after the paint has dried, the showing of art in galleries continued to exert its importance, as did writing about and contextualizing art in group exhibitions that were

10 Rex Reason [David Robbins], "Brie Popcorn: An Interview with the Directors of Nature Morte Gallery," in Katzeff and Lawson, *REALLIFE Magazine: Selected Writings and Projects*, p. 172. The interview was originally published in a 1983–84 issue of *REALLIFE* and appears in full on pp. 146–49 of this volume.

11 This was a work by Meyer Vaisman, possibly *Painting of Depth* (1986–88).

12 Walter Robinson's paintings based on pulp-novel imagery certainly predate that imagery's mining by Richard Prince in recent years, just as Robinson's "spin paintings" came ahead of those of Damien Hirst, who increased their size. This serves as a reminder that in art, it is never a matter of who does something first: valuation is determined financially rather than temporally. All else is a matter of footnotes.

more socially, politically, and critically engaged. This triangulation, which formed the very locus of meaningful exchange, has splintered today, when so much seems merely market driven and duly rewarded. At the risk of valorizing those days gone by, one may characterize the 1980s as being *in the thick of things*, while nowadays, despite the volume of art expeditiously produced, promoted, sold, and resold, and all the attendant *noise*, one feels more and more to be *in the thinness of things*, to be surrounded, if not by peace, then by silence. This lack of depth is nothing if not alienating. While today they *brand apart*, the writers, self-made curators, and artists of the 1980s—particularly those artists who opened galleries—may be thought to have briefly banded together.

The artist collectives and collaborations that characterized the first half of the 1980s, specifically those encouraging the connections between art and the larger culture, art as provocation and agitprop, have much in common with the spirit of Malevich and Chasnik's time, as Sherrie Levine no doubt suspected. The title of her show, *1917*, not coincidentally made reference to the year of the Russian Revolution, and the announcement card **(fig. 6)** featured an enigmatic quote with which Levine has long been associated: "We like to imagine the future as a place where people loved abstraction before they encountered sentimentality."

In terms of contemporary art and critical discourse, the 1980s may be thought of as a decade without a sentimental bone in its body (though this turns out not to have been the case entirely). In Levine's statement, we identify abstraction as the power of the mind, an ability to conceptualize, a seeing beyond, whereas sentimentality represents vulnerable emotion, a past by which one may be swayed, held back. In other words, revolution versus conservatism. As a way of framing the present, Levine's statement could be rephrased: *We like to imagine the future as a place where people loved art before they became enamored of it as a means to an end*. Yet no imagination is necessary, because that future has arrived and seems to be here to stay. And what exactly is that end? Is it status and wealth, a goal not only of the system—driven by its manipulators and facilitators, the dealers, collectors, art advisory services, the whole apparatus outside of creation—but also, once again, of the artists themselves?

Estelle Schwartz, one of the more influential art consultants active in New York in the 1980s (and no relation to Gene Schwartz), said to me of the artists at that time, "They wanted to be bought and we bought them." She was no doubt defending, and laying claim to, her own role in the ascendancy of Koons, Halley, Vaisman, and others. Her remark instantly summons a definitive work produced in this period, Barbara Kruger's *Untitled* of 1984 **(fig. 7)**, which proclaims an eternal promise of consumption: "Buy Me—I'll

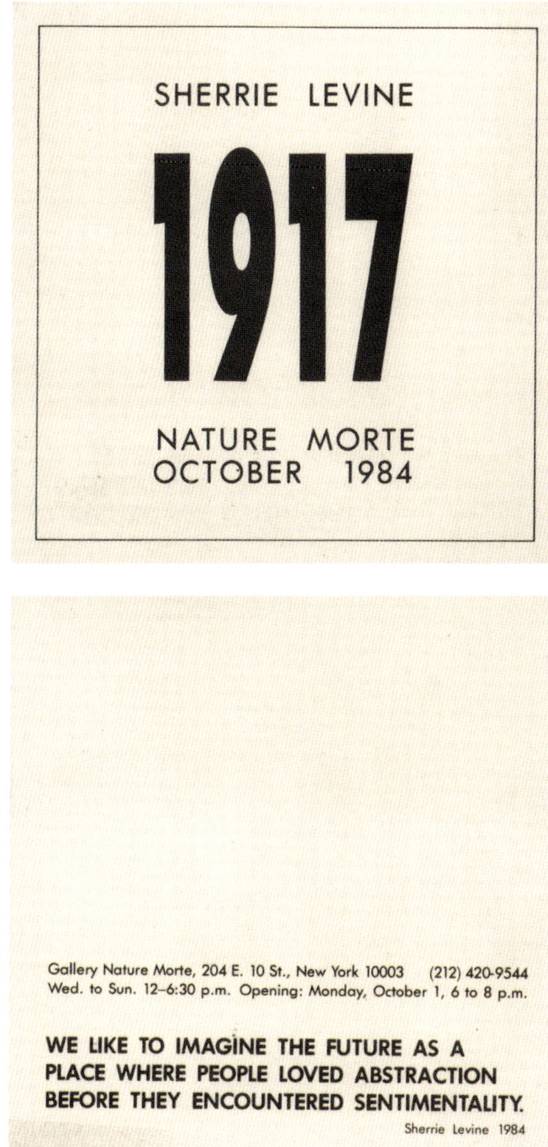

Fig. 6 Announcement (front and back) for Sherrie Levine's exhibition *1917*, Gallery Nature Morte, New York, 1984

Change Your Life." While that phrase can be understood as embedded in the postwar 1950s, from which Kruger's generation emerged (in terms of a housewife being sold a washing machine, for example), her intention was, in large part, to use that idealized world of plenty to skewer the consumption of contemporary art in the 1980s—or, as it might be referred to, the wishing machine. Dating to the 1940s, 1950s, and 1960s, many of the black-and-white images serving as the grounds for Kruger's texts are retro in every sense of the word, meant to appear out of time in the 1980s; their vintage effect is even more pronounced today. Among the artists who ushered in the decade and went on to define this glance backward, Annette Lemieux, Walter Robinson,[12] Cindy Sherman, and Laurie Simmons either relied on or re-created images that were evocative of these past eras, suggesting a period oddly enamored with what can only

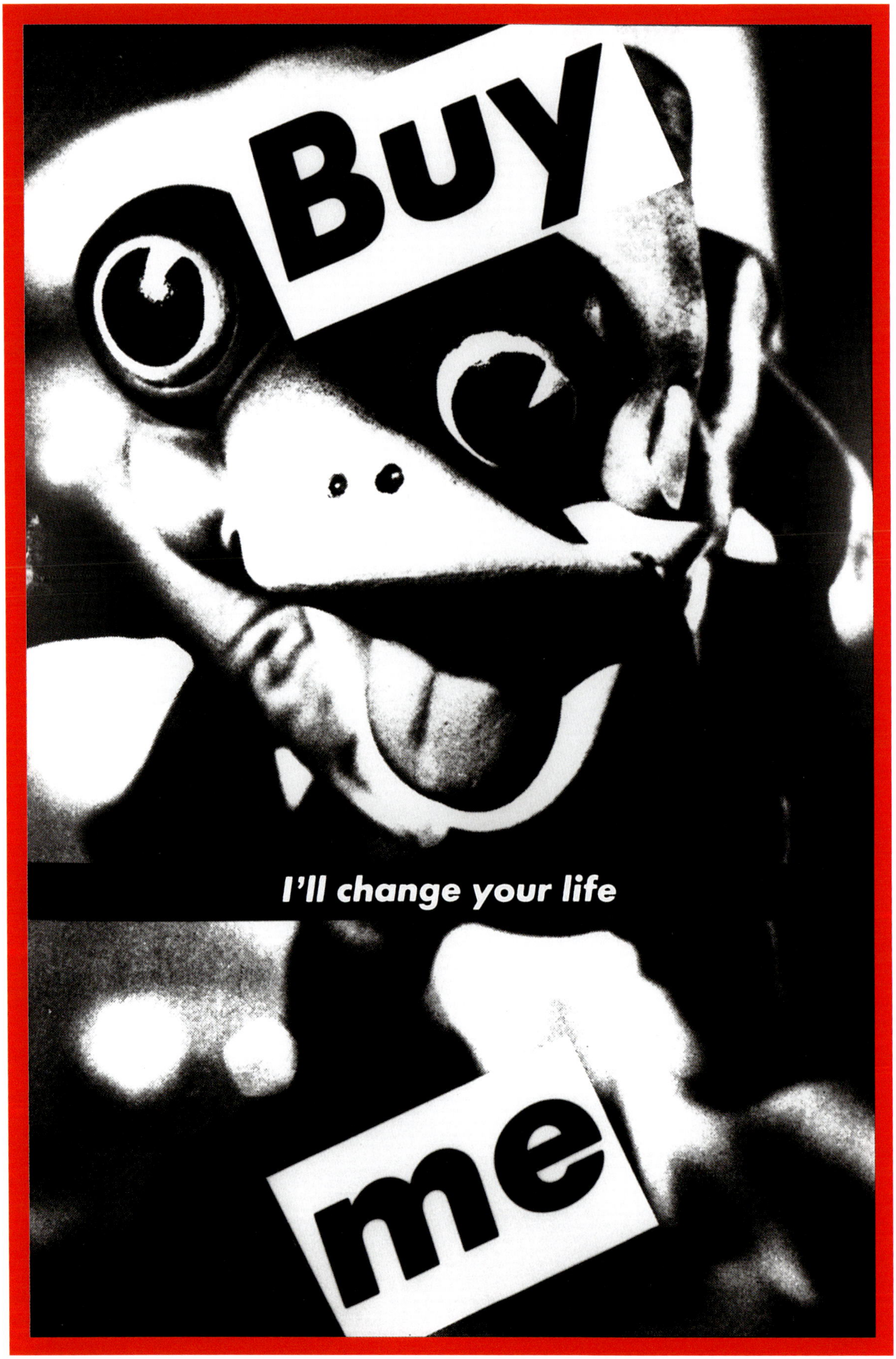

Fig. 7 Barbara Kruger. *Untitled (Buy me I'll change your life)*, 1984. Photograph

be called *retro pictures*. We have seen that, in the initial period of "post-time," the past was never more present; yet to what extent is a mining of what has passed a matter of criticality, nostalgia, or ambivalence? Affection and disaffection may find no greater entwinement than in art, with conflicts orchestrated by artists equally for themselves and for their public. If Pop art mined the plentitude of the supermarket, Neo-Pop, Neo-Geo, and the new readymades of the 1980s demanded more than product, marketing, and supply-and-demand. Trading in futures, as much as trading in the past, required the retelling of fables, cautionary tales one and all: supply-and-desire.

The pictorial background for Barbara Kruger's *Untitled* is a rubbery bath toy, possibly a frog unlikely to transform into a prince–if kissed, destined to remain reptilian. In hindsight, we see that the lives potentially changed in the buying and selling of art were not simply those of the "bad guys"–the collectors, museum board members, middlemen, and dealers–but those of the artists as well. This work changed Kruger's life as well as yours, mine, and, in these sped-up times, everyone's. Who knows what Estelle Schwartz, if she returned to art consultancy, would make of the acceleration from that time to now? Would she be in any way bemused or appalled? Would she jump in to make money once more? Although we may claim that artists are now, more than ever, willing to be bought, hasn't this always been the case? The game and the rules remain nearly the same–there are still none to speak of, save for the few in place that are there to be broken. Only the players have changed, although their numbers are now greater than ever. Schwartz would have seen it all before, not on this scale, of course, what with so many intersecting vectors, each propelled by a velocity that in its blur reduces all art to abstraction no matter how realistic, quote/unquote political, or unsentimental the work may be. In the end, we are left to imagine a final exchange between Donald Barthelme and Sherrie Levine.

DB: Maybe, once again, it's time to start worrying about art-as-commodity.

SL: My sentiments exactly.

Pages 146–49 Rex Reason (pseud. for David Robbins). "Brie Popcorn: An Interview with the Directors of Nature Morte Gallery," ***REALLIFE Magazine***, Winter 1983

Brie Popcorn

an interview
with the directors
of Nature Morte Gallery

by Rex Reason

Peter Nagy: Wouldn't it be great if Leo Castelli were like Burger King, and you had a Leo Castelli in every town across America.

Rex Reason: Franchises. . . well, it's like that now with him.

PN: Yeah, and then we need a farm system. It could be so big! One in Indianapolis, one in Cape Cod. The farm system would be set up so that young artists could get experience in other parts of the country and then slowly feed into New York. . .

Alan Belcher: The only problem at this point is that there is a lot of work being shown, written about, and sold that is very quickly appreciated; it's either very graphic or aggressive or colorful or pleasing, illustrational, and it just pops off of the wall instantly and people say, "Oh, yeah, this is a really nice painting," without thinking about it twice. But maybe this is just the first step.

RR: Towards what—the grand democratization of art?

AB: Perhaps.

PN: Often the seed of art comes out of the lower class or middle class, and an intellectual elite approves it. The elite fabricates the career. At this point, the New York Art World in 1983 is the ultimate cliche of the American dream. Keith Haring is the Henry Ford of the 1980s.

RR: But that is evidence of a profound change, of what kind of success an artist wants to have or what kind of artist to be. All these middle class kids going to art school and learning about art in universities are then shot out into a world in which they simply graft their art aspirations onto their middle class aspirations. It's the diminution of the adverserial culture. They reject nothing. This happened almost without art knowing it.

PN: Hopefully, the dogma of art will rise above the dogma of business.

RR: I'm not sure it does. Art gains much of its meaning from the tension caused by its "otherness" and opposition to prevailing conditions.

PN: The need for opposition changes, and I'm not sure that's art's role anyway. I've always thought if there were a utopia it would be when everyone is an artist and everyone is looking at every aspect of life as art. . . a total work of art as your life, which many artists have done—Beuys, Warhol. Maybe the only really concrete way of achieving utopia is if everyone's a Joseph Beuys!

RR: Who's going to clean the streets? The people who naturally love doing that?

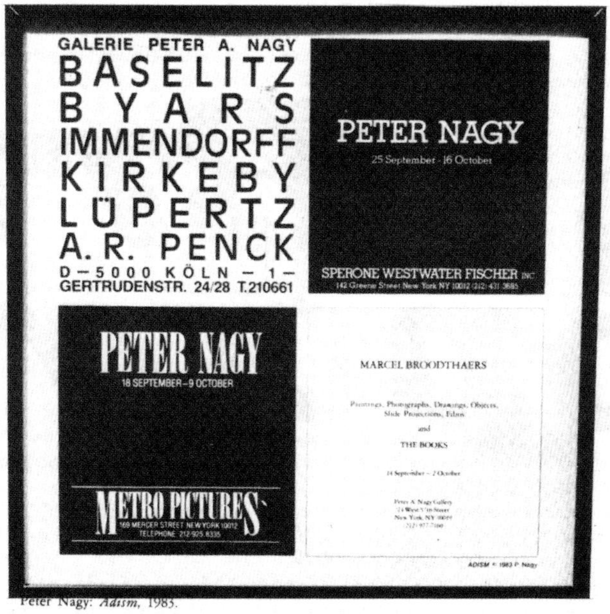

Peter Nagy: *Adism*, 1983.

AB: *We* have jobs during the day.

PN: Due to massive hype and exposure, the art world is on the verge of becoming something it's never been before. More in the vein of popular culture, movies, television, fashion. It's competing for that segment of *Newsweek* magazine, that four-page color spread.

RR: There's a statement attributed to you guys, "In the Fifties everyone wanted to have a car, in the Sixties and Seventies everyone wanted to be a rock star, and in the Eighties everyone wants to be an artist."

PN: Yeah, or a gallery owner.

AB: A painter.

PN: In '78 you open a nightclub, in '82 you open a gallery, a dayclub. The whole change in atmosphere can be attributed to Mary Boone-ism and Julian Schnabelism. It's the mass movement of popular youth culture from music into art. The whole music thing coalesced in the late Seventies, and now our stars aren't Debbie Harry and Joey Ramone, they're Keith Haring and Futura 2000. Music flopped into art. Mary Boone gave confidence to a lot of young artists. Artists were taken more seriously, getting more press, so at least it seemed like the market, the whole environment was much more open to younger artists, to unknown people, because of the success of the biggies. The general excitement in the art world over all...

AB: Of course you get a lot of schlocky work because you have more people looking at and thinking about art that had never previously done it. But it also means that soon in the future we'll be able to have art everywhere.

RR: How do you feel about trademark-ism in art: objects that are instantly recognizable as made by a certain artist?

PN: It's very important. It's the way our whole society functions.

AB: I think it's great. Especially now with such a large population.

PN: It's certainly necessary for survival. We're both artists and we have a gallery, but we tell every artist we handle, "Look, you're going to have to be as much your own dealer as we're going to be. You've got to hype your career just as much."

AB: If not more.

PN: We don't want you just sitting home making paintings.

RR: Not to be gloomy, but what is that attitude's effect on art? Trademark-ism indicates to me that an artist constrains creative development to the issues raised by the last series of pieces, conceptual serialism...further variations on the last theme in order to support its place in the market.

PN: My background is in media, and I've always seen that as a necessary part of it—so you could get that necessary feedback so you could go out and make more. It's just economics.

RR: The trademark is so you can *sell* it so you can make more. To say, "Oh, it's just economics" is to sweep it under the rug—and definitely relegate the content and quality of what is made to economic concerns, which I think is newish, certainly "after-Warhol".

PN: You're advocating a quicker turnover of the product?

RR: I'm saying I'd rather make William Wegman's drawings than Robert Longo's: there's an infinitely greater area of play that one gives oneself access to.

PN: You feel the artists' desires should be the bottom line.

RR: Yes, as far as the content and range of art is concerned.

PN: I don't see trademark as being that limited. Beuys has a trademark, but it's more of a material or an essence. There's always been a lot of trademark in art: Duchamp, Man Ray had a lot of it.

RR: No! They were completely not about that. The variation in the look and content of the object was for them much broader.

PN: I disagree. And Sherrie Levine introduced a further confusion, she took on this sort of martyr position: when you don't have to worry about being original, you're completely liberated. Copies of copies of copies is generative, and regenerative. And most of those artists who are strongly trademarked are doing other things which you never see, like Twombly's 3-D collages.

AB: Warhol's Piss Paintings.

RR: Are people "expressing" themselves all over the map?

PN: People don't have anything to express, except the trademark. The void is inside us. We hardly have original thoughts all the time. We're fed information all the time.

AB: We're filters.

PN: We're hardly ourselves. You make an object to fill the void. You're nothing inside so you make a concrete object to see yourself. It's the concrete self.

AB: Especially if you die tomorrow. But you're not just filling it, you're saying something about it as well. And a gallerist just picks out of the atmosphere bits one relates to.

PN: You look for things that remind you of what you never remembered before.

RR: You're known as having a policy of no-policy, as far as aesthetics are concerned.

PN: That harmed us during our first year because the media didn't have a label they could pin on us. We knew that we didn't want to show what was being seen in most galleries, which was neo-expressionist figurative paintings. The 90% of that that you see is pretty useless. So from the beginning that was our only direction—we knew we weren't showing neo expressionism. We were going to concentrate on other media and other imagery, and mix things up. Pluralism certainly didn't die with the Seventies.

AB: Our policy of no-policy is one of survival: we feel that if we become known for a certain type of work, then people will only come to see us for a few months, and then never come again. We want a long shelf life.

PN: But we are getting more focused—it takes a gallery a few years, especially when you've started out really fast like us, it takes a few years to coalesce into a style. We're on our way to having a definite outlook.

AB: It's becoming more apparent: we tend to go for either the primitive or the slick, or hard-edged.

PN: Serious, intelligent work: those are our artful requirements. We never wanted to show cliche East Village art—kitschy religious art or punky aggressive paintings. Even though 90% of our artists are working in the East Village, they're certainly not making that kind of stuff.

RR: How do you find your artists?

AB: They find us, mostly. Friends of friends.

PN: We still look at slides, and it's getting a little out of hand, but we feel it's something we have to do, to at least let people know there's an outlet. FUN won't look at anything.

AB: Our shows are planned through April, and we've got most of the people we want to work with, so even though we're looking at slides, it's a little futile.

PN: Even if we liked the work we couldn't deal with it for a year.

RR: Do you see yourselves as functioning as filters for the gallery system?

AB: That's one of our motives: one of our principles is to show new people previously unshown, and then having them get shows in other galleries afterwards. Also having dealers, collectors, writers, coming here and knowing they're going to be competing with each other.

PN: We don't have a stable. We don't sign people.

AB: Basically we always want to have fun showing work—if we had to keep showing the same people we'd just hire someone to run the place.

PN: We're not threatened by people stealing our artists.

AB: We're all for it—if they steal it just makes us valid, it proves we're showing what people respond to.

RR: But of course this completely plugs into the extant gallery system. It's the food chain—artists are plankton, you guys are minnows, and so on.

AB: But it's working.

PN: We didn't feel revolt against that system. Basically that system has a lot of good in it, and it takes care of a lot of artists.

RR: In order to draw meaning from the incredible variety of objects, styles, and aims that constitutes pluralism, doesn't pluralism presuppose such an intense and constant involvement with the art world that it continues and accentuates the ghettoization of artists? Kosuth said the only people who pay attention to art are artists, anyway, so let's just admit it and make art for artists, and that spirals upwards to esoterica.

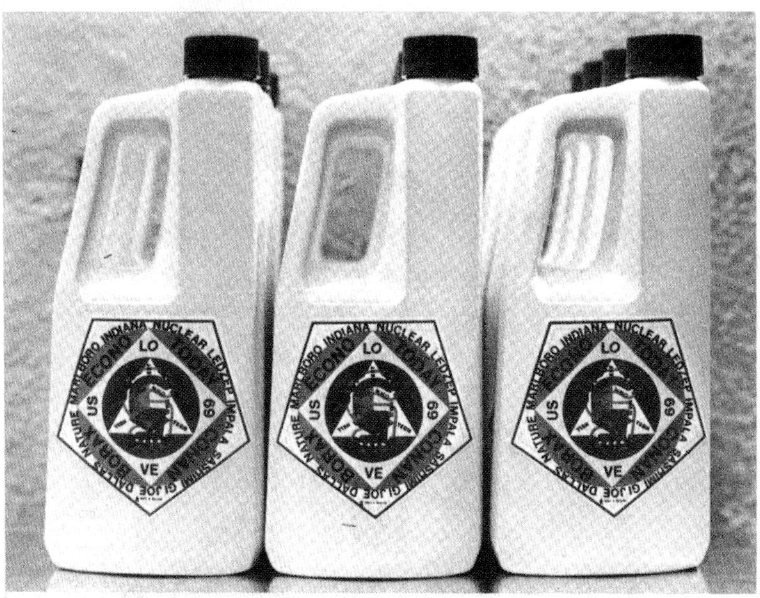

Alan Belcher: *$51.49*, 1983.

PN: I live breathe think sleep art.

AB: There's nothing else to do now.

PN: It's been ghetto-ized but it's self-preservation.

AB: Everybody has their ghetto.

PN: Golf, whatever. The only way in which pluralism works against us is with the collectors—they may see two things they like next to four things they don't like. That doesn't make them shell out the money too fast.

AB: The product really needs packaging and promotion to sell it. And if it's not shown a lot and written about, then it's not packaged.

PN: As far as ads go, the art world is the pits right now.

AB: It's all just type.

PN: Mary Boone, Sperone Westwater. . . it's the same little format every month. We have lots of art magazines from the Sixties and the ads were art in themselves.

RR: What's the difference between art and any other product?

PN: In the marketplace, nothing. Art is something different when you're making it and when you're admiring it—the difference is in the quality of the consumption.

RR: So in the marketplace the art object is without pretensions to meaning?

PN: Pretty much.

RR: Maybe there's not enough time anymore for the deep stuff—things keep moving faster and faster.

PN: That's the natural flow of society—things get more and more complex, weirder and weirder, faster and faster. You have to learn to just groove on it.

RR: Do you invest less and less of yourself with each microrevolution?

PN: Yeah. The key to survival is staying on top of the wave.

RR: Surfing.

AB: Stay on the board.

RR: You guys are so modern. What do you look for in an object? What qualities?

AB: Right now we like either black, white, and gray, or generic color.

PN: We're pretty anti-color.

RR: By generic you mean red as "red" rather than modulations of it?

AB: Yeah.

PN: So many people bring us slides that are just like Salle, Basquiat, or Roberto Juarez. These poor kids are out there going to the galleries and they say, "This is what I have to do to have a show." So they run home and paint them. We don't want that—we want stuff we've never seen in a gallery before.

RR: And what do you think is the best art? What influenced the shaping of your taste?

AB: Right now, we like pretty classic late modern stuff: Pop Art, Paolozzi, Indiana for logos, Duchamp, Manzoni, Beuys, Klein. Scarpitta's a favorite of mine.

PN: We think Op Art is highly underrated, Bridget Riley. That's corporate psychedelia, the orgasm of modernism.

AB: We started the gallery because we really just wanted to get our voices in.

PN: And chose the name "Nature Morte" for its Fifties-jazz, pseudo-continental appeal. Ersatz European. Franco-American Chef Boy-ar-dee.

AB: We wanted to be the Leper Gallery.

PN: But then I thought of the Wallet Gallery.

RR: Great!

AB: We gotta get MasterCharge. I want to see the stickers in the window.

PN: We'd love to build a sliver.

AB: Coop Nature Morte, Cafe Nature Morte, Cinema Nature Morte Quad.

PN: Brie popcorn. See, that's what I mean about trademarks: the image is succinct but the meaning can't be battened down.

October, 1983

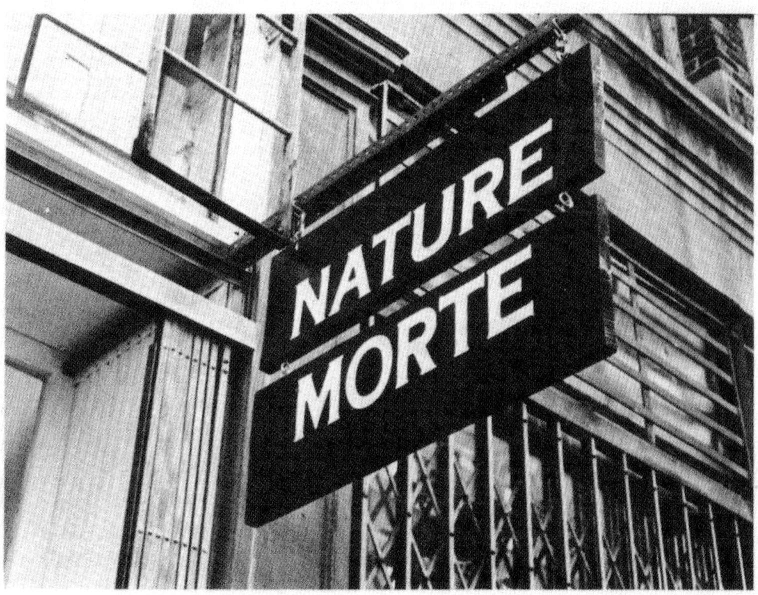

Mary Agnes Smith: *Nature Morte sign.*

1987–89
Dissemination & Contamination

1987

Jay Gorney moves his gallery from East 10th Street in the East Village to Greene Street in Soho, following the blossoming careers of artists with whom he has worked such as Barbara Bloom, Sarah Charlesworth, Haim Steinbach, and James Welling. Gorney is the first to show Bloom's installation *The Reign of Narcissism*, which later finds its way into the important Los Angeles show *A Forest of Signs* (see May 1989).

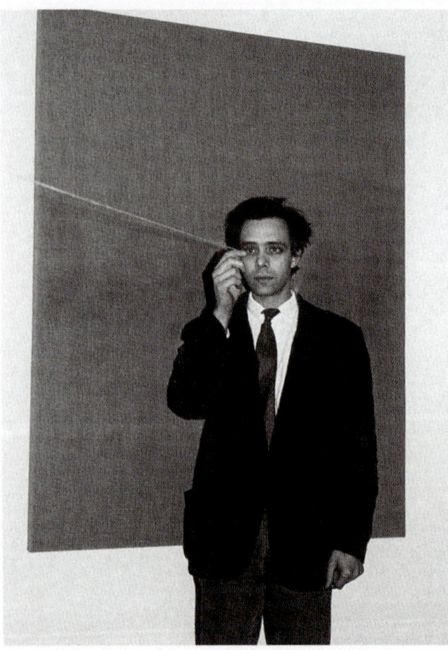

David Robbins. *The Art Dealers' Optical Tests, #2: To Colin de Land of American Fine Arts, the string appears single wherever it is fixated, double elsewhere*, 1987

Colin de Land opens his gallery American Fine Arts, Co., at 40 Wooster Street in Soho, bringing with him his critique of—and intimacy with—the art market from his former East 6th Street gallery, Vox Populi. Vibrant with experimentation even as it remains firmly in the commercial scene, the gallery shows work by artists such as Cady Noland and even the filmmaker John Waters.

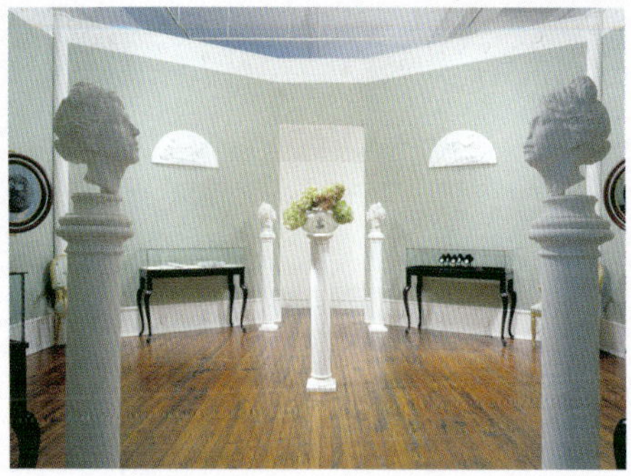

Barbara Bloom. *The Reign of Narcissism*, 1988–89

CASH/Newhouse Gallery closes instead of relocating, the owners citing a desire to focus on their own art practices. It is the first of the so-called conceptual galleries in the East Village to close.

SILENCE = DEATH posters and stickers start showing up around New York City in response to the AIDS crisis. The Reagan administration, which had not mentioned the word "AIDS" until a point when thousands of people (mostly gay men) had already died, continues to receive flak for slow and subdued action in response to the epidemic.

Jean Baudrillard conducts a lecture tour sponsored by the Whitney Museum of American Art, Columbia University, and the School of the Art Institute of Chicago. He tells the audience at Columbia that he rejects art that cites his philosophy and that he "cannot get involved in explaining this new art of simulation. In the world of simulation, there is no object. There is a misunderstanding in taking me as a reference for this work."[18]

February

Resistance (Anti-Baudrillard), an exhibition curated by **Group Material**, opens at White Columns, critiquing Jean Baudrillard's theory that there is no reality, only simulation; participating artists include Gretchen Bender, Jenny Holzer, Barbara Kruger, and Louise Lawler. An accompanying panel discussion is held among Judith Barry, Peter Halley, William Olander, Julia Wachtel, and Oliver Wasow, moderated by Doug Ashford and Julie Ault of Group Material.

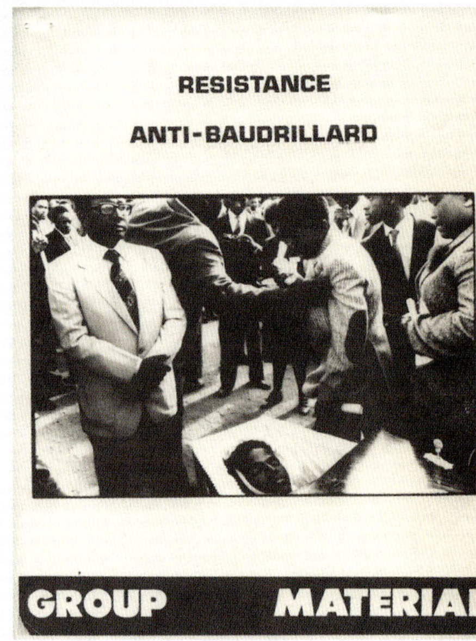

Poster for Group Material's *Resistance (Anti-Baudrillard)*, White Columns, New York, 1987

Andy Warhol dies on February 22 at the age of 58 after gallbladder surgery. On hearing the news, Leo Castelli (Warhol's dealer of 23 years) says: "Of all the painters of his generation he's still the one most influential on the younger artists—a real guru."[19] Warhol had once written about death: "I'm so sorry to hear about it. I just thought that things were magic and that it would never happen."[20]

April

The 1987 **Whitney Biennial,** curated by Lisa Phillips, Richard Armstrong, and Richard Marshall, includes only three "Simulationists": Peter Halley, Jeff Koons, and Philip Taaffe. Says the *New York Times* in its review: "Each is presented in a different gallery, thereby making a point that they are really not a group—that the differences between them are more important than what they share. The Biennial has definitely not given them the same kind of attention it gave the Neo-Expressionists, against whom the 'Simulationists' were partly reacting." Some of the other artists in the show are R. M. Fischer, Joseph Kosuth, Barbara Kruger, and Richard Prince.[21]

July
The *New York Times* announces "Art Boom Slows in the East Village."[22] **Gracie Mansion** is quoted as saying that "there used to be a sense of community. Now, it's just another art neighborhood. There's Madison Avenue, 57th Street, SoHo and the East Village."[23]

October
On October 19—which comes to be known as **Black Monday**—the stock market crashes. Money starts to pour into the art market and auctions instead of into the unstable stock market.

Dia Center for the Arts opens to the public in Chelsea, giving individual contemporary artists space to produce new work and exhibit existing work and foretelling the neighborhood's destiny as New York's next major gallery hub.

November
New Museum curator William Olander organizes the exhibition *Let the Record Show . . .*, which includes work by Gran Fury and ACT UP. This is the first showing of the neon sign *SILENCE = DEATH*, although the phrase had been coined earlier by another anonymous collective. **ACT UP (AIDS Coalition To Unleash Power)** had been formed earlier in the year by a group of activists, including Olander and other artists and arts workers. **Gran Fury**, the collective that will produce all the media for ACT UP in addition to other visual art projects, emerges from this group.

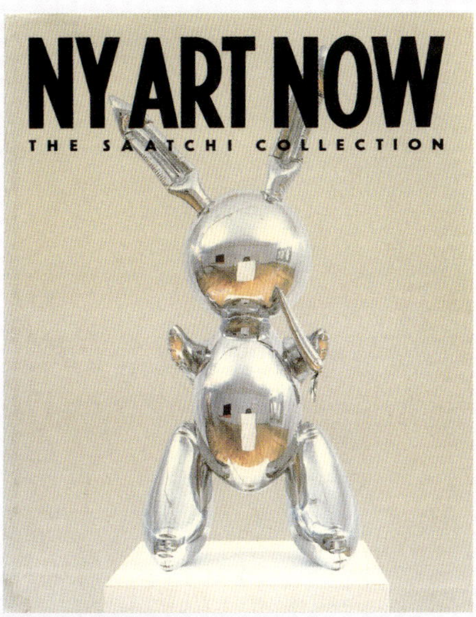

Cover of exhibition catalogue for *NY ART NOW: The Saatchi Collection* (Giancarlo Politi Editore, 1992), Saatchi Gallery, London, with photograph of Jeff Koons's *Rabbit*

December
Prominent collector **Charles Saatchi** (known to make the East Village rounds with his wife, Doris) presents a group of New York artists in the show *NY ART NOW* in London, influencing a generation that would later become known as the Young British Artists, or YBAs (see July 1988). Included in the exhibition are Ashley Bickerton, Ross Bleckner, Robert Gober, Peter Halley, Jeff Koons, Tim Rollins & K.O.S., Haim Steinbach, Philip Taaffe, and Meyer Vaisman.

1988

Both **Nature Morte** and **Cable Gallery** close their doors, signaling the approaching end of the East Village alternative gallery scene. Despite Cable's short lifespan, in 2008, art critic Jerry Saltz includes it in his "New York Canon" of the past forty years.[24] **P•P•O•W** shutters its East Village location and moves to 532 Broadway in Soho.

January
Jeffrey Deitch curates *Cultural Geometry*, a collaboration between the DESTE Foundation for Contemporary Art and the House of Cyprus in Athens. The show, with its installation designed by Haim Steinbach, juxtaposes ancient art from the collection of the National Archaeological Museum with contemporary art from the collection of Dakis Joannou (one of the most important Greek collectors of contemporary art), including works by Steinbach himself, John M Armleder, Ashley Bickerton, John Dogg, R. M. Fischer, Peter Halley, Jenny Holzer, and others. The catalogue indicates the curator's intention of tracking the ways in which "cultural artifacts and commodities function as symbols and images of desire."[25]

April
Fourteen months after **Andy Warhol**'s death, 10,000 items from his collection are auctioned over the course of ten days at Sotheby's New York. Bidders and browsers swarm the auction house, and the first day brings in \$5.3 million—more than double the most optimistic estimate. Collector and philanthropist Ronald Lauder: "The most important things are the cookie jars."[26]

July
Damien Hirst organizes the exhibition *Freeze* at the Surrey Docks in South East London. He and many of the other participating artists, who come to be known as the Young British Artists, or YBAs, are inspired by all that has recently transpired in the New York art world. Charles Saatchi, a champion of the YBAs, sponsors a rise

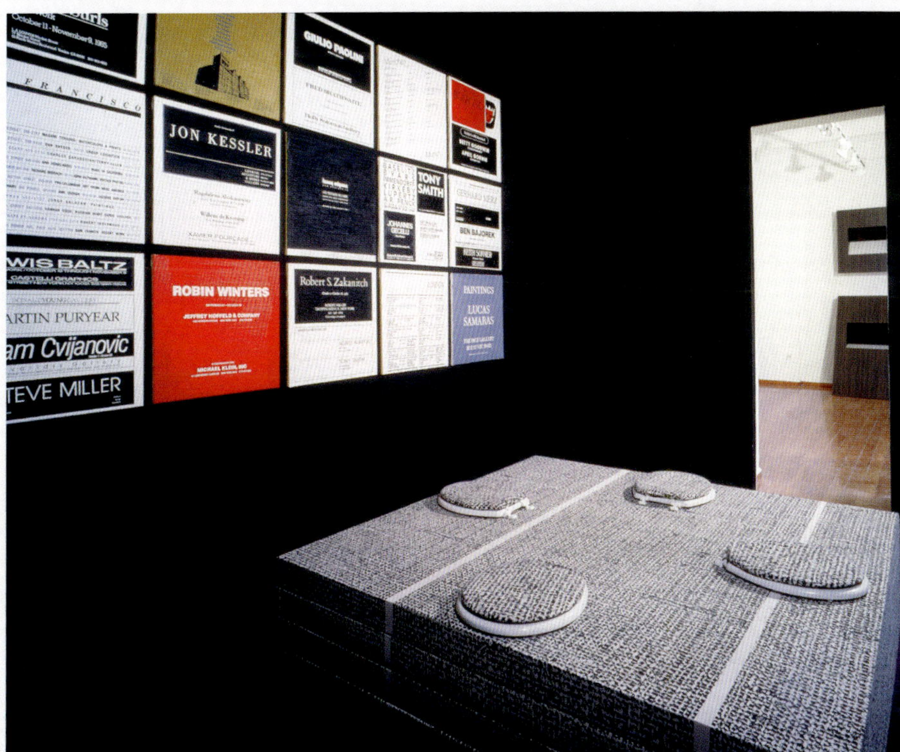

Installation view, *Cultural Geometry*, House of Cyprus, Athens, 1988

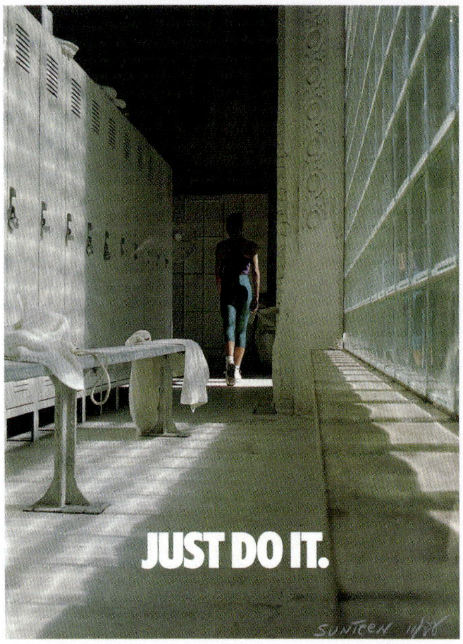

Nike advertisement by Wieden+Kennedy, 1988

of art and commodity in London comparable to New York's.

Nike, Inc., launches its first advertising campaign featuring the slogan JUST DO IT.

August
Jean-Michel Basquiat dies in his East Village home at the age of 27. The artist, who had a close, well-publicized relationship with Andy Warhol, had been heavily affected by Warhol's death the previous year. In 1985, the two artists had collaborated on a series of works featuring Basquiat's signature scrawls over corporate logos.

1989

March
Tim Berners-Lee, a British software engineer working at CERN (European Organization for Nuclear Research) in Geneva, submits to his supervisor a document called "Information Management: A Proposal." The system he describes becomes, later the next year, the embryonic **World Wide Web**.

May
***A Forest of Signs**: Art in the Crisis of Representation*, curated by Ann Goldstein and Mary Jane Jacob, opens at the Museum of Contemporary Art (MOCA), Los Angeles, featuring older and new work by Gretchen Bender, Dara Birnbaum, Barbara Bloom, Sarah Charlesworth, Louise Lawler, Sherrie Levine, Peter Nagy, and Haim Steinbach. The show stresses the complexity of artistic practice and production in the context of artists' professionalization and delves into the question of commodity art and appropriation since the *Pictures* exhibition.

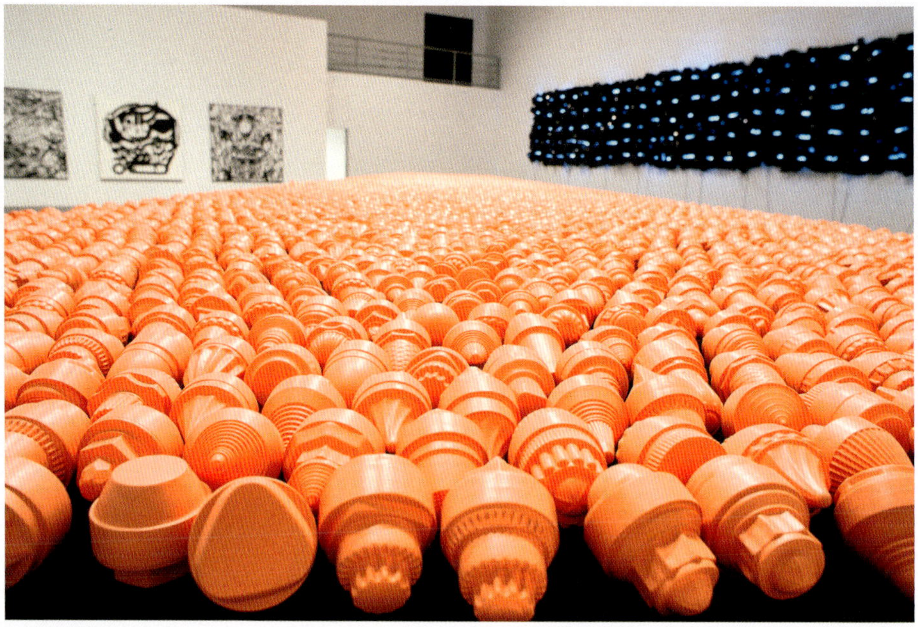

Installation view, *A Forest of Signs*, Museum of Contemporary Art, Los Angeles, 1989

June
A retrospective exhibition of works by the photographer **Robert Mapplethorpe**, who had died in March from complications of AIDS, is canceled by the Corcoran Gallery of Art in Washington, DC. The museum cites its concern that the show's content might "trigger a political storm on Capitol Hill."[27] The canceled show prefigures other AIDS-related political controversies, such as that involving the exhibition *Witnesses: Against Our Vanishing* (see November 1989).

September
ACT UP members infiltrate the New York Stock Exchange, chaining themselves to the VIP balcony and unfurling a banner that reads "SELL WELLCOME." Burroughs Wellcome is the maker of the only anti-AIDS medication available at the time, azidothymidine, or AZT. In 1990, *Rolling Stone* lauds ACT UP for having "developed a behind-the-scenes sophistication that has

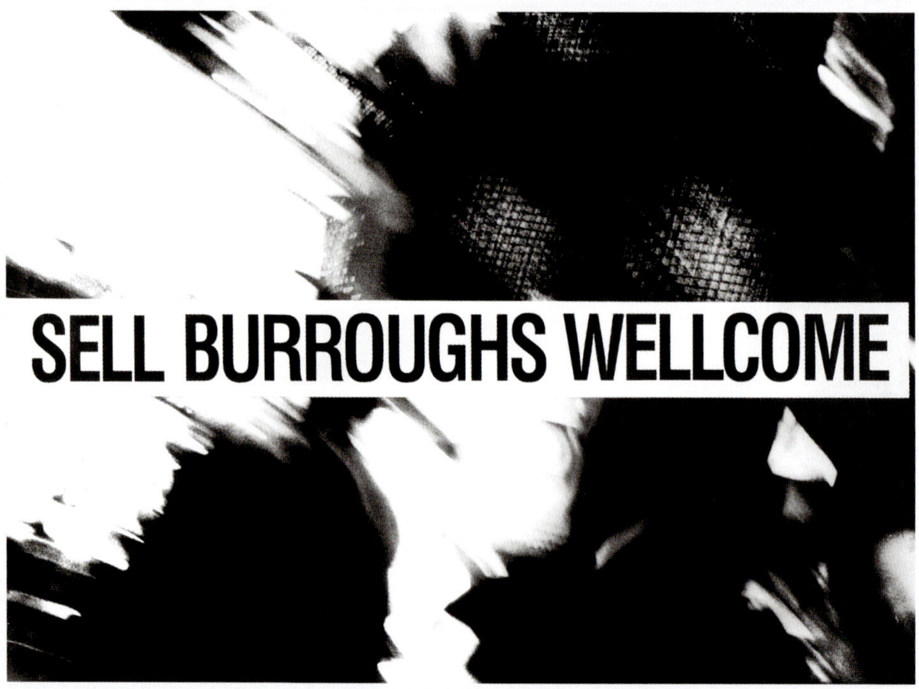

Unidentified artist. *Sell Burroughs Wellcome*, ca. 1987

enabled it to have a major voice in governmental policy. In 1989, the group not only helped get the price of AZT reduced but also helped speed the release of at least four new AIDS-related treatments."[28]

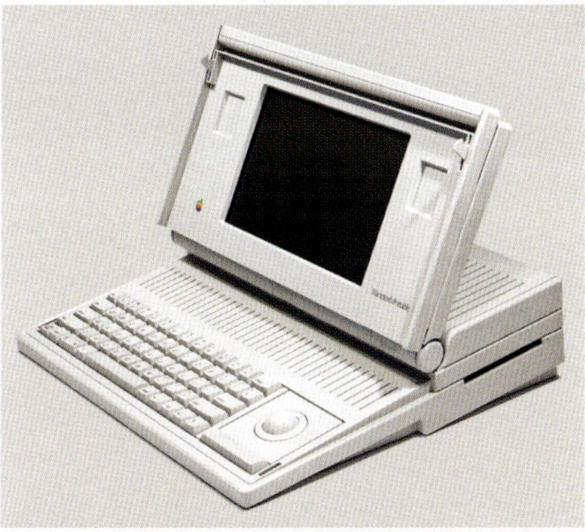

Macintosh Portable computer, released September 20, 1989

September
Apple releases its first portable, battery-powered computer, the Macintosh Portable. Available for purchase at $6,500, the machine weighs 16 pounds and features what *Time* magazine describes in its September 25 issue as an "active-matrix screen" and a "cursor-control device called a trackball."

October
Energizer launches the first advertising campaign featuring its now-iconic **Energizer Bunny**. In a parodic appropriation, the character echoes the lesser-known Duracell Bunny, which is no longer used in Duracell's branding in the United States.

November
Nan Goldin curates *Witnesses: Against Our Vanishing*, an exhibition of artists working in response to the AIDS crisis, at Artists Space. For the catalogue, **David Wojnarowicz** contributes the essay "Postcards from America: X-Rays from Hell," which criticizes a number of right-wing politicians, including Senator Jesse Helms and U.S. Representative William E. Dannemeyer, for their policies discouraging education about safe-sex practices. The essay finds its way to the desk of recently elected chairman of the National Endowment for the Arts John Frohnmayer, which leads to the withdrawal of a $10,000 grant for the exhibition. After much debate, the grant is partially restored, but without funding for the catalogue.

Image World: Art and Media Culture, curated by Marvin Heiferman, Lisa Phillips, and John G. Hanhardt, opens at the Whitney Museum of American Art, presenting post-Pop/postconceptual artists "vacillating between critique and complicity."[29] Sponsored by the Polaroid Corporation, ***Image World*** "demonstrates that a great deal of the most astute and acutely political work over the last two decades has been done by women."[30] Although the focus of the exhibition is the development of the image through technological and cultural advancements, it also demonstrates the use of the commodity image in political works by Barbara Bloom, Sarah Charlesworth, Gran Fury, Barbara Kruger, Annette Lemieux, and others.

The **Berlin Wall** falls on November 9, marking what many pundits view as the triumph of capitalism. Western lifestyle and commodity culture begin to flow eastward, quickly becoming a dominant global culture.

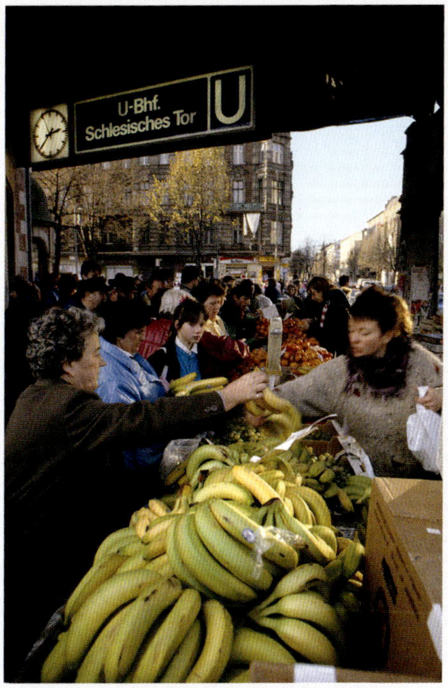

Residents of East Berlin buying bananas, Schlesisches Tor, Berlin, 1989

December
The organization Visual AIDS coordinates the first annual **Day Without Art**. More than 800 other art organizations, galleries, and museums opt to close their doors, sending staff members to volunteer at AIDS organizations; others shroud one or more works of art, replacing them with information about HIV and safer sex, or schedule HIV/AIDS-related exhibitions, programs, and performances in the name of public awareness.

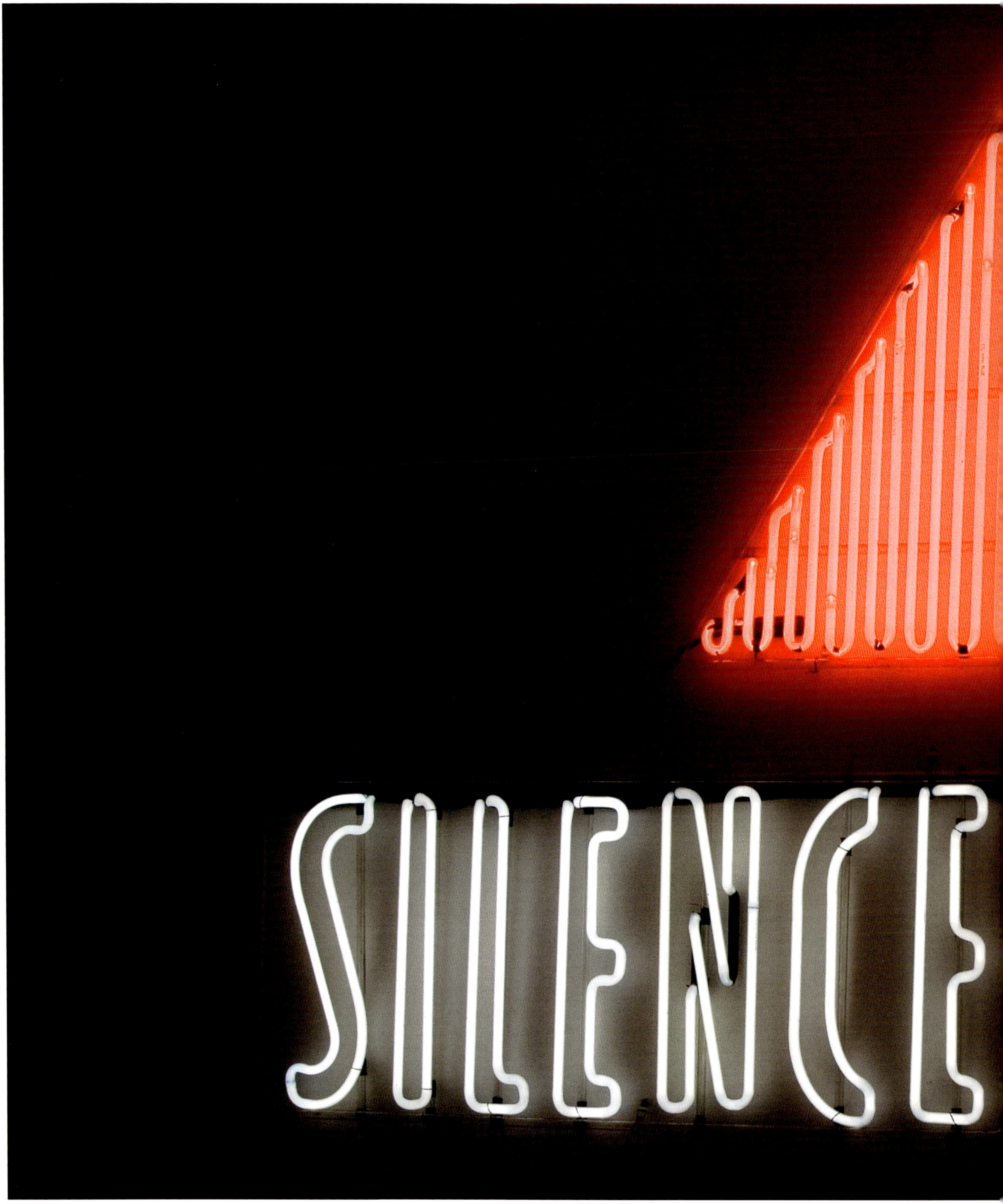

ACT UP (Gran Fury). ***SILENCE = DEATH***, 1987. Neon sign in two colors, 48 × 79 in. (121.9 × 200.7 cm). New Museum, New York, William Olander Memorial Fund

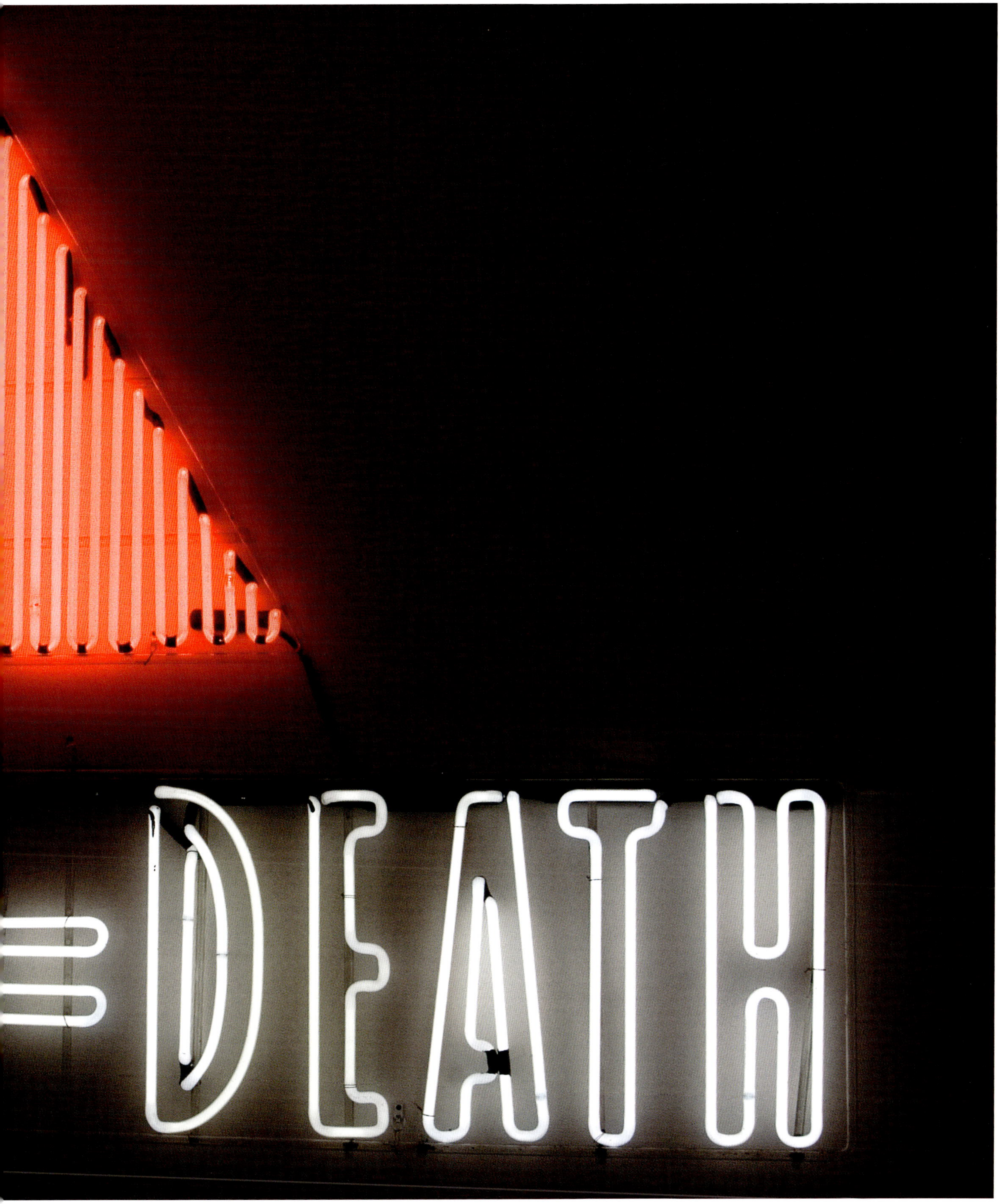
=DEATH

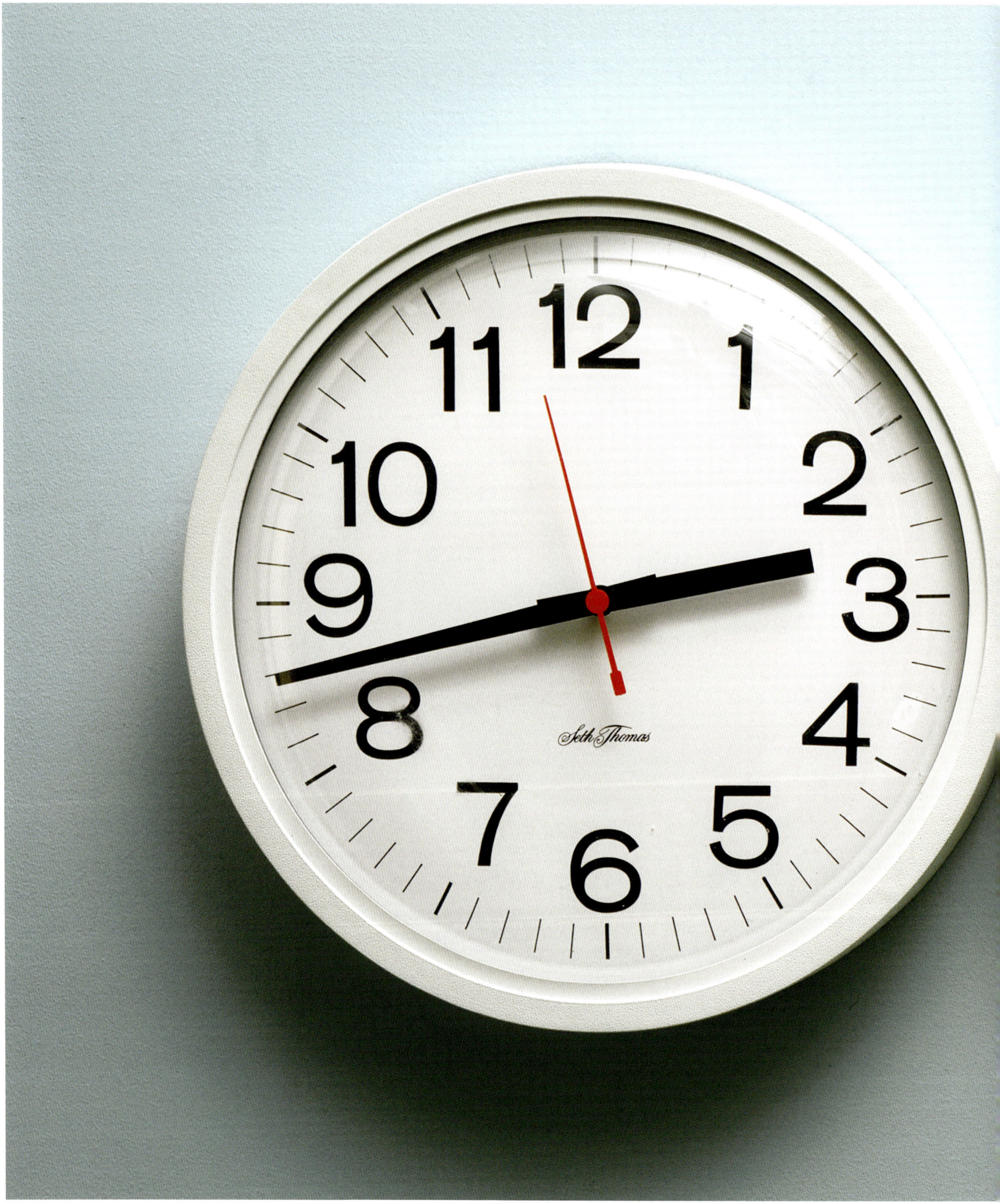

Felix Gonzalez-Torres. *"Untitled" (Perfect Lovers)*, 1991. Two wall clocks, paint on wall, diam. of each clock 13½ in. (34.3 cm), overall dimensions variable. Ed. of 3 with 1 artist's proof. The Museum of Modern Art, New York, Gift of the Dannheisser Foundation

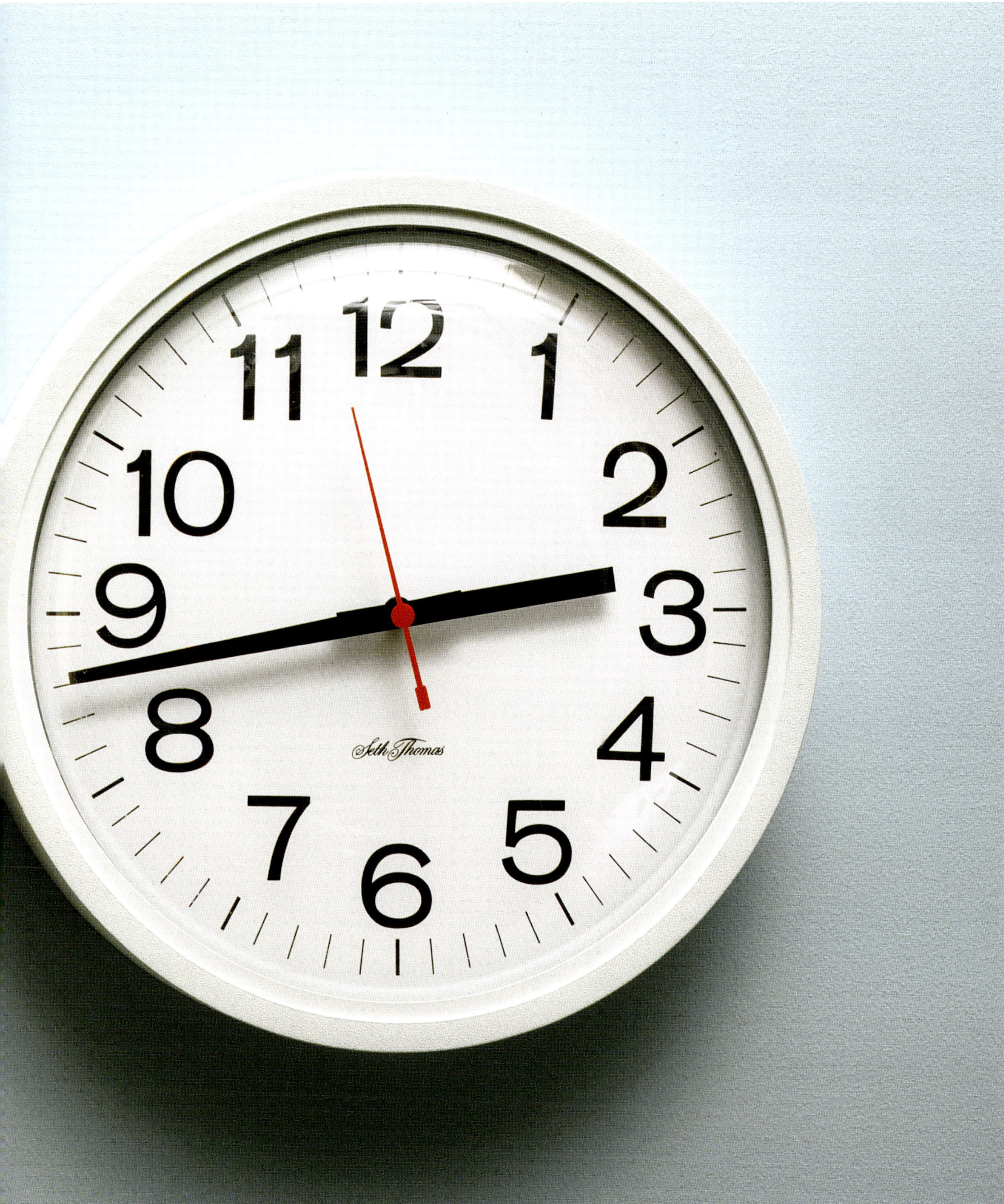
Seth Thomas

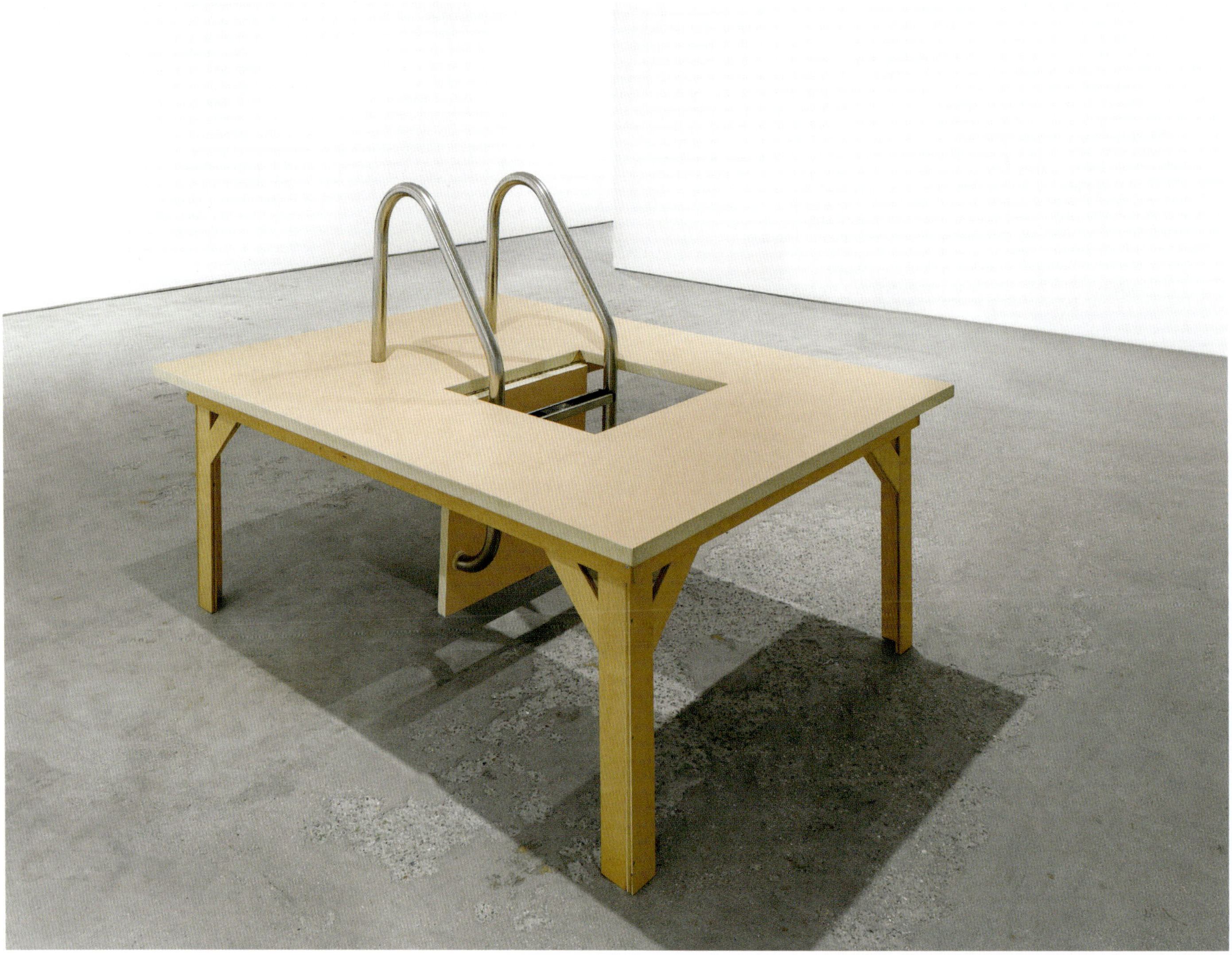

Joan Wallace. *The Pool Ladder Painting, No. 2*, 2004 (after *The Pool Ladder Painting*, 1985).
Latex paint on canvas, wood, stainless-steel pool ladder, 54 × 84 × 60 in. (137.2 × 213.4 × 152.4 cm).
Courtesy of the artist and Elizabeth Dee, New York

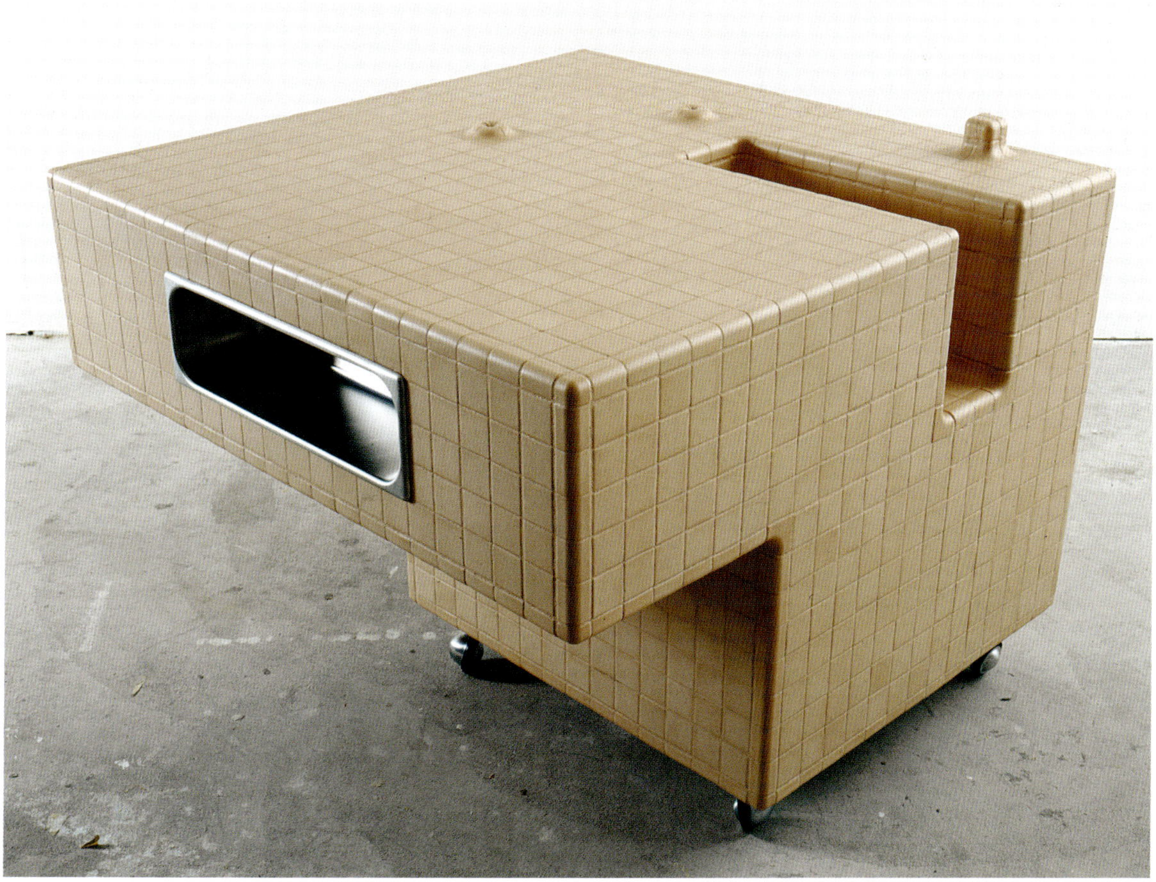

Tishan Hsu. ***Biocube***, 1988. Porcelain tile, rubber, acrylic, stainless steel, plywood, 35½ × 44½ × 44½ in. (90.2 × 113 × 113 cm). Courtesy of the artist
Following spread: ***Biocube*** (detail)

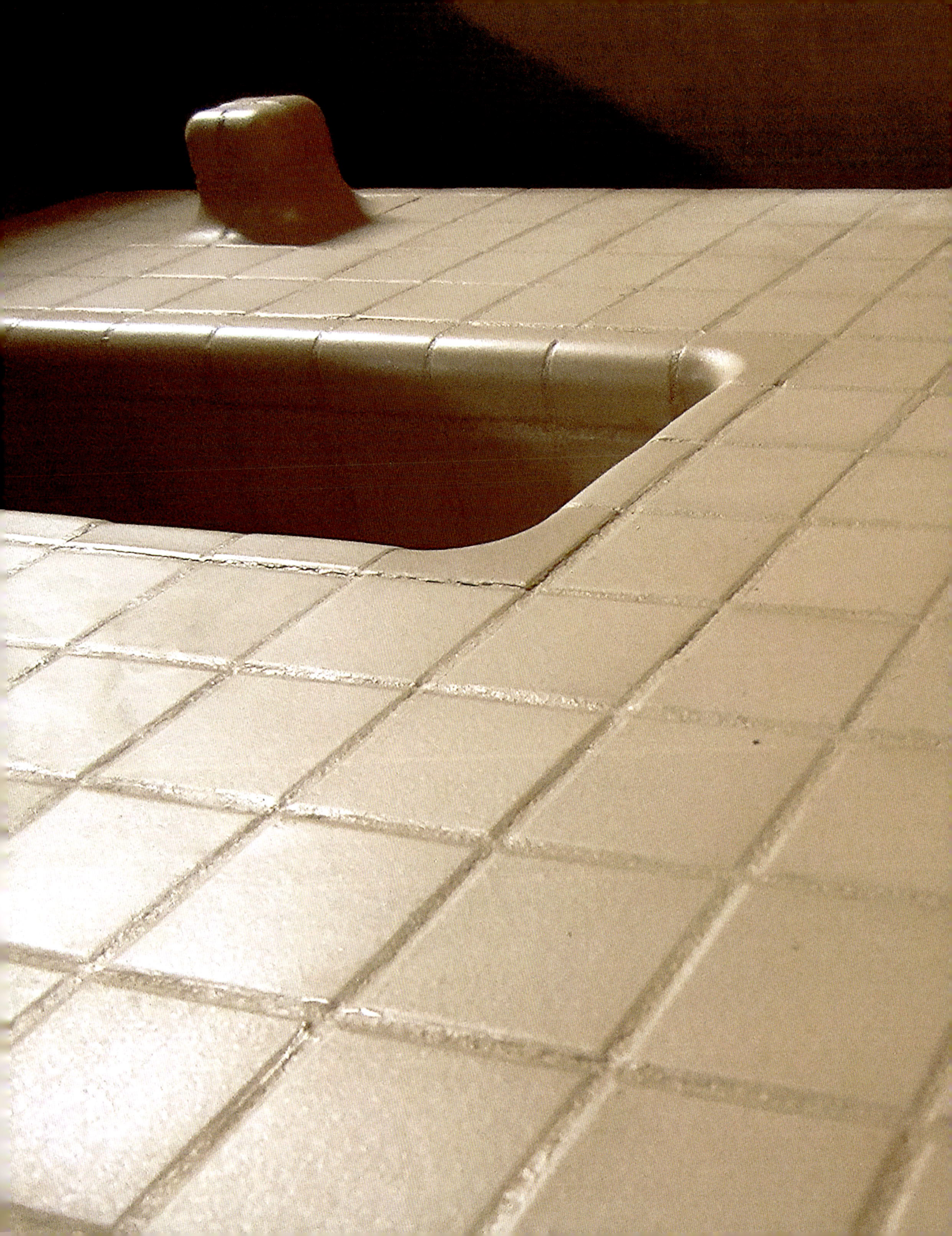

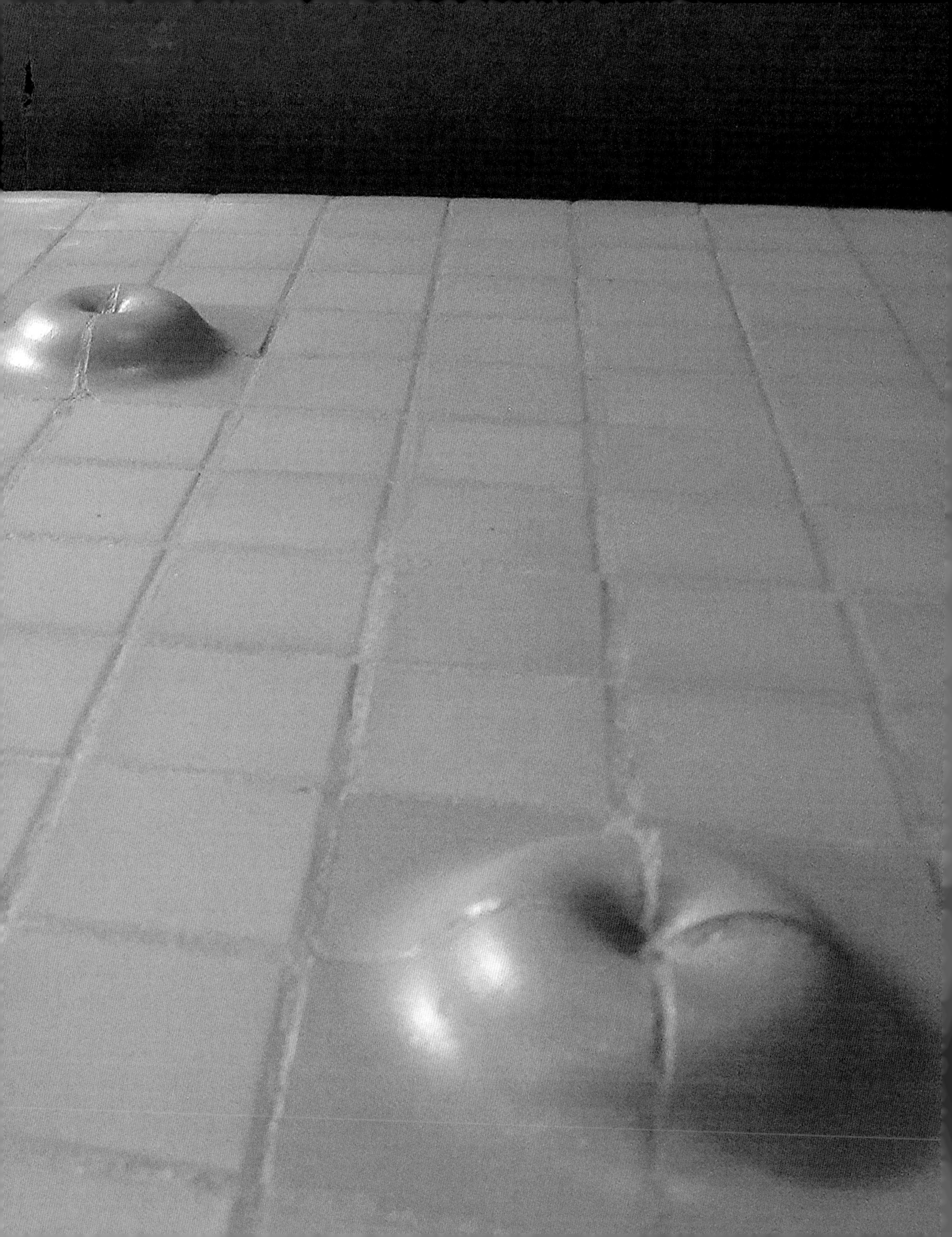

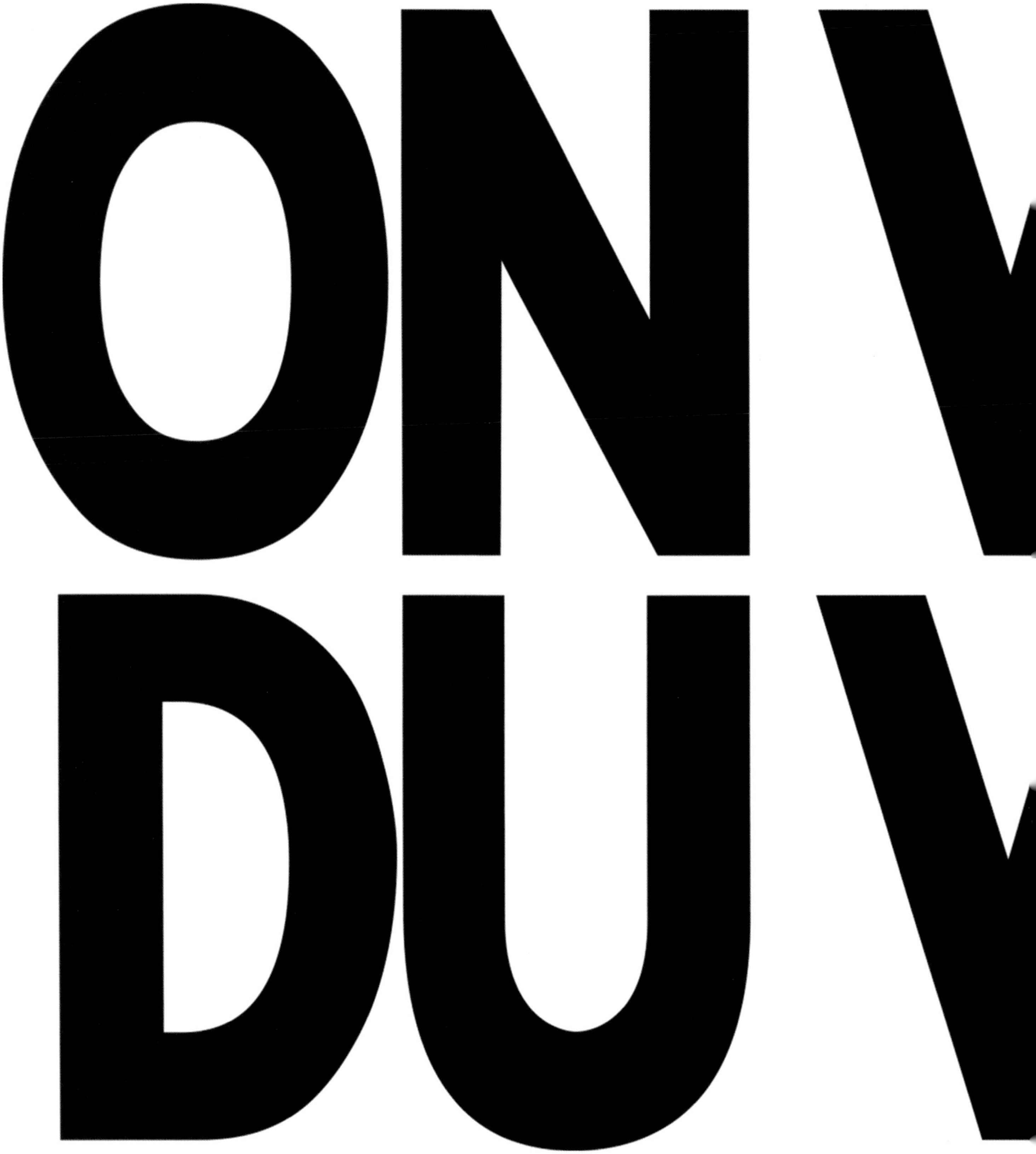

Haim Steinbach. ***on vend du vent***, 1988. Text in matte black latex paint or vinyl letters applied to wall, dimensions variable. CAPC musée d'art contemporain de Bordeaux

VEND
VENT.

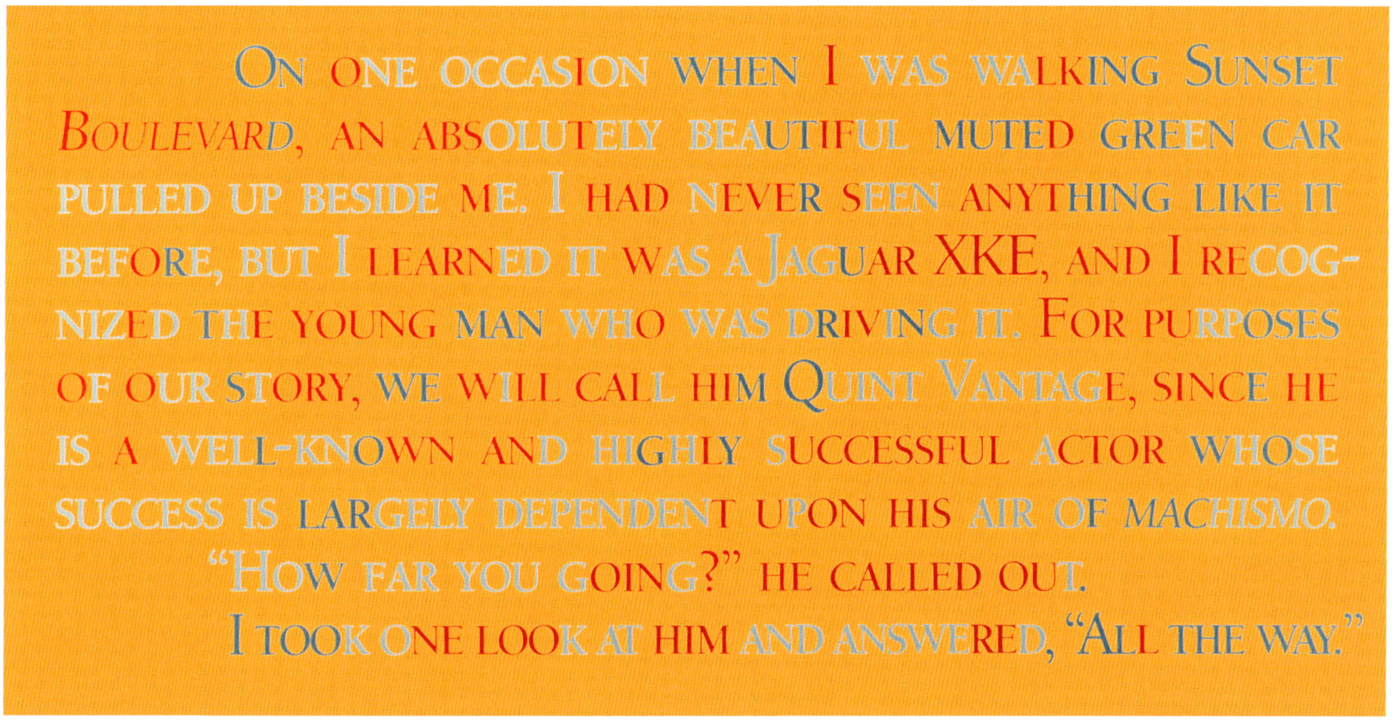

Larry Johnson. ***Untitled (I Had Never Seen Anything Like It)***, 1988. Color coupler print, framed 45¾ × 90¾ in. (116.2 × 230.5 cm). Walker Art Center, Minneapolis, T. B. Walker Acquisition Fund, 1996

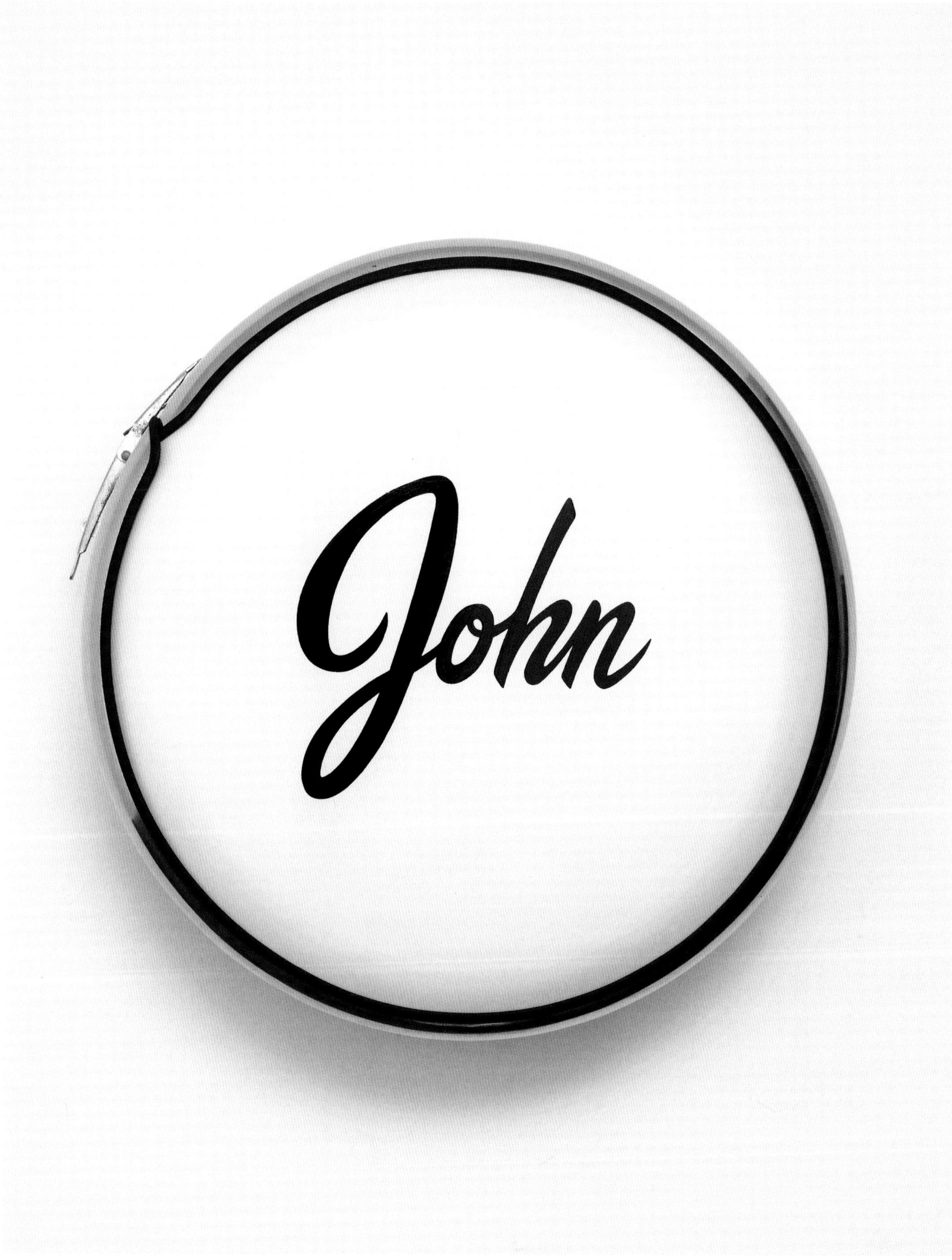

John Dogg. *John, Not Johnny*, 1987. Painted stainless-steel spare-tire cover, diam. 29 in. (73.7 cm).
Collection of Adam Lindemann

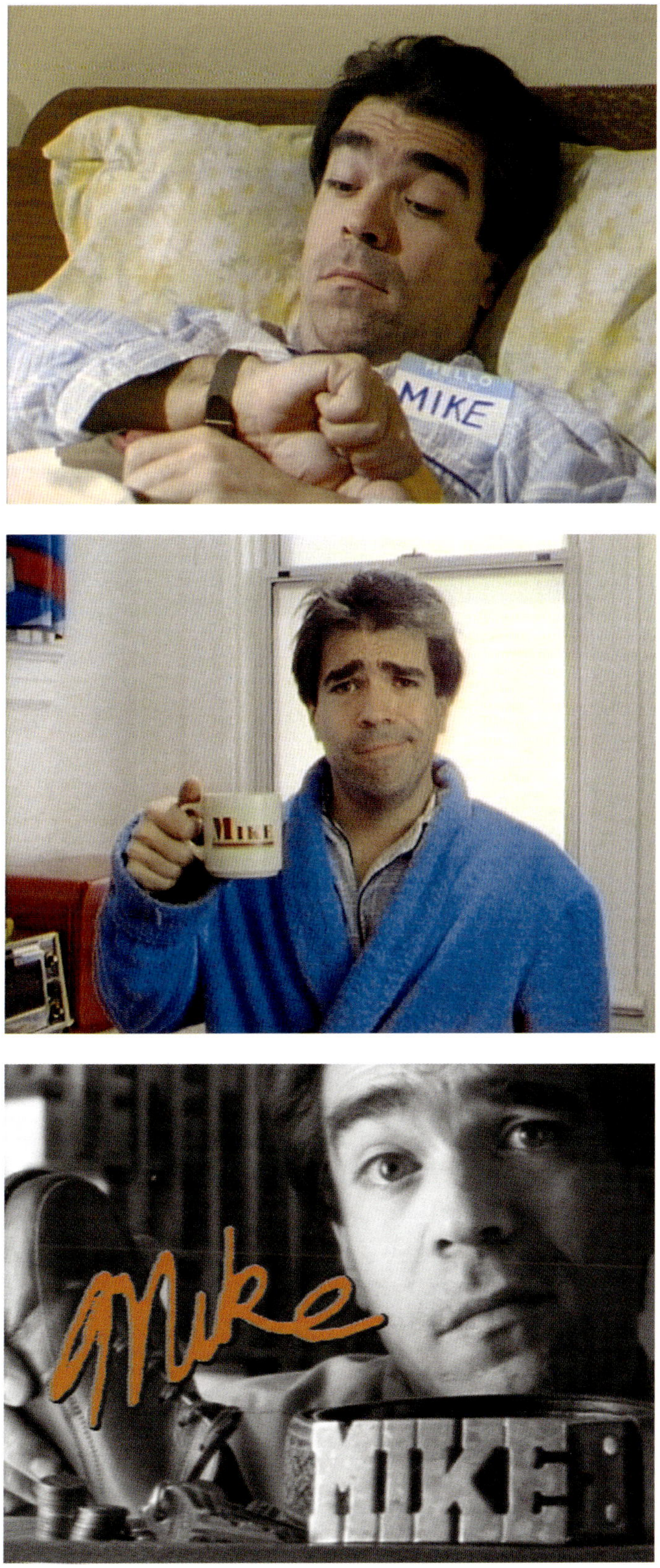

Michael Smith. Stills from ***Mike***, 1987. Video, black-and-white and color, sound, 2:43 min.
Courtesy of Electronic Arts Intermix (EAI), New York

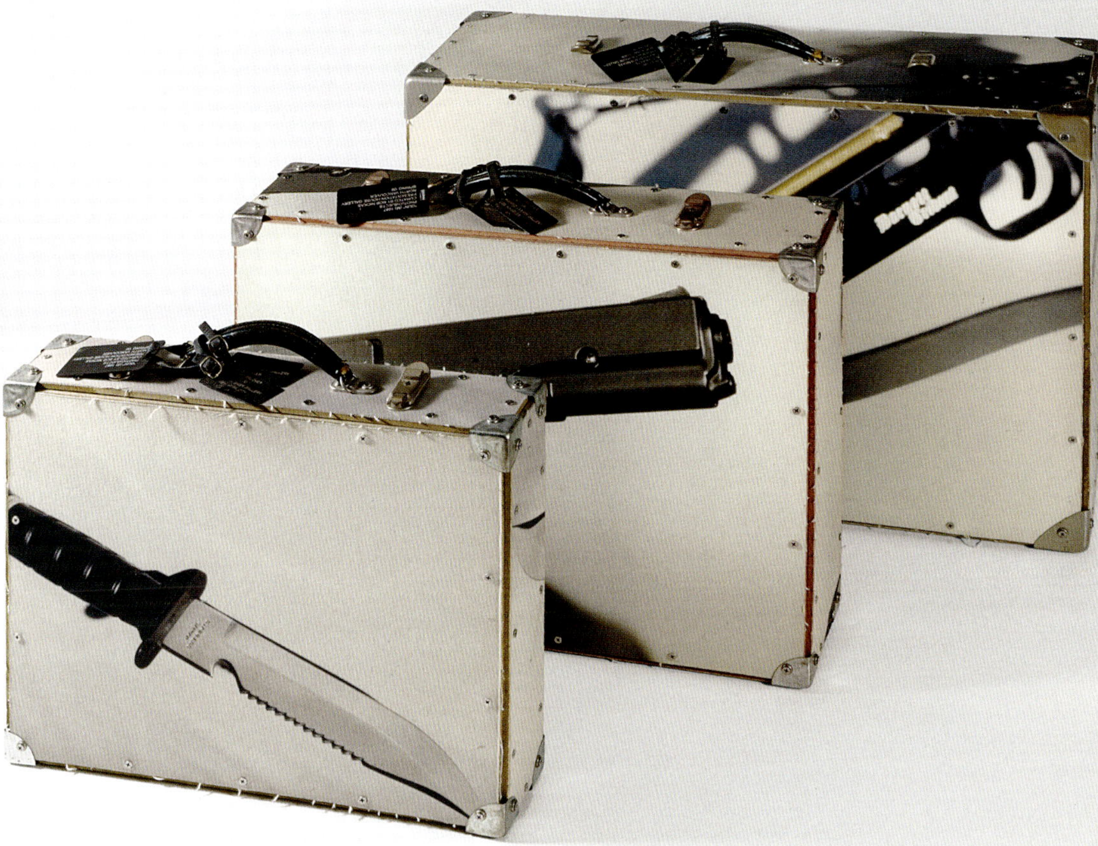

Alan Belcher. *Gun*, 1987. Color photographs laminated to canvas, stainless-steel hardware, leather handles, identification tags (set of 3), largest 20 × 30 × 10 in. (50.8 × 76.2 × 25.4 cm), smallest 16 × 20 × 4½ in. (40.6 × 50.8 × 11.4 cm). Ed. of 2. Ruth and William Ehrlich
Following spread: ***Gun*** (detail)

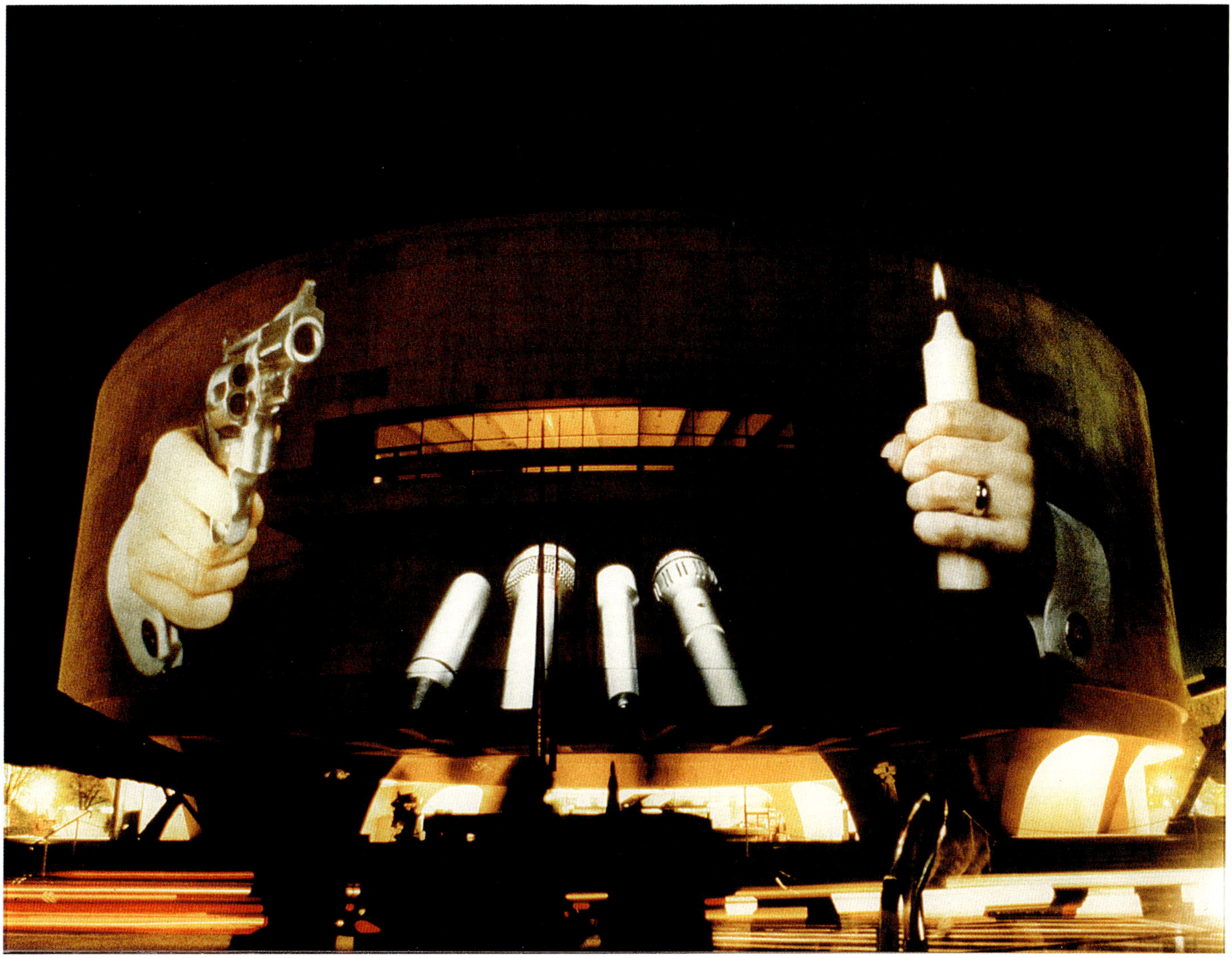

Krzysztof Wodiczko. *Hirshhorn Museum, Washington, DC*, October 25–27, 1988. Public projection at the Hirshhorn Museum and Sculpture Garden, Smithsonian Institution, Washington, DC

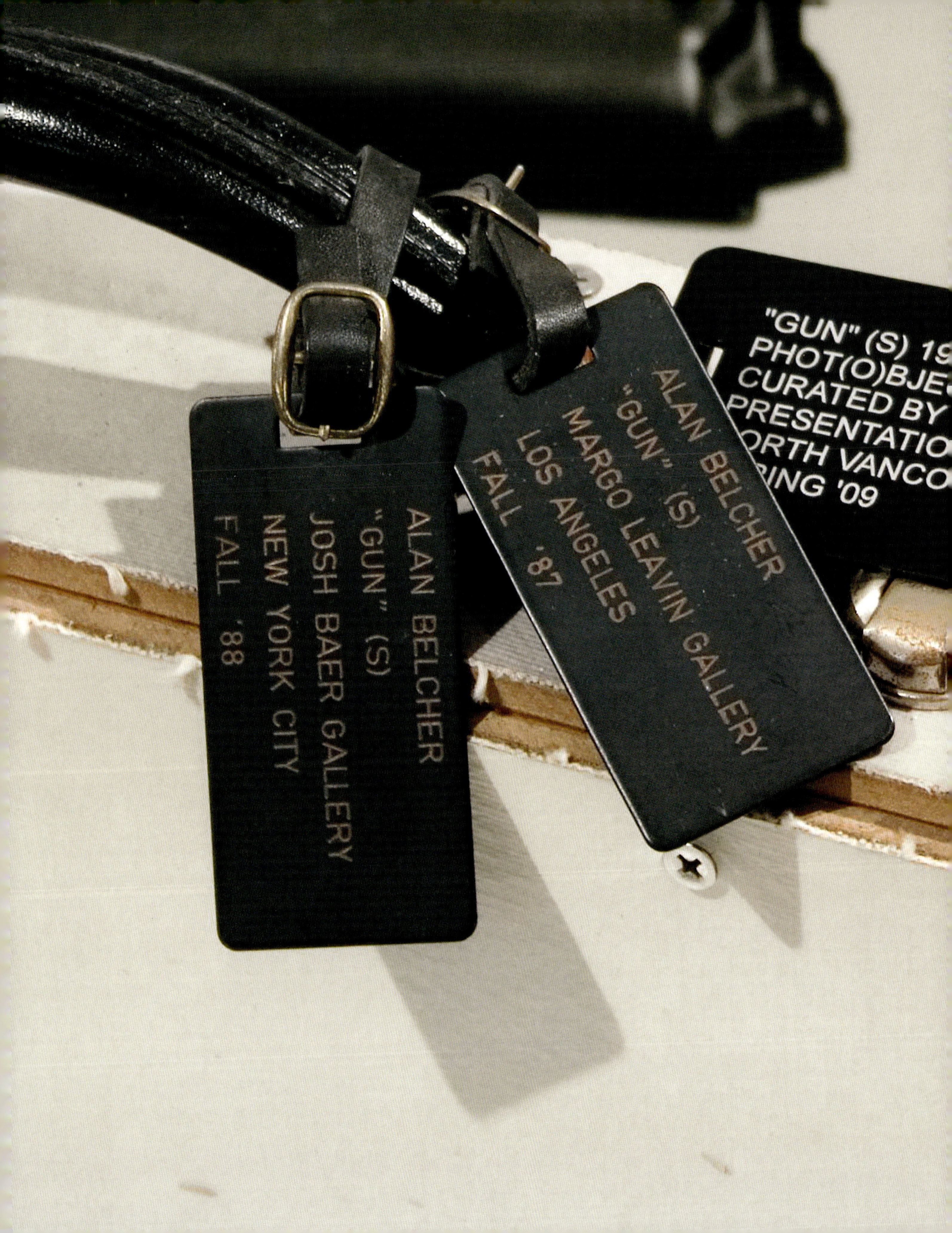
ALAN BELCHER
"GUN" (S)
JOSH BAER GALLERY
NEW YORK CITY
FALL '88
ALAN BELCHER
"GUN" (S)
MARGO LEAVIN GALLERY
LOS ANGELES
FALL '87
"GUN" (S) 19
PHOT(O)BJE
CURATED BY
PRESENTATIO
ORTH VANCO
RING '09

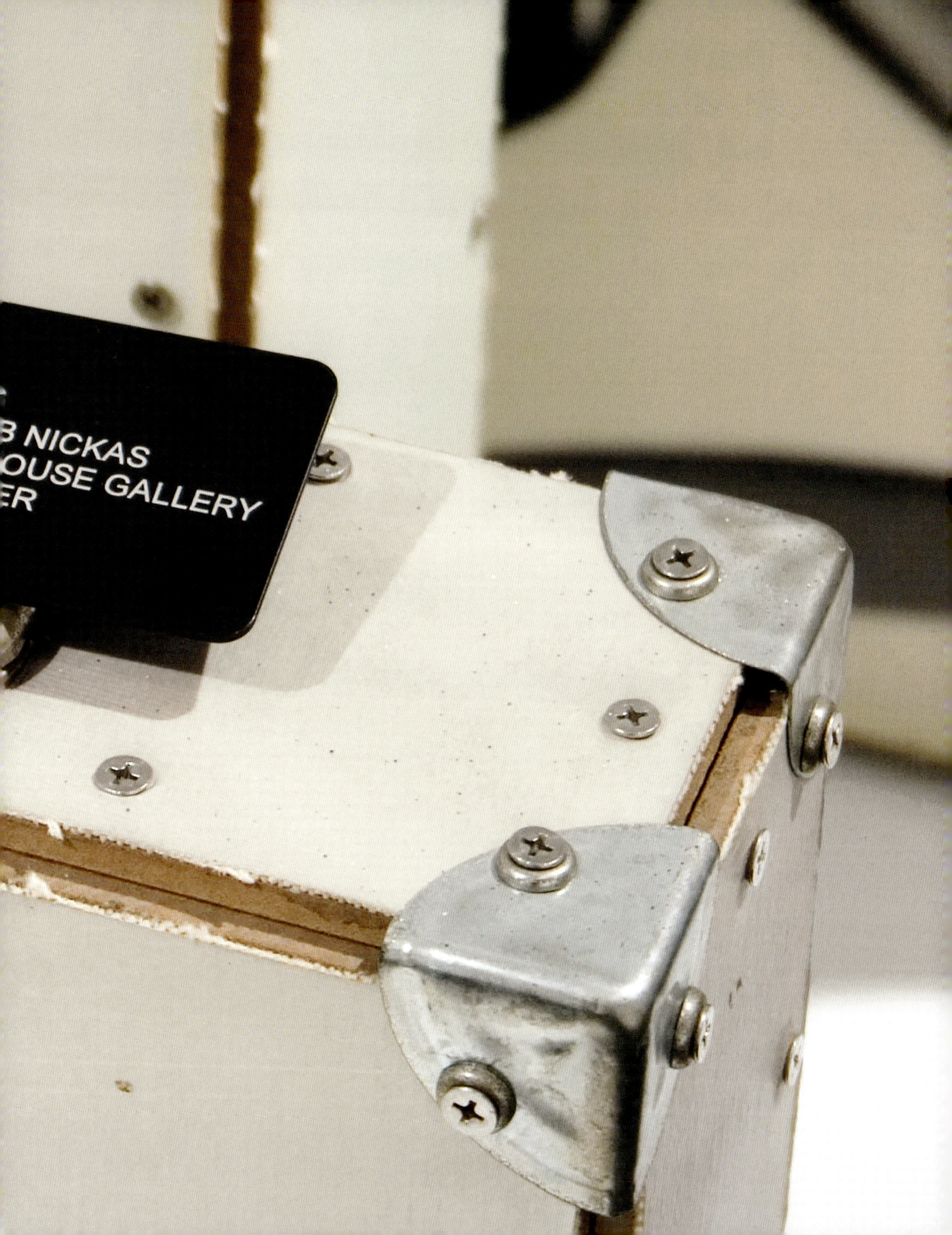
B NICKAS
OUSE GALLERY
ER

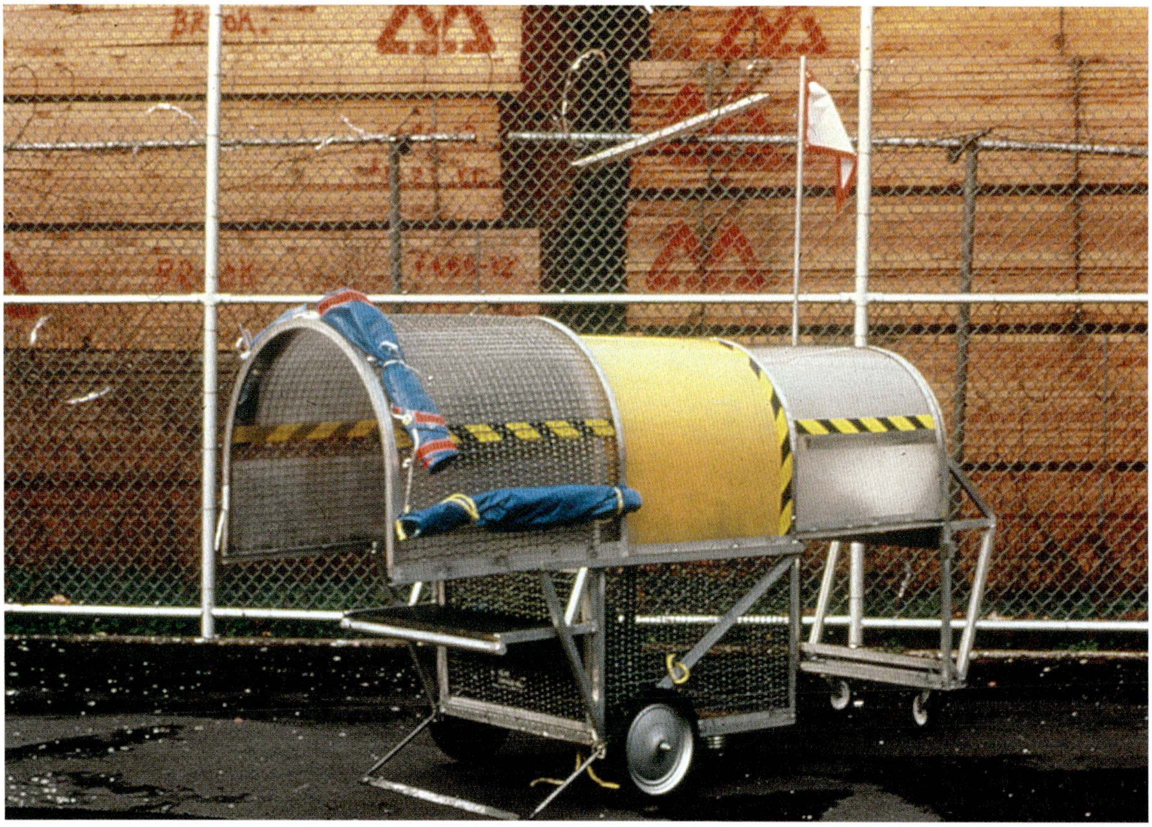

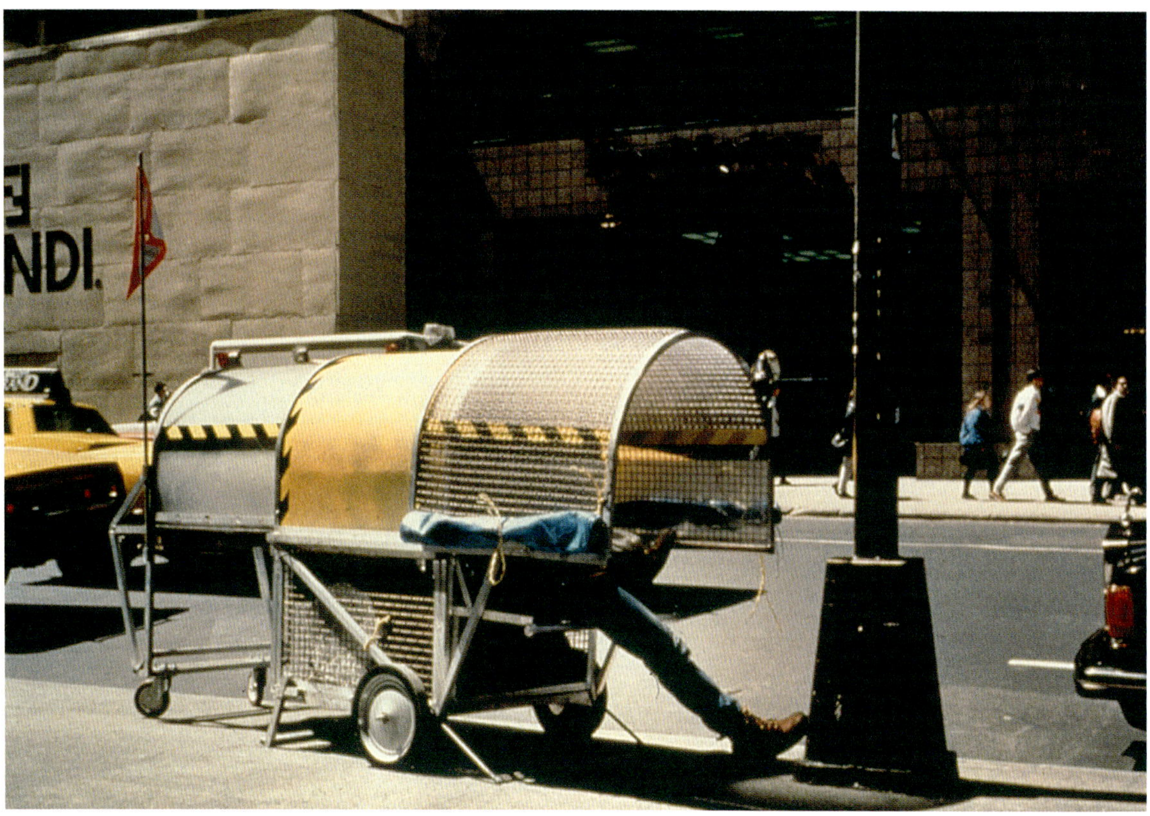

 Krzysztof Wodiczko. Photographs of ***Homeless Vehicle***, 1988

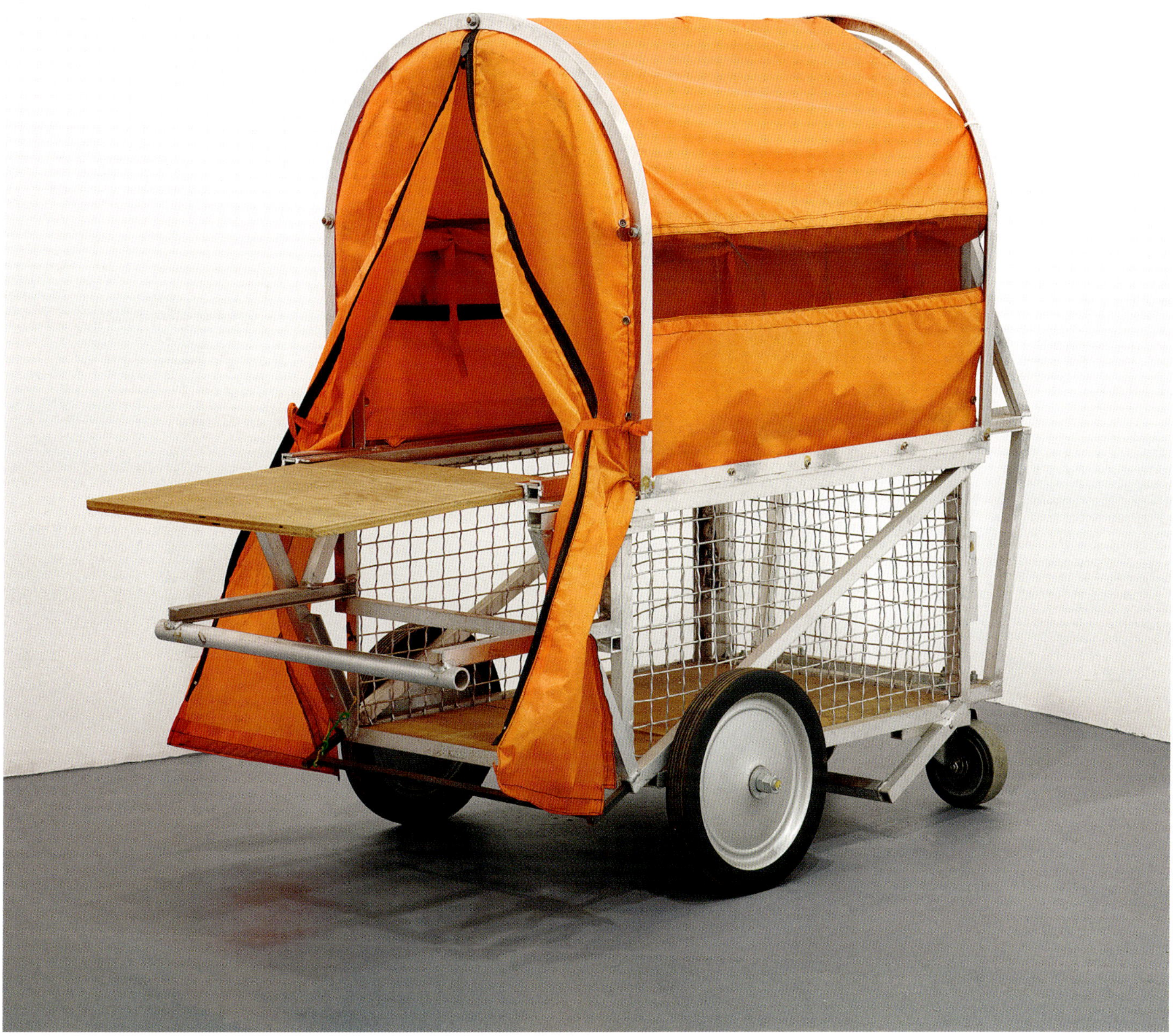

Krzysztof Wodiczko. ***Homeless Vehicle, Variant 5***, 1988. Aluminum, fabric, wire cage, hardware, 60 × 36 × 56 in. (152.4 × 91.4 × 142.2 cm). Hirshhorn Museum and Sculpture Garden, Smithsonian Institution, Washington, DC

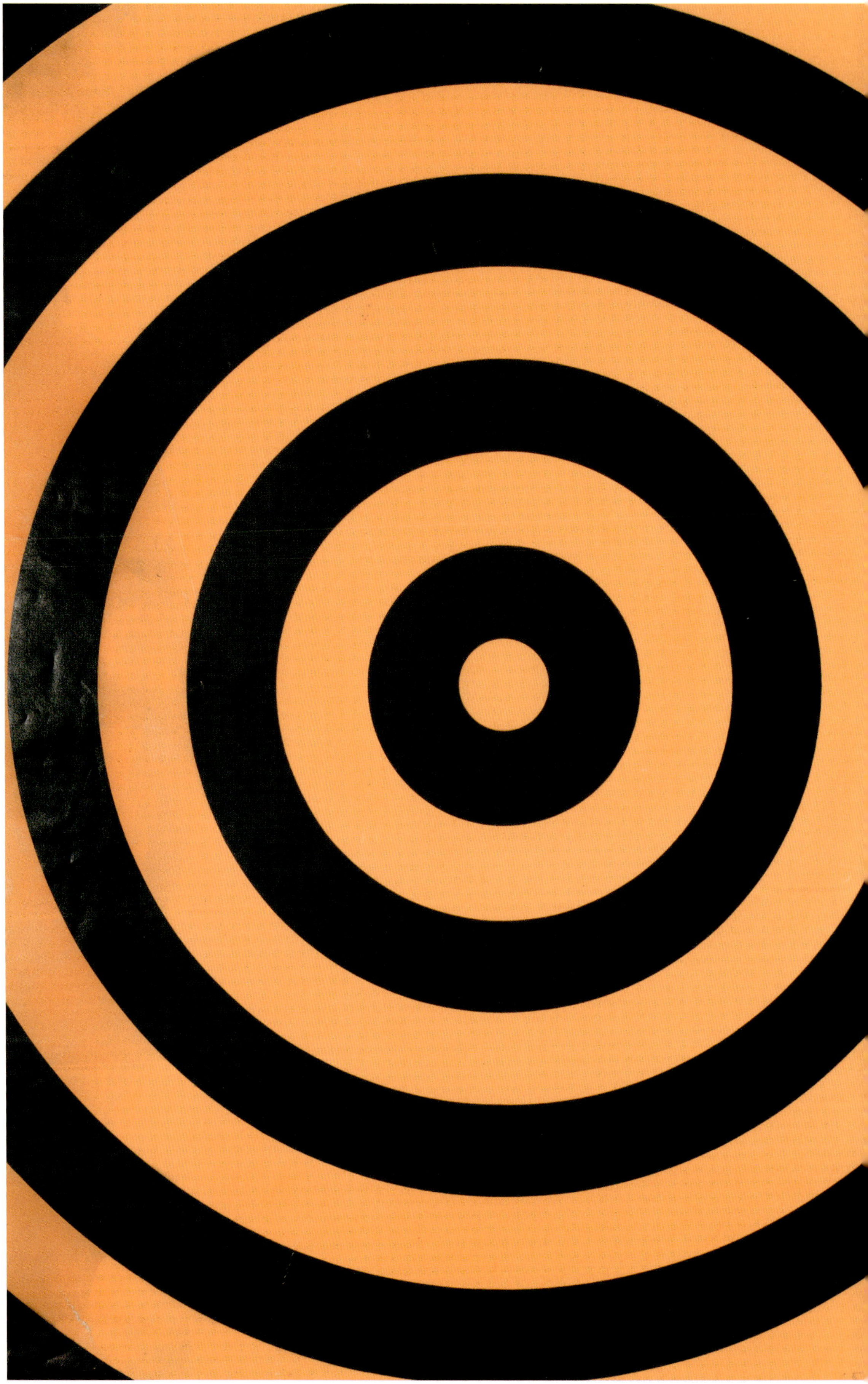

Donald Moffett. ***He Kills Me***, 1987. Offset lithograph, 23½ × 37½ in. (59.7 × 95.3 cm).
International Center of Photography, New York, Purchase, with funds provided by the ICP Acquisitions Committee, 2000

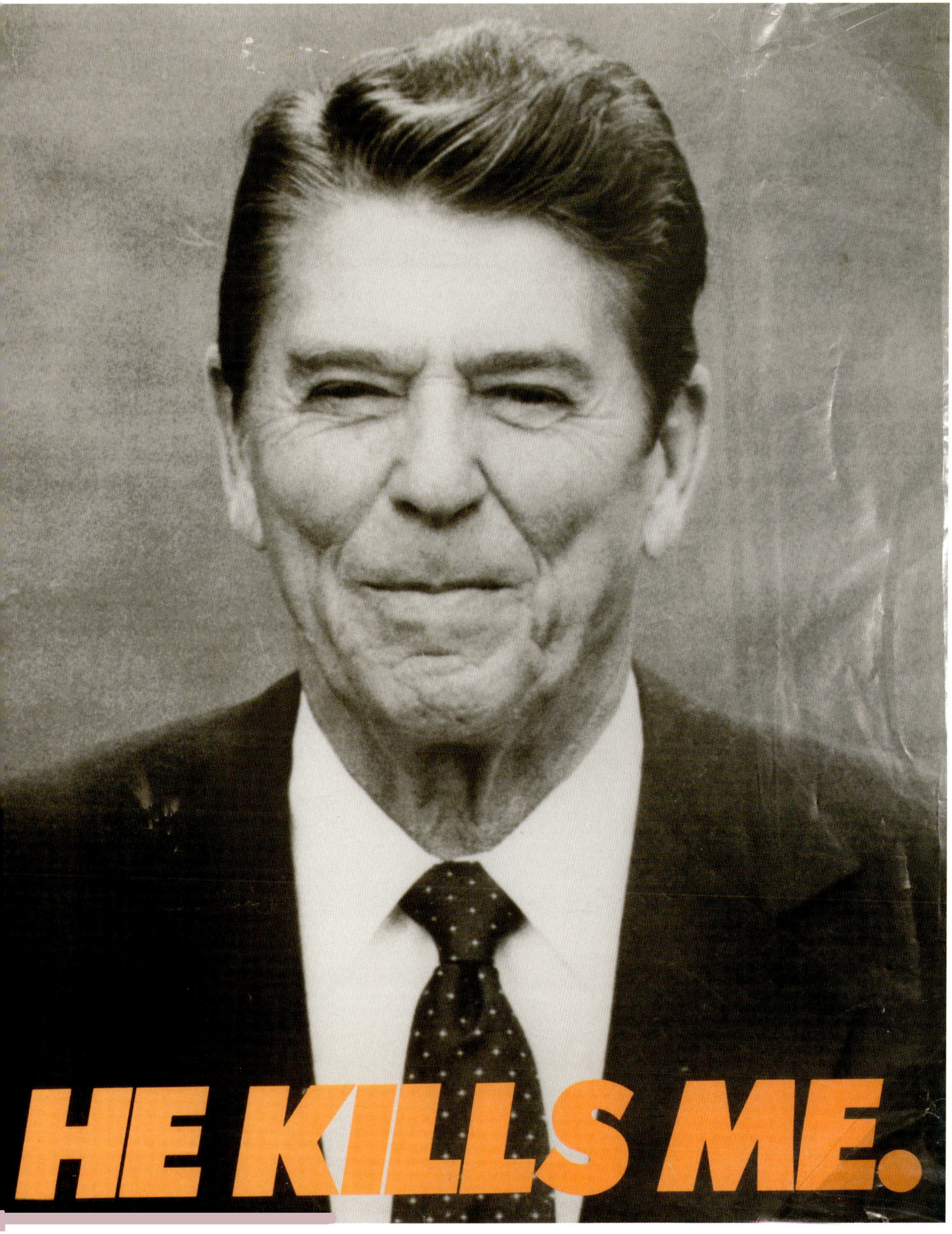
HE KILLS ME.

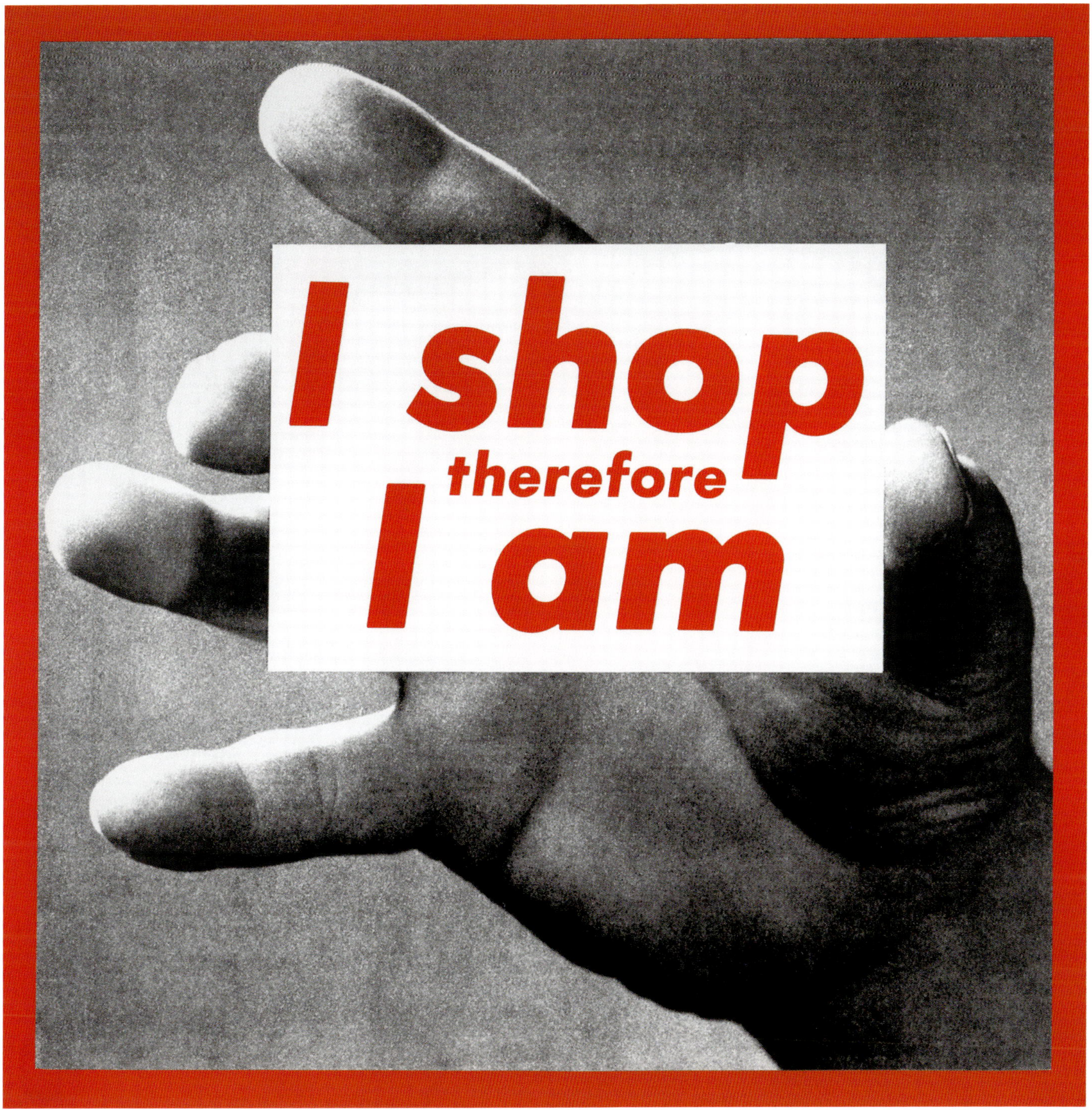

Barbara Kruger. ***Untitled (I Shop therefore I am)***, 1987. Photographic silkscreen on vinyl, 9 ft. 3 in. × 9 ft. 5 in. (281.9 × 287 cm). Glenstone, Potomac, Maryland

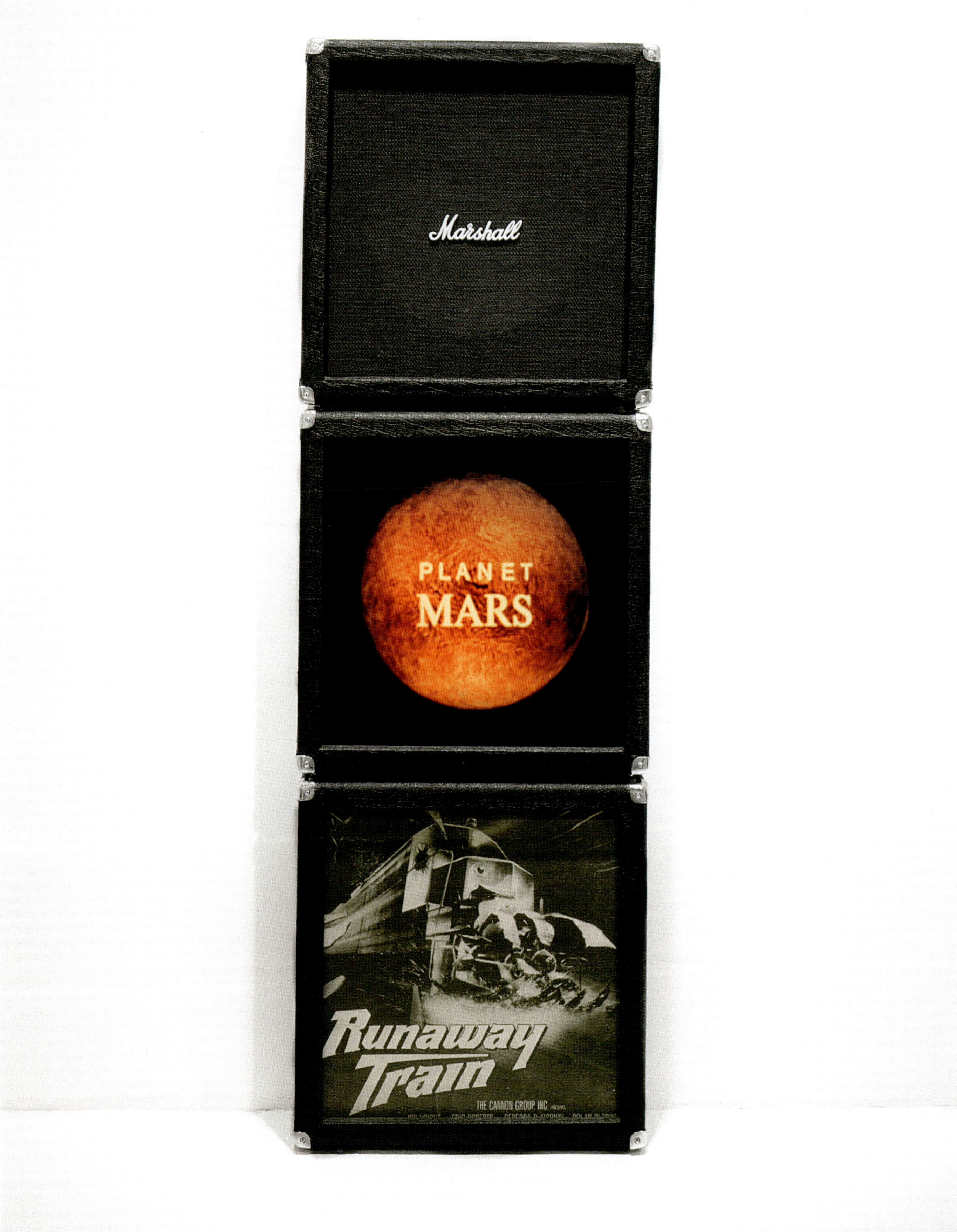

Jennifer Bolande. *Marshall Stack*, 1987. Three handmade wood-and-vinyl speaker cabinets, color photographs, Marshall-brand speaker cloth, accessories, and plastic logo, 69 × 22½ × 6½ in. (175.3 × 57.2 × 16.5 cm). Collection of the artist

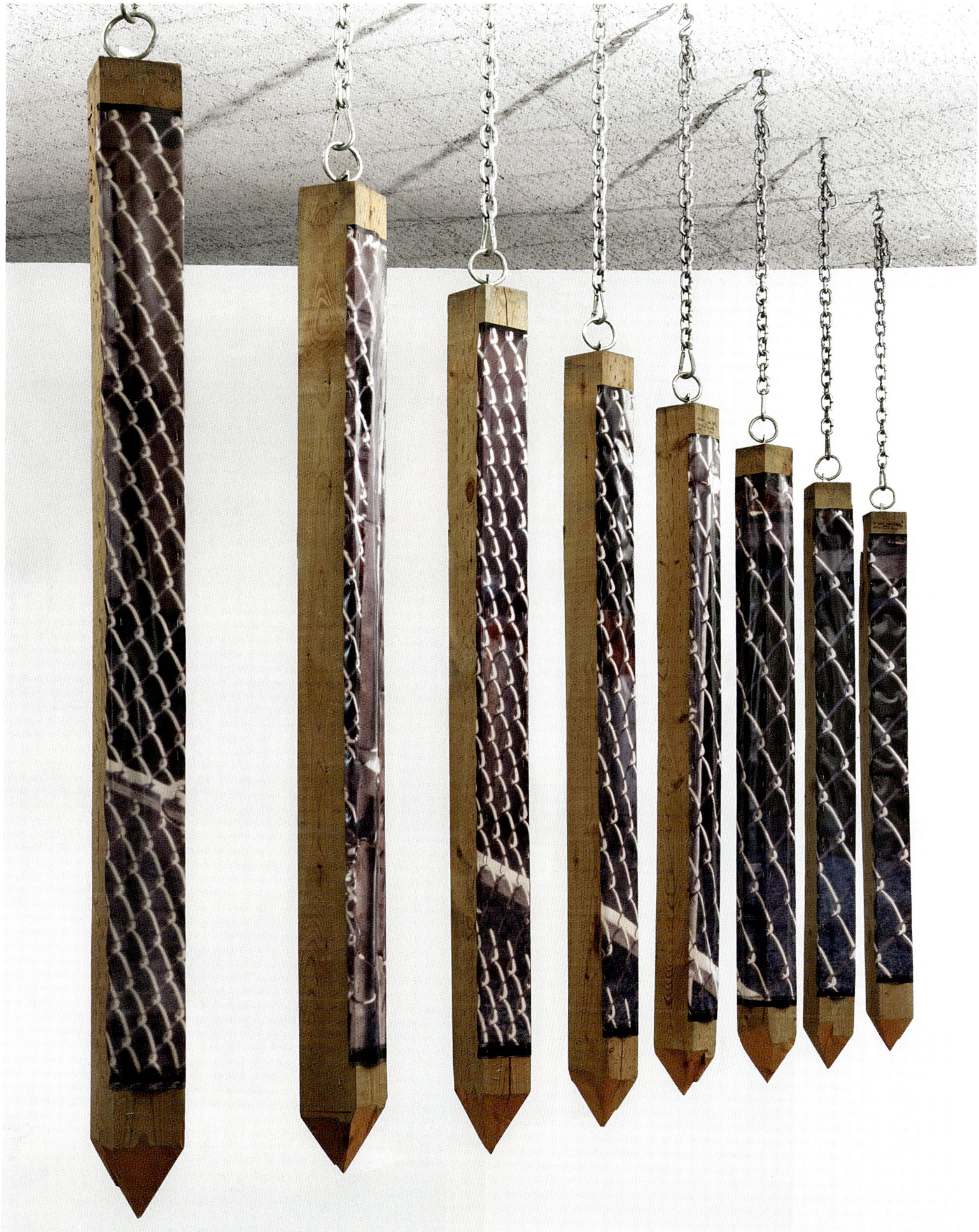

Alan Belcher. ***Fence Posts***, 1987. Color photographs stapled to sharpened wood posts, hanging from metal chains, h. of each 60 in. (152.4 cm). Ruth and William Ehrlich

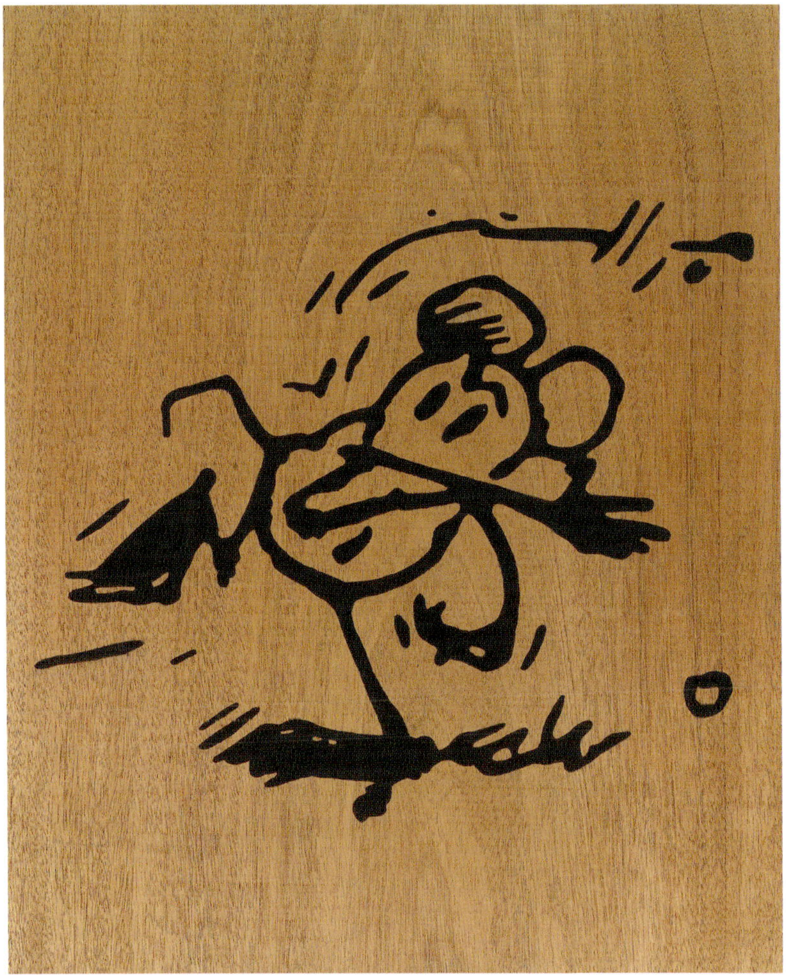

Sherrie Levine. *Ignatz: 6*, 1988. Casein on wood, 24 × 19⅞ × ⅞ in. (61 × 50.5 × 2.2 cm).
Walker Art Center, Minneapolis, T. B. Walker Acquisition Fund, 1992

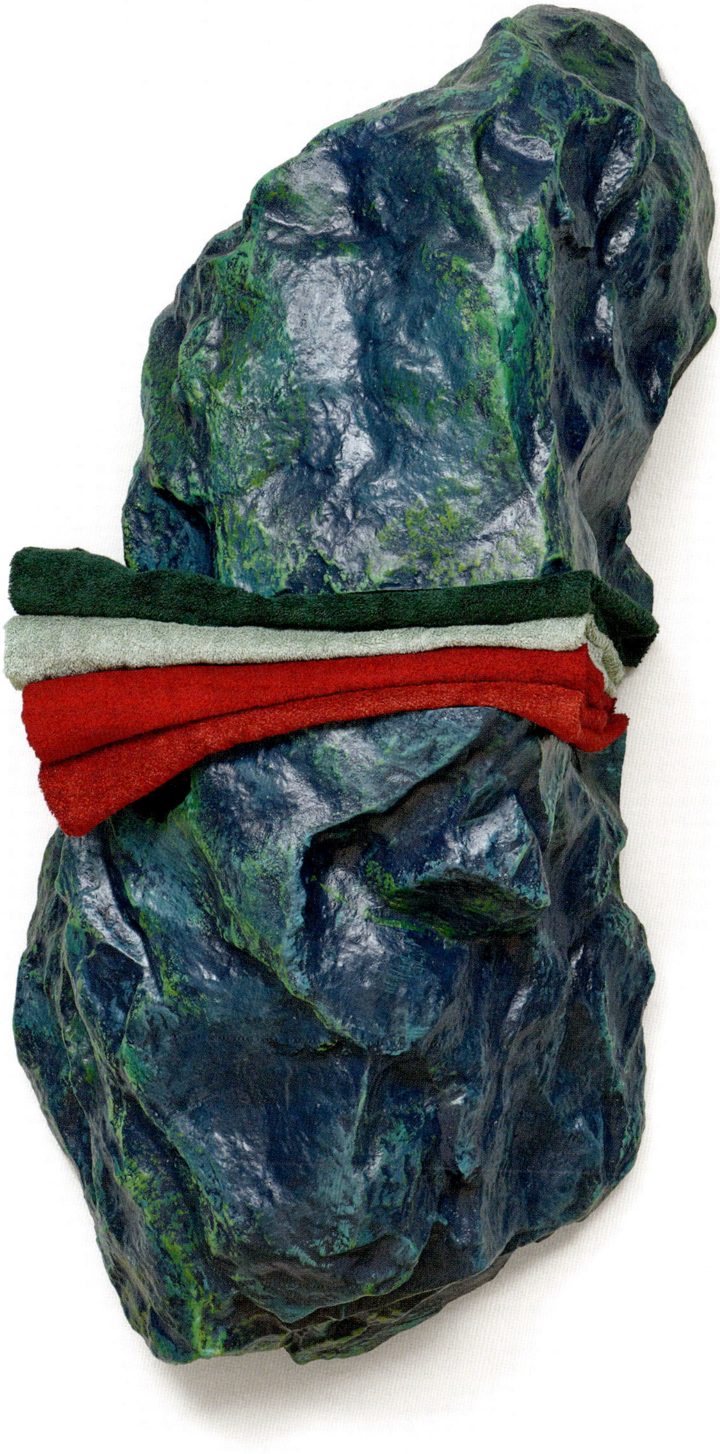

Mark Stahl. ***Leisure World***, 1987. Fiberglass rocks, bath towels, 52 × 28 × 17 in. (132.1 × 71.1 × 43.2 cm). Courtesy of Pierre Huber, Geneva

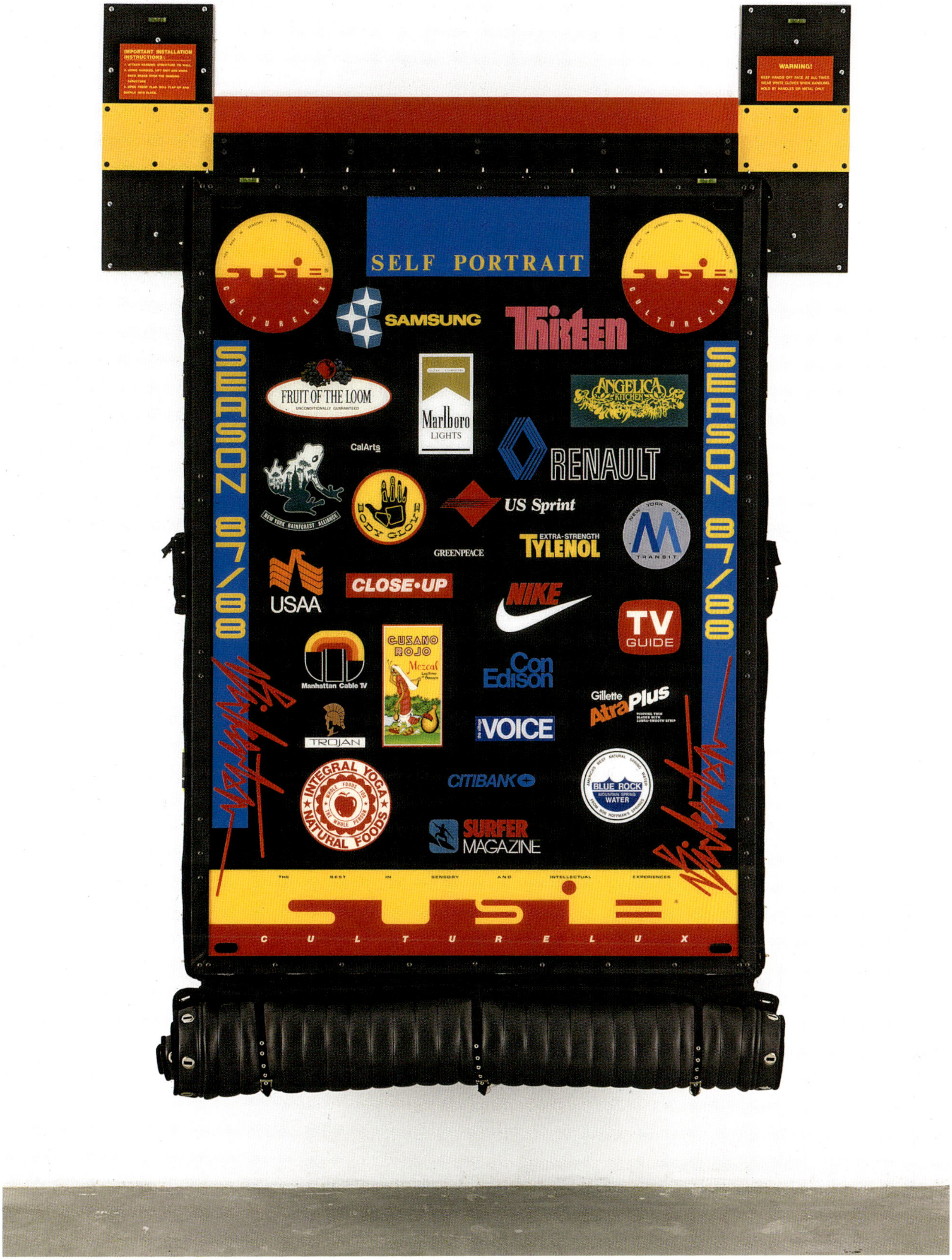

Ashley Bickerton. ***Tormented Self-Portrait (Susie at Arles) No. 2***, 1988. Mixed media, 90 × 68½ × 20 in. (228.6 × 174 × 50.8 cm). Des Moines Art Center, Purchased with funds from the Edmundson Art Foundation, Inc.

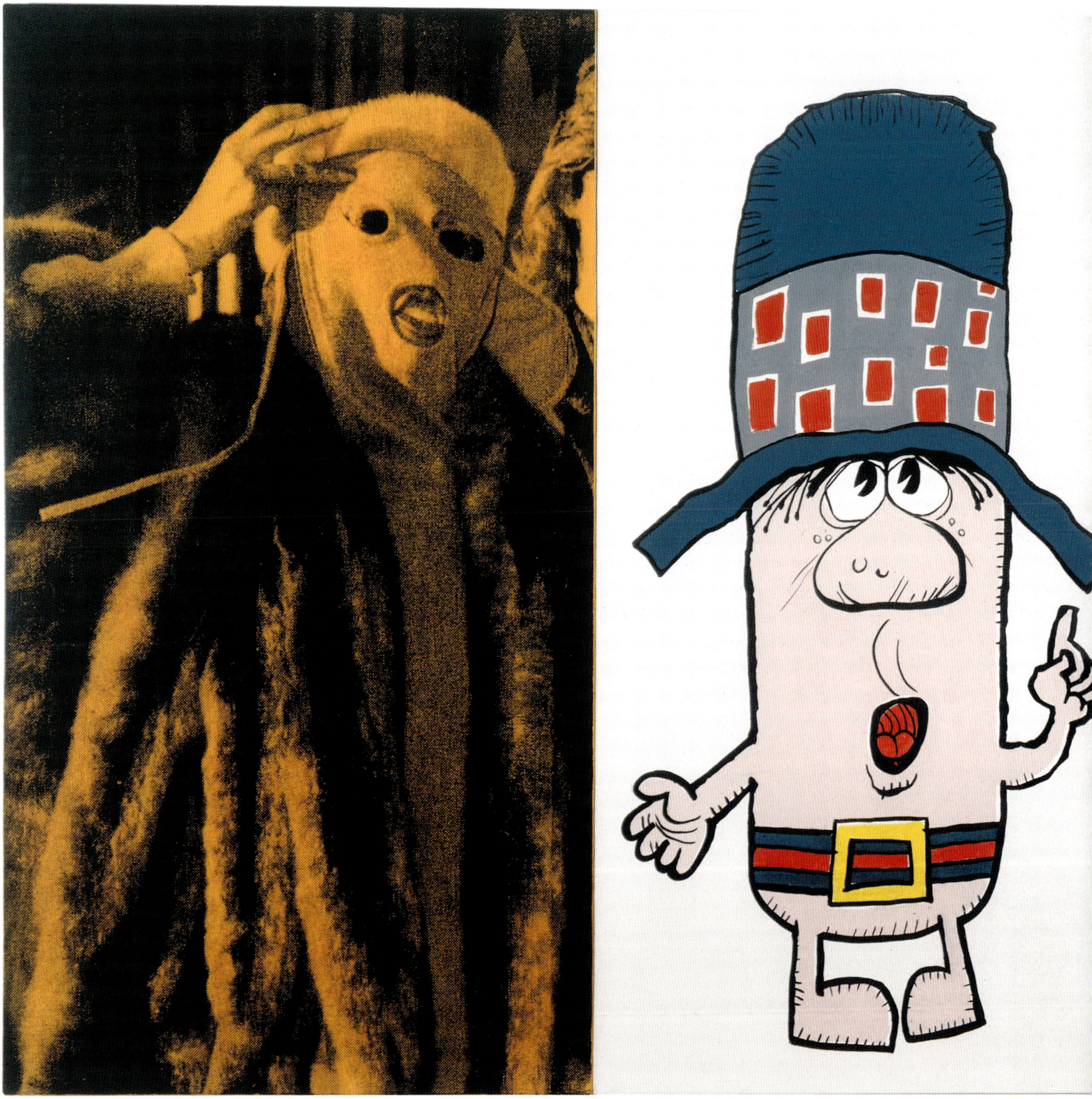

Julia Wachtel. *what, what, what*, 1988. Oil, Flashe, and lacquer ink on canvas, 52 in. × 9 ft. 3 in. (132.1 × 281.9 cm). Courtesy of the artist and Elizabeth Dee, New York

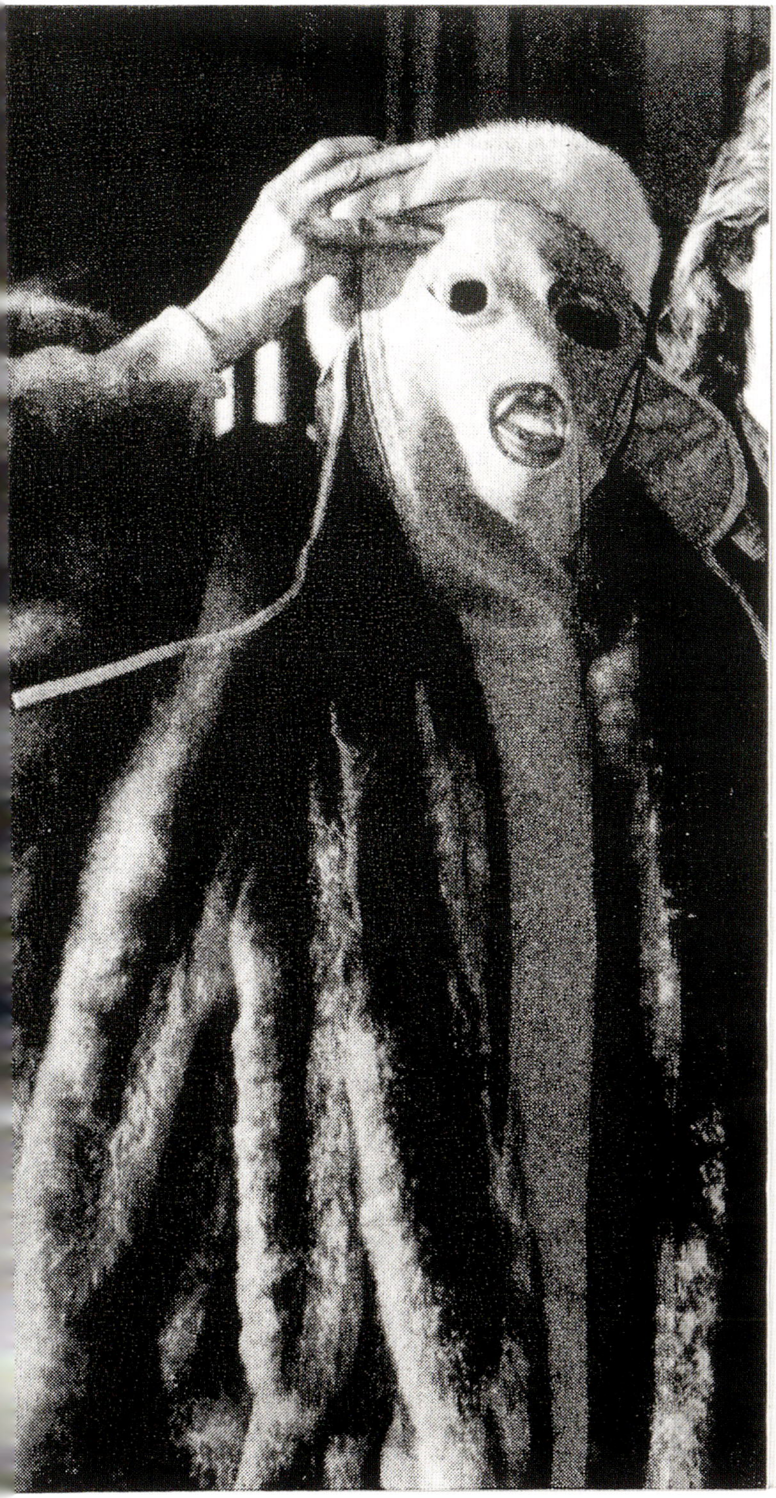

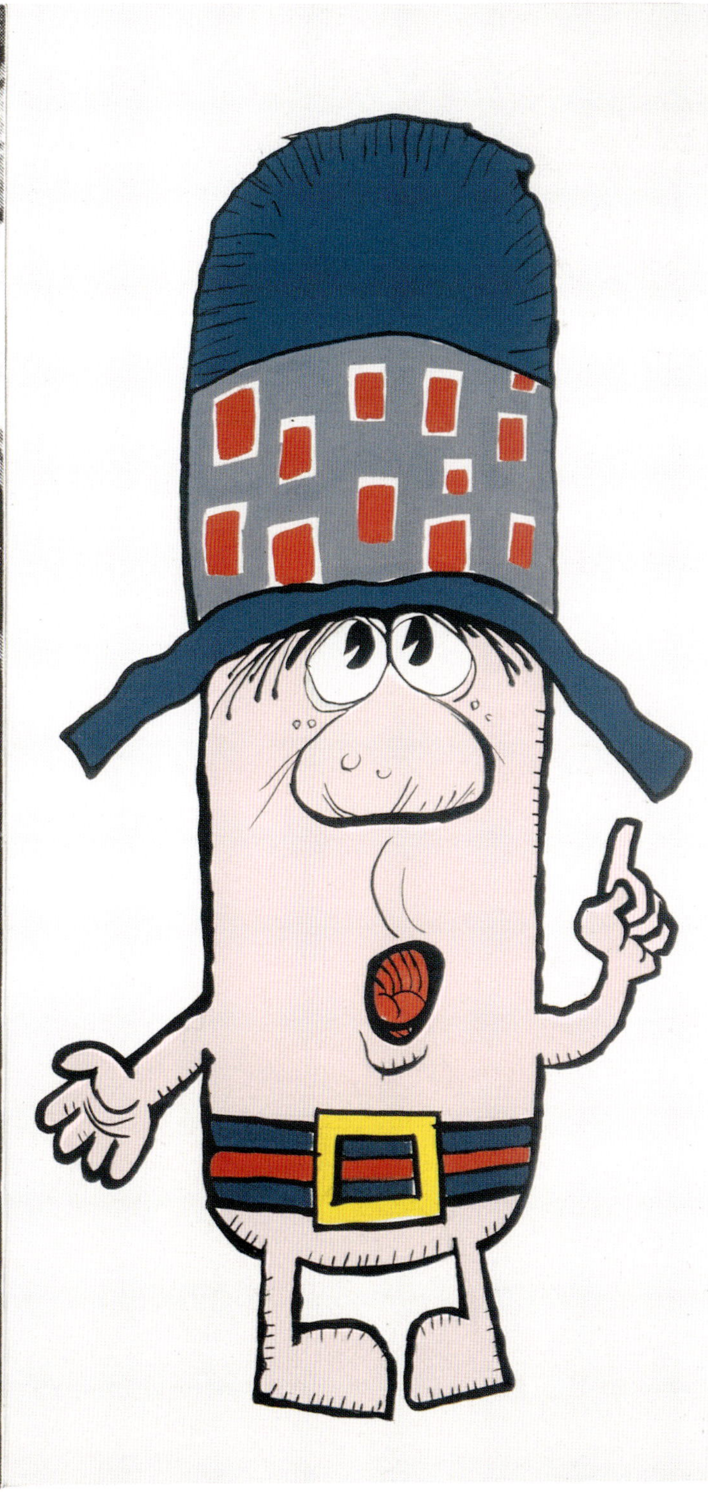

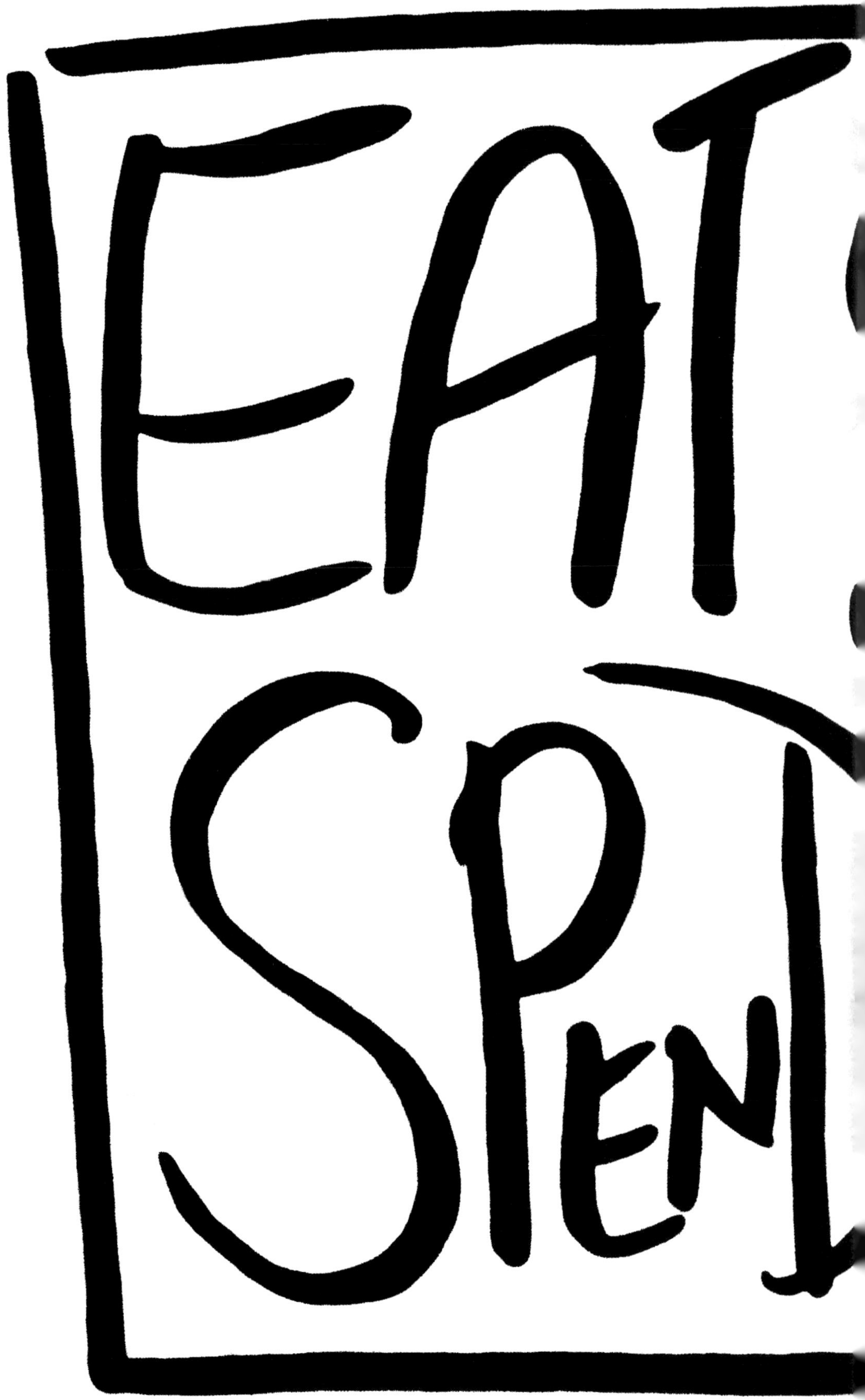

Jessica Diamond. ***T.V. Telepathy (Black-and-White Version)***, 1989. Acrylic on wall, dimensions variable. Ed. 1/3. Courtesy of the artist

SUGAR MONEY

Chronology Endnotes

1 Elizabeth Hess, "Home-Style Looking," *Village Voice*, January 28–February 3, 1981.

2 *Lower Manhattan Drawing Show* [press release], 1981.

3 Quoted in Jane Gross, "Homosexuals Stepping up AIDS Education," *New York Times*, September 22, 1985.

4 Anthony Haden-Guest, "The New Queen of the Art Scene," *New York*, April 19, 1982, p. 28.

5 John Passmore, "The Rise and Fall of the East Village Art Scene," NYPR Archives and Preservation, accessed July 5, 2017, http://www.wnyc.org/story/rise-and-fall-east-village-art-scene.

6 Grace Glueck, "Gallery View; A Gallery Scene That Pioneers in New Territories," *New York Times*, June 26, 1983; "New Prosperity Brings Discord to the East Village," December 19, 1983; Lisa Belkin, "The Gentrification of the East Village," September 2, 1984.

7 Rita Reif, "50 Paintings to Be Sold from Tremaine Estate," *New York Times*, June 7, 1991.

8 Walter Robinson and Carlo McCormick, "Slouching towards Avenue D," *Art in America*, Summer 1984, pp. 135–61.

9 See Mira Schor, *Wet: On Painting, Feminism, and Art Culture* (Durham, NC, and London: Duke University Press, 1997), p. 88.

10 Therese Lichtenstein. "Review: Louise Lawler/Allan McCollum," *Arts*, December 1984, p. 34.

11 Gallery Nature Morte, *Louise Lawler: Interesting* [press release], April 1985.

12 Brian Wallis, "A Product You Could Kill For," in Brian Wallis, *Damaged Goods: Desire and the Economy of the Object* (New York: New Museum of Contemporary Art, 1986), p. 33.

13 Ibid.

14 "Pop Shop," The Keith Haring Foundation website, accessed July 5, 2017, http://www.haring.com/!/pop-shop.

15 Brian Wallis, "Acknowledgments," in Wallis, *Damaged Goods*, p. 7.

16 Hal Foster, "The Future of an Illusion, or The Contemporary Artist as Cargo Cultist," in Yve-Alain Bois et al., *Endgame: Reference and Simulation in Recent Painting and Sculpture* (Boston: Institute of Contemporary Art; Cambridge, MA: MIT Press, 1986), p. 100.

17 Bob Nickas, *Catalog of the Exhibition, 1984–2011* (Los Angeles: 2nd Cannons Publications, 2011), n.p. See http://www.2ndcannons.com/catalogoftheexhibition.htm (accessed July 5, 2017).

18 E. Heartney, "Reluctant Prophet (Jean Baudrillard)," *Art News* 86, no. 7 (September 1987), p. 18.

19 Douglas C. McGill, "Andy Warhol, Pop Artist, Dies," *New York Times*, February 23, 1987.

20 Andy Warhol, *The Philosophy of Andy Warhol (from A to B and Back Again)* (New York: Harcourt Brace Jovanovich, 1975), p. 121.

21 Michael Brenson, "Art: Whitney Biennial's New Look," *New York Times*, April 10, 1987.

22 Douglas C. McGill, "Art Boom Slows in the East Village," *New York Times*, July 25, 1987.

23 Ibid.

24 Jerry Saltz, "The New York Canon," *New York*, April 7, 2008.

25 Jeffrey Deitch, *Cultural Geometry*, exh. cat. (Athens: DESTE Foundation for Contemporary Art, 1988), p. 27.

26 Rita Reif, "Bidders Throng Warhol Auction," *New York Times*, April 24, 1988.

27 Barbara Gamarekian, "Corcoran, to Foil Dispute, Drops Mapplethorpe Show," *New York Times*, June 14, 1989.

28 David Handelman, "Act Up in Anger," *Rolling Stone*, March 8, 1990.

29 David Rimanelli, "Time Capsules: 1986–1990," *Artforum*, April 2003, p. 108.

30 Michael Kimmelman, "Review/Art; At the Whitney, 100 Works from the Last 30 Years," *New York Times*, November 10, 1989.

Captions and Credits for Chronology Images

Page numbers appear in **boldface**.

36 left: Jenny Holzer/Coleen Fitzgibbon. *Manifesto Show* poster, 1979. Courtesy of online Gallery 98. **36 right:** Poster for Sonic Youth concert at the Mudd Club, 1981. Collection of Tom McQuown. **37:** Advertisement for A. More Store, with drawing by Tom Otterness, published in *East Village Eye*, Winter 1980. Courtesy of online Gallery 98. **38 left:** Barbara Kruger. *Pictures and Promises* poster, 1981. The Kitchen videos and records, Getty Research Institute, Los Angeles (2014.M.6). © Barbara Kruger. Courtesy of Mary Boone Gallery, New York. **38 right:** Jenny Holzer. *Untitled*, 1982. Spectacolor light board with computer animation. Installation view, *Messages to the Public*, Times Square, New York, 1982. Photo by John Marchael; artwork courtesy of Jane Dickson, Project Initiator and Animator; courtesy of Public Art Fund, NY. **39 top:** Poster for Fashion Moda designed by Stefan Eins, with photograph of work by John Ahearn, 1980. Courtesy of online Gallery 98. **39 bottom:** Advertisement for Gallery Nature Morte's inaugural group exhibition, published in *BOMB*, Spring 1982. **74 left:** Cover of Hal Foster's *The Anti-Aesthetic* (Seattle: Bay Press, 1983), with photograph by Richard Prince. **74 right:** Janet Koenig and Gregory Sholette. Poster for Group Material's project *Subculture*, New York, 1983. Courtesy of the ABC No Rio Book Collection. **75 left:** Photograph by Stefan Lupino of Peter Nagy and Alan Belcher at Sherrie Levine's exhibition *1917*, Gallery Nature Morte, New York, published in *L'Uomo Vogue*, December 1984. **75 right:** Installation view, *The New Capital*, White Columns, New York, 1984–85. Courtesy of White Columns, New York. **76 left, top:** Poster by the Guerrilla Girls, 1985. © Guerrilla Girls; courtesy of guerrillagirls.com. **76 left, bottom:** Dara Birnbaum. Still from MTV's *Art Break*, 1987. Courtesy of Electronic Arts Intermix (EAI), New York. **76 center, top:** Cover of the Coca-Cola Company's first-quarter progress report, 1985. David M. Rubenstein Rare Book and Manuscript Library, Duke University, Durham, NC, Stuart Elliot Papers, John W. Hartman Center for Sales, Advertising and Marketing History. **76 center, bottom:** Louise Lawler. *Portrait (Blue)*, 1984. Cibachrome. Courtesy of the artist and Metro Pictures, New York (MP# LL–88). **76 right:** Installation view, Jeff Koons's *Equilibrium*, International With Monument, 1985. © Jeff Koons. **77 left, top:** Julia Wachtel. *Absolut Wachtel*, 1989. Acrylic and silkscreen on canvas, mounted on wood. Courtesy of Spritmuseum, Stockholm. **77 left, bottom:** Cover of exhibition catalogue for *Damaged Goods: Desire and the Economy of the Object*, New Museum of Contemporary Art, New York, 1986. Courtesy of New Museum. **77 center:** Installation view, *Ashley Bickerton, Peter Halley, Jeff Koons, Meyer Vaisman*, Sonnabend Gallery, New York, 1986. Courtesy of Sonnabend Gallery, New York; photo by Fred Scruton. **77 right:** Barbara Kruger. Six matchbooks, 1986. Black-and-white photolithographs on black cardboard. Courtesy of Swann Auction Galleries. **150 left:** David Robbins. *The Art Dealers' Optical Tests, #2: To Colin de Land of American Fine Arts, the string appears single wherever it is fixated, double elsewhere,* 1987. Gelatin silver print. Courtesy of David Robbins. **150 center:** Barbara Bloom. *The Reign of Narcissism,* 1988–89. Mixed-media installation. The Museum of Contemporary Art, Los Angeles, Gift of the Frederick R. Weisman Art Foundation. Courtesy of the artist and David Lewis, New York. **150 right:** Poster for Group Material's *Resistance (Anti-Baudrillard)*, White Columns, New York, 1987. Courtesy of White Columns, New York. **151 left:** Cover of exhibition catalogue for *NY ART NOW: The Saatchi Collection* (Giancarlo Politi Editore, 1992), Saatchi Gallery, London, with photograph of Jeff Koons's *Rabbit*. Courtesy of the Saatchi Gallery, London. **151 right:** Installation view, *Cultural Geometry*, House of Cyprus, Athens, 1988. Courtesy of DESTE Foundation. **152 left:** Nike advertisement by Portland, Oregon, advertising firm Wieden+Kennedy, 1988. David M. Rubenstein Rare Book and Manuscript Library, Duke University, Durham, NC, Competitive Advertisements Collection, John W. Hartman Center for Sales, Advertising and Marketing History. **152 right, top:** Installation view, *A Forest of Signs: Art in the Crisis of Representation*, The Temporary Contemporary, Los Angeles, 1989. Courtesy of The Museum of Contemporary Art, Los Angeles; photo by Gene Ogami. **152 right, bottom:** Unidentified artist. *Sell Burroughs Wellcome*, ca. 1987. Lithograph. International Center of Photography, New York, Purchase, with funds provided by the ICP Acquisitions Committee, 2000 (1184.2000). **153 left:** Macintosh Portable computer, released September 20, 1989. Photo courtesy of theregister.co.uk. **153 right:** Residents of East Berlin buying bananas, Schlesisches Tor, 1989. Alamy stock photo by Norbert Michalke

Works in the Exhibition

1979–82

Gretchen Bender
Untitled (The Pleasure Is Back), 1982
Photographic silkscreen on enamel sign tin (5 parts)
Overall 72 × 72 in. (182.9 × 182.9 cm)
Courtesy of the Gretchen Bender Estate and OSMOS

Ashley Bickerton
Susie, 1982
Polymer and latex paint on Masonite
48 × 96 in. (121.9 × 243.8 cm)
Courtesy of the artist and Lehmann Maupin, New York and Hong Kong

Dara Birnbaum
Rémy/Grand Central: Trains and Boats and Planes, 1980
Video, color, sound, 4:18 min.
Courtesy of the artist and Electronic Arts Intermix (EAI), New York

Barbara Bloom
Planned Abandon, 1981
Wall mural, backdrop paper, information table, poster rack with fake travel posters
Dimensions variable
Courtesy of the artist and David Lewis, New York

R. M. Fischer
Elbow Macaroni Lamp, 1979
Multimedia lamp
93 × 26 × 42 in. (236.2 × 66 × 106.7 cm)
Rubell Family Collection, Miami

General Idea
The Boutique from the 1984 Miss General Idea Pavilion, 1980
Galvanized metal and plexiglass, prints, posters, publications
Overall (installed) 60¼ in. × 10 ft. 11⅞ in. × 8 ft. 6⅜ in. (153 × 335 × 260 cm)
Art Gallery of Ontario, Toronto, Gift of Sandra Simpson, 1998 (98/355)

Peter Halley
Glowing and Burnt-Out Cells with Conduit, 1981
Acrylic, Day-Glo acrylic, and Roll-A-Tex on canvas
64 × 96 in. (162.6 × 243.8 cm)
Collection of B. Z. + Michael Schwartz

Peter Halley
Pepsi Please, 1980
Acrylic on Canvasette
20 × 16 in. (50.8 × 40.6 cm)
Collection of the artist

Jenny Holzer
The Inflammatory Essays, 1979–82
Offset lithographs on colored paper
Each 17 × 17 in. (43.2 × 43.2 cm)
Courtesy of the artist and Hauser & Wirth

Barbara Kruger
Untitled (You Rule by Pathetic Display), 1982
Offset lithograph and silkscreen
73 × 49 in. (185.4 × 124.5 cm)
Krannert Art Museum, University of Illinois at Urbana-Champaign, Museum Purchase (1986-36-1)

Ken Lum
Untitled Furniture Sculpture, 1980–present
Couches, side tables, table lamps
Dimensions variable
Courtesy of the artist

Allan McCollum
40 Plaster Surrogates, 1982–90
Enamel on Hydrocal
Overall dimensions variable
Hirshhorn Museum and Sculpture Garden, Smithsonian Institution, Washington, DC, Joseph H. Hirshhorn Purchase Fund, 1990 (90.22)

Matt Mullican
Untitled (Death), 1980
Lead paint on paper, mounted on canvas
60 × 42 in. (152.3 × 106.7 cm)
Courtesy of the artist, Mai 36 Galerie, and Peter Freeman, Inc.

Matt Mullican
Untitled (Sign), 1982
Acrylic on paper
50 × 37 in. (127 × 94 cm)
Courtesy of the artist, Mai 36 Galerie, and Peter Freeman, Inc.

Richard Prince
Untitled (Hand with cigarette and watch), 1980
Chromogenic print
Sheet 39¹⁵⁄₁₆ × 60 in. (101.4 × 152.4 cm), mount 39¹⁵⁄₁₆ × 60 × ¼ in. (101.4 × 152.4 × 0.6 cm)
Whitney Museum of American Art, New York, Promised gift of Thea Westreich Wagner and Ethan Wagner (P.2011.317)

Martha Rosler
Martha Rosler Reads "Vogue," 1982
Video, color, sound, 25:22 min.
Courtesy of Electronic Arts Intermix (EAI), New York

Haim Steinbach
Shelf with Ajax, 1981
Wood and plastic shelf, Ajax cleaner can
22 × 14 × 14 in. (55.9 × 35.6 × 35.6 cm)
Courtesy of the artist and Tanya Bonakdar Gallery, New York

1983–86

Apple Inc.
Chiat\Day (advertising agency);
Ridley Scott (director)
1984, 1983
Television commercial, color, sound, 1 min.
Courtesy of Apple Inc.

John M Armleder
Untitled, 1986
Synthetic polymer paint and China ink on canvas, two chrome-and-vinyl chairs
Canvas 8 ft. ¼ in. × 48⅛ in. (244.3 × 122.3 cm), each chair 18½ × 20 × 28 in. (47 × 50.8 × 71.1 cm)
The Museum of Modern Art, New York, Gift of Raymond J. Learsy and Gabriella De Ferrari, 1991 (222.1991.a-c)

Alan Belcher
$51.49, 1983
Dye transfer prints on bottles of Solo fabric softener
Each 8¾ × 3¾ × 1⅞ in. (22.2 × 9.5 × 4.8 cm), 16 fl. oz. (473.2 ml)
Courtesy of Alan Belcher

Alan Belcher
$51.49, 1983
Dye transfer prints on bottles of Solo fabric softener
Each 8¾ × 3¾ × 1⅞ in. (22.2 × 9.5 × 4.8 cm), 16 fl. oz. (473.2 ml)
Collection of Lisa Beck and Kevin Jones

Alan Belcher
$51.49, 1983
Dye transfer prints on bottles of Solo fabric softener
Each 8¾ × 3¾ × 1⅞ in. (22.2 × 9.5 × 4.8 cm), 16 fl. oz. (473.2 ml)
Collection of R. A. Weglinski

Gretchen Bender
Dumping Core, 1984
Four-channel video, color, sound, 13 min.; 13 monitors
Dimensions variable
Courtesy of the Gretchen Bender Estate and OSMOS

Gretchen Bender
Untitled (People with AIDS), 1986
Television with live broadcast, vinyl lettering, steel shelf
20 × 15 × 15 in. (50.8 × 38.1 × 38.1 cm)
Courtesy of the Gretchen Bender Estate and OSMOS

Mike Bidlo
Mike Bidlo Presents: The Factory at PS1, 1984
Performance
Documented in digital slide projection of photographs by Tom Warren
Tom Warren Portrait Studio

Mike Bidlo
Not Warhol (Cow Wallpaper, 1966), 1984
Wallpaper repeat on adhesive vinyl
Dimensions variable
Courtesy of Mike Bidlo and Galerie Bruno Bischofberger

Sarah Charlesworth
Golden Boy, 1983–84
Cibachrome with lacquered wood frame
42 × 32 in. (106.7 × 81.3 cm)
Courtesy of the Estate of Sarah Charlesworth and Maccarone, NY/LA

Sarah Charlesworth
Virgin, 1986
Cibachrome with lacquered wood frame
42 × 32 in. (106.7 × 81.3 cm)
Courtesy of the Estate of Sarah Charlesworth and Maccarone, NY/LA

Clegg & Guttmann
Our Production, the Production of Others, 1986/2012, CD Cover Version II, 1986/2012
Chromogenic print (2 panels)
Overall 91⁵⁄₁₆ × 105½ in. (231.9 × 268 cm)
The Metropolitan Museum of Art, New York, Purchase, Vital Projects Fund Inc. Gift, through Joyce and Robert Menschel, 2013 (2013.501a, b)

Drexel Burnham Lambert
Print advertisement featuring Andy Warhol, 1986
Published in *New York Times Magazine*,
November 23, 1986
University of Wisconsin-Madison Memorial Library

General Idea
Sans titre (Marlboro), from the series
Pasta Paintings, 1986–87
Acrylic and dried pasta on canvas
48 × 40⅛ in. (122 × 102 cm)
MUDAM Luxembourg, Musée d'Art Moderne
Grand-Duc Jean

Robert Gober
Three Parts of an X, 1985
Plaster, wood, wire lath, steel, semigloss enamel paint
82 × 82 × 26½ in. (208.3 × 208.3 × 67.3 cm)
Hirshhorn Museum and Sculpture Garden,
Smithsonian Institution, Washington, DC,
Joseph H. Hirshhorn Purchase Fund, 1993 (93.16)

Guerrilla Girls
These Galleries Show No More Than 10% Women Artists or None at All, 1984–85
Offset lithograph
11 × 17 in. (27.9 × 43.2 cm)
Hirshhorn Museum and Sculpture Garden,
Smithsonian Institution, Washington, DC,
Joseph H. Hirshhorn Purchase Fund, 2017 (14.9.2)

Guerrilla Girls
What Do These Artists Have in Common? 1985
Offset lithograph
11 × 17 in. (27.9 × 43.2 cm)
Hirshhorn Museum and Sculpture Garden,
Smithsonian Institution, Washington, DC,
Joseph H. Hirshhorn Purchase Fund, 2014 (14.9.1)

Peter Halley
Copies Simulated, 1984
Kodalith (photosensitive Mylar print)
17½ × 22¼ in. (44.5 × 56.5 cm)
Ed. 2/2
Collection of the artist

Jeff Koons
New! New Too! 1983
Lithographic billboard, mounted on cotton
10 ft. 3 in. × 22 ft. 8 in. (312.4 × 690.9 cm)
Private collection, New York

Louise Lawler
Gift Certificate for Leo Castelli Gallery, New York, 1983
Printed matter
3⁹⁄₁₆ × 6½ in. (9 × 16.5 cm)
Courtesy of the artist and Metro Pictures, New York

Louise Lawler
Who Are You Close To? (Red), 1984/1990
Cibachrome
39¼ × 61¾ in. (99.7 × 156.9 cm)
Ed. 3/5
Hessel Museum of Art, Center for Curatorial Studies,
Bard College, Annandale-on-Hudson, NY, Marieluise
Hessel Collection

Annette Lemieux
Courting Death, 1985
Pigment print on Epson Luster paper
48 × 38 in. (121.9 × 96.5 cm)
Hirshhorn Museum and Sculpture Garden,
Smithsonian Institution, Washington, DC

Sherrie Levine
Chair Seat: 5, 1986
Casein and wax on wood
18 × 18⅜ × 2¼ in. (45.7 × 46.7 × 5.7 cm)
Courtesy of the artist and David Zwirner,
New York/London

Frank Majore
Four O'Clock, 1985
Silver-dye bleach print
24 × 20 in. (61 × 50.8 cm)
Collection of the artist

MICA-TV
R. M. Fischer: An Industrial, 1983
Video, color, sound, 3:30 min.
Courtesy of Electronic Arts Intermix (EAI), New York

Matt Mullican
Untitled (Before Birth), 1984
Lead paint on paper, mounted on canvas
59⅛ × 41⅞ in. (150.3 × 106.5 cm)
Courtesy of the artist, Mai 36 Galerie,
and Peter Freeman, Inc.

Matt Mullican
Untitled (Subjective), 1985
Lead paint on board
50 × 38¹⁄₁₆ in. (127 × 96.7 cm)
Courtesy of the artist, Mai 36 Galerie,
and Peter Freeman, Inc.

Peter Nagy
Adism, 1983
Black-and-white photocopy
10 × 10 in. (25.4 × 25.4 cm)
Courtesy of the artist and Magenta Plains, New York

Peter Nagy
Entertainment Erases History, 1983
Black-and-white photocopy
Dimensions variable
Courtesy of the artist and Magenta Plains, New York

Joel Otterson
Devil/Jesus, 1986
Found table with copper pipes
19 × 39 × 72 in. (48.3 × 99.1 × 182.9 cm)
Ruth and William Ehrlich

Joel Otterson
Perfect Misuse, 1985
Cast trophy figurine, baseballs, wood and aluminum
baseball bats, copper piping, cast concrete,
steel plates
100 × 12 × 12 in. (254 × 30.5 × 30.5 cm)
Courtesy of the artist and Elizabeth Dee, New York

Adrian Piper
Vanilla Nightmares #8, 1986
Charcoal on newspaper
22 x 14 in. (55.9 x 35.6 cm)
Richard and Ellen Sandor Family Collections, LLC

David Robbins
Talent, 1986
Eighteen framed black-and-white photographs
Each 11 × 9 in. (27.9 × 22.9 cm)
Courtesy of Jessica R. Wolff and Stephen A. Wanta

Walter Robinson
Lube Landscape, 1985
Acrylic on canvas
24 × 36 in. (61 × 91.4 cm)
Collection of Gracie Mansion, New York

Cindy Sherman
Untitled #121, 1983
Chromogenic print
40 × 27½ in. (101.5 × 69.8 cm)
Hirshhorn Museum and Sculpture Garden,
Smithsonian Institution, Washington, DC,
Gift of Dr. William H. Goldiner, 1998 (98.19)

Haim Steinbach
supremely black, 1985
Plastic-laminated wood shelf, two ceramic pitchers,
three cardboard detergent boxes
29 × 66 × 13 in. (73.7 × 167.6 × 33 cm)
Ed. of 4
Courtesy of the artist and Tanya Bonakdar Gallery,
New York

Philip Taaffe
Undercurrent, 1984
Mixed media on canvas
88 × 88 in. (223.5 × 223.5 cm)
Collection of the artist

Meyer Vaisman
The Stretch Painting, 1986
Laminated process ink on canvas
71½ × 51½ × 7½ in. (181.6 × 130.8 × 19 cm)
Collection of B. Z. + Michael Schwartz

Julia Wachtel
Love Thing, 1983
Acrylic on canvas
96 × 64 in. (243.8 × 162.6 cm)
Courtesy of the artist and Elizabeth Dee, New York

Joan Wallace
The Pool Ladder Painting, No. 2, 2004
(after ***The Pool Ladder Painting***, 1985)
Latex paint on canvas, wood, stainless-steel
pool ladder
54 × 84 × 60 in. (137.2 × 213.4 × 152.4 cm)
Courtesy of the artist and Elizabeth Dee, New York

Andy Warhol
Self-Portrait, 1986
Synthetic polymer and silkscreen ink on linen
80 × 80¼ in. (203 × 203.4 cm)
Hirshhorn Museum and Sculpture Garden,
Smithsonian Institution, Washington, DC, Partial Gift
of the Andy Warhol Foundation for the Visual Arts and
Partial Purchase, Smithsonian Collections Acquisition
Program and Joseph H. Hirshhorn Bequest (95.1)

James Welling
Tile Photograph 1, 1985
Vintage gelatin silver print
20 × 16 in. (50.8 × 40.6 cm)
Ed. of 3 with 2 artist's proofs
Courtesy of the artist and David Zwirner,
New York/London

James Welling
Tile Photograph 3, 1985
Vintage gelatin silver print
20 × 16 in. (50.8 × 40.6 cm)
Ed. of 3 with 2 artist's proofs
Courtesy of the artist and David Zwirner,
New York/London

James Welling
Tile Photograph 4, 1985
Vintage gelatin silver print
20 × 16 in. (50.8 × 40.6 cm)
Ed. of 3 with 2 artist's proofs
Courtesy of the artist and David Zwirner,
New York/London

David Wojnarowicz
USDA Choice Beef, 1985
Acrylic on found supermarket poster
42 × 31½ in. (106.7 × 80 cm)
Courtesy of the Estate of David Wojnarowicz and P•P•O•W, New York

B. Wurtz
Three Orange Mops, 1986
Three mops, wood stretcher bars
50 × 38 × 3 in. (127 × 96.5 × 7.6 cm)
Courtesy of Martos Gallery, New York

1987–89

ACT UP (Gran Fury)
SILENCE = DEATH, 1987
Neon sign in two colors
48 × 79 in. (121.9 × 200.7 cm)
New Museum, New York, William Olander Memorial Fund

Alan Belcher
Fence Posts, 1987
Color photographs stapled to sharpened wood posts, hanging from metal chains
H. of each 60 in. (152.4 cm)
Ruth and William Ehrlich

Alan Belcher
Gun, 1987
Color photographs laminated to canvas, stainless-steel hardware, leather handles, identification tags (set of 3)
20 × 30 × 10 in. (50.8 × 76.2 × 25.4 cm);
18 × 24 × 6 in. (45.7 × 61 × 15.2 cm);
16 × 20 × 4½ in. (40.6 × 50.8 × 11.4 cm)
Ed. of 2
Ruth and William Ehrlich

Ashley Bickerton
Tormented Self-Portrait (Susie at Arles) No. 2, 1988
Mixed media
90 × 68½ × 20 in. (228.6 × 174 × 50.8 cm)
Des Moines Art Center, Purchased with funds from the Edmundson Art Foundation, Inc. (1994.334)

Jennifer Bolande
Marshall Stack, 1987
Three handmade wood-and-vinyl speaker cabinets, color photographs, Marshall-brand speaker cloth, accessories, and plastic logo
69 × 22½ × 6½ in. (175.3 × 57.2 × 16.5 cm)
Collection of the artist

Jessica Diamond
T.V. Telepathy (Black-and-White Version), 1989
Acrylic on wall
Dimensions variable
Ed. 1/3
Courtesy of the artist

John Dogg
John, Not Johnny, 1987
Painted stainless-steel spare-tire cover
Diam. 29 in. (73.7 cm)
Collection of Adam Lindemann

Tishan Hsu
Biocube, 1988
Porcelain tile, rubber, acrylic, stainless steel, plywood
35½ × 44½ × 44½ in. (90.2 × 113 × 113 cm)
Courtesy of the artist

Larry Johnson
Untitled (I Had Never Seen Anything Like It), 1988
Color coupler print
Framed 45¾ × 90¾ in. (116.2 × 230.5 cm)
Walker Art Center, Minneapolis, T. B. Walker Acquisition Fund, 1996 (1996.175)

Jeff Koons
Art Magazine Ad (Art in America), 1988–89
Lithographic print
45 × 37¼ in. (114.3 × 94.6 cm)
Rubell Family Collection, Miami

Jeff Koons
Art Magazine Ad (Artforum), 1988–89
Lithographic print
45 × 37¼ in. (114.3 × 94.6 cm)
Rubell Family Collection, Miami

Jeff Koons
Art Magazine Ad (Arts), 1988–89
Lithographic print
45 × 37¼ in. (114.3 × 94.6 cm)
Rubell Family Collection, Miami

Jeff Koons
Art Magazine Ad (Flash Art), 1988–89
Lithographic print
45 × 37¼ in. (114.3 × 94.6 cm)
Rubell Family Collection, Miami

Barbara Kruger
Untitled (I Shop therefore I am), 1987
Photographic silkscreen on vinyl
111⅝ × 113¼ × 2½ in. (283.5 × 287.7 × 6.4 cm)
Glenstone, Potomac, Maryland

Sherrie Levine
Ignatz: 6, 1988
Casein on wood
24 × 19⅞ × ⅞ in. (61 × 50.5 × 2.2 cm)
Walker Art Center, Minneapolis, T. B. Walker Acquisition Fund, 1992 (1992.154)

Ken Lum
Alex Gonzalez Loves His Mother and Father, 1989
Chromogenic print on Sintra, mounted on acrylic with screenprinted ink text
45⅞ × 80 × 2⅛ in. (116.5 × 203.3 × 5.5 cm)
Courtesy of the artist

Donald Moffett
He Kills Me, 1987
Offset lithograph
23½ × 37½ in. (59.7 × 95.3 cm)
International Center of Photography, New York Purchase, with funds provided by the ICP Acquisitions Committee, 2000 (1253.2000)

David Robbins
Prop, 1987
Bronze
6 × 12 × ⅜ in. (15.4 × 30.5 × 1 cm)
MAMCO (Musée d'art moderne et contemporain), Geneva, Gift of Galerie 1900–2000, Paris

Erika Rothenberg
Freedom of Expression Drugs, 1989
Three pill bottles, three mouthwash bottles, two ointment boxes, hand-colored printed sign (9 parts)
Overall 14 × 18 × 24 in. (35.6 × 45.7 × 61 cm)
Collection of the artist

Michael Smith
Mike, 1987
Video, black-and-white and color, sound, 2:43 min.
Courtesy of Electronic Arts Intermix (EAI), New York

Mark Stahl
Leisure World, 1987
Fiberglass rocks, bath towels
52 × 28 × 17 in. (132.1 × 71.1 × 43.2 cm)
Courtesy of Pierre Huber, Geneva

Haim Steinbach
on vend du vent, 1988
Text in matte black latex paint or vinyl letters applied to wall
Dimensions variable
CAPC musée d'art contemporain de Bordeaux

Julia Wachtel
what, what, what, 1988
Oil, Flashe, and lacquer ink on canvas
52 in. × 9 ft. 3 in. (132.1 × 281.9 cm)
Courtesy of the artist and Elizabeth Dee, New York

Krzysztof Wodiczko
Hirshhorn Museum, Washington, DC, October 25–27, 1988
Public projection at the Hirshhorn Museum and Sculpture Garden, Smithsonian Institution, Washington, DC
Courtesy of the artist and Galerie Lelong, New York

Krzysztof Wodiczko
Homeless Vehicle, Variant 5, 1988
Aluminum, fabric, wire cage, hardware
60 × 36 × 56 in. (152.4 × 91.4 × 142.2 cm)
Hirshhorn Museum and Sculpture Garden, Smithsonian Institution, Washington, DC

Krzysztof Wodiczko
Homeless Vehicle in New York City, 1988–89
Six color photographs
Each 11 × 17 in. (27.9 × 43.2 cm)
Hirshhorn Museum and Sculpture Garden, Smithsonian Institution, Washington, DC

Works Exhibited in Vitrines

"Art Stars: Out of the Studios into the Glossies," 1985
Illustrated feature in *ZG*, no. 14 (Summer 1985)
22 × 16½ in. (55.9 × 41.9 cm)
GJ Archive, New York

Jane Dickson (image and design) and **Charlie Ahearn** (design)
Poster for *Times Square Show*, 1980
Silkscreen and paint on paper
22½ × 28½ in. (57.2 × 72.4 cm)
Courtesy of online Gallery 98

Stefan Eins
Poster for Fashion Moda, 1980
Offset lithograph
13 × 13½ in. (33 × 34.3 cm)
Courtesy of online Gallery 98

Stefan Eins for Fashion Moda
T-shirt, 1982
Offset printing on cotton
Courtesy of online Gallery 98

Fashion Moda
Sign for documenta 7, 1982
Mixed media on Masonite
16 × 39½ in. (40.6 × 100.3 cm)
Courtesy of online Gallery 98

Bobby G (Robert Goldman)
Money Talks, 1980
Hand-crafted pin (photocopy of black-and-white drawing dry-mounted on rag paper and colored by hand with red gouache)
4¼ × 2¼ in. (10.8 × 5.7 cm)
Courtesy of online Gallery 98

Christof Kohlhofer
25 Billion Dollars, 1979
Centerfold in *East Village Eye*, September 1979 (shown in the "Money, Love and Death" room at *Times Square Show*, 1980)
21½ × 15¾ in. (54.6 × 40 cm)
Courtesy of online Gallery 98

Stefan Lupino
Photograph of Peter Nagy and Alan Belcher at Sherrie Levine's exhibition *1917*, Gallery Nature Morte, October 1984
Published in *L'Uomo Vogue*, December 1984
Courtesy of Alan Belcher

Dick Miller
Shopping bag for A. More Store, 1980
Spray stencil on paper
17 × 13 in. (43.2 × 33 cm)
Courtesy of online Gallery 98

Tom Otterness (cover art)
Collaborative Projects & Printed Matter Inc. Present Art Direct, Items for the Home or Office, 1982
Offset-printed booklet (40 pages)
5¼ × 8¼ in. (13.3 × 21 cm)
Courtesy of online Gallery 98

Tom Otterness
Libra, from the series ***Zodiac Love***, 1982–87
Painted Hydrocal
Approx. 6 × 4 × 4 in. (15.2 × 10.2 × 10.2 cm)
Courtesy of online Gallery 98

Tom Otterness (drawings)
and **John Ahearn** (notations)
Floor plan and artist list for *Times Square Show*, 1980
Offset printing on yellow paper
Each 8½ × 14 in. (21.6 × 35.6 cm)
Courtesy of online Gallery 98

Christy Rupp
T-shirt for documenta 7, 1982
Silkscreen on cotton
Courtesy of online Gallery 98

Teri Slotkin
Exterior of the A. More Store, a Colab-sponsored artists' outlet selling low-priced multiples for the holidays, on Broome Street in Soho, 1980
Photograph
Full-frame image 6 × 9 in. (15.2 × 22.9 cm), sheet 8 × 10 in. (20.3 × 25.4 cm)
Collection of Teri Slotkin

The vitrine containing the following objects is curated by Leah Pires:

David Amico
Group portrait of the members of the Offices of Fend, Fitzgibbon, Holzer, Nadin, Prince & Winters at *Pleasure/Function*, 616 South Broadway, Los Angeles, 1980
Color photograph
4 × 6 in. (10.2 × 15.2 cm)
Courtesy of Peter Nadin

Jenny Holzer and **Peter Nadin**
***Here to There* statement**, 1979
Printed paper
11 × 8½ in. (27.9 × 21.6 cm)
Courtesy of Peter Nadin

Louise Lawler
Matchbook for *Arrangements of Pictures*, Metro Pictures, New York, 1982
Printed cardboard
2 × 1¹³⁄₁₆ in. (5.1 × 4.6 cm)
Courtesy of the artist and Metro Pictures, New York

Louise Lawler
Matchbook for *Borrowed Time*, Baskerville and Watson Gallery, New York, 1983
Printed cardboard
2 × 1¹³⁄₁₆ in. (5.1 × 4.6 cm)
Courtesy of the artist and Metro Pictures, New York

Louise Lawler
Matchbook for *An Evening with Julian Schnabel*, 1982
Printed cardboard
2 × 1¹³⁄₁₆ in. (5.1 × 4.6 cm)
Courtesy of the artist and Metro Pictures, New York

Louise Lawler
Poster for ___________ *, Louise Lawler, Adrian Piper and Cindy Sherman Are Participating in an Exhibition Organized by Janelle Reiring*, Artists Space, New York, September 23–October 28, 1978, 1978
Offset lithograph
17¹⁄₁₆ × 11¹⁄₁₆ in. (43.3 × 28.1 cm)
Courtesy of the artist and Metro Pictures, New York

Louise Lawler
Stationery for documenta 7, 1982
Two sheets of printed paper, envelope
Each sheet 11 × 8½ in (27.9 × 21.6 cm)
Courtesy of the artist and Metro Pictures, New York

Sherrie Levine
Announcement for *Two Shoes for Two Dollars*, 3 Mercer Street, New York, April 16–23, 1977, 1977
Printed postcard, 3½ × 5⅛ in. (9 × 13 cm)
Collection of Thomas Lawson and Susan Morgan

Sherrie Levine
Two Shoes, 1992
Pair of children's brown leather shoes
Each 6½ × 2½ × 2½ in. (15.8 × 6 × 5.8 cm)
Signed and numbered ed. of 99 + XXXVI for *Parkett*, no. 32
Courtesy of Parkett Publishers and Sherrie Levine

The Offices of Fend, Fitzgibbon, Holzer, Nadin, Prince & Winters
Advertisement in *REALLIFE Magazine*, March 1980
Printed paper
11 × 8½ in. (27.9 × 21.6 cm)
Courtesy of Coleen Fitzgibbon

The Offices of Fend, Fitzgibbon, Holzer, Nadin, Prince & Winters
Announcement for *A Moment of Truth, with Drinks*, 112 Workshop Consultation, 1980
Printed paper
Courtesy of Coleen Fitzgibbon

The Offices of Fend, Fitzgibbon, Holzer, Nadin, Prince & Winters
Business card, 1980
Printed card
Approx. 2½ × 4⅜ in. (6.4 × 11 cm)
Courtesy of Coleen Fitzgibbon

The Offices of Fend, Fitzgibbon, Holzer, Nadin, Prince & Winters
Business card (recto); **Invitation to *Pleasure/Function*, 616 South Broadway, Los Angeles** (verso), 1980
Printed card
Approx. 2½ × 4⅜ in. (6.4 × 11 cm)
Courtesy of Peter Nadin

The Offices of Fend, Fitzgibbon, Holzer, Nadin, Prince & Winters
Flyer for *Pleasure/Function*, 616 South Broadway, Los Angeles, 1980
Printed paper
11 × 8½ in. (27.9 × 21.6 cm)
Courtesy of David Amico

The Offices of Fend, Fitzgibbon, Holzer, Nadin, Prince & Winters
Invitation to reception at 305 Broadway, February 29, 1980, 1980
Printed card
5½ × 3½ in. (14 × 8.9 cm)
Courtesy of Peter Nadin

The Offices of Fend, Fitzgibbon, Holzer, Nadin, Prince & Winters
Notes on *Pleasure/Function*, 616 South Broadway, Los Angeles, 1980
Handwriting on paper
11 × 8½ in. (27.9 × 21.6 cm)
Courtesy of David Amico

A Picture Is No Substitute for Anything
Announcement for *A Picture Is No Substitute for Anything*, James Turcotte Gallery, Los Angeles, 1982
Printed card, envelope
Card 3½ × 5½ in. (8.9 × 14 cm)
Courtesy of the artist and Metro Pictures, New York

A Picture Is No Substitute for Anything
Announcement for *A Picture Is No Substitute for Anything—Sherrie Levine*, 407 Greenwich Street, New York, 1981
Printed card
3½ × 5 in. (8.9 × 12.7 cm)
Courtesy of the artist and Metro Pictures, New York

A Picture Is No Substitute for Anything
"A Picture Is No Substitute for Anything," 1982
Illustrated feature in *Wedge*, no. 2 (Fall 1982)
10¹⁄₁₆ × 17⅛ in. (25.6 × 43.4 cm)
Courtesy of the artist and Metro Pictures, New York